Warren Gay

SAMS

Teach Yourself Linux Programming in 24 Hours

SAMS

201 West 103rd St., Indianapolis, Indiana, 46290 USA

Sams Teach Yourself Linux Programming in 24 Hours

International Standard Book Number: 0-672-31582-3

Library of Congress Catalog Card Number: 98-89430

Printed in the United States of America

First Printing: May 1999

01 00 99 4 3 2 1

Trademarks

Warning and Disclaimer

Executive Editor
Brian Gill

Acquisitions Editor
Brian Gill

Development Editor
Jeff W. Durham

Managing Editor
Jodi Jensen

Senior Editor
Susan Ross Moore

Copy Editor
Chuck Hutchinson

Indexer
Johnna VanHoose

Proofreaders
Mona Brown
Ben Berg

Technical Editor
Richard Blum

Software Development Specialist
Dan Scherf

Interior Design
Gary Adair

Cover Design
Aren Howell

Copy Writer
Eric Borgert

Layout Technicians
Stacey DeRome
Ayanna Lacey
Heather Miller
Amy Parker

Contents at a Glance

Contents

About the Author

Warren Gay is a supervisor of Investment Management Systems at Mackenzie Financial Corporation in Toronto. Warren also holds an Advanced Amateur Radio license and is active on 75 meters with callsign VE3WWG when time permits. Using the 2-meter band on August 3, 1991, he made contact with the Musa Manarov, callsign U2MIR, aboard the Soviet MIR space station by using his PC and packet radio gear. During this time period, Warren also contributed the DOVE3WWG.ZIP DOS software package to the SIMTEL archives. This program is able to decode the DOVE amateur satellite telemetry codes into temperature and battery level readings.

Before entering Ryerson Polytechnical in 1976, Warren built a microcomputer system from his own design. This system used the first 8-bit Intel microprocessor known as the 8008, which preceded the popular 8080. This computer system required programs to be entered by octal rotary switches and sported a total static RAM capacity of 1 kilobytes.

Warren has been programming professionally since 1980, using many assembler languages, PL/I, C, and C++. He has been programming for UNIX since 1986, and started programming for Linux in 1994. Linux has allowed him to contribute such software packages as the `ftpbackup` program and the rewrite of the popular `wavplay` program. These and his other Linux packages can be found at the ftp site `sunsite.unc.edu` and its mirror sites.

Warren lives in St. Catharines, Ontario, Canada with his wife Jacqueline, and his three children Erin, Laura, and Scott.

Dedication

This book is dedicated to my son Scott, whom I hope will grow up into a Linux-based world. This work is also dedicated to the memory of my grandfather, Charles Henry Gay, who loved to read books.

Acknowledgments

A published book of any nature is a group effort. This book has been no exception, and consequently I owe thanks to many people. Initially, I must express my thanks to Ron Gallager, the Acquisitions Editor who signed me up for this project. This came at a time in my life when I least expected to be writing a book. Ron helped me get started in this effort, and offered me much encouragement.

Special thanks also belong to Jeff W. Durham, the Development Editor, for his careful and patient proofreading of the manuscript. Without his thoughtful suggestions and insight, the book would have been quite a different animal. I am especially thankful for his patience when I was impatient, and for his ability to suggest important improvements to each chapter.

Thanks also go to Brian Gill, the Executive Editor, for overseeing the whole process, and for responding to my numerous questions. I also want to express my thanks to Richard Blum, the Technical Editor of this book. Through his careful efforts, a number of errors were caught early in the process. His assistance was invaluable for checking out the programming examples on other Linux distributions that he had at his disposal.

I am also indebted to Chuck Hutchinson, the Copy Editor, for turning my English into prose. His efforts concerning those publishing details like punctuation are greatly appreciated, as I was spared from having to worry about them too much.

There are many others to whom I owe thanks. These include the formatters, illustrators, and all of those who had a hand in the production of this book. I am also grateful to those on the marketing side who decide what is to be published, and for those who helped market this work.

I must also thank those who have helped me in my involvement with Linux, and in my professional career. Special thanks go to Darie Urbanky for the initial Linux CDs that he gave me in 1994, which started me using Linux at home. I am also thankful for the object-oriented C techniques that Babak Morshedizadeh managed to teach me in the workplace, despite my own stubbornness. These techniques were used effectively within the TQL demonstration program of Chapter 23. Finally, I would like to thank Steve

Gligic for his generosity in providing me with old UNIX systems that I was able to learn from in my basement. This was especially helpful to me in the years preceding 1994.

I am grateful for the patience of my wife Jacqueline, and my children Erin, Laura, and Scott. Without their quiet patience and sacrifice with my virtual absence, this work would not have been accomplished.

Last of all, I offer my apologies to my dog Pepper, who could not understand why I didn't have time to play ball.

Tell Us What You Think!

As the reader of this book, *you* are our most important critic and commentator. We value your opinion and want to know what we're doing right, what we could do better, what areas you'd like to see us publish in, and any other words of wisdom you're willing to pass our way.

As an Associate Publisher for Sams Publishing, I welcome your comments. You can fax, email, or write me directly to let me know what you did or didn't like about this book—as well as what we can do to make our books stronger.

Please note that I cannot help you with technical problems related to the topic of this book, and that due to the high volume of mail I receive, I might not be able to reply to every message.

When you write, please be sure to include this book's title and author as well as your name and phone or fax number. I will carefully review your comments and share them with the author and editors who worked on the book.

Fax: 317-581-4770

Email: `adv_prog@mcp.com`

Mail: Bradley L. Jones
Associate Publisher
Sams Publishing
201 West 103rd Street
Indianapolis, IN 46290 USA

Introduction

Using a hands-on approach, this book quickly introduces you to the essentials of Linux application development in the C programming language. After reading this book, you will be able to write professional applications, client programs, and server daemons that run under the Linux operating system.

This book focuses on Linux topics that are of practical importance to C programmers. The carefully organized lessons cover the essential topics early and progress toward the more advanced features. Each lesson is logically organized, full of examples, and has systematic instructions. Furthermore, you will appreciate the strong Linux and GNU content bias in this book.

Who Should Read This Book

If you're a beginning programmer, you will find this book indispensable for getting started. If you're an experienced programmer, you should find this book to be a handy reference for application development. If you're a Linux enthusiast, you will find that this book contains the practical examples and advice you need to get started creating quality programs.

Conventions Used in This Book

This book uses different typefaces to differentiate between code and regular English, and also to help you identify important concepts.

Text that you type and text that should appear on your screen is presented in `monospace` type.

```
It will look like this to mimic the way text looks on your screen.
```

Placeholders for variables and expressions appear in *`monospace italic`* font. You should replace the placeholder with the specific value it represents.

This arrow (➥) at the beginning of a line of code means that a single line of code is too long to fit on the printed page. Continue typing all characters after the ➥ as though they were part of the preceding line.

A Note presents interesting pieces of information related to the surrounding discussion.

A Tip offers advice or teaches an easier way to do something.

A Caution advises you about potential problems and helps you steer clear of disaster.

NEW TERM New Term icons provide clear definitions of new, essential terms. The term appears in italic.

HOUR 1

Getting Started

Introducing Linux

This book focuses on C program development for Linux. Most of what you will learn is directly transferable to a commercial UNIX platform that you might find in the workplace.

In this lesson, I'll introduce you to the GNU `gcc` compiler and tell you which options you need to perform successful compiles. I'll also describe the compile options that are needed to allow the GNU `gdb` debugger to debug your programs. I'll describe the core file and outline the steps you need to perform to look at it using the debugger.

In this lesson, you'll look at how the GNU `gcc` compiler warning levels help save you time and make your programs more reliable. You'll also learn some tips on how to get rid of compiler warnings for valid C constructs that occur in everyday practice. Finally, you'll perform a short procedure to check out the operation of your `gcc` compiler to make sure that it is working.

Before you begin, it is important for you to distinguish between Linux itself and the tools that are used on Linux. This distinction will help when you must report problems to the Internet or ask for advice on Usenet. Linux is the operating system component. Often Linux is called the *UNIX kernel*. The kernel manages files, memory resources, processes, and devices.

The other important component is the set of development tools that are available on the Linux host. They include the GNU C compiler, the GNU `make` command, and the GNU RCS tools for source control, to name but a few. When you're reporting problems or asking for advice on Usenet, do not confuse these tools with the Linux kernel.

Introducing GNU gcc

The C compiler for Linux is the GNU `gcc` command. Generally, knowing what version of the compiler you are working with is a good idea, especially if you need to report problems with it. You can easily determine the version by performing the following command:

```
bash$ gcc --version
2.7.2.3
```

> On most other UNIX platforms, the C compiler is invoked with the `cc` command. On Linux systems, the `cc` command and the `gcc` command refer to the same C compiler.

The GNU `gcc` compiler expects and compiles ANSI C code statements, although it does silently accept the older non-ANSI–styled C code. This is good news for you because you do not require any additional compiler options for `gcc`, unlike some commercial C compilers.

Selecting the GNU Standard

C programs often include *header* files like the following:

```
#include <stdio.h>
```

This statement causes the compiler to compile and read the text file /usr/include/stdio.h. In fact, the C compiler may end up reading and compiling several more files, depending on whether the stdio.h file includes other include files. While the compiler processes these files with its preprocessor, different C source code is compiled, or alternative source files are included. This activity is controlled by the current state of the macros currently defined in the compile process. The designers of the GNU C libraries have carefully crafted these include files to define programming constructs—things with slight variations to accommodate different standards that are available for UNIX.

You may have heard people say that "one of the nice things about standards is that there are so many of them!" The standard that you will be writing to and compiling to is the *GNU* standard. Under Linux, this standard presently represents the superset of all the various other standards available with the GNU C libraries.

To choose between these standards requires the use of a macro definition. In this case, you simply must define a macro named `_GNU_SOURCE`. You don't need to assign a value to this macro; the macro value needs only to exist. The accepted way of defining this macro is to specify the `-D` option on the compiler command line:

```
bash$ gcc -D_GNU_SOURCE hello.c
```

Using the `-D` option is actually equivalent to the following C language statement:

```
#define _GNU_SOURCE
```

> The default executable output file produced by the compiler is named a.out.

Specifying the Compiler Output

The compile examples so far have used the default output filename a.out. Normally, however, you specify the name of the output file explicitly. You do so by using the `-o` option:

```
bash$ gcc -D_GNU_SOURCE hello.c -o hello
```

Running the Compiled Program

After compiling a program, you should be ready to run it. To run it, you invoke it using the shell:

```
bash$ ./hello
```

> The use of the dot and slash may appear redundant. Using this method is a good practice, however, so that you can avoid the possibility of running another command that has the same name as your program's executable filename, found because of your shell's `PATH` variable. When you're logged in as root, this practice also helps you avoid the possibility of running a *Trojan horse* program.

Compiling for Debugging

Under Linux, the normal debugging tool to use is the `gdb` command. You should check for its availability on your system because you will likely want to make use of it as you develop new programs. It's also quite useful for performing a "postmortem" on a program that has died. So, check for it now as follows:

```
bash$ gdb --version
GDB 4.16 (i586-unknown-linux), Copyright 1996 Free Software
➥ Foundation, Inc.
bash$
```

If, instead, you get

```
bash$ gdb
bash: gdb: command not found
bash$
```

then you either don't have `gdb` installed, or you might not have your shell `PATH` environment variable set up correctly.

No matter what your debugging tool of choice is, you need a compiler option to enable the compiler to write special debugging information to the final executable file. When you're developing new programs or debugging problem programs, always compile with the debug option:

```
bash$ gcc -g -D_GNU_SOURCE hello.c -o hello
```

Option `-g` causes the final executable to contain some additional information that allows the debugger to link machine instructions back to lines of source code. If you don't compile with `-g`, the debugger cannot tell you much in human-friendly terms.

Most debuggers have many commands. Here, I'll just show you the most important ones to know to get started.

When a program runs and encounters a fault, the Linux kernel causes the program to abort. When this situation occurs, the operating system causes a file to be written to the current directory named core. This core file is a memory image of the program that existed at the time of failure. It is your key to perform a "postmortem analysis."

Listing 1.1 shows a simple program with an attitude. Lines 2 and 4 have been purposely coded to provoke a memory violation. Line 2 sets the pointer `cp` to a `null` pointer. Line 4 tries to store the exclamation point by using the `null` pointer `cp`. Because the pointer is `null`, a `core` file will be created by the Linux kernel and the program terminated.

LISTING 1.1 01LST01.C—A C PROGRAM WITH ATTITUDE

```
1:    static void fun1(void) {
2:        char *cp = 0;
3:
4:        *cp = '!'; /* Take that! */
5:    }
6:    int main(int argc,char **argv) {
7:        fun1();
8:        return 0;
9:    }
```

Compile this program now, run it, and allow the program to abort. Doing so causes the Linux kernel to create a `core` file for you to analyze.

```
bash$ gcc -g -D_GNU_SOURCE 01LST01.c -o wipe_out
bash$ ./wipe_out
Segmentation fault (core dumped)
bash$
```

Detail is everything in this business. You can see that the program died of a *Segmentation fault*. It is your first clue to the nature of the problem. Segmentation faults occur because a bad memory reference has been made. It usually means that you attempted to dereference a bad pointer, but often it's a null pointer (a pointer with a zero address).

In this case, the source of the problem is in line 4 of Listing 1.1. The pointer is `null`, but you try to store an exclamation point character at location zero anyway. The Linux operating system forbids this use, raises a Segmentation fault instead, and leaves you with this core file:

```
bash$ ls -l core
-rw-------   1 student1 user       98304 Nov 25 23:41 core
```

If this program had been made up of thousands of C language functions, deducing the source of the problem would be less than trivial. At this point, a postmortem becomes crucial. Here, you can see how to begin your postmortem analysis:

```
bash$ gdb ./wipe_out core
GDB is free software and you are welcome to distribute copies of it
 under certain conditions; type "show copying" to see the conditions.
There is absolutely no warranty for GDB; type "show warranty" for
➥ details.
GDB 4.16 (i586-unknown-linux), Copyright 1996 Free Software
➥ Foundation, Inc...
Core was generated by './wipe_out'.
Program terminated with signal 11, Segmentation fault.
```

```
#0  0x8048550 in fun1 () at 01LST01.c:4
4          *cp = '!'; /* Take that! */
(gdb) where
#0  0x8048550 in fun1 () at 01LST01.c:4
#1  0x8048568 in main (argc=1, argv=0xbffffb54) at 01LST01.c:7
(gdb) quit
bash$
```

To perform the postmortem, you invoke `gdb` with the name of the executable that was used as the first command-line argument. The second argument must be the name of the core file. After you invoke the debugger, `gdb` analyzes both the executable and the core file. You see that `gdb` identifies itself as version 4.16 and that the core file was generated by the program ./wipe_out. It regurgitates the fact that the core file was created due to a Segmentation fault. Finally, `gdb` tells you that the fault occurred in 01LST01.c line 4. Then it even proceeds to show you line 4, comments and all.

Sometimes knowing which function called which is important to explain how it got called in the first place. At other times, this information can help expose recursion problems. By entering the `where` command, you get a trace of the stack. Here, you see that `fun1()` was called by `main()` from line 7 of 01LST01.c. Even the `main()` function arguments are shown. All this good information shows you the actual cause of the program abort.

To exit the debugger, you simply issue the `quit` command, and control is returned to the shell. `gdb` can do considerably more for you, but this description will take care of your most immediate needs.

Examining Compiler Warning Levels

The C compiler often reports messages. These messages can be divided into *error messages* and *warning messages*. Error messages indicate things that must be corrected for the compile to succeed. Warnings, on the other hand, alert the programmer about bad practices and problems that might occur later when the program is run.

With the maximum `gcc` warning level set, the compiler reports on the smallest of infractions but does so intelligently and diligently. Sometimes warnings are issued for valid C programming practices, and some developers use compiler options to disable these warnings from being generated. However, by doing so, they prevent the C compiler from providing useful advice.

The best advice I can provide here is to always use the maximum warning level available. Doing so forces the developer to address all source code issues until the warnings disappear from the compilation. The only justifiable reason for going to a lower warning level is a situation in which you've inherited someone else's source code, and you do not have the luxury of time to fix all causes of warnings.

> Always compile with the maximum warning level turned on. Time spent up front eliminating causes of warning messages can save an order of magnitude of time later while you're debugging your program.

The following shows how to use `gcc` with the maximum warning level turned on:

```
bash$ gcc -Wall -D_GNU_SOURCE hello.c -o hello
```

Notice the use of the `-Wall` option on the command line. The `-W` option is used to specify a warning option to the `gcc` compiler. The argument that follows specifies the warning level to use. With the GNU `gcc` command, you can specify the `-W` option more than once. This capability permits you to specify multiple warning options that may apply in concert. The best practice is to just use the one `-Wall` option and correct your program until the warnings are all addressed properly. That is the approach you will take in this book, and it should help to teach good C language practices in the process.

> Most Linux command-line options do not require a space to appear between the option letter and the option's argument. For example, you can specify the option as `-Wall` or `-W all` because they are equivalent.

Working with Compiler Warning Messages

When a high warning level is used by the compiler, every possible warning message is reported. A low warning level reports only the most important messages and suppresses the rest.

Using a high warning level with your C compiler presents one drawback. Sometimes you receive warning messages for valid C language constructs. Well-designed compilers allow you to cope with these problems, however, and GNU's `gcc` is very good at using these levels.

Warnings About Assignments

Programmers often love the economy of expression in the C language. By this, I mean that programmers employ the fewest number of statements or operators to accomplish a task. Sometimes this approach involves doing an assignment and a test for nonzero all in one step. Consider the `if` statement in Listing 1.2.

Listing 1.2 01LST02.c—Warnings About Value Assignment in the `if` Statement

```
1:     #include <string.h>
2:
3:     char *
4:     Basename(char *pathname) {
5:         char *cp;           /* Work Pointer */
6:
7:         if ( cp = strrchr(pathname,'/') )
8:             return cp + 1; /* Return basename pointer */
9:         return pathname;   /* No directory component */
10:    }
```

The following is the compile session for Listing 1.2:

```
bash$ gcc -c -D_GNU_SOURCE -Wall 01LST02.c
01LST02.c: In function 'Basename':
01LST02.c:7: warning: suggest parentheses around assignment used as
➥ truth value
bash$
```

In Listing 1.2, notice the statement in line 7. The compiler flags this statement as a possible error because often the C programmer really means to use the comparison operator == to compare values instead of assigning a value. The compiler has no way of confirming whether the actual assignment is correct or whether a comparison was intended. The developer is left to decide the issue, after the compiler has issued the warning.

> The `-c` compile option tells the compiler not to link the final program. As a result, the source code is compiled into an intermediate object file, which will participate in a link step at a later time.

Note that the statement cannot be called incorrect, nor is it clear that the statement truly reflects the programmer's real intentions. Some people might be tempted to argue that comparison is normal in the `if` statement and that the assignment in an `if` statement is unusual and should be reported as an error. The fact remains that the C language is defined such that both are equally valid expressions.

Compiler writers have developed clever tricks for dealing with these types of issues. This particular case is resolved this way: If an assignment is coded as shown in Listing 1.2, it is flagged as a warning because it represents a possible error on the programmer's part. If it indeed represents an error, the programmer goes back and repairs the single equal sign to a double equal sign and compiles the code again. If, on the other hand, this assignment is valid, the programmer encloses the assignment within a set of brackets. When this is done, the compiler assumes that the programmer knows what he or she is doing.

Listings 1.3 and 1.4 show two different strategies for resolving this issue in favor of the assignment.

Listing 1.3 01LST03.c—One Way to Resolve Assignments in the `if` Statement Warning

```
1:    #include <string.h>
2:
3:    char *
4:    Basename(char *pathname) {
5:        char *cp;           /* Work Pointer */
6:
7:        if ( ( cp = strrchr(pathname,'/') ) )
8:            return cp + 1; /* Return basename pointer */
9:        return pathname;   /* No directory component */
10:   }
```

Listing 1.4 01LST04.c—The Preferred Way to Avoid an Assignment Warning

```
1:    #include <string.h>
2:
3:    char *
4:    Basename(char *pathname) {
5:        char *cp;     /* Work Pointer */
6:
7:        if ( ( cp = strrchr(pathname,'/') ) != 0 )
8:            return cp + 1; /* Return basename pointer */
9:        return pathname;   /* No directory component */
10:   }
```

Note the extra pair of parentheses around the assignment in line 7 of both Listings 1.3 and 1.4. The language here does not require the parentheses, but the compiler takes this use as a cue that the developer knows what he or she is doing. Although Listing 1.3 shows a solution acceptable to GNU's `gcc` compiler, some other commercial compilers insist on the construct shown in Listing 1.4. For this reason, the solution that is offered in Listing 1.4 is probably preferred and is a little more clear to the reader.

> You no longer need to economize in C language expressions for the sake of optimization. Today's optimizing compilers are very effective at arriving at optimal code without any help from the programmer. For this reason, making an expression easier to read is better than reducing it to the fewest number of operators.

I have made an example out of the C language `if` statement, but the same issue applies to other C language statements, including the `switch` and `while` statements.

Warnings About Unused Arguments

Some compilers complain about unused arguments. The thinking appears to be that if the argument is defined, then it was meant to be used. The truth of the matter is that the function arguments define an interface. Fully using the interface that is defined is not really required because an interface may plan for future uses.

An example of the unused argument problem is the ubiquitous `main()` program. The `main` program interface is often defined as follows:

```
extern int main(int argc,char *argv[]);
```

If the program being written does not use these arguments, does that mean these arguments don't exist in the interface? Certainly not. For this reason, always defining your function arguments is preferable, whether or not they are used in the program.

If, however, your compiler whines about unused arguments, you might be tempted to remove them from its definition. For this reason, Listing 1.5 shows how to avoid this problem so that you don't need to leave out function arguments.

LISTING 1.5 01LST05.C—PROPERLY ADDRESSING UNUSED ARGUMENTS

```
#include <stdio.h>
int main(int argc,char **argv) {

    (void) argc;
    (void) argv;

    puts("Hello World!");
    return 0;
}
```

If you remember your C language programming rules, you know that referencing a value all by itself in a statement is perfectly valid. Normally, this construct is not useful because it has no useful side effect. It can be used as a useful compiler-side effect, however, and this is exactly what is done. By referencing the argument's value and then discarding it with the `(void)` cast, you tell the compiler that the argument is referenced but that you are happy to discard the referenced value.

The current GNU `gcc` compiler does not warn about unused arguments. Depending on your point of view, this lack of warning may or may not be a feature. Perhaps the choice not to warn about unused arguments was made by the `gcc` people so that programmers are not tempted to remove these arguments from the interface definition. If gcc should change its position on this issue in the future, however, you will be prepared.

Resolving Unused Variable Warnings

Sometimes the compiler warns you about unused variables that you have declared in your code. These warnings might strongly tempt you to remove these variables from your code immediately. You should exercise great care, however, before doing so.

> Be extremely careful about removing unused variables and buffers. Make sure that you fully evaluate the C preprocessing directives of the source code before you assume that these values are never used. Sometimes compiling a program with different macro settings can cause a need for these variable declarations.

The problem of unused variables often occurs in code that is designed to be portable to many different UNIX platforms, including Linux. The specific problem is normally that the original developer never properly allowed for the unused declarations at the right time with the help of the correct C preprocessing directives. What often happens in practice is that the source code becomes patched and modified by several people, and those changes never get fully tested or fixed on the other platforms it was meant to compile on.

To illustrate this problem, take a look at Listing 1.6.

LISTING 1.6 01LST06.C—AN EXAMPLE OF UNUSED VARIABLE DECLARATIONS

```
#include <stdio.h>
#include <unistd.h>
#include <sys/types.h>
/* #define SHOW_PID */ /* MACRO NOT DEFINED */

int main(int argc,char **argv) {
    pid_t PID;          /* Process ID */

    (void) argc;
    (void) argv;

#ifdef SHOW_PID
    PID = getpid();   /* Get Process ID */
    printf("Hello World! Process ID is %d\n",
        (int)PID);
#else
```

continues

LISTING 1.6 CONTINUED

```
17:     puts("Hello World!");
18: #endif
19:     return 0;
20: }
```

The compile session for Listing 1.6 appears as follows:

```
bash$ gcc -c -D_GNU_SOURCE -Wall 01LST06.c
01LST06.c: In function 'main':
01LST06.c:7: warning: unused variable 'PID'
```

If you were to compile this program with line 4 commented out as it is shown, the compiler would complain that the declared variable `PID` in line 7 is not used because the macro `SHOW_PID` is not defined, so line 17 would be compiled in place of lines 13 to 15. If you take that warning message at face value and remove or comment out line 7, then you solve the immediate problem but create another longer-term problem.

By commenting out line 7 and then compiling the program with line 4 uncommented (macro `SHOW_PID` defined), as shown in Listing 1.7, the compiler then compiles lines 13 to 15 instead of line 17. When that happens, the compiler reports the error that variable `PID` is not declared.

LISTING 1.7 01LST07.C—ERROR COMPILING PROGRAM WITH A MISSING VARIABLE DECLARATION

```
1:  #include <stdio.h>
2:  #include <unistd.h>
3:  #include <sys/types.h>
4:  #define SHOW_PID        /* MACRO IS DEFINED */
5:
6:  int main(int argc,char **argv) {
7:  /*  pid_t PID;          // Commented Out */
8:
9:      (void) argc;
10:     (void) argv;
11:
12: #ifdef SHOW_PID
13:     PID = getpid();     /* Get Process ID */
14:     printf("Hello World! Process ID is %d\n",
15:         (int)PID);
16: #else
17:     puts("Hello World!");
18: #endif
19:     return 0;
20: }
```

The compile session for Listing 1.7 looks like this:

```
bash$ gcc -c -D_GNU_SOURCE -Wall 01LST07.c
01LST07.c: In function 'main':
01LST07.c:13: 'PID' undeclared (first use this function)
01LST07.c:13: (Each undeclared identifier is reported only once
01LST07.c:13: for each function it appears in.)
```

The compiler error message tells you immediately that the variable `PID` was not declared in line 13 when the variable name was encountered. The problem is that the removal of the variable declaration is the wrong solution to the original warning. The real problem was the lack of some needed C preprocessing directives. Listing 1.8 shows the correct way to correct this problem.

LISTING 1.8 01LST08.C—THE CORRECT WAY TO ADDRESS UNUSED VARIABLES

```
1:    #include <stdio.h>
2:    #include <unistd.h>
3:    #include <sys/types.h>
4:    #define SHOW_PID       /* MACRO IS DEFINED */
5:
6:    int main(int argc,char **argv) {
7:    #ifdef SHOW_PID
8:        pid_t PID;         /* Process ID */
9:    #endif
10:
11:       (void) argc;
12:       (void) argv;
13:
14:   #ifdef SHOW_PID
15:       PID = getpid();    /* Get Process ID */
16:       printf("Hello World! Process ID is %d\n",
17:           (int)PID);
18:   #else
19:       puts("Hello World!");
20:   #endif
21:       return 0;
22:   }
```

Notice the addition of lines 7 and 9 around the declaration of the variable in line 8. The addition of these two preprocessing directives now allows the program to compile without warnings, with or without the definition of the macro `SHOW_PID`.

Resolving Unreferenced String Warnings

Unreferenced string constants also cause warnings to be generated. Sometimes programmers leave string constants in a program so that they become part of the final executable. A common practice is to define version strings in a program so that the executable file can be dumped and matched up with a particular version of a source module.

The solution to these warnings is simply to define them as a constant using the `const` keyword. The compiler does not complain about unreferenced constants. Listing 1.9 shows an embedded RCS string that is unreferenced. (Note that embedded RCS strings will be covered in Hour 2, "Managing Your Source Code.")

> To eliminate compiler warnings about unreferenced string constants, simply declare the string constant as a constant by using the C language `const` keyword.

LISTING 1.9 01LST09.C—EXAMPLE OF AN UNREFERENCED RCS STRING

```
1:    static char rcsid[] = "@(#)01LST09.c $Revision: 1.3$";
2:
3:    #include <stdio.h>
4:    int main(int argc,char **argv) {
5:
6:        (void) argc;
7:        (void) argv;
8:
9:        puts("Hello World!");
10:       return 0;
11:   }
```

The compile session for Listing 1.9 follows:

```
bash$ gcc -c -D_GNU_SOURCE -Wall 01LST09.c
01LST09.c:1: warning: 'rcsid' defined but not used
```

Note line 1 where the string array `rcsid` is declared. The purpose of this declaration will become evident when source control is covered later. This declared string is never referenced in the program, so the compiler issues a warning about it. You can easily fix this problem by adding the `const` compiler keyword, as shown in Listing 1.10.

LISTING 1.10 01LST10.C—ELIMINATING THE UNUSED STRING CONSTANT WARNING

```
static const char rcsid[] = "@(#)01LST10.c $Revision: 1.3$";

#include <stdio.h>
int main(int argc,char **argv) {

    (void) argc;
    (void) argv;

    puts("Hello World!");
    return 0;
}
```

Testing Your C Compiler

Before you begin your programming adventures under Linux, checking out your compiler with a simple test is a good idea. Often the software itself or the software developer gets blamed for what is frequently an improperly installed or administered piece of software. Here, you will use that old familiar "Hello World" program one more time. This program tests that your compiler is properly configured and is operating correctly.

> Before you email to developers or post to Usenet news about a software difficulty, take all reasonable measures to make sure that you have installed and operated the software correctly. Frequently, the problem is the failure to follow instructions, especially installation instructions.

Type the simple hello.c program using your favorite editor (many people use vi for this purpose). Alternatively, use the hello.c file on the supplied CD. The listing is shown in Listing 1.11.

> Remember not to type the line numbers if you are keying in the program. They are shown for ease of reference only.

LISTING 1.11 HELLO.C—THE SIMPLE "HELLO WORLD" CHECKOUT PROGRAM

```
#include <stdio.h>
int main(int argc,char **argv) {

    (void) argc;
    (void) argv;

    puts("Hello World!");
    return 0;
}
```

Perform a compile and then a link, and then invoke the program as shown in Listing 1.12. You should complete this process in three separate steps to aid in the problem analysis.

LISTING 1.12 LINUX COMPILE, LINK, AND EXECUTE TEST OF HELLO.C

```
1:     bash$ gcc -c -Wall -D_GNU_SOURCE hello.c -o hello.o
2:     bash$ gcc hello.o -o hello
3:     bash$ ./hello
4:     Hello World!
5:     bash$ echo $?
6:     0
7:     bash$
```

Line 1 of Listing 1.12 shows the compile of the source module into the object module hello.o. Line 2 shows the link step, where the hello.o object file is linked with the C libraries and the final executable file hello is written out.

Line 3 invokes the newly compiled C program and causes it to run. Line 4 shows the program's announcement. Finally, in line 5, you display the program's exit code, which prints as zero (line 6). If you made it to line 7 with no problems, then you are ready to start your new programming adventures with Linux.

Troubleshooting Compiler Difficulties

If you experienced problems in line 1 of Listing 1.12, then these problems are usually a sign that the compiler is not properly installed, or its include files in directory /usr/include are missing or incorrect.

If the second step in line 2 failed, this failure indicates a problem with your compiler, your linker, or possibly with your libraries. Often the C libraries are missing or incorrectly installed when problems appear at this stage.

If the program compiled and linked all right, but it failed to execute properly in line 3, then this failure may point to incorrect or corrupted libraries installed on your system.

The value displayed in line 6 should be zero. If you do not get zero, first check that the hello.c file is returning a zero with a `return` statement. Also, make sure you did *not* define function `main()` as returning type `void`. If these points check out okay, one of your support C libraries might still be incorrect or faulty.

> The shell variable `$?` is valid only immediately after the command or program has exited. This value changes with each command that the shell executes.

I hope that your compiler and debugger checked out okay. Getting a good report will keep you smiling as you progress to the next lesson.

1

Summary

In this lesson, you became acquainted with the Linux gcc compiler and examined some compiler options. You learned the reasons for defining the C macro _GNU_SOURCE and looked at the -g option as it affects debugging. You also learned how to use the gdb debugger to analyze a core file and determine the source of the problem.

You learned the merits of using a high warning level for your compiles. You also looked at some of the consequences of using a high warning level and learned how to avoid unnecessary warnings.

Q&A

Q Why do I need to declare arguments like those in the main program, even when they are not used?

A It is important to declare the interface to your function as it actually is. The implementation of the function may change in a future revision of the source code that may depend on those values being defined.

Q Why is it not a good practice to be too efficient in C source language statements?

A Making the program easier to read and understand is better. You no longer need to help the compiler to produce efficient translations. Modern compiler optimization is quite good at this task.

Q Why do I need to use the -g compile option when compiling a program I plan to debug?

A The -g option causes the compiler to produce extra information in the resulting object code. This information assists the gdb debugger so that it knows how to locate your source statements and provides information about your variable names, and so on.

Workshop

You are encouraged to work through the following exercises to help you retain what you have learned in this lesson. You should complete these exercises before proceeding to the next lesson.

Quiz

1. Is the GNU `gcc` command the compiler, linker, or both?
2. What is a *.c file called? a *.h file?
3. What is a *.o file called?
4. What kind of file is the a.out file?
5. What is the difference between a compiler error and a warning?
6. Why is it a good idea to use the dot slash method of invoking an executable? Why is this an especially good idea for root users?
7. What does the `void` type cast mean? Why is it useful?

Exercises

1. Using the source code from Listing 1.6 (file 01LST06.c), compile and execute the program to show the process ID in addition to the message `Hello World`, without modifying the source code in any way.
2. Again using the source code from Listing 1.6 (file 01LST06.c), compile the program with the option `-DSHOW_PID=13` and run it. Did you find a difference? Why or why not?

HOUR 2

Managing Your Source Code

The Benefits of Using Source Control

The UNIX platform has long been recognized as a platform that has a rich set of tools. Some of the tools in this arsenal include tools to manage different revisions of source code. They naturally are also available under Linux.

Despite the availability of source control tools, many programmers fail to take advantage of them. Usually not until they get involved with a large project or a team of developers are they forced into using such tools. Not using these tools beforehand is regretful because source control can provide a number of benefits to the individual developer as well as the team.

What Tool Choices Exist?

On the Linux platform, you basically have the following three mainstream choices:

- SCCS Source Code Control System originated by Marc Rochkind ("The source code control system, IEEE Trans. on Software Engineering, 1975).
- RCS Revision Control System Walter F. Tichy, RCS—A System for Version Control, Software—Practice & Experience 15, 7 (July 1985), 637-654.
- CVS Concurrent Versions System Authors Dick Grune : was the original author of the cvs shell script version that was posted to comp.sources.unix, volume6 (December 1986). Dick has been credited with much of the conflict resolution algorithms.

  Brian Berliner: Wrote and designed the cvs program in April, 1989 based upon Dick's original work.

  Jeff Polk: Assisted Brian with the design of cvs and vendor branch support. He is the author of the checkin(1) shell script, which is the ancestor of the 'cvs import'.

SCCS was one of the earliest forms of source control for UNIX. I avoid describing it in this text because it lacks the flexibility to create separate branches of changes (such as when two users want to make changes at the same time to the same source program). SCCS takes the simple view that only one person is permitted to change a source file at one time.

RCS was written as a better and more powerful replacement for the SCCS tool. You'll use this tool here because it is quite flexible and easy to use.

CVS is built upon the RCS framework and enjoys the advantage that it can operate over a network. Many large Internet development efforts are carried out with the help of a CVS server that is made available to the participating authors. CVS, however, is much more complex to set up and administer and is beyond the scope of this book.

Setting Up RCS for a Project

To learn how to use RCS, you can start by coding the shell of a program that you'll develop further in Hour 3, "Writing a Linux Utility." This way, you have a new source module to start experimenting with.

Normally, you would be wise to create a directory dedicated to the project. Creating such a directory allows you to keep all files related to one project together and all other unrelated files out of the way. The following steps are required to start a new project, as illustrated in Listing 2.1:

1. Pick a project name.
2. Review which directory you are in by using the `pwd` shell command. If you are not in the correct place, then change to another appropriate directory using the shell `cd` command.
3. Create a new directory using your selected project name by using the shell `mkdir` command.
4. Change to your new project directory by using the `cd` shell command.

LISTING 2.1 CREATING A PROJECT DIRECTORY

```
1:    bash$ cd
2:    bash$ pwd
3:    /home/student01
4:    bash$ mkdir dos_cvrt
5:    bash$ cd ./dos_cvrt
6:    bash$ pwd
7:    /home/student01/dos_cvrt
8:    bash$
```

Listing 2.1 shows how you create a directory for your project. Following the procedure outlined, you complete these steps:

1. Select the project name dos_cvrt.
2. Lines 1 and 2 of Listing 2.1 show how you establish and review the current starting directory. The `cd` command in line 1 moves you to the home directory. The `pwd` command allows you to review the current directory.
3. Line 4 shows how you create the project directory named dos_cvrt.
4. Line 5 shows how to change to the new project directory. In line 6, you verify that you are in the new project directory with the use of the `pwd` command.

> When you're changing to a subdirectory, you should use the dot slash convention for subdirectories if you have the shell CDPATH variable defined. The optional CDPATH shell variable lists directories that you might frequently visit. This method allows you to change to these directories with an abbreviated name.
>
> With the CDPATH variable defined, you might be surprised where you end up sometimes. The dot slash method ensures that you change relative to your current directory.

Creating a New Source File

Now you are ready to work with a new source file. You either can create the file shown in Listing 2.2 with your favorite editor, or you can simply choose to copy the file 02LST02.c from the CD provided to your new directory as file dos_cvrt.c. Listing 2.2 shows the new program in its infancy.

LISTING 2.2 02LST02.C—EARLY BEGINNINGS OF THE DOS_CVRT UTILITY

```
/* dos_cvrt.c */
#include <stdio.h>

int
main(int argc,char **argv) {
    puts("dos_cvrt.c");
    return 0;
}
```

The program is so new that RCS does not know about it yet. The way that you introduce a new program to RCS is to simply check it in. The following steps are necessary to create a new file, under revision control, as illustrated in Listing 2.3:

1. Use the RCS `ci` command to start the check-in process.
2. When you're prompted by RCS, enter the description of this file. Usually, you describe what the source program is for, but you might add a description of other types of text files.
3. End your description input. Either enter a period on a line by itself, or use your end-of-file character (which is often a Ctrl+D character).

LISTING 2.3 SUBMITTING A NEW SOURCE MODULE TO RCS

```
bash$ ls -l
total 1
-rw-r--r--   1 student1 user        110 Nov 21 00:37 dos_cvrt.c
bash$ ci dos_cvrt.c
dos_cvrt.c,v  <--  dos_cvrt.c
enter description, terminated with single '.' or end of file:
NOTE: This is NOT the log message!
>> The beginning of a new DOS text utility
>> CTRL+D
initial revision: 1.1
done
bash$ ls -l
total 1
```

```
14:    -r--r--r--    1 student1 user          330 Nov 21 00:45 dos
➥_cvrt.c,v
15:    bash$
```


Listing 2.3 shows a sample check-in session. The `ls` command is used to show the before and after sizes and permissions of the affected files. The revision number is now 1.1, as shown in line 10. Notice that after the check-in is complete, the original file dos_cvrt.c is gone, and a new file dos_cvrt.c,v is created with only read permissions (see line 14).

The dos_cvrt.c,v file is actually a special RCS file. As a developer, you normally don't touch files with names that end in a comma and the letter *v*. This file is larger because the RCS system keeps some additional information in this file. It keeps version information, the description just typed in, the change history, and so on. In fact, attempts to work with this file directly would likely be futile. You would be wise to leave RCS to manage its contents. Notice again that the file is set to read-only permission to protect it from your tampering.

> Never tamper with an RCS file. Altering its contents may render it unusable. RCS filenames normally end with a comma and the letter *v*.

Viewing an RCS-Controlled File

You might be asking yourself how to view this file now that it's under RCS control. After all, you may just want to read it or perhaps even compile or print it. (These requests seem to be reasonable, don't they?) The current form of the file is not very useful to you.

Obtaining a Working Copy of a File

What you need is a working copy of the file. You can ask RCS for one at any time, with the help of the `co` command, as shown in Listing 2.4. Note that even though you are checking out the file, it is not being checked out for editing. I'll explain this issue fully later.

LISTING 2.4 CHECKING OUT A SOURCE MODULE FOR INSPECTION

```
bash$ ls -l
total 1
-r--r--r--    1 student1 user          330 Nov 21 00:45 dos
➥_cvrt.c,v
bash$ co dos_cvrt.c
```

continues

LISTING 2.4 CONTINUED

```
5:    dos_cvrt.c,v  -->  dos_cvrt.c
6:    revision 1.1
7:    done
8:    bash$ ls -l
9:    total 2
10:   -r--r--r--   1 student1 user         110 Nov 21 01:18 dos
       ➥_cvrt.c
11:   -r--r--r--   1 student1 user         330 Nov 21 00:45 dos
      ➥_cvrt.c,v
12:   bash$ cat dos_cvrt.c
13:   /* dos_cvrt.c */
14:   #include <stdio.h>
15:
16:   int
17:   main(int argc,char **argv) {
18:       puts("dos_cvrt.c");
19:       return 0;
20:   }
21:   bash$
```

Listing 2.4 shows a sample session in which you extract a working copy of the file dos_cvrt.c.

1. Lines 1 through 3 demonstrate that you have only the RCS file dos_cvrt.c,v to start with.
2. In line 4, you use the `co` command to request a working copy of the dos_cvrt.c source file.
3. Lines 8 to 11 show that you now get a read-only copy of dos_cvrt.c to use.
4. Lines 12 through 20 show that you indeed have your original source program back.

Using an RCS Subdirectory

In Listing 2.4, you can see that the working copy of the source module and the RCS copy of the file are both in the same directory. When only a few source modules are involved, this arrangement may be acceptable. Many people find that this arrangement adds too much clutter to their project directory and that it can lead to an accidental deletion of a master source file. Use the following steps, as demonstrated in Listing 2.5, to change RCS to use a subdirectory:

1. Starting from your project directory, create a subdirectory named RCS (in uppercase), using the shell `mkdir` command.
2. Move any existing RCS files into your new RCS subdirectory. Only the files with names ending in a comma and the letter *v* should be moved.

3. Use the `ls` command and the recursive list option `-R` to ensure that all files are in their correct places.

LISTING 2.5 ADJUSTING RCS TO KEEP FILES IN A SUBDIRECTORY

```
1:    bash$ mkdir RCS
2:    bash$ mv dos_cvrt.c,v ./RCS/.
3:    bash$ ls -lR
4:    total 1
5:    drwxr-xr-x   2 student1 user        1024 Nov 21 01:29 RCS/
6:
7:    RCS:
8:    total 1
9:    -r--r--r--   1 student1 user         330 Nov 21 00:45 dos
      ➥_cvrt.c,v
10:   bash$ co dos_cvrt.c
11:   RCS/dos_cvrt.c,v  -->  dos_cvrt.c
12:   revision 1.1
13:   done
14:   bash$ ls -l
15:   total 2
16:   drwxr-xr-x   2 student1 user        1024 Nov 21 01:29 RCS/
17:   -r--r--r--   1 student1 user         110 Nov 21 01:29 dos
      ➥_cvrt.c
18:   bash$
```

Listing 2.5 shows how you change RCS to use the new subdirectory.

1. In line 1, you create the subdirectory named RCS. Note that it must be in capital letters.
2. Line 2 shows how to move the existing RCS file dos_cvrt.c,v into the new subdirectory RCS.
3. Lines 3 to 9 show a full list of the current directory and subdirectories.
4. As an extra step, you do a checkout in lines 10 to 13 to make certain that RCS is still functioning. Line 11 shows where the file was derived from. Lines 14 to 17 show that you are successful.

This method of keeping the master copies of the RCS files under the subdirectory of RCS works well for most users. This way, you can keep the master files out of the way of your normal project files. However, you also can use RCS in other ways and configure it in other ways. One method includes defining a shell environment variable `RCSINIT`. You can simply stick to the practice of using the RCS subdirectory for both convenience and simplicity in this book.

Checking Out Source for Editing

You covered a lot of ground in the preceding sections. To summarize, you created a subdirectory RCS to keep its files in. You simply used the `ci` command to submit a new source file to source control. You also used the `co` command to obtain a working copy of the source code under management. Now you'll examine how you can start a set of changes.

To check out a work file for changes, you simply tell the `co` command to "lock the file," as shown in Listing 2.6. Locking the file registers your intent to make changes to that file, and it causes RCS to take certain measures to prevent someone else from making changes at the same time. You lock the file because having two people change one file simultaneously is normally undesirable. After you've accomplished this task, you get a working copy that is writable. It is your cue that you can now make changes.

LISTING 2.6 CHECKING OUT SOURCE CODE TO MAKE CHANGES

```
1:    bash$ ls -l
2:    total 2
3:    drwxr-xr-x   2 student1 user       1024 Nov 21 01:29 RCS/
4:    -r--r--r--   1 student1 user        110 Nov 21 01:29 dos
      ➥_cvrt.c
5:    bash$ co -l dos_cvrt.c
6:    RCS/dos_cvrt.c,v  -->  dos_cvrt.c
7:    revision 1.1 (locked)
8:    done
9:    bash$ ls -l
10:   total 2
11:   drwxr-xr-x   2 student1 user       1024 Nov 21 01:57 RCS/
12:   -rw-r--r--   1 student1 user        110 Nov 21 01:57 dos
      ➥_cvrt.c
13:   bash$
```

Listing 2.6 shows the procedure you use to indicate your desire to edit the file dos_cvrt.c. In this session, you accomplish the following:

1. In line 1, you list the current set of files. Note that, currently, the copy of dos_cvrt.c is read-only (line 4).
2. You issue the `co` command again, but this time you use the `-l` (dash el) option to request that the file be locked. Locking is confirmed in the display on line 7.
3. You list the files again in lines 9 to 12 and note that the file dos_cvrt.c is now writable (line 12).

> The `-l` option is used with the `co` command to check out a file for editing. It locks the file against editing by other users.

Editing Your Changes

Now that you have the working copy dos_cvrt.c checked out to allow edits to it, you can apply a small change. Listing 2.7 shows the resulting changed file. The following alterations were made:

1. Line 3 is the added line for including the `stdlib.h` include file. It defines many of the standard C functions such as `strtoul()`, which I will cover in a later lesson.
2. Line 4 is another line added to include the file `unistd.h`. This file defines a number of UNIX standard functions such as `read()` and `write()`.

LISTING 2.7 02LST07.C—ALTERING LOCKED SOURCE CODE

```
1:    /* dos_cvrt.c */
2:    #include <stdio.h>
3:    #include <stdlib.h>
4:    #include <unistd.h>
5:
6:    int
7:    main(int argc,char **argv) {
8:        puts("dos_cvrt.c");
9:        return 0;
10:   }
```

Displaying Your Changes

One of the nice things about source control is that you can demand to be shown what changes you actually made. You can do so before you make the changes permanent with the help of the `rcsdiff` command. Listing 2.8 shows an example of this command in use.

LISTING 2.8 DISPLAYING CHANGES MADE TO A SOURCE MODULE BEING EDITED

```
bash$ rcsdiff dos_cvrt.c
===================================================================
RCS file: RCS/dos_cvrt.c,v
retrieving revision 1.1
```

continues

LISTING 2.8 CONTINUED

```
5:    diff -r1.1 dos_cvrt.c
6:    2a3,4
7:    > #include <stdlib.h>
8:    > #include <unistd.h>
9:    bash$
```

In line 1 of Listing 2.8, you invoke the `rcsdiff` command with the name of the work file. Lines 7 and 8 show the two lines added to this file (in `diff` format).

Registering Your Changes

You've so far been able to check out a file for change, make those changes, and even display the differences you have made to the working copy (as compared to the master RCS source file). It's now high time you registered your new changes with RCS.

As you might have suspected, this process is as simple as checking in the work file. You register changes in the same way that you register a new file for source control. Listing 2.9 illustrates the procedure.

LISTING 2.9 CHECKING IN SOURCE CODE CHANGES

```
1:    bash$ ci dos_cvrt.c
2:    RCS/dos_cvrt.c,v  <--  dos_cvrt.c
3:    new revision: 1.2; previous revision: 1.1
4:    enter log message, terminated with single '.' or end of file:
5:    >> Added include files stdlib.h and unistd.h
6:    >> CTRL+D
7:    done
8:    bash$ ls -lR
9:    total 1
10:   drwxr-xr-x   2 student1 user       1024 Nov 21 02:23 RCS/
11:
12:   RCS:
13:   total 1
14:   -r--r--r--   1 student1 user        515 Nov 21 02:23 dos
      ➥_cvrt.c,v
15:   bash$
```

In Listing 2.9, you do the following:

1. You invoke the `ci` command to register the new edited file (line 1). This process is known as *checking in* your changes.
2. You type in a description of the change you have just made (line 5).
3. You end your message by pressing Ctrl+D. You could also have just typed one period and pressed Enter.

4. Lines 8 to 14 show that your working copy of the source file has been removed and that the RCS file has grown in size.

Depending on your work habits, you might not want to have the work file disappear after a check-in. You can override that behavior by using the `-u` option on the `ci` command line. Using this option leaves a read-only copy of the work file behind, in place of the original edited work file.

> To keep a work file around, simply add a `-u` option prior to the filename that you are checking in. Using this option causes a read-only work file to be left in the place of the edited file.

Listing History with the `rlog` Command

Sometimes when you're reviewing a project under RCS control, you want to check the editing history of a source module. You can easily accomplish this task with the help of the `rlog` command, as shown in Listing 2.10.

LISTING 2.10 LISTING CHANGE HISTORY ON A SOURCE MODULE

```
bash$ rlog dos_cvrt.c

RCS file: RCS/dos_cvrt.c,v
Working file: dos_cvrt.c
head: 1.2
branch:
locks: strict
access list:
symbolic names:
keyword substitution: kv
total revisions: 2;     selected revisions: 2
description:
The beginning of a new DOS text utility
----------------------------
revision 1.2
date: 1998/11/21 07:23:08;  author: student1;  state: Exp;
Added include files stdlib.h and unistd.h
----------------------------
revision 1.1
date: 1998/11/21 05:44:54;  author: student1;  state: Exp;
Initial revision
=============================================================================
bash$
```

Listing 2.10 shows an example of the `rlog` command being used. In this session, you do the following:

1. You invoke the `rlog` command, providing the name of the source file as an argument (line 1).
2. The description of the source module is shown in line 12.
3. Lines 13 through 21 display the revision comments in a most recent to least recent sequence.

Embedded Substitutions

RCS can perform a number of automatic substitutions for you as you check in your source code. Here, you'll look at the most useful ones. For more information under Linux, do a `man lookup` on `rcsintro(5)` and `co`.

To try these substitutions, you must check out the program again and edit into the source code some special RCS strings. When these strings are present, RCS replaces them with substituted values. The general procedure that you will use is as follows:

1. Check out the source file for editing. Listing 2.11 shows an example.
2. Add special string xe “”constants `$Id$` (line 3), `$Log$` (lines 5 to 7), and `$Revision$` (line 14) to the program. Listing 2.12 shows where these strings are edited into the program.
3. Check in the changes. An example is shown in Listing 2.13. Here, you use the `-l` option to keep the working copy of dos_cvrt.c around so that you can view the results of the RCS substitutions.
4. Listing 2.14 shows the new working copy of the file dos_cvrt.c. The special RCS strings have now been substituted with values.

> Remember to use the `-l` option on the `co` command line when you want to lock the source file for editing purposes.

LISTING 2.11 EDITING SOME RCS STRINGS INTO DOS_CVRT.C

```
bash$ co -l dos_cvrt.c
RCS/dos_cvrt.c,v  -->  dos_cvrt.c
revision 1.2 (locked)
done
bash$ vi dos_cvrt.c
```

LISTING 2.12 02LST12.C—CHANGES WITH RCS SUBSTITUTION STRINGS INCLUDED

```
/* dos_cvrt.c */

static const char rcsid[] = "$Id$";

/* REVISION HISTORY:
 * $Log$
 */
#include <stdio.h>
#include <stdlib.h>
#include <unistd.h>

int
main(int argc,char **argv) {
    puts("dos_cvrt.c version $Revision$");
    return 0;
}
```


LISTING 2.13 CHECKING IN SOURCE WITH RCS SUBSTITUTION STRINGS

```
bash$ ci -l dos_cvrt.c
RCS/dos_cvrt.c,v  <--  dos_cvrt.c
new revision: 1.3; previous revision: 1.2
enter log message, terminated with single '.' or end of file:
>> Demonstration of RCS substitutions
>> CTRL+D
done
bash$
```

Listing 2.14 shows the new current work file dos_cvrt.c.

LISTING 2.14 02LST14.C—LISTING OF DOS_CVRT.C AFTER RCS SUBSTITUTIONS

```
/* dos_cvrt.c */

static const char rcsid[] = "$Id: dos_cvrt.c,v 1.3
➥ 1998/11/21 22:49:39 student1 Exp student1 $";

/* REVISION HISTORY:
 * $Log: dos_cvrt.c,v $
 * Revision 1.3  1998/11/21 22:49:39  student1
 * Demonstration of RCS substitutions
 *
 */
#include <stdio.h>
#include <stdlib.h>
#include <unistd.h>

```

continues

LISTING 2.14 CONTINUED

```
15:   int
16:   main(int argc,char **argv) {
17:       puts("dos_cvrt.c version $Revision: 1.3 $");
18:       return 0;
19:   }
```

Line 3 in Listing 2.14 got quite a bit longer. Notice how the simple string `$Id$` was replaced with a number of pieces of information. Lines 6 to 8 now show some revision history. Note that the history does not start from the beginning but instead starts at the first release that the `$Log$` string appears in. For this reason, you would be wise to start using `$Log$` from the module's start.

Displaying Embedded RCS Information

If you compile and run the program from Listing 2.14, you can see that it is able to use the revision information, as shown in Listing 2.15 (though it is not very beautiful here).

LISTING 2.15 02LST15.SH—COMPILING THE SUBSTITUTED PROGRAM AND TESTING ITS VERSION

```
1:    bash$ gcc -Wall -D_GNU_SOURCE dos_cvrt.c -o dos_cvrt
2:    bash$ ./dos_cvrt
3:    dos_cvrt.c version $Revision: 1.3 $
4:    bash$ ident dos_cvrt
5:    dos_cvrt:
6:         $Id: dos_cvrt.c,v 1.3 1998/11/21 22:49:39 student1
           ➥ Exp student1 $
7:         $Revision: 1.3 $
8:    bash$
```

Listing 2.15 shows an example of a compile and execute session. The third step in the session shows something new:

1. First, the program is compiled (line 1).
2. The program is invoked in line 2. The program then displays the RCS revision information (line 3).
3. The `ident` command is used on the executable file dos_cvrt to extract RCS embedded strings. Lines 6 and 7 show the embedded `$Id$` and `$Revision$` strings.

Command `ident`, under Linux, looks through the executable named and displays any special RCS strings it can find. In this case, it finds the `rcsid` string you added and the additional text added to the `puts()` function call. Naturally, it doesn't find any of the `$Log$` text because it is placed into the C source comment lines. This type of tool is very useful for identifying, after the fact, the source module revisions that went into building the executable.

> Some UNIX platforms and competing source control tools use different conventions for embedded identification. For example, the `what` command is used under HP-UX to locate SCCS-styled strings that begin with `@(#)` embedded within an executable.

Using Source File Templates

After you get comfortable with a certain development style, you'll likely want to develop source file templates: one for *.c files and another for *.h files. Creating these templates saves you time and provides your source files with consistency.

A Source Program Template

Listing 2.16 shows a sample template for a *.c file.

LISTING 2.16 02LST16.C—A SAMPLE C LANGUAGE TEMPLATE FILE

```
/* $Header$
 * My Name          $Date$
 *
 * <Description_Here>
 *
 * $Log$
 */
static const char rcsid[] =
    "$Id$";

#include <stdio.h>
#include <stdlib.h>
#include <unistd.h>

/* End $Source$ */
```

An include File Template

Listing 2.17 shows a template for include files. It is a bit different from the template shown in Listing 2.16 because you need to use a convention that prevents the same include file from being compiled more than once. This precaution is necessary because include files often include other files, and including them all in the correct order is frequently difficult. In fact, this task is impossible for programs that must compile on all flavors of UNIX.

LISTING 2.17 02LST17.H—A SAMPLE INCLUDE FILE TEMPLATE

```
1:     /* $Header$
2:      * My Name      $Date$
3:      *
4:      * <My_Description_Here>
5:      *
6:      * $Log$
7:      */
8:     #ifndef _myhfile_h_
9:     #define _myhfile_h_  "@(#)myhfile.h $Revision$"
10:
11:    <Code_Goes_Here>
12:
13:    #endif /* _myhfile_h_ */
14:
15:    /* $Source$ */
```

Listing 2.17 shows how the C preprocessing directives in lines 8, 9, and 13 take care of preventing the same source code from being compiled more than once. Note that the macro named in the listing as `_myhfile_h_` should be changed to match the name of the include file being created. You do so for consistency and to avoid macro name clashes with other include files or program-defined macros.

Line 9 requires only that the macro `_myhfile_h_` be defined, but defining it with a version string is sometimes useful because the macro can be used elsewhere to embed the versions of included files in a program. The best practice is to define the macro with a version string even when you don't plan to use it. This approach allows you the option of using an include file version string later, should it become necessary or desirable.

Undoing a Locked Checkout

Sometimes you check out and lock a source module for editing, and you decide not to proceed with the changes made. At other times, you might just decide not to make any changes at all. RCS provides for this contingency, if you use the `rcs` command and the `-u` option, as shown in Listing 2.18.

LISTING 2.18 UNDOING A LOCKED CHECKOUT

```
bash$ rcs -u dos_cvrt.c
RCS file: RCS/dos_cvrt.c,v
1.3 unlocked
done
bash$
```

Listing 2.18 shows how a locked work file dos_cvrt.c is unlocked. However, you probably should use this procedure to avoid confusion:

1. Use the `rcs` command with the `-u` option to undo a locked file. Listing 2.18 shows an example.
2. Delete the working file. The `rcs` command does not remove the work file; it merely unlocks the status of the source file. The work file should be deleted to prevent you from compiling or subsequently editing the file.
3. If you need to keep a work file present, use the `co` command (with no options) to immediately obtain a new read-only copy of this source file. This copy does not contain any changes that were discarded in step 1.

> When you're undoing a check-out with `rcs -u`, make sure that you always remove the leftover work file, or replace it with a fresh read-only work file by invoking the `co` command.

Summary

In this lesson, you learned how to use the `rcs` command under Linux to manage your source files. You also learned how to set up a new project and how a subdirectory named RCS can help keep RCS master files separate from your working files. You went through the whole cycle of checking out a source file for editing. You also checked in those changes and even had RCS display what those changes were.

In addition to `rcs`, you learned how the Linux `ident` command can be used to spot revision information in executable files.

In the next lesson, you will write a small Linux utility program.

Q&A

Q A writable work file in my project directory usually means what?

A A writable work file usually means that the source file is checked out and locked for editing. However, it can also indicate a file that has never been checked in.

Q How do I tell what changes have been made to my work file?

A Use the `rcsdiff` utility to list the differences between the work file and the last checked-in file.

Q Why is it a good idea to create the RCS subdirectory in my project directory?

A This subdirectory separates the RCS master source files from your working copies. Separating the files provides file safety as well as removes the clutter from your current project directory.

Q What is the disadvantage of a program that does not contain any embedded version information in its executable file?

A The executable cannot by itself identify which source code versions contributed to its build. This is a significant handicap in an environment in which the program has been distributed or installed in many places and then has problems that need to be solved. Neither the user nor the developer can trace the instance of the executable back to a specific set of contributing source code modules for further investigation.

Workshop

You are encouraged to answer the quiz questions and to work through the exercises to aid in your understanding of the principles of source control and gain confidence in your use of the tools.

Quiz

1. Which RCS command is used to put a new source module under source control?
2. Which RCS command is used to get a read-only working copy of a source module?
3. Which RCS command (and options if any) is used to check out a source module for editing?
4. What is the full RCS command that cancels a locked checkout for editing?
5. Which RCS command checks in changes?
6. How is a locked checkout different from a normal checkout?

Exercises

1. Create a brand new project directory named show_time. Set up that project directory for use with RCS, copy file 02LST02.c into it, and name it show_time.c. Then check in that program as the initial version.
2. Check out the program show_time.c from exercise 1, and modify the program to obtain and display the current date and time. (**Hint:** Use function `ctime()`). After applying and testing your changes, check in the program, compile it, and run it one more time.
3. Show the revision history of your show_time.c program from exercise 2.

HOUR 3

Writing a Linux Utility

Starting Project dos_cvrt

In this lesson, I will present the very basics of a Linux utility program using a primitive but simple command-line interface. This utility program will perform a conversion of DOS format text files into UNIX text format, and vice versa. You'll also look at how this utility can be invoked by different names and cause different actions to occur.

At the end of the lesson, you'll look at the labor-saving techniques of command-line editing. This knowledge will help you work through the remainder of the book in a more efficient manner.

The dos_cvrt utility that you'll write here will convert DOS text files into UNIX text files, and vice versa. Some UNIX hosts provide tools for this task, but these tools tend to be clumsy to use because they do not work as filters or work only with fixed numbers of arguments. Others may not have a tool at all. Before you reach the end of this book, you will have a full-featured DOS-to-UNIX text conversion utility tool. Here, you'll start with the basics, but as you progress through the book, you'll tweak and enhance the tool.

Planning for Your Project

You need a plan before you go running off to create C files. To keep things simple at the start, you also should keep the requirements simple. To this end, you'll begin by designing a program that decides what type of conversion it does based on the name of the program that it is invoked with. If the program is invoked with the name unix_cvrt, for example, the program expects the input data to be UNIX-formatted text and produce DOS-formatted text as output. You can also assume that if the program is invoked with the name dos_cvrt, or any other name, the input is in DOS text format and the program produces UNIX-formatted text as output.

The first command argument is the input filename to be opened for input, and the output is simply written to standard output.

Checking Out dos_cvrt.c for Editing

You started the shell of the program in Hour 2, "Managing Your Source Code." Listing 2.14 showed the present condition of the file dos_cvrt.c. Let's check out this file and apply some changes to it:

```
bash$ co -l dos_cvrt.c
RCS/dos_cvrt.c,v  -->  dos_cvrt.c
revision 1.3 (locked)
done
bash$
```

If you left a writable working copy of the work file dos_cvrt.c from Hour 2, then you might get a session that looks like this:

```
bash$ co -l dos_cvrt.c
RCS/dos_cvrt.c,v  -->  dos_cvrt.c
revision 1.3 (locked)
writable dos_cvrt.c exists; remove it? [ny](n): y
done
bash$
```

If the file should be removed, simply answer by typing `"y"` to indicate that it can be removed and replaced with the actual file that will be checked out.

Selecting the include Files

Usually, when you begin writing a C program, you try to anticipate what include files you need. Here, you will be using the standard C I/O functions, so you know that you need the stdio.h include file. Unless you have a good reason to omit these files, you should also include files stdlib.h and unistd.h when programming for UNIX. The stdlib.h file includes definitions of the common C language library functions, such as the `exit()` function. The include file unistd.h defines many commonly used UNIX functions, such as `read()`, `write()`, and `close()`. The unistd.h file also defines the external environment variable `environ`, which you'll learn about in Hour 8, "The Linux `main` Program and Its Environment."

All three of these files are already included in the shell of the C program that you have in file dos_cvrt.c, from Hour 2. As it turns out, you also need the help of a string function, so you can add the include file for string.h as well.

Writing the dos_cvrt Utility with Stubs

A good place to begin is to determine how the command is being invoked. Remember that you have a requirement for the command to behave differently, depending on the name of the command as it is invoked.

To code for this requirement and to allow you test it, you can code your utility with stubs in place of the actual code that will be provided later. A "*program stub*" is a statement or function that substitutes for the real code.

Listing 3.1 shows how to use stubs.

LISTING 3.1 03LST01.C—DOS_CVRT.C TESTS HOW THE COMMAND IS INVOKED

```
/* dos_cvrt.c */

static const char rcsid[] =
    "$Id: dos_cvrt.c,v 1.3 1998/11/21 22:49:39 student1 Exp
    ➥ student1 $";

/* REVISION HISTORY:
 * $Log: dos_cvrt.c,v $
 * Revision 1.3  1998/11/21 22:49:39  student1
 * Demonstration of RCS substitutions
 */
#include <stdio.h>
#include <stdlib.h>
#include <unistd.h>
#include <string.h>

int
main(int argc,char **argv) {
    char *base_name = 0;     /* Basename of command */

```

continues

LISTING 3.1 CONTINUED

```
20:     /*
21:      * Determine the basename of the command name. This
22:      * is necessary since this command could be invoked
23:      * with a pathname. For example, argv[0] could be
24:      * "/usr/local/bin/unix_cvrt" if it was installed
25:      * in the system that way.
26:      */
27:     if ( ( base_name = strrchr(argv[0],'/') ) != 0 )
28:         ++base_name;        /* Skip over '/' */
29:     else
30:         base_name = argv[0];/* No dir. component */
31:
32:     /*
33:      * Now that we know the basename of the command
34:      * name used, we can determine which function we
35:      * must carry out here.
36:      */
37:     if ( !strcmp(base_name,"unix_cvrt") ) {
38:         /* Perform a UNIX -> DOS text conversion */
39:         puts("UNIX to DOS conversion");
40:     } else {
41:         /* Perform a DOS -> UNIX text conversion */
42:         puts("DOS to UNIX conversion");
43:     }
44:
45:     return 0;
46: }
```

Listing 3.1 shows the result of the following editing steps:

1. The string constant `rcsid[]` is added (line 3).
2. A revision history is added in lines 6 to 10. RCS provides the information in lines 7 to 9.
3. The `"puts("dos_cvrt.c")"` call is removed from the dos_cvrt.c (revision 1.2) used in Hour 2.
4. Lines 18 to 44 are added to fill in the rest of the new utility.

> The changes to dos_cvrt.c shown in Listing 3.1 have not been checked into RCS yet. You still have the writable dos_cvrt.c work file. When you actually check in these changes, this source file will become revision 1.4.

The major chunk of code added to the `main()` function requires some explanation:

1. The main program begins by extracting the basename of the command name in lines 27 to 30 of Listing 3.1. The C function `strrchr()` is used to determine where the last slash is located.
2. If no slash is located in the pathname, `strrchr()` returns a `null` pointer. It tells you that variable `argv[0]` contains the basename already.
3. If, however, `strrchr()` does return a pointer, you increment past the slash character in line 28. This causes the variable `base_name` to point to the basename within the pathname.
4. Line 37 tests to see whether the basename matches the string `"unix_cvrt"`. If so, then you know that you are doing the UNIX-to-DOS text conversion according to your program specifications.
5. Otherwise, in line 40, you assume that if you don't have a name match in line 37, the required conversion is DOS text format to UNIX format.

> A *basename* is the filename component of a pathname. It is the file's name without any directory component attached. For example, the pathname /usr/local/bin/dos_cvrt can be broken into the directory component /usr/local/bin and the basename component dos_cvrt.

In lines 39 and 42, notice that you simply put calls to `puts()` there to tell you what is happening. These calls are program "stubs" that will be filled in with real code after preliminary testing.

> Using stubs in programs under development can help you debug a program. Testing with stubs can often point out early design problems.

Testing the Utility with Stubs in Place

With your stubs in place, you are now ready to test the improvements to this program. Before you do that, however, check in the changes made in Listing 3.1. After you do so, that edit becomes known to RCS as revision 1.4.

By using the `ci` command with the `-l` option, you can perform a checkpoint release:

```
bash$ ci -l dos_cvrt.c
RCS/dos_cvrt.c,v  <--  dos_cvrt.c
new revision: 1.4; previous revision: 1.3
enter log message, terminated with single '.' or end of file:
>> Coded basename test
>> CTRL+D
done
bash$ gcc -Wall -D_GNU_SOURCE dos_cvrt.c -o dos_cvrt
bash$
```

This operation accomplishes two things at once:

1. It checks in the changes you made (shown in Listing 3.1). They are registered as revision 1.4.
2. It checks out and locks a new work file dos_cvrt.c, which will later become revision 1.5.

Now it is time to test the program's functionality. You can easily test the DOS-to-UNIX conversion process by simply invoking the program:

```
bash$ ./dos_cvrt dos_file
DOS to UNIX conversion
bash$
```

Note that the output shows the intention to do the "DOS to UNIX conversion." To test the other conversion, you need to invoke this command with another name—namely unix_cvrt. You can easily accomplish this feat under Linux by linking this second name to the first:

1. Link the dos_cvrt executable to the name unix_cvrt using the `ln` command.
2. Invoke the link name unix_cvrt instead of dos_cvrt.

The following is an example of what that session might look like:

```
bash$ ln ./dos_cvrt ./unix_cvrt
bash$ ./unix_cvrt unix_file
UNIX to DOS conversion
bash$
```

You see that this operation indeed does work. Note that the command-line argument `unix_file` does not actually exist presently as a file, but the command pays no attention to this fact.

Replacing the Stubs

Now it's time to fill in the rest of the program and replace the stubs. This time, assume that you've edited the program dos_cvrt.c to replace the stubs with the actual conversion code that you need. Now you can check in the finalized code by using the `ci` command and the `-u` option:

```
bash$ ci -u dos_cvrt.c
RCS/dos_cvrt.c,v  <--  dos_cvrt.c
new revision: 1.5; previous revision: 1.4
enter log message, terminated with single '.' or end of file:
>> Completed utility & tested ok.
>>
done
bash$
```

The check-in procedure here accomplishes the following two things in one command:

1. It checks in the current edit. This process registers the changes made to replace the program stubs.
2. The `-u` option causes `ci` to leave behind a read-only copy of the source file dos_cvrt.c. This copy of revision 1.4 now includes the registered changes to the stubs.

Listing 3.2 shows what the final source code looks like. This time, these changes have been checked in, so the comments in line 8 reflect the true version of the file that you are looking at.

LISTING 3.2 03LST02.C—THE WORKING DOS_CVRT.C UTILITY

```
1:   /* dos_cvrt.c */
2:
3:   static const char rcsid[] =
4:       "$Id: dos_cvrt.c,v 1.5 1998/11/23 05:32:21 student1 Exp $";
5:
6:   /* REVISION HISTORY:
7:    * $Log: dos_cvrt.c,v $
8:    * Revision 1.5  1998/11/23 05:32:21  student1
9:    * Completed utility & tested ok.
10:   *
11:   * Revision 1.4  1998/11/23 05:04:23  student1
12:   * Coded basename test
13:   *
14:   * Revision 1.3  1998/11/21 22:49:39  student1
15:   * Demonstration of RCS substitutions
16:   */
17:  #include <stdio.h>
18:  #include <stdlib.h>
19:  #include <unistd.h>
20:  #include <string.h>
21:
```

continues

Listing 3.2 CONTINUED

```
int
main(int argc,char **argv) {
    char *base_name = 0;    /* Basename of command */
    int ch;                 /* Current input character */
    int cr_flag;            /* True when CR prev. encountered */
    FILE *in = 0;           /* Input file */

    /*
     * Determine the basename of the command name. This
     * is necessary since this command could be invoked
     * with a pathname. For example, argv[0] could be
     * "/usr/local/bin/unix_cvrt" if it was installed
     * in the system that way.
     */
    if ( ( base_name = strrchr(argv[0],'/') ) != 0 )
        ++base_name;        /* Skip over '/' */
    else
        base_name = argv[0];/* No dir. component */

    /*
     * Open the input file:
     */
    if ( argc != 2 ) {
        fprintf(stderr,"Missing input file.\n");
        return 1;
    }
    if ( !(in = fopen(argv[1],"r")) ) {
        fprintf(stderr,"Cannot open input file.\n");
        return 2;
    }

    /*
     * Now that we know the basename of the command
     * name used, we can determine which function we
     * must carry out here.
     */
    if ( !strcmp(base_name,"unix_cvrt") ) {
        /* Perform a UNIX -> DOS text conversion */
        while ( (ch = fgetc(in)) != EOF ) {
            if ( ch == '\n' )
                putchar('\r');
            putchar(ch);
        }
    } else {
        /* Perform a DOS -> UNIX text conversion */
        cr_flag = 0;    /* No CR encountered yet */
        while ( (ch = fgetc(in)) != EOF ) {
            if ( cr_flag && ch != '\n' ) {
                /* This CR did not precede LF */
```

```
71:                 putchar('\r');
72:             }
73:             if ( !(cr_flag = ch == '\r') )
74:                 putchar(ch);
75:         }
76:     }
77:
78:     fclose(in);
79:
80:     return 0;
81: }
```


The following changes have been made to the program in Listing 3.2:

1. To support the changes, variables are added in lines 25 to 27. Variable `ch` is simply the current character read. The `FILE` variable `in` is a pointer to the opened input file. The DOS-to-UNIX text conversion code uses variable `cr_flag`.
2. Lines 44 to 47 must make sure that the command line includes the filename argument. Note that you test for a count of two arguments because the command name in `argv[0]` counts as one.
3. In lines 48 to 51, you have code installed to open the input file or exit with a status `2` if unsuccessful. The error message in line 49 is not too friendly to the user here, but you'll remedy that problem later.
4. The UNIX-to-DOS conversion code is shown in lines 60 to 64. The program simply reads one character at a time into variable `ch` until it encounters "end of file." Within the loop at line 61, the program tests whether the character is a newline (linefeed) character. If it is, the DOS return character is put to standard output before the newline is.
5. The DOS-to-UNIX conversion code is added in lines 67 to 75.

Performing the DOS-to-UNIX Conversion

The DOS-to-UNIX conversion code in lines 67 to 75 of Listing 3.2 requires a bit of explanation. You might be tempted to simply assume that you can strip all DOS return characters out of the input stream and allow the normal newline characters to go out on their own. In practice, this method may work most of the time. The problem with this approach, however, is that sometimes a return character may be embedded in a DOS text line before the end of the line. This type of coding is often done for overtyping on impact printers for extra boldness or overstriking. Allowing those characters to go through as is requires a slightly different approach, as you can see here:

1. Line 67 initializes `cr_flag` to `false`. This flag is set to `true` whenever a return character is encountered.
2. A character is read (line 68) until the end of file is reached.

3. If the `cr_flag` is not `true`, then proceed to step 5.
4. If the `cr_flag` is true, and the character read in step 2 is not a newline (linefeed) character, then you emit a return character. You do so because you did not get a return and newline pair.
5. Line 73 notes whether you got a return character by setting `cr_flag`. If `cr_flag` is set to `false`, indicating that you did not get a return character, then you immediately emit that character because it requires no further processing.
6. At the bottom of the loop in line 75, you return back to step 2.

Testing the Utility

Now you can try this utility. You might not have a DOS text file readily available, but this is no problem because this wonderful utility can convert both ways. The procedure you'll use is as follows:

1. Compile the new utility.
2. Remove the existing unix_cvrt executable link, if it still exists. If it exists, it references an old executable.
3. Link the newly created dos_cvrt executable to the name unix_cvrt.
4. Using the new unix_cvrt utility, convert the UNIX-formatted text in dos_cvrt.c to a file named dos.txt. This new file will be in DOS text format.
5. Using the `cat` command with the `-v` option, verify that the new file dos.txt is indeed in DOS format.
6. Provided that step 5 succeeds, convert the DOS text file dos.txt back into a UNIX text file using the dos_cvrt utility you just compiled. The file created will be named unix.txt.
7. Using the `cat` command with the `-v` option again, display the tail end of the unix.txt file to see whether it has been converted successfully back to UNIX format.

Listing 3.3 shows a sample session using the procedure just outlined.

LISTING 3.3 TESTING THE COMPLETED DOS_CVRT UTILITY

```
bash$ gcc -Wall -D_GNU_SOURCE dos_cvrt.c -o dos_cvrt
bash$ rm unix_cvrt
bash$ ln dos_cvrt unix_cvrt
bash$ ./unix_cvrt dos_cvrt.c >dos.txt
bash$ cat -v dos.txt | tail
                }^M
                if ( !(cr_flag = ch == '\r') )^M
```

```
                putchar(ch);^M
            }^M
        }^M
    ^M
        fclose(in);^M
    ^M
        return 0;^M
    }^M
    bash$ ./dos_cvrt dos.txt >unix.txt
    bash$ cat -v unix.txt ¦ tail
                }
                if ( !(cr_flag = ch == '\r') )
                    putchar(ch);
            }
        }

        fclose(in);

        return 0;
    }
    bash$
```

> Be careful when you're working with linked files. After a recompile, your link may be stale. Always remove it and re-establish the link afterward to be sure.

> To test whether two particular filenames are linked to the same physical file, you can use the `-i` option in the Linux `ls` command to list the i-node numbers. If these files are on the same file system, and the i-node numbers match, then they are linked to the same file.

Step 6 of the procedure allows for a visual inspection of the final text file unix.txt. You know, however, that the resulting file unix.txt should be identical to the file you started with in step 4. Using the Linux `diff` command as follows, you should be able to prove that no differences have crept in:

```
bash$ diff dos_cvrt.c unix.txt
bash$
```

Apparently, there are no differences. The utility is a success. Don't get too hasty in your celebration, however, because there is still plenty of room for improvement.

Reviewing the Project

Even though the conversion utility gets the job done, looking at the program now is useful to see how you can improve on it. You might be tempted to immediately start to enhance the program without paying attention to the other important details such as improving its error handling and its messages. However, a developer should not stop working on a program simply because it seems to work. The program may have usability problems and reliability problems that you've not yet encountered in your testing. Perhaps you've already noted some of the weaknesses in your program.

One problem with the program at present is that it is not modular. All the code is contained in one source module, and even worse, all the code is contained within the `main()` program. If this was the full extent of the program, leaving it this way might be acceptable. However, you already know that you plan to enhance this utility, so this structure will not do.

If this program were larger, this structure would not be the best for longer term maintenance. Small changes become more difficult because you must adjust a lot more code. Small changes also invoke large compiles instead of small ones. You'll look at the modularity issues in Hour 4, "Modular Programming in C."

Another weakness in this program is the error message that the user gets if the program is unable to open the input file. Look at the following command session:

```
bash$ ./dos_cvrt oink >out.txt
Cannot open input file.
bash$
```

Here, you get a terse message saying that the program cannot open the input file. "Well, thank you very much," you might be inclined to say, as a user of this utility, "but why can't it open that file?" The reasons may vary from the file not existing to a lack of permissions to open it.

Not only is the reason for the open failure missing, but also, the identity of the file that failed to open is missing. This information will become important when you enhance the utility to allow for more than one input file. Even as it stands, however, if this program were invoked from a shell script with a number of other commands, the message identifying both the reason for failure and the filename would be much better for troubleshooting.

More user unfriendliness comes from the message when you don't specify an input file:

```
bash$ ./dos_cvrt
Missing input file.
bash$
```

Notice that the message tersely says "`Missing input file`". "Well, thank you very much, but how do I use this thing?" might be the grumble of your users. The users don't know whether they should use shell input redirection or provide the filename on the command line. A message showing how the command should be used would be helpful, or at least a short message telling the users how to obtain such documentation from the command is needed.

To support additional enhancements to this utility, you need command-line option processing. You'll look at this topic in Hour 6, "Linux Command-Line Option Processing."

Before you leave this program review, note that one more weakness to this program has not been looked at. You have avoided any form of error checking when you actually do the conversion on the text files. You do not check for read errors when reading, and you don't check that all our output gets written. A common problem is to run out of disk space. Yet your program glibly assumes upon completion that all is well and returns a status code of zero to the shell. If a shell script checks this code, it then also assumes that the text conversion was a success, which could be dangerous. You'll look at error reporting in Hour 7, "Error Handling and Reporting."

Using Command-Line Editing

If you have been working through the examples I've provided, you might have found that typing in the long command lines for each compile can be a bit of a nuisance. In fact, you may even have a shell alias or shell script defined by now to make your job easier. In any case, take a quick look at the Linux bash shell facilities for editing and recalling command lines. You may be unaware of this capability, which might save you a lot of effort.

The GNU bash was created by the Free Software Foundation and named from the acronym for "Bourne-Again SHell". The Bourne shell is the standard shell on most UNIX systems, whereas bash is an advanced version of this shell. Its functionality actually borrows heavily from the newer UNIX shell known as the Korn shell.

Selecting a Command-Line Editing Mode

One of the new features of the UNIX shell is the capability to provide command-line editing (both bash and Korn). When you catch on to this feature, you'll be amazed at the bare editing facilities of the NT DOS prompt.

The default for the bash shell is to use the emacs-styled editing mode. You can also activate this shell at any time you are in another mode by typing the following:

```
bash$ set -o emacs
```

When you're in this mode, you have a subset of the emacs commands at your disposal. For example, if you want to retrieve the last command that you typed, you can press Ctrl+P and then press Enter (Ctrl+P is an emacs way of moving to the previous line).

Many users, of course, like the vi editor's way of doing things. Bash caters to this whim by allowing you to select vi mode, as follows:

```
bash$ set -o vi
```

Now that you have this mode set, you can use vi keystrokes to get things done. Note, however, one small difference: In vi, you are normally in command mode, and you use "`i`" or some other command to enter an "input mode". For command lines, you are in input mode by default and must press the Escape key to enter a command mode. For example, to back up to the previous command, you press Escape to enter command mode and then press the "`K`" key ("k" in vi moves up to the previous line). To append to the current line, you might enter the "`A`" and then start typing. The command is initiated when you press Enter. You might find that using vi mode takes a bit of practice.

Performing Command-Line Searches

Bash also can conveniently search back through your command history.

Using emacs Mode Searches

In emacs mode, you can perform the following:

1. Press Ctrl+R (emacs reverse incremental search).
2. Type in a fragment of the command that you are looking for.
3. If the first search is not what you require, press Ctrl+R again to repeat the search.
4. When the required result has been located, press Enter to execute that command. Otherwise, apply other emacs commands to edit the result before executing it.

Next, you can set emacs mode and perform a search. Press Ctrl+R, and immediately bash prompts you with "`(reverse-i-search)`" (this means reverse incremental search). Then you type in **`vi`** to search back to the prior vi setting command, and immediately the search yields the text "`set -o vi`" to the right of where you're typing:

```
bash$ set -o emacs
(reverse-i-search)'vi': set -o vi
```

1. You set emacs mode (just in case you have vi mode set). Then you press Ctrl+R to start a reverse incremental search.
2. You then type the fragment "`vi`".
3. The bash shell immediately shows you the command "`set -o vi`" as a result.

4. To use this result as is, press Enter. However, you could start editing that command if you enter some other emacs editing commands.

Using vi Mode Searches

In vi mode, you follow a slightly different procedure:

1. Press the Escape key to enter "vi command mode". By default, bash allows you to "enter data".
2. Type in one (forward) slash. For Microsoft types, this is the "`/`" character. This slash indicates a backward search through your command history.
3. Enter a command fragment to base your search on. In the example shown next, you'll use the fragment "**`o emacs`**".
4. Press Enter to start the search.
5. The search result is displayed on the command line. To execute it, press Enter. Otherwise, you can apply other vi commands to edit this command.
6. To repeat the search because the incorrect entry was shown, type a single slash character again and go to step 4.

An example of how this procedure might look is shown here:

```
bash$ /o emacs
```

After you press Enter to activate the search, the command line shows the prior "`set -o emacs`" command from the command history as the current line, as you can see here:

```
bash$ set -o emacs
```

Using Forward vi Mode Searches

In vi mode, the slash searches backward through your command history, and the question mark searches forward. This use may seem a bit counterintuitive because normal vi editor behavior is the opposite of this in a file. However, it just works this way (presumably because the slash is the easier thing to type).

Listing Your Command History

The bash shell has another trick up its sleeve: You can list your recent command-line history. This capability can be useful when you want to see what has been done recently. This history can also be useful when you are having difficulty finding the command you want. Finally, this history display is necessary if you want to recall a command using command recall by number. Consider the following:

```
bash$ fc -l
485     clear
486     set -o vi
```

```
487     fc -l
488     clear
489     mount
490     man bash
491     set -o emacs
492     ls -l /usr/local/bin
493     echo $PATH
494     emacs ~/.profile
495     ps -ax
496     pine
497     lpstat -t
498     clear
499     ls -l
500     pwd
501     sync
bash$
```

The `fc` command is a built-in command of the bash shell program. It lists all recently used commands. You can recall any one of these commands by number:

```
bash$ !500
pwd
/home/student1/
bash$
```

You simply precede the number with an exclamation mark, and the command that gets executed is shown on the following line.

This lesson provided a very brief introduction to some of the most essential aspects of command-line editing. I've included this information to help equip you for more work tofollow.

Summary

In this lesson, you did some project planning and started writing the utility program with stubs. You later replaced those stubs with the actual code that performed the conversion. You also practiced using RCS, as you built up the program. You tested the program by converting text to DOS format and then converted it back to UNIX format. You concluded that section with a look at the present limitations of the project.

In the remainder of the lesson, you learned about the command-line editing features that are available in the bash shell. Mastering these features will make you much more efficient as a developer.

Q&A

Q The utility program dos_cvrt.c does two different text file conversions. How does it determine which conversion to perform?

A The program looks at the command name provided to the `main()` program in `argv[0]`. The same executable file can be invoked by different links to it. Based on which link name is used, the program can make a choice.

Q Why is the basename of the executable filename used for comparison? Why not just use the `argv[0]` value as it is supplied?

A Using the basename is the only reliable way to test for the command name because the same program can be invoked from multiple directories and in multiple ways in the current directory. For example, the command can be invoked using the dot slash method, as well as just by using the bare command name. In short, using the basename eliminates the need to test for all the possibilities.

Q What is a stub in a program?

A A stub is a simple piece of programming that substitutes for the real thing. Often it is just a `print` statement.

Q Why is it necessary to remove the alternate link of unix_cvrt after each compile of dos_cvrt?

A Depending on the current behavior of the `gcc` command, it might remove the link to dos_cvrt before writing out the new dos_cvrt executable. If this happens, the old link unix_cvrt still points to the old executable program. For this reason, you should always remove the alternate link (unix_cvrt) and then link the new executable with the alternate link name.

Workshop

To practice what you have learned in this lesson, you are encouraged to answer the quiz and work through the exercises.

Quiz

1. What is the value of `argc` if the program is provided two command-line arguments?
2. What is the value of `argc` if the program is provided one option and two command-line arguments?
3. Given two links to a file on the same file system, how do you prove that they point to the same physical file without changing the file's contents?

4. Can a link exist to your executable from two different file systems? Why or why not?
5. What are two reasons why a file might not be successfully opened for input?
6. Why might an output operation to standard output fail?
7. Is `bash` part of Linux, or is it a program that runs on top of the Linux kernel?
8. How do you set vi command-line editing mode?
9. How do you display recent command-line history?

Exercises

1. Copy the program 03LST02.c to a new work area for your experiments. Modify the program to accept more than one input file.
2. Modify the finished program from exercise 1 so that it works with zero input files if none are given—that is, to accept input from standard input. When a program operates this way, what is it called?

HOUR 4

Modular Programming in C

Programming in Modules

A modular program is broken into smaller components, thus making it easier to understand. A well-understood program is easier to enhance or fix. Although modular programs also tend to reuse code more, the main advantage of using such programs is making work easier for the programmer.

In this lesson, you are going to take the nonmodular dos_cvrt.c and make it modular. After the program is broken into functions and then into smaller modules, a number of new issues arise. How to use external function prototypes, the need for a new include file, and the need for static definitions are systematically discussed.

Adding New Functionality

To learn how modularization helps make enhancing the program easier, you are going to add a new program requirement to dos_cvrt in this lesson. The new dos_cvrt program must accept one or more input files. These input files will be processed in sequence, and their output will be combined. This aspect of dos_cvrt will be much like the Linux `cat` command.

Making dos_cvrt.c Modular

In this section, you are going to edit the single dos_cvrt.c program into a few smaller source files. Making smaller files helps you organize this utility program into subprograms that are easier to understand and manage.

Checking Out dos_cvrt.c for Editing

To break the source program into smaller modules, you must first check out the source code for editing, as follows:

```
bash$ co -l dos_cvrt.c
RCS/dos_cvrt.c,v  -->  dos_cvrt.c
revision 1.5 (locked)
done
bash$
```

Splitting dos_cvrt.c into Functions

Now you can separate the code that does the actual text conversions. Remember that you have two different text conversions in this utility: a UNIX text conversion and a DOS text conversion. Both of these operations deserve to be in their own separate functions. Listing 4.1 shows the result of this change, though the overall functionality of the program has not been changed just yet.

LISTING 4.1 04LST01.C—CONVERSION CODE BROKEN OUT INTO FUNCTIONS

```
/* dos_cvrt.c */

static const char rcsid[] =
    "$Id: dos_cvrt.c,v 1.6 1998/11/27 01:01:28 student1 Exp $";

/* REVISION HISTORY:
 * $Log: dos_cvrt.c,v $
 * Revision 1.6  1998/11/27 01:01:28  student1
 * Separated conversions into unix2dos() and
 * dos2unix() functions.
 *
 * Revision 1.5  1998/11/23 05:32:21  student1
 * Completed utility & tested ok.
 *
 * Revision 1.4  1998/11/23 05:04:23  student1
```

```
 * Coded basename test
 *
 * Revision 1.3  1998/11/21 22:49:39  student1
 * Demonstration of RCS substitutions
 */
#include <stdio.h>
#include <stdlib.h>
#include <unistd.h>
#include <string.h>

/*
 * Convert file named by pathname to DOS
 * text format, on standard output:
 */
int
unix2dos(const char *pathname) {
    int ch;                 /* Current input character */
    FILE *in = 0;           /* Input file */

    if ( !(in = fopen(pathname,"r")) ) {
        fprintf(stderr,"Cannot open input file.\n");
        return 2;
    }

    while ( (ch = fgetc(in)) != EOF ) {
        if ( ch == '\n' )
            putchar('\r');
        putchar(ch);
    }

    fclose(in);
    return 0;
}

/*
 * Convert file named by pathname, to
 * UNIX text file format on standard output:
 */
int
dos2unix(const char *pathname) {
    int ch;                 /* Current input character */
    int cr_flag;            /* True when CR prev. encountered */
    FILE *in = 0;           /* Input file */

    if ( !(in = fopen(pathname,"r")) ) {
        fprintf(stderr,"Cannot open input file.\n");
        return 2;
    }

```


continues

LISTING 4.1 CONTINUED

```
    cr_flag = 0;   /* No CR encountered yet */
    while ( (ch = fgetc(in)) != EOF ) {
        if ( cr_flag && ch != '\n' ) {
            /* This CR did not preceed LF */
            putchar('\r');
        }
        if ( !(cr_flag = ch == '\r') )
            putchar(ch);
    }

    fclose(in);
    return 0;
}

int
main(int argc,char **argv) {
    char *base_name = 0;    /* Basename of command */
    int rc = 0;             /* Command return code */

    /*
     * Determine the basename of the command name. This
     * is necessary since this command could be invoked
     * with a pathname. For example, argv[0] could be
     * "/usr/local/bin/unix_cvrt" if it was installed
     * in the system that way.
     */
    if ( ( base_name = strrchr(argv[0],'/') ) != 0 )
        ++base_name;        /* Skip over '/' */
    else
        base_name = argv[0];/* No dir. component */

    /*
     * Check for missing input file:
     */
    if ( argc != 2 ) {
        fprintf(stderr,"Missing input file.\n");
        return 1;
    }

    /*
     * Now that we know the basename of the command
     * name used, we can determine which function we
     * must carry out here.
     */
    if ( !strcmp(base_name,"unix_cvrt") ) {
        /* Perform a UNIX -> DOS text conversion */
        rc = unix2dos(argv[1]);
    } else {
        /* Perform a DOS -> UNIX text conversion */
```

```
114:         rc = dos2unix(argv[1]);
115:     }
116:
117:     return rc;
118: }
```

The following is a systematic summary of the changes made:

1. The UNIX conversion code has now been moved to function `unix2dos()` (lines 30 to 48).
2. The DOS conversion code has been moved to function dos2unix() (lines 54 to 77).
3. Functions `unix2dos()` and `dos2unix()` receive a copy of the `fopen()` code segment that was previously in the `main()` program. This change entails a bit of planning to arrive at the new requirements later.

Note that the functions `unix2dos()` and `dos2unix()` are defined prior to the `main()` program. Seasoned programmers take advantage of the fact that defining the functions ahead of their use saves extra effort later. Had the `main()` program appeared first, you would be required to supply two additional `extern` statements:

```
extern int unix2dos(const char *pathname);
extern int dos2unix(const char *pathname);
```

This point may seem trite, but Linux developers like to save code.

Notice how simple the `main()` program appears now. The function calls replace the original code in lines 111 and 114. The `main()` program now has fewer lines of code and fewer variables. This change makes it more pleasing to look at, and it will be easier for the next person who gets to maintain your code.

Enhancing dos_cvrt

The `main()` program still contains the inline basename code that should be cleaned up. It's now time that you make the new program comply with the new requirements. Listing 4.2 shows the new dos_cvrt.c.

LISTING 4.2 04LST02.C—THE MULTI-INPUT FILE DOS_CVRT.C

```
/* dos_cvrt.c */

static const char rcsid[] =
    "$Id: dos_cvrt.c,v 1.7 1998/11/27 01:31:39 student1 Exp $";

```

continues

LISTING 4.2 CONTINUED

```
/* REVISION HISTORY:
 * $Log: dos_cvrt.c,v $
 * Revision 1.7  1998/11/27 01:31:39  student1
 * Now handles multiple input files, plus
 * put basename code into its own Basename()
 * function.
 *
 * Revision 1.6  1998/11/27 01:01:28  student1
 * Separated conversions into unix2dos() and
 * dos2unix() functions.
 *
 * Revision 1.5  1998/11/23 05:32:21  student1
 * Completed utility & tested ok.
 *
 * Revision 1.4  1998/11/23 05:04:23  student1
 * Coded basename test
 *
 * Revision 1.3  1998/11/21 22:49:39  student1
 * Demonstration of RCS substitutions
 */
#include <stdio.h>
#include <stdlib.h>
#include <unistd.h>
#include <string.h>

/*
 * Convert file named by pathname to DOS
 * text format, on standard output:
 */
int
unix2dos(const char *pathname) {
    int ch;                 /* Current input character */
    FILE *in = 0;           /* Input file */

    if ( !(in = fopen(pathname,"r")) ) {
        fprintf(stderr,"Cannot open input file.\n");
        return 2;
    }

    while ( (ch = fgetc(in)) != EOF ) {
        if ( ch == '\n' )
            putchar('\r');
        putchar(ch);
    }

    fclose(in);
    return 0;
}
```

```

/*
 * Convert file named by pathname, to
 * UNIX text file format on standard output:
 */
int
dos2unix(const char *pathname) {
    int ch;                     /* Current input character */
    int cr_flag;                /* True when CR prev. encountered */
    FILE *in = 0;               /* Input file */

    if ( !(in = fopen(pathname,"r")) ) {
        fprintf(stderr,"Cannot open input file.\n");
        return 2;
    }

    cr_flag = 0;    /* No CR encountered yet */
    while ( (ch = fgetc(in)) != EOF ) {
        if ( cr_flag && ch != '\n' ) {
            /* This CR did not preceed LF */
            putchar('\r');
        }
        if ( !(cr_flag = ch == '\r') )
            putchar(ch);
    }

    fclose(in);
    return 0;
}

/*
 * Return the pointer to the basename component
 * of a pathname:
 */
char *
Basename(const char *path) {
    char *base_name = 0;

    if ( ( base_name = strrchr(path,'/') ) != 0 )
        ++base_name;                         /* Skip over '/' */
    else
        base_name = (char *) path;           /* No dir. */
    return base_name;
}

int
main(int argc,char **argv) {
    char *base_name = 0;    /* Basename of command */
    int rc = 0;             /* Command return code */
```


continues

LISTING 4.2 CONTINUED

```
103:     int (*conv)(const char *pathname); /* Conv. Func. Ptr */
104:     int x;
105:
106:     /*
107:      * Determine the basename of the command name. This
108:      * is necessary since this command could be invoked
109:      * with a pathname. For example, argv[0] could be
110:      * "/usr/local/bin/unix_cvrt" if it was installed
111:      * in the system that way.
112:      */
113:     base_name = Basename(argv[0]);
114:
115:     /*
116:      * Check for missing input file:
117:      */
118:     if ( argc < 2 ) {
119:         fprintf(stderr,"Missing input file(s).\n");
120:         return 1;
121:     }
122:
123:     /*
124:      * Now that we know the basename of the command
125:      * name used, we can determine which function we
126:      * must carry out here.
127:      */
128:     if ( !strcmp(base_name,"unix_cvrt") )
129:         conv = unix2dos;
130:     else
131:         conv = dos2unix;
132:
133:     /*
134:      * Perform a text conversion
135:      */
136:     for ( x=1; x<argc; ++x )
137:         if ( (rc = conv(argv[x])) != 0 )
138:             break;      /* An error occurred */
139:
140:     return rc;
141: }
```

The program has certainly been through some changes here. The basename code is broken out into its own function in lines 88 to 97 of Listing 4.2. This change makes the `main()` program look less cluttered in line 113.

The other important change in Listing 4.2 is the addition of the function pointer variable named `conv` in line 103. Because both conversion functions have identical interfaces, you can simplify this whole program by arriving at the function pointer to use in lines

128 to 131. After you've settled on the conversion to perform, the operations for either are identical. For this reason, lines 136 to 138 now are used for both the UNIX-to-DOS and the DOS-to-UNIX text file conversions. This small change makes the `main()` program even easier to read.

Notice the new `for` loop in line 136. It now addresses the capability to allow for multiple input files. Note that `x` starts at the value `1` because `argv[0]` is the command name.

Splitting dos_cvrt into Separate Source Modules

At this point, you've managed to organize dos_cvrt.c into separate functions, which is a very good start. For this size of program, leaving it in its present form is acceptable. For a large project, however, having a large source file makes the program less manageable for editing. Large source modules also require large compiles whenever a change is made. Therefore, to see how larger projects should be split into separate source files, you can modularize the dos_cvrt.c program as a simple example.

Often the `main()` function is separated into its own file called main.c. However, if you separate it here, you lose the nice RCS history that you have been diligently maintaining. What you can do instead is retain the `main()` function and the `Basename()` function in this dos_cvrt.c source module. You can split the two different text conversion functions into their own source modules, unix2dos.c and dos2unix.c.

Check out the source module dos_cvrt.c again for editing. You can create the new files by cutting lines of code from dos_cvrt.c and pasting them to the new files unix2dos.c and dos2unix.c, respectively. After these new modules are checked into RCS, they have new revision numbers of 1.1. However, that code is derived from the dos_cvrt.c version 1.7 file that you are currently editing. The new dos_cvrt.c is soon to become version 1.8.

Having split up the source into its three different source files now, you then have one more requirement left to take care of. The `main()` program calls on functions `unix2dos()` and `dos2unix()`. They are now defined externally to the dos_cvrt.c source module, so you need interface definitions to be made available to the `main()` program.

Creating File dos_cvrt.h

You could put the `extern` statements in the dos_cvrt.c module. For your immediate needs, this approach would do for this small project, but try to imagine a large project with hundreds or possibly thousands of functions defined. What you need is your own include file. Listing 4.3 illustrates the new dos_cvrt.h include file.

Listing 4.3 04LST03.h—Include File for Modular dos_cvrt.c

```
1:  /* $Header: /home/student1/dos_cvrt/RCS/dos_cvrt.h,v 1.1 ...
2:   * Basil Fawlty      $Date: 1998/11/27 02:28:57 $
3:   *
4:   * Header File for the dos_cvrt utility program:
5:   *
6:   * $Log: dos_cvrt.h,v $
7:   * Revision 1.1  1998/11/27 02:28:57  student1
8:   * Initial revision
9:   *
10:  */
11: #ifndef _dos_cvrt_h_
12: #define _dos_cvrt_h_ "@(#)dos_cvrt.h $Revision: 1.1 $"
13:
14: extern int unix2dos(const char *pathname);
15: extern int dos2unix(const char *pathname);
16:
17: #endif /* _dos_cvrt_h_ */
18:
19: /* $Source: /home/student1/dos_cvrt/RCS/dos_cvrt.h,v $ */
```

Most of this include file appears to be comments, but you do have the important `extern` declarations in lines 14 and 15 of Listing 4.3.

Creating the unix2dos.c Source Module

Listing 4.4 shows the new unix2dos.c source module after it has been edited and checked into RCS.

Listing 4.4 04LST04.c—The New unix2dos.c Source Module

```
/* $Header: /home/student1/dos_cvrt/RCS/unix2dos.c,v 1.1 ...
 * Basil Fawlty     $Date: 1998/11/27 02:29:21 $
 *
 * UNIX to DOS text format conversion.
 *
 * $Log: unix2dos.c,v $
 * Revision 1.1  1998/11/27 02:29:21  student1
 * Initial revision
 *
 */
static const char rcsid[] =
    "$Id: unix2dos.c,v 1.1 1998/11/27 02:29:21 student1 Exp $";

#include <stdio.h>
#include <stdlib.h>
#include <unistd.h>
#include "dos_cvrt.h"
```

```
18:
19:  /*
20:   * Convert file named by pathname to DOS
21:   * text format, on standard output:
22:   */
23:  int
24:  unix2dos(const char *pathname) {
25:      int ch;                  /* Current input character */
26:      FILE *in = 0;            /* Input file */
27:
28:      if ( !(in = fopen(pathname,"r")) ) {
29:          fprintf(stderr,"Cannot open input file.\n");
30:          return 2;
31:      }
32:
33:      while ( (ch = fgetc(in)) != EOF ) {
34:          if ( ch == '\n' )
35:              putchar('\r');
36:          putchar(ch);
37:      }
38:
39:      fclose(in);
40:      return 0;
41:  }
42:
43:  /* End $Source: /home/student1/dos_cvrt/RCS/unix2dos.c,v $ */
```


In line 17 of Listing 4.4, notice that the file dos_cvrt.h is included, although there is currently no need for it in file unix2dos.c. You include it to allow the compiler to check the `extern` declaration for the function `unix2dos()` in the include file against the actual function definition in unix2dos.c. If any disagreement occurs in the definition, the compiler produces warnings or errors.

Creating the dos2unix.c Source Module

Listing 4.5 is similar to Listing 4.4, except that it shows the new dos2unix.c source module, which has a slightly different type of text conversion process. Note again, you include the file dos_cvrt.h as a compiler check in line 17.

LISTING 4.5 04LST05.C—THE NEW DOS2UNIX.C SOURCE MODULE

```
1:   /* $Header: /home/student1/dos_cvrt/RCS/dos2unix.c,v 1.1 ...
2:    * Basil Fawlty     $Date: 1998/11/27 02:29:37 $
3:    *
4:    * The DOS to UNIX text conversion:
5:    *
6:    * $Log: dos2unix.c,v $
```

continues

LISTING 4.5 CONTINUED

```
 * Revision 1.1  1998/11/27 02:29:37  student1
 * Initial revision
 *
 */
static const char rcsid[] =
    "$Id: dos2unix.c,v 1.1 1998/11/27 02:29:37 student1 Exp $";

#include <stdio.h>
#include <stdlib.h>
#include <unistd.h>
#include "dos_cvrt.h"

/*
 * Convert file named by pathname, to
 * UNIX text file format on standard output:
 */
int
dos2unix(const char *pathname) {
    int ch;                    /* Current input character */
    int cr_flag;               /* True when CR prev. encountered */
    FILE *in = 0;              /* Input file */

    if ( !(in = fopen(pathname,"r")) ) {
        fprintf(stderr,"Cannot open input file.\n");
        return 2;
    }

    cr_flag = 0;   /* No CR encountered yet */
    while ( (ch = fgetc(in)) != EOF ) {
        if ( cr_flag && ch != '\n' ) {
            /* This CR did not preceed LF */
            putchar('\r');
        }
        if ( !(cr_flag = ch == '\r') )
            putchar(ch);
    }

    fclose(in);
    return 0;
}

/* End $Source: /home/student1/dos_cvrt/RCS/dos2unix.c,v $ */
```

Checking In the Improved dos_cvrt.c Module

Now that you've edited out the various functions that have moved to their own source module unix2dos.c and dos2unix.c, you have a much smaller dos_cvrt.c. The improved dos_cvrt.c has been checked in as version 1.8, and this file is illustrated in Listing 4.6. It contains the following improvements:

1. The basename is determined in one statement by a function call to `Basename()` (line 66).
2. All the file open logic has been moved to the `unix2dos()` or `dos2unix()` functions. This change simplifies the `main()` program.
3. You use the function pointer `conv` to determine the type of the text conversion (lines 81 to 84).
4. The text conversion itself is processed by the function call (line 90). This call reduces the number of source statements you need to read at this level. If you're interested in the conversion itself, you can inspect the appropriate source module unix2dos.c or dos2unix.c.

LISTING 4.6 04LST06.C—THE NEW, MORE MODULAR DOS_CVRT.C

```
1:   /* dos_cvrt.c */
2:
3:   static const char rcsid[] =
4:       "$Id: dos_cvrt.c,v 1.8 1998/11/27 02:29:54 student1 Exp $";
5:
6:   /* REVISION HISTORY:
7:    * $Log: dos_cvrt.c,v $
8:    * Revision 1.8  1998/11/27 02:29:54  student1
9:    * Separated out the text conversion
10:   * functions to make this project
11:   * more modular.
12:   *
13:   * Revision 1.7  1998/11/27 01:31:39  student1
14:   * Now handles multiple input files, plus
15:   * put basename code into its own Basename()
16:   * function.
17:   *
18:   * Revision 1.6  1998/11/27 01:01:28  student1
19:   * Separated conversions into unix2dos() and
20:   * dos2unix() functions.
21:   *
22:   * Revision 1.5  1998/11/23 05:32:21  student1
23:   * Completed utility & tested ok.
24:   *
25:   * Revision 1.4  1998/11/23 05:04:23  student1
26:   * Coded basename test
27:   *
28:   * Revision 1.3  1998/11/21 22:49:39  student1
29:   * Demonstration of RCS substitutions
```


continues

Listing 4.6 continued

```
 */
#include <stdio.h>
#include <stdlib.h>
#include <unistd.h>
#include <string.h>
#include "dos_cvrt.h"

/*
 * Return the pointer to the basename component
 * of a pathname:
 */
static char *
Basename(const char *path) {
    char *base_name = 0;

    if ( ( base_name = strrchr(path,'/') ) != 0 )
        ++base_name;                       /* Skip over '/' */
    else
        base_name = (char *) path;         /* No dir. */
    return base_name;
}

int
main(int argc,char **argv) {
    char *base_name = 0;    /* Basename of command */
    int rc = 0;             /* Command return code */
    int (*conv)(const char *pathname); /* Conv. Func. Ptr */
    int x;

    /*
     * Determine the basename of the command name. This
     * is necessary since this command could be invoked
     * with a pathname. For example, argv[0] could be
     * "/usr/local/bin/unix_cvrt" if it was installed
     * in the system that way.
     */
    base_name = Basename(argv[0]);

    /*
     * Check for missing input file:
     */
    if ( argc < 2 ) {
        fprintf(stderr,"Missing input file(s).\n");
        return 1;
    }

    /*
     * Now that we know the basename of the command
```

```
78:         * name used, we can determine which function we
79:         * must carry out here.
80:         */
81:        if ( !strcmp(base_name,"unix_cvrt") )
82:            conv = unix2dos;
83:        else
84:            conv = dos2unix;
85:
86:        /*
87:         * Perform a text conversion
88:         */
89:        for ( x=1; x<argc; ++x )
90:            if ( (rc = conv(argv[x])) != 0 )
91:                break;      /* An error occurred */
92:
93:        return rc;
94:    }
```

The `include` of dos_cvrt.h in line 35 of Listing 4.6 is mandatory for this source module because it contains the necessary interface definitions for the two text conversion functions.

Declaring `static` Functions

You make another change to line 41 of the dos_cvrt.c module in Listing 4.6. Here, you make the function `Basename()` static. The C language keyword `static` in this context simply tells the compiler that this function will only be used locally by the current source file. The advantage of making this change here is that you don't unnecessarily pollute the linker name space. What do I mean by this?

Another example might help. Say you have to maintain a very large application consisting of hundreds of source modules. In one of these modules is a function definition like this:

```
/* Round to the nearest integer */
double round(double value) {
```

This particular function simply rounds a `double` floating-point value to the nearest integer number in a `double`. Furthermore, only that particular source module needs access to this function.

However, because rounding is so common, in another module among the hundreds, you have yet another function defined with the same name. Again, that source module accesses only this particular rounding function:

```
/* Round to the nearest decimal place */
double round(double value,unsigned short decplaces) {
```

Now you have a conflict, and the function interfaces are different. When the loader attempts to establish the linkages at link time, it notices that it has two functions with the name `round()`. The link ends in error as a result.

You can avoid this entire problem if you keep the function name `round()` out of the linking process. Only the individual source modules need local access to their corresponding versions of the `round()` function. By declaring both of these functions static, you avoid this clash.

Keep this idea of static functions in mind. Later, you will have another reason to review it when you look at creating C libraries in Hour 10, "Static and Shared Libraries."

Summary

In this lesson, you looked at the modularity of programs. You practiced creating modularity by taking the single source module dos_cvrt.c and splitting it into several C functions. Then you modularized it at the source module level by separating some of the functions into individual source modules. You also learned about the usefulness of having an include file to declare the external function declarations. Finally, you looked at the reasons for encouraging the use of statically declared functions when external definitions are not necessary.

Q&A

Q Why is nonmodular programming a bad practice?

A A nonmodular program, if large, is difficult to adapt to new program requirements. It also requires longer compiles when the program is undergoing a number of iterative changes. If the program is large enough, editing can also be a problem.

Q What are the two levels of modularity covered in this lesson?

A Modularity begins at the function level and then at the source module level.

Q How is a static function different from an extern function?

A An extern function can be called by separate source modules. A static function can only be referenced locally in the current source module.

Workshop

You are encouraged to answer the quiz and perform the work in the exercises to demonstrate and practice what you have learned.

Quiz

1. When does a program become modular?
2. How does modularity help the software engineering process?
3. How do external definitions play a role in modular programs?
4. How do static definitions help in modular programs?

Exercise

Create a new work project directory for your experiments. Copy the source modules 04LST03.h, 04LST04.c, 04LST05.c, and 04LST06.c to this directory. Take the static function `Basename()` out of the source module 04LST06.c, and create a new one for it in basename.c. Make all necessary tweaks and modifications to make the group of modules link together and function as before.

Hour 5

Introducing Makefiles

Why Use `make`?

Perhaps you looked at the Makefile that came with GNU `gcc` when you recompiled a newer version of it and felt your head starting to hurt.

Given the complexity level that a make file can reach, you might reasonably ask, "Why use `make`?" After all, even Albert Einstein said, "It must be simple, but not simpler."

If you consider a very large project consisting of dozens, perhaps hundreds, of modules, you're probably not very eager to recompile all those modules every time you change one line of code and want to test it. Imagine making one small change to your Linux kernel source code and then having to rebuild it from scratch. Yet determining which compiles to skip can be complicated, and skipping necessary compiles causes trouble. The `make` command is good at precisely this kind of task.

The `make` command can draw conclusions about the dependencies between different files. The `make` command has other features that make it powerful. It can define macros and additional targets that help you get your work done efficiently.

Another advantage that `make` possesses is that the build instructions are recorded in the make file. You don't have to memorize all the command-line options you used on a project from a year ago, for example. Better still, you don't have to document what you used to build that project for someone else.

The Makefile

When you start the `make` command and do not explicitly name a make file on the command line (with option `-f`), the GNU `make` utility looks for three different default filenames in the current directory in the following sequence:

1. GNUmakefile
2. makefile
3. Makefile

Testing `make`'s Built-In Capabilities

In fact, the GNU `make` is so smart that if it doesn't find your make file, it even checks the file out of RCS if it finds the master RCS source file. See for yourself in Listing 5.1.

LISTING 5.1 THE `make` COMMAND FETCHING ITS MAKE FILE FROM RCS

```
bash$ pwd
/home/student1/make
bash$ ls -lR
total 1
drwxr-xr-x   2 student1 user        1024 Nov 27 12:27 RCS/

RCS:
total 1
-r--r--r--   1 student1 user         231 Nov 27 12:27 Makefile,v
bash$ make
co  RCS/Makefile,v Makefile
RCS/Makefile,v  -->  Makefile
revision 1.1
done
echo /home/student1/Makefile
/home/student1/Makefile
bash$
```

Here is the basic procedure used in Listing 5.1:

1. You identify that you have the correct starting directory by using the `pwd` command (line 1).
2. You perform a recursive list using the `ls` command to illustrate which files you're starting with (line 3). Note that you have only the master source file RCS/Makefile,v present.
3. You invoke `make` (line 10), but it fails to find a file named GNUmakefile, makefile, or even Makefile. In each case, the `make` command tries many built-in rules to arrive at a make file from other sources. In this case, it discovers the file RCS/Makefile,v, and a built-in rule tells it how to check out a working copy of that file in line 11. In line 12, RCS tells you that it created a Makefile in the current directory.
4. Here, a simple Makefile is used; it just echoes its pathname for this experiment (lines 15 and 16 show the results).

Naming Your Makefile

The usual practice is to use a file named Makefile, and as always, keeping it under source control is good practice. What you just saw, however, is that if you forget to keep a working copy of that Makefile in your project directory, `make` knows how to get one from RCS.

Using Makefile

The name Makefile with the uppercase first letter works best because when you list your files, it sorts near the beginning of your listed files display.

Using GNUmakefile

The GNU `make` documentation suggests that you should avoid using the filename GNUmakefile. You should use this name only if you use features that are supported by the GNU `make` command. If the feature set employed is the standard UNIX `make` feature set, then use the filenames Makefile or makefile.

Using makefile

When the normal name Makefile (with an uppercase "*M*") is used, you are left with one preemption option. If you download a source package from the Internet but discover that you need to change the Makefile provided, you can test your changes without changing the supplied Makefile. To do so, simply perform the following steps:

1. Copy Makefile to the new file named makefile.
2. Edit makefile to suit your needs.

3. Run the make command. The makefile is used instead of Makefile because makefile is chosen first if it exists.

Makefile Targets

The make command starts with the notion of a target. The very first target, as you saw earlier, is always the make file itself. In the preceding section, the command tried three default target filenames, of which Makefile was the last tried. When it realized that Makefile did not exist, the command thought to itself "if I have an RCS file RCS/Makefile,v, then I can create my target." And you saw that it did. After you have a make file to process, however, the make command must process at least one target from that file, or nothing gets accomplished. In fact, if you give make a make file without a target, it becomes unhappy about the situation, as you can see here:

```
bash$ make
make: *** No targets.  Stop.
bash$
```

Defining Targets

Listing 5.2 shows a very simple Makefile with three different targets in it. Lines 4, 7, and 10 contain the three targets, named one, two, and three, respectively. A target name always starts at the beginning of the line and is followed by a colon.

LISTING 5.2 05LST02.MK—A SIMPLE MAKEFILE WITH THREE TARGETS

```
1:   # $Source: /home/student1/make/RCS/Makefile,v $
2:   # $Date: 1998/11/27 17:55:54 $
3:
4:   one:
5:      @echo One
6:
7:   two:
8:      @echo Two
9:
10:  three:
11:     @echo Three
12:
13:  # End Makefile
```

Invoking Makefile Targets

To invoke a target, you simply specify its name on the command line. The following command, for example, invokes target two:

```
bash$ make two
Two
bash$
```

make completely ignores targets one and three in this example.

Invoking Multiple Targets

You can also invoke multiple targets on the same command line:

```
bash$ make three one two
Three
One
Two
bash$
```

Notice how the targets are processed in command-line argument sequence.

The Default Target

The `make` command assumes that the very first target it encounters in the make file is the default target. Consider this example:

```
bash$ make
One
bash$
```

`make` invokes the first target encountered, which is named `one` in line 4 of Listing 5.2. Target names `two` and `three` are considered alternate targets and are not invoked.

Standard Target Names

Although no formal standard exists for target names, you will commonly come across conventions in widespread use when you examine the make files of publicly downloadable sources. The following is a list of some commonly accepted target names:

- `'all'` is often used as the first, thus default, target name. Its purpose is usually to name the real target names, which can be one or more other targets. Using this target builds the entire project.
- `'install'` is normally used to install a built project into its Linux system directories, complete with the correct permissions and ownership applied, and any subdirectories created as necessary.
- `'clean'` is often used to allow you to remove all object files (*.o), core files, and other temporary files that might be created in the build process. This target leaves the built executables and libraries, however.
- `'clobber'` is often used to remove the project targets that are built (usually executables and libraries). You remove these targets to completely rebuild the project from scratch.
- `'distclean'` is often used by Linux and GNU developers to clean the project file of everything but the original files that were distributed over the Internet. Going beyond `clobber`, this target removes project configuration files and so on.

Dependencies

In Hour 3, "Writing a Linux Utility," before dos_cvrt.c was modularized, you compiled the module dos_cvrt.c directly into the executable file dos_cvrt. You could say that the executable file dos_cvrt depends on dos_cvrt.c. If you make a change to the source file dos_cvrt.c, then you must recompile that source and generate a new dos_cvrt executable file.

The `make` command understands this process at a more mechanical level: If the date and time stamp of the source file dos_cvrt.c is more recent than the date and time stamp of the target executable dos_cvrt, then `make` has to act. In this case, `make` had better recompile dos_cvrt.c into a new executable file dos_cvrt. This process works because when you edit the source file, the saved source file has its modified date and time stamp changed.

Using Standard Dependencies

Some dependencies between the accepted target names are commonly accepted. As a developer, you should be aware of the following:

- Target `install` usually depends on `all`.
- Target `clobber` usually depends on `clean`.
- Target `distclean` usually depends on `clobber`.

If you have `install` depend on the target `all`, the project is built first, if necessary, before installation is attempted. Otherwise, no project would be available for installation. However, software is often installed with root privileges, so building your project while operating as root is generally not a good idea. If you feel strongly enough about this point, you might omit this dependency in your project.

Target `clobber` depends on `clean` usually for convenience. Target `clean` takes care of some of the work, and then you need to define only the additional work for `clobber`. Target `distclean` works on that same principle.

Defining Dependencies

Listing 5.3 shows a new make file with dependencies added to it. Here, target `three` depends on target `two` (line 10), and target `two` now depends on target `one` (line 7). Notice that dependencies are simply listed after the target name and the colon. Additional targets are separated by space(s). At least one space should separate the target's colon character and the first dependency.

LISTING 5.3 05LST03.MK—A MAKEFILE WITH DEPENDENCIES

```
# $Source: /home/student1/make/RCS/Makefile,v $
# $Date: 1998/11/27 18:48:31 $

one:
   @echo One

two:   one
   @echo Two

three: two
   @echo Three

# End Makefile
```

Testing Target Dependencies

Now if you invoke the make file shown in Listing 5.3 with the target name `three`, you'll see that the `make` command actually ends up processing all three targets:

```
bash$ make three
One
Two
Three
bash$
```

Are you surprised by the order? Target `one` is carried out first because target `two` depends on it, and target `three` depends on `two`. So, before anything can be performed for target `three`, its dependencies must be satisfied first. Although target `three` is invoked, the chain of dependencies is such that `make` has to invoke target `one` first to satisfy the other two targets in the dependency chain.

Defining `make` Macros

One of the powerful aspects of shell scripting is the capability to use and manipulate shell variables and environment variables. The `make` command has its own brand of this functionality and can draw on environment variables as well.

A `make` macro can hold a string value like a filename or a parameter value. A macro allows the value to be defined once in the Makefile, yet it can be used in several places. When a change is required, only the macro assignment requires a change. When the assignment is altered, the change is immediately reflected wherever the macro is used.

Listing 5.4 shows a new rendition of the demo Makefile. Line 5 shows how you declare a macro named `OBJECT` and set its value equal to the value "`Pear`". You also remove the dependencies used before and add a more conventional default target name of `all` in line 7. Note that this target depends on all three targets—`one`, `two`, and `three`. A larger project is often structured this way in a make file.

LISTING 5.4 05LST04.MK—MAKEFILE WITH A MACRO DEFINITION

```
1:   # $Source: /home/student1/make/RCS/Makefile,v $
2:   # $Revision: 1.3 $
3:   # $Date: 1998/11/27 19:08:32 $
4:
5:   OBJECT= Pear
6:
7:   all: one two three
8:
9:   one:
10:     @echo One $(OBJECT)
11:
12:  two:
13:     @echo Two $(OBJECT)s
14:
15:  three:
16:     @echo Three $(OBJECT)s
17:
18:  # End Makefile
```

Lines 10, 13, and 16 show how the macro values can be used. The macro's value is substituted for the dollar sign and the macro name that follows in parentheses. The parentheses are not required if the macro name is one letter," such as `$X`". Generally speaking, however, using descriptive macro names is good practice. Now invoke this make file and look at its results:

```
bash$ make
One Pear
Two Pears
Three Pears
bash$
```

Notice how nicely the value is substituted. Note also that the target line 7 has no action statements. This line serves only to tie one target to the other dependents named.

Overriding Macro Values

The `make` command also permits you to override a macro value. Using the same make file in Listing 5.4, you can do the following:

```
bash$ make OBJECT=apple
One apple
Two apples
Three apples
bash$
```

Even though line 5 of Listing 5.4 assigns the value "`Pear`" to the macro `OBJECT`, the command-line assignment "`OBJECT=apple`" overrules it. To generalize, then, the `make` command does all the macro assignments in the make file first and then performs any additional macro assignments by scanning the command line.

Using Environment Variables

The `make` command can also take values from the environment. Still using the make file from Listing 5.4, see whether you can overrule a macro based on an exported environment variable:

```
bash$ OBJECT=walnut make
One Pear
Two Pears
Three Pears
bash$
```

This is nuts; it appears that this test doesn't work. Indeed, it turns out that environment variables do not overrule macro assignments in the make file. Had no macro named `OBJECT` been defined in that make file, you would have influenced the substitution. To prove this point, you can comment out line 5 in Listing 5.5, and try this test again:

```
bash$ OBJECT=walnut make
One walnut
Two walnuts
Three walnuts
bash$
```

Now because no macro assignments appear in the Makefile, the environment variable value for `OBJECT` persists and is used as you expect.

LISTING 5.5 05LST05.MK—MAKEFILE WITH MACRO ASSIGNMENT COMMENTED OUT

```
1:   # $Source: /home/student1/make/RCS/Makefile,v $
2:   # $Revision: 1.4 $
3:   # $Date: 1998/11/27 19:38:15 $
4:
5:   # OBJECT= Pear
6:
7:   all:        one two three
8:
9:   one:
10:     @echo One $(OBJECT)
11:
12:  two:
13:     @echo Two $(OBJECT)s
```

continues

LISTING 5.5 CONTINUED

```

three:
	@echo Three $(OBJECT)s

# End Makefile
```

Using the make -e Option

One little make option, -e, permits the environment to overrule the macros in the make file. However, be careful with its use because the environment may change more than you bargained for. Using the original make file from Listing 5.4, you can test this theory:

```
bash$ co -r1.3 Makefile
RCS/Makefile,v  -->  Makefile
revision 1.3
done
bash$ OBJECT=walnut make
One Pear
Two Pears
Three Pears
bash$ OBJECT=walnut make -e
One walnut
Two walnuts
Three walnuts
bash$
```

The procedure you use is as follows:

1. You first check out version 1.3 of the Makefile (note the -r1.3 option). This Makefile is illustrated in Listing 5.4.
2. You export the environment variable OBJECT and run the make command, but the OBJECT variable has no effect.
3. You export the environment variable OBJECT again but this time run make with the -e option. This time, the OBJECT environment variable affects the results.

> When you're relying on environment variables in a make file, be sure that the environment variables are exported from your shell. Also, be sure that you understand what the export built-in command accomplishes in the bash shell.

Examining File Suffixes

The `make` command is very much driven by the use of file suffixes. File suffix conventions permit the `make` command to deduce what type of file it is. This way, it can apply inference rules by default. Before you get to inference rules, look at some of the suffixes that `make` knows about in Table 5.1.

TABLE 5.1 SOME `make`-RECOGNIZED FILE SUFFIXES

File Suffix	*Description*
.c	C language source module
.h	C language header file
.cc	C++ language source module
.o	Compiled object file

Understanding Inference Rules

Part of the `make` command's power lies in its inference rules. It can also be a source of frustration if it is not well understood.

Testing the Default Inference Rules

Copy the hello.c program that you used in Hour 1, "Getting Started," into a private work area. Then you can test `make`'s default inference rules, as shown in Listing 5.6, to see what kind of mileage you get.

LISTING 5.6 TESTING GNU `make`'S INFERENCE RULE FOR HELLO.O

```
1:   bash$ mkdir experiment
2:   bash$ cd experiment
3:   bash$ cp /cdrom/hello.c .
4:   bash$ >Makefile
5:   bash$ make hello.o
6:   cc    -c hello.c -o hello.o
7:   bash$ type cc
8:   cc is /usr/bin/cc
9:   bash$ ls -dl /usr/bin/cc
10:  lrwxrwxrwx   1 root   root   3 Jan 6 1998 /usr/bin/cc -> gcc
11:  bash$
```

You follow these steps to complete this experiment:

1. You create a directory to work in (line 1).
2. You change to that directory (line 2).

3. You copy your hello.c program to the current directory (line 3). Note that the directory of the source copy of hello.c may be different for you.
4. You quickly create an empty Makefile for `make` to work with (line 4).
5. You invoke `make` with the empty Makefile in the current directory (line 5). Note that you explicitly give `make` the target name hello.o because the Makefile has no defined targets.
6. The `make` command runs, showing how its built-in rule deduces that hello.c must be compiled by a C compiler to produce hello.o (line 6).
7. You ask the shell to tell you where the `cc` comes from (line 7). The shell tells the pathname in line 8.
8. You invoke the `ls` command with the `-dl` options (line 9) to discover that the `cc` command is a symbolic link to the `gcc` command (line 10).

Apart from the fact that the rule does not supply the options `-D_GNU_SOURCE` and `-Wall`, it does very well with no help from you. Because this result may not be exactly what you have in mind, you should explicitly define a rule that suits your needs.

Defining an Inference Rule

Listing 5.7 shows a demo make file that contains an inference rule.

LISTING 5.7 A `make` INFERENCE RULE

```
1:  CC = gcc
2:  STD = _GNU_SOURCE
3:
4:  .c.o:
5:      $(CC) -c -Wall $(CFLAGS) -D$(STD) $< -o $@
```

Line 1 shows the conventional way to choose your compiler in a make file with the `CC` macro. Here, you point it directly to the `gcc` compiler. Line 2 defines the `STD` macro in order to choose the standard that you want to compile to. Line 4 is a special kind of target. This target is composed of the starting file suffix, followed by the target file suffix. By defining a target in this form, you are actually defining an inference rule to `make`.

> Never define any dependencies for an inference rule. The `make` command ignores dependencies for inference rules. On some UNIX platforms, the rule is not interpreted as an inference rule at all if it has dependencies listed.

Line 4 begins to define an inference rule that says if you have a target that is an object file (*.o), and you find that you have the corresponding input file with the .c suffix (that is newer), apply the actions that follow.

Action Statements

Line 5 of Listing 5.7 is the single action statement. An action statement must begin with a tab character. Space characters are not acceptable here. You can have more than one action, but here you need only one. Note also that if the action command starts with a leading '`@`' character, it causes `make` to suppress printing the command to standard output. You might have noticed this back in Listing 5.2 in lines 5, 8, and 11.

> Action lines in a make file must start with a tab character. Some editors insist on using blanks when you press the Tab key. Make certain that the first character is an ASCII tab character; otherwise, `make` does not accept it as an action statement.

Line 5 of Listing 5.7 outlines a compile statement and draws heavily on macros. Most of the named macros are easily understood, so I will defer the discussion of `CFLAGS` for the moment. That leaves two funny-looking macros: "`$<`" and "`$@`".

Built-in Macros

The `make` command supports at least six built-in macros. They are different from the user-defined macros because they never need to be defined. These macros are maintained internally by the `make` command and change in value as an inference rule is being carried out.

The most important of these macros are those shown in Table 5.2.

TABLE 5.2 SOME BUILT-IN `make` MACROS

Macro Name	*Description*
`$*`	This macro provides the filename component of the current dependent (with the suffix removed).
`$@`	This macro provides the full target name, with suffix, for the current target.
`$<`	This macro provides the full dependent filename, complete with suffix.

In the session depicted in Listing 5.6, line 5 names hello.o as the target. Inside the inference rule on lines 5 and 6 of Listing 5.7, you would have the values as shown in Table 5.3.

TABLE 5.3 Built-In make File Macro Values for Listing 5.6

Macro Name	*Macro Value*
`$*`	`"hello"`
`$@`	`"hello.o"`
`$<`	`"hello.c"`

Remember that these built-in macros have values only inside an inference rule. The `$<` macro has one small exception, and at least two other built-in macros have other applications. I want to keep things simple here, so you can ignore them for now.

The CFLAGS Macro

The `CFLAGS` macro is used to hold any additional C compiler options. If this macro is left undefined within the make file, then you are free to optionally set an environment variable to alter the compiles being performed in your current terminal session.

Using CFLAGS from the Shell

One commonly used practice is to use the `CFLAGS` macro for compiling in debug mode (or not). Notice how this procedure works in this developer session:

```
bash$ rm hello.o
bash$ export CFLAGS=-g
bash$ make hello.o
gcc -c -Wall -g -D_GNU_SOURCE hello.c -o hello.o
bash$
```

The steps used here are as follows:

1. You make sure to get rid of the last hello.o you made (otherwise, `make` does not feel obligated to make it again).
2. You define and export the `CFLAGS` environment variable with the `gcc` debug option `-g`.
3. Now and subsequently when you compile, the `make` command automatically picks up the exported `CFLAGS` value and applies it in the command line. (Notice that the `-g` option appears in the `gcc` command.)

The same technique can be used to recompile for optimization instead of debugging. This trick is especially helpful when you have the Makefile under RCS source control, eliminating the need to change it.

Using a Makefile for dos_cvrt

Now that you know how the Makefile works, it's time you created one for the dos_cvrt project. Creating a Makefile allows you to build the project without remembering all those command-line options for `gcc` and so on.

Creating the Makefile

Listing 5.8 shows a make file that you might use for the dos_cvrt utility project.

LISTING 5.8 05LST08.MK—A MAKEFILE FOR THE MODULAR DOS_CVRT PROJECT

```
1:  # $Source: /home/student1/dos_cvrt/RCS/Makefile,v $
2:  # $Revision: 1.1 $
3:  # $Date: 1998/11/27 22:17:18 $
4:
5:  CC=        gcc
6:  STD=       _GNU_SOURCE
7:  OBJS=      dos_cvrt.o unix2dos.o dos2unix.o
8:
9:  .c.o:
10:    $(CC) -c -Wall $(CFLAGS) -D$(STD) $<
11:
12: all:       dos_cvrt unix_cvrt
13:
14: dos_cvrt: $(OBJS)
15:    $(CC) $(OBJS) -o dos_cvrt
16:
17: unix_cvrt: dos_cvrt
18:    rm -f unix_cvrt
19:    ln dos_cvrt unix_cvrt
20:
21: clean:
22:    rm -f *.o core
23:
24: clobber: clean
25:    rm -f dos_cvrt unix_cvrt
26:
27: # End Makefile
```


The new Makefile has the following content:

- Macro definitions for the C compiler (`CC`), the standard you want to use (`STD`), and the list of object modules you need to generate (`OBJS`) are defined (lines 5 to 7). The main purpose of the `OBJS` macro is to save repetition throughout the Makefile.
- An inference rule is defined to tell `make` how to compile a *.c file into an object file (*.o) (lines 9 and 10). You can leave out the unnecessary `-o` option here because

the compiler's default actions are acceptable for this operation. The advantage to this approach is a shorter command line. (These lines get too long in some projects.)

- A default target is defined for `'all'` (line 12). It tells the `make` command that the `'all'` target depends on targets dos_cvrt and unix_cvrt. This causes `make` to build both of those executables.
- The target dos_cvrt is defined (line 14). Notice that you use the macro `OBJS` to list all the object files that must be made before building this target. Each of these object files is built by the inference rule in lines 9 and 10. Finally, when all the object modules have been written out by the compiles, you perform the final step of linking these objects all together into an executable file dos_cvrt.
- The target unix_cvrt is defined (line 17). Notice that this target lists dos_cvrt as a dependency to ensure that `make` builds dos_cvrt first. Line 18 shows the `rm` command, which removes the old link to a prior version of the dos_cvrt executable. The `rm` command's `-f` option keeps it silent if there is no file to delete. Line 19 then shows that the unix_cvrt target is created simply by linking with the existing new dos_cvrt executable file (line 15).
- The `'clean'` target is defined (line 21). The actions for the `'clean'` target allow you to clean out all unnecessary object files and the core file if it exists. However, if dos_cvrt and unix_cvrt executables exist, they remain.
- The `'clobber'` target is defined (line 24). The action lines for the `clobber` target allow you to completely gut your project directory to the original source files. Because target `clean` is listed as a dependency, it is performed first. Then line 25 removes the executables if they exist.

Testing the New Makefile

Now test the new Makefile. The following session assumes that you have checked out working copies of all the *.c and *.h files required for the compile:

```
bash$ make clobber
rm -f *.o core
rm -f dos_cvrt unix_cvrt
bash$ make
gcc -c -Wall -g -D_GNU_SOURCE dos_cvrt.c
gcc -c -Wall -g -D_GNU_SOURCE unix2dos.c
gcc -c -Wall -g -D_GNU_SOURCE dos2unix.c
gcc dos_cvrt.o unix2dos.o dos2unix.o -o dos_cvrt
rm -f unix_cvrt
ln dos_cvrt unix_cvrt
bash$
```

Because you've built this project a number of times, you first use "`make clobber`" to be sure that you are starting from scratch. Then you use the usual "`make`". Notice how nicely `make` gets all the modules compiled and does the link to create the dos_cvrt executable. Finally, it takes care of all the fuss to properly set up the link name unix_cvrt. This is automation at its best.

Testing a Partial Compile

To demonstrate the advantage of using `make` in a large project, pretend that you made a change to dos2unix.c to fix a bug. You can cheat here with the `touch` command, but pretend that you have to edit the file:

```
bash$ ls -l dos2unix.c dos_cvrt
-r--r--r--   1 student1 user        1243 Nov 27 01:15 dos2unix.c
-rwxr-xr-x   2 student1 user       19567 Nov 27 17:37 dos_cvrt
bash$ touch -m 11271738 dos2unix.c
bash$ ls -l dos2unix.c dos_cvrt
-r--r--r--   1 student1 user        1243 Nov 27 17:38 dos2unix.c
-rwxr-xr-x   2 student1 user       19567 Nov 27 17:37 dos_cvrt
bash$
```

You list the date and time stamp on the dos2unix.c source file, and then using the `touch` command, you make it one second newer than the executable file dos_cvrt. Now you can run `make` to see what happens:

```
bash$ make
gcc -c -Wall -D_GNU_SOURCE dos2unix.c
gcc dos_cvrt.o unix2dos.o dos2unix.o -o dos_cvrt
rm -f unix_cvrt
ln dos_cvrt unix_cvrt
bash$
```

5

Notice that this test only recompiles dos2unix.c. You get this result because dos2unix.c is newer than the executable. However, the executable depends on object file dos2unix.o, so that file has to be regenerated by doing a compile from file dos2unix.c. Because dos_cvrt is re-created, the link unix_cvrt also requires updating. The `make` command smartly performs only the work that it is necessary.

Summary

In this lesson, you learned how `make` works and how to put this command to work. You learned about the three different "make files" that `make` looks for by default. You also gained an understanding of how to write a make file for a new project. Finally, you learned how to control `make` through the shell environment variables, command-line options, and macro assignments.

Q&A

Q What is the advantage of using a make file named Makefile instead of makefile?

A When it lists your files, Makefile sorts before lowercased filenames and appears earlier in the list.

Q When is it useful to use the make file named makefile instead of Makefile?

A Because makefile has priority over Makefile, you can use this file as a temporary modified copy of the original Makefile. This way, `make` uses your customized makefile without having to make any changes to the original Makefile that came with the project.

Q What is the purpose of defining a `CFLAGS` macro in the make file if the macro value is never assigned to it in the make file?

A The `CFLAGS` value can be obtained from your shell environment. This way, you can choose to compile with debugging turned on or instead to compile with some level of optimization without requiring any change to the make file.

Workshop

You are encouraged to work through the following exercises to help you retain what you have learned in this lesson. You should complete these exercises before proceeding to the next chapter.

Quiz

1. Is it an error to reference a macro that is not defined? Why or why not?
2. If the target filename is newer than the dependent file, are the target actions carried out by `make`? Why or why not?
3. Do macro assignments override environment variables? What `make` command-line option alters this behavior?
4. Does a target have to represent a file that is being built?
5. What character must precede the definition of an action line in the make file?
6. What character prevents `make` from echoing an action line to standard output?
7. What character separates multiple dependents on a target specification line?

Exercises

1. Assume that the target name is unix2dos.o and the dependency filename is unix2dos.c. Write out the values of the macros `$@`, `$*`, and `$<` during the processing of an inference rule.
2. Create a new subdirectory for this exercise. Copy your dos_cvrt project source files and Makefile to it (no need to establish RCS here). Perform a complete rebuild of the project by using "`make clobber all`". Now list the dates and times of files unix2dos.c, unix2dos.o, and dos_cvrt. Using the `touch` command, set the date and time of unix2dos.c and unix2dos.o files to exactly the same modification date and time that show for the executable dos_cvrt. Now "use `make`". Does the `make` do anything? Why or why not?
3. Using the same exercise subdirectory and files from exercise 2, use the `touch` command to change the time of unix2dos.o to one second newer than dos_cvrt. Run `make` and explain its actions.
4. Using the subdirectory and files from exercise 3, use the `touch` command to make the unix2dos.c file one second newer than dos_cvrt. Explain why the results are different from the results in exercise 3.
5. The make file presented in Listing 5.8 is not 100 percent complete. If the include file dos_cvrt.h is modified, `make` presently does not recompile the *.c modules that include that file. Modify the Makefile to "make it so."
6. Write out an inference rule that compiles a single source file directly into its executable. For example, it should be able to compile hello.c directly into the executable hello in one compile step. Note that the target hello has no file suffix to be used in the inference rule (this exercise requires that you do a little research).

HOUR 6

Linux Command-Line Option Processing

Introducing Command-Line Processing

Anyone who uses Linux at the command prompt for a period of time unwittingly becomes acquainted with the general way that UNIX commands work. Some of the most basic and frequently used commands are `ls`, `mv`, `cp`, `rm`, and `ln`. In all these cases, and in most other cases, the command lines all follow the same general convention.

This convention does not occur by coincidence, however. To achieve this level of consistency, the convention had to be defined, and a mechanism to encourage this convention had to be in place. In this lesson, you will look at the UNIX command-line conventions. Then you will examine command-line parsing and how it is normally accomplished by a C program. GNU extensions to the convention, as it affects Linux, will also be covered.

Understanding Command-Line Conventions

At the most basic level, the general convention used for most Linux commands is as follows:

```
bash$ command_name [-options] [arg1 [arg2 [argn]]]
```

The square brackets show optional items (or zones) on the command line. An option always begins with a hyphen character and is followed by a letter or some other option character. Arguments, when used, always follow the options, if present. The number of valid arguments is determined by the command being invoked. A concrete example of this convention in use is the `rm` command:

```
bash$ rm -f core
```

Here, the option is given by the hyphen and the letter *f*. It is then followed by one argument, which in this case represents the name of a file in the current directory.

Using Multiple Options

A command line can have more than one option. The following example uses multiple options:

```
bash$ ls -l -u b*
```

This command uses both of the options `-l` and `-u`. The options are followed by a wildcard filename.

Combining Multiple Options

Options can be combined together behind a hyphen. This command is functionally equivalent to the preceding command:

```
bash$ ls -lu b*
```

This example leads to another principle of standard command-line processing: Option characters can be grouped following the initial hyphen character.

Using Options with Arguments

Some options, however, take arguments of their own. Remember that the GNU `gcc` option `-W` is like that:

```
bash$ gcc -c -Wall prog.c
```

You also learned previously that the following construct is equally valid:

```
bash$ gcc -c -W all prog.c
```

Options that take an argument can have the argument value immediately follow the option letter, or they can be specified next on the command line like a regular argument.

Identifying Options or Arguments

You might ask, "How can I tell when what follows the option letter is an option argument or more options?" You cannot be certain from the appearance of the command line. This behavior is defined by the definition of the option itself, which comes from within the program. I'll show how this use is defined later in this lesson, when I discuss the `getopt()` library function.

Examining Arguments That Look Like Options

You may have encountered a situation in which you wanted to specify an argument that started with a hyphen, and your command complained about the improper options that were being used. For example, say you want to use `grep` to find a source program for the string `--help`:

```
bash$ grep --help dos_cvrt.c
grep: illegal option -- -
usage: grep [-[[AB] ]<num>] [-[CEFGVchilnqsvwx]] [-[ef]] <expr>
➥ [<files...>]
bash$
```

Depending on the version of GNU `grep` you have installed, you might see the display shown, or you might be presented with "help" information from `grep`. Either way, the command does not accomplish what you set out to do. It turns out that this little problem has not gone unnoticed. The following example shows how you can avoid this problem:

```
bash$ grep -- --help dos_cvrt.c
```

You can tell the command to stop processing options by including a double hyphen argument. This argument tells the command's parser function that no more options follow—that only arguments may follow. As you can see from the `grep` example, `grep` is able to accomplish the task that you gave it.

Introducing `getopt()`

The ingredient that makes so many Linux commands appear consistent in their command-line parsing is that they all use a common library function. This function, named `getopt()`, is shown in Listing 6.1.

LISTING 6.1 THE `getopt()` FUNCTION

```
#include <unistd.h>

int getopt(int argc,char *const *argv,const char *optstring);

extern char *optarg;  /* Ptr to option argument */
extern int optind;    /* argv[] index */
extern int opterr;    /* Controls error processing */
```

The `getopt()` External Values

Before you can utilize `getopt()`, you need to be aware of how the external values are used by it. The two most important of these variables are the `optarg` and `optind` variables.

Using the `optarg` External Variable

The `optarg` external pointer variable is set to point to the argument supplied for the option being processed. However, this is done only for those options that take arguments (I'll say more about this issue later). So if `getopt()` is processing the option `-Wall` or `-W all`, the variable `optarg` points to the C string `all` after the `getopt()` call returns.

Using the `optind` External Variable

The external variable `optind` is initially set to the value `1`. `getopt()` uses it to point to the next `argv[]` value to be used. By having the initial value set to `1`, the `getopt()` command starts processing options in `argv[1]`. When the command reaches the end of the options on the command line, the value of `optind` indicates where on the command line the first argument is. For example, if this command were to be processed

```
bash$ rm -f core
```

then the `optind` value after all options are processed is the value `2`. This value indicates that `argv[2]` has the first argument (in this example, it is the file named core).

Using the `opterr` External Variable

The final external value advertised in the `getopt()` interface is the variable `opterr`. This value is initialized to the value `1` (indicating `true`) and is used as input to the `getopt()` function. When variable `opterr` is `true`, and an unrecognized option character is encountered, `getopt()` prints a message to `stderr` indicating the unrecognized option. When `opterr` is set to `0` (`false`) by your program, `getopt()` suppresses the error message if an unrecognized option character is encountered. The message is usually suppressed when your program reports the error message instead or when your error message must go somewhere other than `stderr`.

Working with the getopt() Function Call

Review Listing 6.1 again, and note that the function getopt() returns an integer value. When your command line is processed, each option character is returned by each call to the function. When the end of the option list is encountered, the value -1 is returned (or you can use the EOF macro as defined by stdio.h). When -1 is returned, you should use the external integer value in optind to extract the command-line arguments.

Assume that you have just started to process the command line for gcc:

```
bash$ gcc -Wall -c prog.c
```

The processing proceeds like this:

1. Function getopt() is called for the first time.
2. The call returns the single character W to indicate that it is processing the option -W.
3. You process for a -W option. The -W option takes an argument causing your program to use the C string pointer in the variable optarg (which points to the string "all").
4. Function getopt() is called a second time.
5. This call returns the character c because it is now processing the -c option.
6. You process for a -c option. Because this option does not take an argument, your program ignores the value optarg.
7. The function getopt() is called again.
8. The call returns EOF (-1). You know from this response that there are no more options to process.
9. Examining value optind, you discover that it has the value 3 and the argc value is 4. This means the program has an argument in argv[3] to process. In this case, it holds the string "prog.c".

Reviewing the getopt() Function Prototype

Listing 6.1 shows the function prototype for the getopt() function. The first argument argc is obvious: It states how many argument values you have in the supplied second argument for the array argv[]. The second argument is an array of C string pointers that point to each command-line argument. Usually, the argc and argv values are supplied directly from the main() function interface.

The last argument to getopt() might look a little puzzling at first. It is the C string that "drives" the getopt() processing. It tells getopt() what options are supported and which options take arguments. This single string determines the whole personality of the command line.

Defining the `optstring` Argument

To support a few gcc options such as -c for compiles without linking, -g for debugging, and -W for warning levels, you define an optstring as follows:

```
int main(int argc,char **argv) {
    static char optstring[] = "cgW:";
```

Note how a colon follows the W in the string. The colon tells getopt() that option -W takes an argument. Option order is not significant in the string. The following would be equally acceptable:

```
int main(int argc,char **argv) {
    static char optstring[] = "gW:c";
```

Whenever getopt() processes an option, it searches this optstring. If the option character is not present, then it is not a supported option character, and it is treated as an error (a question mark character is returned). When the option character is found within optstring, the getopt() function checks the next immediate character in the optstring. If it finds a colon there, then getopt() knows that it must extract an argument to go with this option. Otherwise, the simple option character alone is returned to your program.

Defining an Option-Processing Loop

Listing 6.2 shows a typical option-processing loop that processes some of the gcc options.

Listing 6.2 06LST02.c—Typical Option-Processing Loop

```
#include <stdio.h>
#include <unistd.h>

int
main(int argc,char **argv) {
    int optch;
    static char optstring[] = "gW:c";

    while ( (optch = getopt(argc,argv,optstring)) != -1 )
        switch ( optch ) {
        case 'c' :
            puts("-c processed.");
```

```
13:             break;
14:         case 'g' :
15:             puts("-g processed.");
16:             break;
17:         case 'W' :
18:             printf("-W '%s' processed.\n",optarg);
19:             break;
20:         default :
21:             puts("Unknown option!");
22:         }
23:
24:     for ( ; optind < argc; ++optind )
25:         printf("argv[%d] = '%s'\n",
26:             optind, argv[optind]);
27:
28:     return 0;
29: }
```

The basic structure of Listing 6.2 is as follows:

1. Line 7 defines the `optstring` for use by `getopt()`. This line sets the personality of the command-line parse by indicating that it will accept option `-g`, option `-W` with an argument, and option `-c`.
2. Function `getopt()` is called in a `while` loop in line 9 until it returns `-1`.
3. Variable `optch` receives the option character being processed (line 9).
4. The options are processed by the appropriate `case` statements in lines 11 through 17.
5. Variable `optch` receives a `?` if an unrecognized option is encountered. The default case in line 20 carries out this processing.
6. The remaining command-line arguments are processed in lines 24 to 26.

The following is a sample run session of this code:

```
bash$ gcc -Wall 06LST02.c
bash$ ./a.out -c -g -Wall -W pedantic prog.c prog2.c
-c processed.
-g processed.
-W 'all' processed.
-W 'pedantic' processed.
argv[6] = 'prog.c'
argv[7] = 'prog2.c'
bash$
```


Now you are armed with yet another tool for Linux development. It's time to enhance your dos_cvrt tool again.

Enhancing dos_cvrt to Use `getopt()`

One of the present limitations of the dos_cvrt utility is that you cannot specify any optional variations in its processing. With the addition of a few options, the command becomes much more user friendly.

Having the command capable of displaying help information is always a welcome addition, even if just a brief synopsis is included. Many commands respond to an option `-h` for that purpose, so you will add that command here.

Another limitation of the present command is that you must use one of the two different command names to specify whether the conversion is DOS to UNIX or UNIX to DOS. Sometimes its preferable to know and use the command by one name, and select the conversion based on an option. Here, you can make that capability possible by allowing the user to give the `-u` option on the dos_cvrt command line to specify that the input is in UNIX format, resulting in a UNIX-to-DOS conversion instead.

Improving the dos_cvrt Utility

Listing 6.3 shows version 1.9 of dos_cvrt.c, which now includes command-line option processing.

LISTING 6.3 06LST03.C—COMMAND-LINE OPTIONS TO THE `main()` PROGRAM

```
/* dos_cvrt.c */

static const char rcsid[] =
    "$Id: dos_cvrt.c,v 1.9 1998/12/04 03:07:13 student1 Exp $";

/* REVISION HISTORY:
 * $Log: dos_cvrt.c,v $
 * Revision 1.9  1998/12/04 03:07:13  student1
 * Added command line processing.
 *
 * Revision 1.8  1998/11/27 02:29:54  student1
 * Separated out the text conversion
 * functions to make this project
 * more modular.
 *
 * Revision 1.7  1998/11/27 01:31:39  student1
 * Now handles multiple input files, plus
 * put basename code into its own Basename()
 * function.
 *
 * Revision 1.6  1998/11/27 01:01:28  student1
 * Separated conversions into unix2dos() and
```

```
 * dos2unix() functions.
 *
 * Revision 1.5  1998/11/23 05:32:21  student1
 * Completed utility & tested ok.
 *
 * Revision 1.4  1998/11/23 05:04:23  student1
 * Coded basename test
 *
 * Revision 1.3  1998/11/21 22:49:39  student1
 * Demonstration of RCS substitutions
 */
#include <stdio.h>
#include <stdlib.h>
#include <unistd.h>
#include <string.h>
#include <getopt.h>
#include "dos_cvrt.h"

extern char *optarg;    /* Option argument */
extern int optind;      /* Option/arg index */
extern int opterr;      /* Error handling flg */

/*
 * Show brief command usage help:
 */
static void
usage(const char *cmd) {

    fprintf(stderr,"Usage: %s [-h] [-u] infile..\n",cmd);
    fputs("\t-h\t\tGives this help display.\n",stderr);
    fputs("\t-u\t\tSpecifies UNIX to DOS conversion.\n\n",
    ➥stderr);
    fputs("Command unix_cvrt converts UNIX to DOS text.\n",
    ➥stderr);
    fputs("while dos_cvrt converts DOS to UNIX, except "
        "when -u is used.\n\n",stderr);
}

/*
 * Return the pointer to the basename component
 * of a pathname:
 */
static char *
Basename(const char *path) {
    char *base_name = 0;

    if ( ( base_name = strrchr(path,'/') ) != 0 )
        ++base_name;                        /* Skip over '/' */
    else
```

continues

LISTING 6.3 CONTINUED

```
        base_name = (char *) path;         /* No dir. */
    return base_name;
}

int
main(int argc,char **argv) {
    char *base_name = 0;    /* Basename of command */
    int rc = 0;             /* Command return code */
    int (*conv)(const char *pathname); /* Conv. Func. Ptr */
    int x;
    int cmdopt_u = 0;       /* -u ; True if UNIX -> DOS */
    int optch;              /* Current option character */
    static char stropts[] = "hu"; /* Supported options */

    /*
     * Determine the basename of the command name. This
     * is necessary since this command could be invoked
     * with a pathname. For example, argv[0] could be
     * "/usr/local/bin/unix_cvrt" if it was installed
     * in the system that way.
     */
    base_name = Basename(argv[0]);
    if ( !strcmp(base_name,"unix_cvrt") )
        cmdopt_u = 1;       /* Pretend that -u was given */

    /*
     * Process all command line options :
     */
    while ( (optch = getopt(argc,argv,stropts)) != EOF )
        switch ( optch ) {
        case 'h' :          /* -h ; Request usage help */
            usage(base_name);
            return 0;
        case 'u' :          /* -u ; Specifies UNIX -> DOS */
            cmdopt_u = 1;
            break;
        default :           /* Unsupported option */
            fputs("Use -h for help.\n",stderr);
            return 1;
        }

    /*
     * Check for missing input file:
     */
    if ( argc - optind < 1 ) {
        fprintf(stderr,"Missing input file(s).\n");
        fputs("Use -h for help.\n",stderr);
        return 1;
    }

```

```
120:     /*
121:      * -u determines the direction of conversion :
122:      */
123:     if ( cmdopt_u != 0 )
124:         conv = unix2dos;
125:     else
126:         conv = dos2unix;
127:
128:     /*
129:      * Perform a text conversion
130:      */
131:     for ( x=optind; x<argc; ++x )
132:         if ( (rc = conv(argv[x])) != 0 )
133:             break;      /* An error occurred */
134:
135:     return rc;
136: }
```

The improvements in Listing 6.3 can be summarized as follows:

1. Variable `optch` is defined to receive each option letter returned by `getopt()` (line 81).
2. Option string `stropts` is defined to configure the command-line options for `getopt()` (line 82).
3. Variable `cmdopt_u` is defined to operate as a flag while processing the `-u` option (line 80). It is initialized to `0` (`false`) but will be set to `true` when the `-u` option is processed.
4. The basename test (line 92) now just sets the variable `cmdopt_u` (line 93) as if the option `-u` had been received. This program considers using the command name `unix_cvrt` to be equivalent to supplying the `-u` option on the dos_cvrt command line.
5. Lines 98 to 109 show the `getopt()` option-processing loop.
6. If you get the `-h` option, you give help by calling upon `usage()` and then exit the command (lines 100 to 102).
7. If you get a `-u` option, you set variable `cmdopt_u` to `true` so that a UNIX-to-DOS conversion will be performed (lines 103 to 105).
8. If control should reach line 106, it happens because the `getopt()` command received an unsupported option. The `getopt()` function writes an error message to `stderr` because `opterr` has a default value of `1`. You simply provide an additional clue about the `-h` option in line 107 and then return an exit code `1` (line 108).
9. The input file argument test is modified (line 114). You no longer have a fixed index for your input file arguments.

10. The type of conversion required is tested (line 123). If variable `cmdopt_u` is `true`, indicating that `-u` is supplied, then a UNIX-to-DOS conversion is defined. Otherwise, a DOS-to-UNIX conversion is assumed. The conversion is selected by setting the function pointer `conv`.
11. Lines 131 to 133 form a loop that processes all input files. Note the use of `optind` to determine where the first argument is.
12. A help display function is added (lines 48 to 57). This function is invoked from the `-h` option case (line 100).

The input file argument test in improvement nine requires more explanation:

1. Subtracting `optind` from `argc` determines how many command-line arguments you have to process (line 114).
2. If you have no arguments, then you have no input files to process. When that situation occurs, the utility program issues a message to `stderr` and then returns an exit code of `1` (lines 115 to 117).
3. Otherwise, you start processing input files at `argv[optind]` until the variable `x` reaches the value of `argc` (line 131).

Understanding the GNU Long Options Extension

Some commands—the GNU `gcc` command, for example—have a large number of options to support. Not only can you run out of characters to use for all those options, but you also might not be able to remember them all. To help users with this problem, GNU came up with the convention of *long options*.

You might remember this long option example shown back in Hour 1, "Getting Started":

```
bash$ gcc --version
2.7.2.3
bash$
```

In this command, the argument `--version` is an example of a long option.

Long options start with two hyphens but must immediately be followed by one or more characters (otherwise, option processing ceases). To process long options, you must call upon the GNU function `getopt_long()`.

Using the GNU getopt_long() Function

The getopt_long() function processes both the traditional short options and the newer GNU long options.

Defining the getopt_long() Function Prototype

The function prototype for the getopt_long() function is as follows:

```
#include <getopt.h>

int getopt_long(int argc, char * const argv[],
    const char *optstring,
    const struct option *longopts,
    int *longindex);
```

The function prototype is almost the same as getopt() except for the two new arguments, longopts and longindex. The argument longindex points to an integer, where an index value is returned.

Understanding the option Structure

The longopts structure pointer points to the array of option structure entries. The option structure is composed of four members:

```
struct option {
    const char *name;    /* Long option name */
    int        has_arg;  /* True if has an arg */
    int        *flag;    /* NULL or ptr to int */
    int        val;      /* Value to return/assign */
};
```

The structure member name points to a C string containing the name of the long option without the leading hyphens. Member has_arg is defined as an integer but is used as a Boolean value. It must be 0 (false) if no argument exists or nonzero (true) if this option does have an argument. The member flag optionally points to an integer or can be null (0). Finally, member val is used in different ways, depending on how member flag is initialized.

Setting Up the option Structure

The last array entry in the option structure array must be initialized with a null (0) pointer for its name member, 0 for the has_arg member, a null (0) pointer for the flag member, and 0 for the val member. This entry indicates to getopt_long() that no more entries appear in that array. The following is an example of two long options defined in the static option structure long_opts[]:

```
static struct option long_opts[] = {
    { "help", 0, 0, 'h' },    /* name, has_arg, flag, val */
    { "version", 0, 0, 'v' }, /* name, has_arg, flag, val */
    { 0, 0, 0, 0 }
};
```

Using a `null` `option.flag` Pointer

The members `flag` and `val` of the `option` structure work together as a team. The easiest way to use them is to use the following procedure:

1. Set the pointer member `flag` to `null` (`0`).
2. Set the `int` member `val` to the value that you want `getopt_long()` to return. Often this value is the ASCII character code for the equivalent short option letter.

Making a Long Option Look Short

A common practice is to set member `val` to the short option letter equivalent of the long option. For example, if a command supports both the options `--help` and `-h`, then `option` member `flag` is set to a `null` (`0`) pointer, and `val` is set to the ASCII value `'h'`. The structure is initialized as follows:

```
static struct option long_opts[] = {
    { "help", 0, 0, 'h' }, /* name, has_arg, flag, val */
    { 0, 0, 0, 0 }
};
```

Processing When `option.flag` Pointer Is `null`

When the `getopt_long()` function processes the long option `--help`, it performs the following basic steps:

1. The `getopt_long()` function scans the `long_opts[]` array, using an index that you can call `x` in this case. It starts with `x=0`.
2. You use `strcmp()` to see whether the option string `"help"` matches the entry in `long_opts[x].name` (`x` is currently the value `0`). Note that the hyphens are already stripped off the option string.
3. The `strcmp()` function returns `0` because the strings match.
4. Now `getopt_long()` knows the correct index value `x`. This value is returned to the caller by using the integer pointer provided in argument five (`longindex`).
5. The pointer in `long_opts[x].flag` is tested for a `null` pointer. If it is `null`, processing proceeds to the next step.

6. The value of `long_opts[x].val` is used as the return value for `getopt_long()`.

A C code fragment illustrates the last three steps:

```
*longindex = x;                /* 4. Return array index */
if ( !long_opts[x].flag )      /* 5. if flag is null then */
    return long_opts[x].val;   /* 6. return 'h' */
```

The options loop within your program is now tricked into thinking the `-h` option was processed instead because the value `'h'` is returned. This is the easiest way to use long options.

Using a Non-`null` `option.flag` Pointer

When the structure `option` member `flag` is a non-`null` pointer, something different happens. Before I can describe what that is, examine Listing 6.4.

LISTING 6.4 AN EXAMPLE OF A NON-`null` `option.flag` MEMBER

```
1:    static int cmdopt_v = 0;       /* Initialized to false */
2:    static struct option long_opts[] = {
3:        { "help", 0, 0, 'h' },     /* name, has_arg, flag, val */
4:        { "version", 0, &cmdopt_v, 1 },
5:        { 0, 0, 0, 0 }
6:    };
```

Listing 6.4 shows how the variables and the `long_opts[]` array are declared. The following points explain the reasoning behind this code:

1. Line 1 declares the `-v` option flag variable `cmdopt_v`. It is initialized to `false` (`0`).
2. Array element `long_opts[1]` is initialized to accept the long option `--version` (line 4).
3. Member `long_opts[1].flag` (line 4) is initialized with a pointer to the variable `cmdopt_v` (in line 1).
4. Member `long_opts[1].val` (line 4) is initialized with the `int` value of `1`.
5. Array element `long_opts[2]` has all members initialized to `null` or `0`. This marks the end of the long options array.

With the declarations arranged as they appear in Listing 6.4, you can now explore the actions of the `getopt_long()` function when it processes the `--version` option:

1. Internally to `getopt_long()`, an array index is initialized to `0`. You can call this variable `x`.
2. You use `strcmp()` to see whether the option string `"version"` matches the entry in `long_opts[x].name` (`x` is currently the value `0`.)

3. The `strcmp()` function returns nonzero because the strings do not match (`long_opts[0].name` points to the C string `"help"`).
4. The `getopt_long()` function increments `x` to the value of `1`.
5. You use `strcmp()` to see whether the option string `"version"` matches the entry in `long_opts[x].name` (`x=1`).
6. The `strcmp()` function returns `0` because the option string `"version"` matches the `long_opts[x].name`, which also points to a string `"version"`.
7. Now `getopt_long()` knows the correct index value `x`. It is returned to the caller by using the integer pointer provided in argument five (`longindex`) (`x=1`).
8. The pointer value `long_opts[1].flag` is tested for `null`. It is not `null`, so the processing proceeds to the next step.
9. The integer value from `long_opts[1].val` is fetched and then stored at the location pointed to by `long_opts[1].flag`.
10. The `getopt_long()` function returns the value `0` to indicate that this special long option has been processed.

Steps 9 and 10 are carried out when the flag member is not `null`. Step 6, in the section titled "Processing When `option.flag` Pointer Is `Null`," is used when the `flag` member is `null`. In step 10 in this procedure, note again how `getopt_long()` returns `0`.

The following code fragment summarizes steps 7 through 10 of the procedure:

```
    *longindex = x;                 /* 7. Return array index */
    if ( !long_opts[x].flag )       /* 8. if flag is null */
        return long_opts[x].val;    /*    return val */
    /* Return val via flag ptr */
    *(long_opts[x].flag) = long_opts[x].val; /* 9. Use ptr */
    return 0;                       /* 10. Indicate flag use */
}
```

Adding GNU Long Options to dos_cvrt

Now you can add the options `--version` and `--help` to the dos_cvrt utility program to make it a bit more user friendly. Option `--version` causes the utility to display its revision number to the user. The `--help` option is an easier-to-remember equivalent of the existing `-h` option already supported.

Enhancing dos_cvrt

Listing 6.5 shows the enhanced dos_cvrt.c program source.

LISTING 6.5 06LST05.C—THE DOS_CVRT UTILITY WITH GNU LONG OPTIONS

```
/* dos_cvrt.c */

static const char rcsid[] =
    "$Id: dos_cvrt.c,v 1.10 1998/12/04 04:43:10 student1 Exp $";

/* REVISION HISTORY:
 * $Log: dos_cvrt.c,v $
 * Revision 1.10  1998/12/04 04:43:10  student1
 * Added GNU long options.
 *
 * Revision 1.9  1998/12/04 03:07:13  student1
 * Added command line processing.
 *
 * Revision 1.8  1998/11/27 02:29:54  student1
 * Separated out the text conversion
 * functions to make this project
 * more modular.
 *
 * Revision 1.7  1998/11/27 01:31:39  student1
 * Now handles multiple input files, plus
 * put basename code into its own Basename()
 * function.
 *
 * Revision 1.6  1998/11/27 01:01:28  student1
 * Separated conversions into unix2dos() and
 * dos2unix() functions.
 *
 * Revision 1.5  1998/11/23 05:32:21  student1
 * Completed utility & tested ok.
 *
 * Revision 1.4  1998/11/23 05:04:23  student1
 * Coded basename test
 *
 * Revision 1.3  1998/11/21 22:49:39  student1
 * Demonstration of RCS substitutions
 */
#include <stdio.h>
#include <stdlib.h>
#include <unistd.h>
#include <string.h>
#include <getopt.h>
#include "dos_cvrt.h"

extern char *optarg;     /* Option argument */
extern int optind;       /* Option/arg index */
extern int opterr;       /* Error handling flg */

```


continues

LISTING 6.5 CONTINUED

```
/*
 * Show brief command usage help:
 */
static void
usage(const char *cmd) {

    fprintf(stderr,"Usage: %s [-h | --help] [--version] "
        "[-u] infile..\n",cmd);
    fputs("\t-h (or --help)\tGives this help display.\n",
    ➥stderr);
    fputs("\t--version\tDisplays program version.\n",stderr);
    fputs("\t-u\t\tSpecifies UNIX to DOS conversion.\n\n",
    ➥stderr);
    fputs("Command unix_cvrt converts UNIX to DOS text.\n",
    ➥stderr);
    fputs("while dos_cvrt converts DOS to UNIX, except "
        "when -u is used.\n\n",stderr);
}

/*
 * Return the pointer to the basename component
 * of a pathname:
 */
static char *
Basename(const char *path) {
    char *base_name = 0;

    if ( ( base_name = strrchr(path,'/') ) != 0 )
        ++base_name;                         /* Skip over '/' */
    else
        base_name = (char *) path;           /* No dir. */
    return base_name;
}

int
main(int argc,char **argv) {
    char *base_name = 0;    /* Basename of command */
    int rc = 0;             /* Command return code */
    int (*conv)(const char *pathname); /* Conv. Func. Ptr */
    int x;
    int cmdopt_u = 0;       /* -u ; True if UNIX -> DOS */
    static int cmdopt_v = 0;/* --version */
    int cmdx = 0;           /* lopts[] index */
    int optch;              /* Current option character */
    static char stropts[] = "hu"; /* Supported options */
    static struct option lopts[] = {
        { "help", 0, 0, 'h' },  /* --help */
        { "version", 0, &cmdopt_v, 1 }, /* --version */
        { 0, 0, 0, 0 }          /* No more options */
```

```
    };

    /*
     * Determine the basename of the command name. This
     * is necessary since this command could be invoked
     * with a pathname. For example, argv[0] could be
     * "/usr/local/bin/unix_cvrt" if it was installed
     * in the system that way.
     */
    base_name = Basename(argv[0]);
    if ( !strcmp(base_name,"unix_cvrt") )
        cmdopt_u = 1;       /* Pretend that -u was given */

    /*
     * Process all command line options :
     */
    while ( (optch = getopt_long(argc,argv,stropts,
      lopts,&cmdx)) != EOF )

        switch ( optch ) {
        case 0 :            /* Processed lopts[cmdx] */
            break;
        case 'h' :          /* -h or --help */
            usage(base_name);
            return 0;
        case 'u' :          /* -u ; Specifies UNIX -> DOS */
            cmdopt_u = 1;
            break;
        default :           /* Unsupported option */
            fputs("Use --help for help.\n",stderr);
            return 1;
        }

    if ( cmdopt_v != 0 ) {
        fprintf(stderr,"Version 1.0\n");
        return 0;
    }

    /*
     * Check for missing input file:
     */
    if ( argc - optind < 1 ) {
        fprintf(stderr,"Missing input file(s).\n");
        fputs("Use --help for help.\n",stderr);
        return 1;
    }

    /*
     * -u determines the direction of conversion :
     */
```


continues

LISTING 6.5 CONTINUED

```
144:     if ( cmdopt_u != 0 )
145:         conv = unix2dos;
146:     else
147:         conv = dos2unix;
148:
149:     /*
150:      * Perform a text conversion
151:      */
152:     for ( x=optind; x<argc; ++x )
153:         if ( (rc = conv(argv[x])) != 0 )
154:             break;      /* An error occurred */
155:
156:     return rc;
157: }
```

The improvements to the program can be summarized as follows:

1. Static `option` structure and its initialization are defined in the `main()` program (lines 90 to 94). To illustrate both methods of using `getopt_long()`, the options `--help` and `--version` are set up differently.
2. Static variable `cmdopt_v` is declared (line 86). This variable must be static because of the static initialized pointer reference you use in line 92 (that is, `&cmdopt_v` has to be a fixed address).
3. The program now calls function `getopt_long()` instead of `getopt()` (lines 110 and 111). Note that function `getopt_long()` updates the value in variable `cmdx` to be the index of the `lopts[]` array member that it is processing, if any.
4. The `case` for when `optch` is `0` is added (lines 114 to 115). This `case` ignores the situation when `getopt_long()` returns `0`. In this program, this result occurs when `--version` is processed. No further processing is required for this option because the variable `cmdopt_v` is automatically set to a value of `1` by the function call.
5. Option `--help` is processed in the same place as the short option `-h` (lines 116 to 118). The setup in `lopts[0]` is such that `getopt_long()` fakes a short option `'h'` value to be returned.
6. The `usage()` function is updated to reflect the new options supported (lines 51 to 62).

Summary

In this lesson, you learned about UNIX command-line conventions and about the GNU long options extension. You also learned how to apply the functions `getopt()` and `getopt_long()` so that you can use them in new programs that you will write.

Q&A

Q How do options help commands?

A Options allow variations in the command's use without requiring a prompt and user-input sequence.

Q Why did GNU introduce a new option convention? Wasn't the original UNIX convention adequate?

A Some commands must support a very large number of options. One example is the GNU `gcc` compiler. When the set of required options becomes large, it is possible to run out of option characters to use. Another problem is that remembering all the options becomes very difficult if many of them are used. For example, the long option `--help` is easy to remember.

Q Where does the first argument start in a program that uses `getopt()` processing?

A The first argument is at `argv[optind]`, after `getopt()` returns `EOF (-1)`.

Q Why is it necessary for `getopt()` to make value `opterr` available to the programmer? Why not just always print errors to `stderr`?

A Library functions must be as flexible as possible to allow widespread use. The caller might not want an error message at all or might want to report a different-from-standard message for that error. It is also possible that the error should be reported to a log rather than `stderr`. The choice should belong to the developer.

Workshop

You are encouraged to complete the following quiz and the exercises so that you can practice what you have learned.

Quiz

6

1. How many characters make up an option, without counting the leading hyphen?
2. How many leading hyphens does a long option have?
3. How do you provide an argument that begins with a hyphen on a command line, without it being interpreted as another option?
4. Where does the option argument come from after calling `getopt()`?
5. Where does the option argument come from after calling `getopt_long()`?
6. How do you disable error messages for unrecognized options for `getopt()` and/or `getopt_long()`?

7. What is returned from `getopt()` when an option given on the command line is not supported by the option string passed to `getopt()` in argument 3?

Exercises

1. Modify the current dos_cvrt project (as shown in Listing 6.5) to include a new `-f` option. Modify the program so that when this option is detected, the dos_cvrt program will behave as a filter program (it takes its input from standard input). If command-line arguments are provided in addition to the `-f` option, they should be processed only after standard input has reached end-of-file.
2. Modify the project from exercise 1 to allow the long option name `--filter` or the original short option `-f` to be used. Define the option structure such that `getopt_long()` returns `'f'` for the `--filter` option.
3. Modify the project from exercise 2 to process the `--filter` option differently: Define an integer `cmdopt_f`, and initialize it to `false` (`0`). Set up the option structure so that `getopt_long()` sets `cmdopt_f` to `1` automatically when the option is encountered (that is, make the `option` member `flag` a non-`null` pointer).

HOUR 7

Error Handling and Reporting

Learning How to Handle Errors

The Linux operating system and its C libraries offer a rich set of function libraries that a developer can call on. In this set, however, a programmer can call very few functions for which an error cannot occur. Reasons for errors include the incorrect use of parameters, insufficient buffer sizes, or lack of file system permissions. Some mechanism must be in place to return the error indication and the cause for the error to the caller of that function.

In this lesson, you will look at the error reporting mechanisms for UNIX, past and present. You'll also see how meaningful error messages can be reported back to users. Error messages reported to the users are especially important for them to do well because the users are going to base their action plans on this very information.

Understanding UNIX Error Reporting

When a C function is called, the programmer is interested in two points upon its return:

- Did the function call succeed?
- If not, then why did it fail?

Indicating Success or Failure

The UNIX convention adopted by most of its library functions is that the return value usually indicates success or failure. Return values fall into two main categories:

- The return value is an integer value (`int` or `long`). Normally, failure is indicated by `-1`.
- The return value is a pointer type (`char` or some structure pointer type). Normally, failure is indicated by a `null` return pointer.

For integer return values, a successful return value is usually anything other than `-1`. Most often, it is a value that is greater than or equal to `0`. For example, the UNIX `open()` call returns a file descriptor that can be `0` or greater. However, `-1` indicates that the `open()` call failed.

For pointer return values, a successful return value is a non-`null` pointer. An example is the `fopen()` function. When it returns a `null` pointer, an error has occurred. When a non-`null` pointer is returned, then you know that the `fopen()` call succeeded.

Determining the Reason for Failure

Knowing when a function call has failed is half of the battle. Some functions can fail for a large number of reasons, so it becomes important for the programmer to know about the precise reason for that failure.

The mechanism that the early developers of UNIX chose (from which Linux has inherited) was to report errors to a special external variable named `errno`. Whenever a function call failed, it would post its reason for failure to this `errno` variable and then return a failure indication in its returned result (`-1` for integers or `null` for pointer return values).

The mechanism used was suitable for early UNIX. However, this older method has some limitations to it, which I will discuss later in this lesson. To address the limitations, the mechanism has been changed somewhat in recent versions of Linux. The change is transparent if used correctly.

The Old errno Value

The original way that a programmer gained access to the posted error code was to declare an external reference to the int value errno:

```
extern int errno;
```

In the program, the programmer could attempt to open a file, for example, and if it failed, he or she could simply query the variable errno to determine the reason for the failure:

```
extern int errno; /* Error code */
int fd;           /* File descriptor */

if ( (fd = open("myfile.dat",O_RDONLY)) < 0 ) {
    printf("errno = %d\n",errno);
    exit(13);
}
```

In this example, when the open call fails, the program simply reports the errno value. This error message is not user friendly, but it certainly is one that a programmer could investigate.

Referencing Error Codes by Name

Using the errno external variable convention for errors required that a series of error codes be agreed upon in advance. Because numeric error codes might vary on different UNIX platforms, a set of C macros was defined to refer to these errors with symbolic macro names. They are defined in the include file errno.h.

```
#include <errno.h>
```

Using symbolic references for error codes means that UNIX C programs can be more portable.

Error codes (or errno values) are nonzero values and usually start at 1 and work up. The value 0 is sometimes used to indicate "no error."

Testing for Specific Errors

Not all errors are reported to the user of a program. Sometimes the program is supposed to take a specific action when a certain condition is detected. For example, the make command looks for the file GNUmakefile first. If this file is "not found", then it tries to open the file named makefile. The following example makes a special case of the "not found" error (ENOENT) by providing a custom error message for it:

```
#include <errno.h>
extern int errno; /* Error code */
```

```
int fd;            /* File descriptor */

if ( (fd = open("myfile.dat",O_RDONLY)) < 0 ) {
    if ( errno == ENOENT ) { /* File Not Found? */
        puts("File myfile.dat does not exist!");
        exit(13);
    }
    printf("Unexpected Error: errno = %d\n",errno);
    exit(13);
}
```

Notice that the program uses the symbolic name `ENOENT` for the error code. This C macro is defined by the include file errno.h.

Applying `errno` Correctly

Novice programmers might be tempted to use the `errno` value to test for success. The `errno` value was originally supposed to be used as a place to post error codes to. As a general policy, then, never expect the `errno` value to be cleared to `0` for success. Only errors are posted to this variable.

A few functions that I will cover later in this book require you to clear the `errno` value to `0` before making the call. These unusual situations will be covered in detail when you examine these functions.

> The `errno` value is updated by library functions only after an error occurs. This value is never cleared to `0` for a successful operation. Always test the function's return value to determine whether an error has occurred. If an error has occurred, then the value of `errno` has meaning.

Testing for Failure with Integer Results

Earlier I discussed how functions that return integer results usually use the value `-1` to indicate that the call has failed. Because `open()` returns a `0` or positive result only for opened file descriptors, the `if` statement simply tests for a negative value:

```
if ( (fd = open("myfile.dat",O_RDONLY)) < 0 ) {
   /* Error Occurred: errno valid */
```

If the `open()` call returns a failed indication by a return value less than `0` (`-1`), then you know that the error code has been posted to the integer `errno`.

Testing for Failure with Pointer Results

Other functions report their failure by returning a `null` pointer. For example, look at how the `fopen()` call does this:

```
FILE *fp = fopen("myfile.dat","r");

if ( fp == 0 ) { /* NULL Returned? */
    /* Open Failed: */
```

Here, the `fopen()` call indicates failure by returning a `null` pointer. Again, when you know that the function has failed, the value in `errno` has the posted error code for the failure.

The New errno Value

If you are a veteran of using C/C++ code for UNIX, and you have been a Linux programmer for a while, then you have probably had to change some old habits over the last year or so. The newer Linux kernel releases have undergone some changes to be able to support threads.

Threads are a welcome addition to Linux. However, threads have forced a number of changes to the C libraries, including the way `errno` is defined and used.

The simple explanation for the new `errno` declaration is that each thread needs its own copy of the `errno` value. Multiple threads sharing a single `errno` variable result in chaos.

To fix the problem for threads, the C libraries had to be reworked extensively. You now are required to include the include file errno.h in your program if you need access to the `errno` value. The old days of declaring `errno` as an external integer are over. If you insist on declaring it that way, your compiler will scold you with error messages.

Declaring the New errno Variable

The new `errno` value can be defined for you as a macro that invokes a function or references an array element or some other exotic thing. The `errno` value of today is meant to be treated as a "black box." Because you can no longer declare it yourself, the new way to declare it is to include the file errno.h:

```
#include <errno.h>
```

Because the new definition for `errno` is different from before, you must not declare it as an external `int` variable. Your compiles will fail if you do. The included errno.h file defines `errno` in a way that is appropriate for your platform.

Using the New errno Variable

After variable `errno` is declared by the include file errno.h, you can still use it as you did before. Consider this example:

```
printf("errno = %d\n",errno);
errno = ENOENT;  /* Set to file not found error */
```

You can obtain its value and change its value just like before. The change in the way `errno` is defined is meant to be transparent to you.

Reporting on errno Values

When an error occurs, the program can simply test for a specific case and act on it. The problem becomes more complex when all you want to do is to report the error back to the users. In general, users do not like to memorize error codes, so you need to find a better way to translate an `errno` code into a message.

You can report a Linux error code as a message in the following ways:

- Report the `errno` code itself. I did this for some of the most basic code examples, but you should never use this approach in normal finished products.
- Use the `perror()` function to generate a message from the `errno` value and report it to `stderr`.
- Use the provided `sys_errlist[]` array of messages.
- Use the `strerror()` function to return a message for the current `errno` value.

Using the perror() Function

One solution provided for reporting errors is to use the library function `perror()`. This function takes one string argument and writes that string to `stderr`, followed by a colon and a space, and then a message for the current `errno` value. The function syntax is as follows:

```
#include <stdio.h>

void perror(const char *s);
```

You can test this function by quite simply assigning an error of your choice to `errno` and then calling `perror()`. Such a test is coded in Listing 7.1.

Listing 7.1 07LST01.c—Test Program for `perror()`

```
1:   #include <errno.h>
2:   int main(int argc,char **argv) {
3:
4:       errno = EIO;
5:       perror("Test EIO Message");
6:       return 0;
7:   }
```

Line 4 shows how you can arbitrarily assign an I/O error to the `errno` variable. Then, in line 5, you can call on `perror()` to do its thing. The following test session shows what happens when you invoke the compiled program:

```
bash$ ./a.out
Test EIO Message: Input/output error
bash$
```

The session output shows the message, followed by a colon and space, and an interpretation of the value `EIO` that was in the variable `errno`.

Evaluating the `perror()` Function

At first sight, the `perror()` function might appear to be a good solution. In reality, this function is not very useful. The first problem with this function is that the message must go to standard error. What if it needs to be written to a log file instead? What if you need it as a string so that you can report it to your X Window GUI session? What if you don't like the reporting format? The preceding are all issues that programmers have with this function. This function works best for simple educational examples.

Using the `sys_errlist[]` Array

If you look up the `perror()` function in the Linux man pages, you will also see that it describes the `sys_errlist[]` array. The syntax of this array is as follows:

```
#include <errno.h>

const char *sys_errlist[];
int sys_nerr;
```

The `sys_errlist[]` array is an external array of pointers to string constants. Each string describes a particular error that corresponds to an `errno` code. The array and the error codes are structured so that the error message can be obtained by using the `errno` value as the subscript into the array:

```
errno = EIO;
printf("The EIO Message is '%s'\n",sys_errlist[errno]);
```

Having access to the error message text for each error code provides you much more flexibility. When an `fopen()` call fails, for example, you can not only report the reason for the failure, but you also can report the pathname and whether you are opening for read or write:

```
FILE *fp = fopen(pathname,"r");

if ( !fp ) {
    fprintf(stderr,"%s: Unable to open %s for read.\n",
        sys_errlist[errno],
        pathname);
    exit(13);
}
```

Using `sys_nerr` to Range Check Errors

The largest error code that is provided for in the `sys_errlist[]` array is given by the external integer value of `sys_nerr` minus one. To be safe, you should always test the `errno` value before using it as a subscript:

```
errno = EIO;
printf("The EIO Message is '%s'\n",
    errno < sys_nerr ? sys_errlist[errno] : "?");
```

Evaluating `sys_errlist[]` Array Method

Although range checking using the `sys_nerr` value is the correct thing to do, it is considered rather tedious and pedantic by many programmers. Therefore, many programmers ignore this test altogether. For this reason, the practice of using the `sys_errlist[]` array has fallen out of favor by many programmers.

Using the `strerror()` Function

The `strerror()` function is the last of all error code conversion methods that you will look at. The syntax of this function is as follows:

```
#include <string.h>

char *strerror(int errnum);
```

> A common mistake is to include the file errno.h instead of string.h for this function. It is commonly assumed that because the function reports an error message, it is declared in the errno.h include file. However, this function is grouped with the string functions instead.

The `strerror()` function gives you the flexibility afforded by the `sys_errlist[]` array, but it also performs the necessary range check on the error code being converted. If the error code is outside the known list of error codes, an unknown error message is returned instead of a bad pointer.

Using the `strerror()` Function

Listing 7.2 shows a short program that you can use to test the `strerror()` function.

LISTING 7.2 07LST02.C—TESTING `strerror()`

```
1:   #include <stdio.h>
2:   #include <errno.h>
3:   #include <string.h>
4:
5:   extern int sys_nerr;
6:
7:   int main(int argc,char **argv) {
8:       int x;
9:       static int ecodes[] =
10:          { -1, EIO, 0 };
11:
12:      /* Get maximum code */
13:      ecodes[2] = sys_nerr;
14:
15:      for ( x=0; x<3; ++x )
16:          printf("%4d = '%s'\n",
17:              ecodes[x],
18:              strerror(ecodes[x]));
19:
20:      return 0;
21:  }
```

This test program uses the following basic procedure:

1. A static integer array `ecodes[]` is declared with two initial values (lines 9 and 10).
2. The third value for `ecodes[]` is copied from the external integer value of `sys_nerr` (line 13).
3. A loop of three iterations is performed. The three elements of `ecodes[]` are passed to `strerror()` and reported to standard output (lines 15 to 18).

Testing the Range Check in `strerror()`

When you compile and run the program shown in Listing 7.2, you get the following results:

```
bash$ ./a.out
  -1 = 'Unknown error 18446744073709551615'
```

```
   5 = 'Input/output error'
 125 = 'Unknown error 125'
bash$
```

The current implementation of `strerror()` appears not to handle the `-1` case very well. It looks like an unsigned conversion except that it is very large for a 32-bit value. In any case, error code `5` shows the normal `EIO` message that you are supposed to get. The last case tries to use the value from `sys_nerr`, which is greater than the last valid error code. Sure enough, `strerror()` appears to treat error code `125` as an unknown error. The important point is that you get an error message for any code you supply.

Applying `strerror()` Correctly

One important point to note about using the `strerror()` function is that the pointer returned by this function is valid only until the next call is made. The following code is incorrect:

```
char *eptr1 = strerror(EIO);
char *eptr2 = strerror(ENOENT);

printf("Msg1='%s', msg2='%s'\n",eptr1,eptr2);
```

This code is not acceptable because the pointer value `eptr1` is considered trash by the time `strerror()` is called the second time and its return value is assigned to `eptr2`. Normally, this functional limitation does not present a problem in practice. If, however, you find that you do need to keep the message text longer, you must copy the message to a local buffer before calling `strerror()` again.

> The value returned by `strerror()` is valid only until the next time `strerror()` is called.

Enhancing dos_cvrt to Be Error-Reporting Friendly

The dos_cvrt utility program has gained quite a bit of functionality over the lessons covered so far. However, one of the features that it really lacks presently is proper error detection and reporting. You will correct this problem in the following sections.

Enhancing Module unix2dos.c

Listing 7.3 illustrates the changes made to the unix2dos.c source module incorporating error tests and reporting.

LISTING 7.3 07LST03.C—UNIX2DOS.C WITH ERROR CHECKING ADDED

```
/* $Header: /home/student1/dos_cvrt/RCS/unix2dos.c,v ...
 * Basil Fawlty     $Date: 1998/12/06 21:34:06 $
 *
 * UNIX to DOS text format conversion.
 *
 * $Log: unix2dos.c,v $
 * Revision 1.2  1998/12/06 21:34:06  student1
 * Added error checking.
 *
 * Revision 1.1  1998/11/27 02:29:21  student1
 * Initial revision
 */
static const char rcsid[] =
    "$Id: unix2dos.c,v 1.2 1998/12/06 21:34:06 student1 Exp $";

#include <stdio.h>
#include <stdlib.h>
#include <unistd.h>
#include <errno.h>
#include <string.h>
#include "dos_cvrt.h"

/*
 * Convert file named by pathname to DOS
 * text format, on standard output:
 */
int
unix2dos(const char *pathname) {
    int ch;                     /* Current input character */
    int rc = 0;                 /* Return code */
    FILE *in = 0;               /* Input file */

    if ( !(in = fopen(pathname,"r")) ) {
        fprintf(stderr,"%s: opening %s for read.\n",
            strerror(errno),pathname);
        return RC_OPENERR;
    }

    while ( (ch = fgetc(in)) != EOF ) {
        if ( ch == '\n' )
            if ( put_ch('\r') ) {
                rc = RC_WRITERR;    /* Write failed */
                goto xit;
            }
        if ( put_ch(ch) ) {
            rc = RC_WRITERR;        /* Write failed */
            goto xit;
```

continues

LISTING 7.3 CONTINUED

```
48:             }
49:         }
50:
51:         /*
52:          * Test for a read error:
53:          */
54:         if ( ferror(in) ) {
55:             fprintf(stderr,"%s: reading %s\n",
56:                 strerror(errno),pathname);
57:             rc = RC_READERR;
58:         }
59:
60: xit:fclose(in);
61:         return rc;
62: }
63:
64: /* End $Source: /home/student1/dos_cvrt/RCS/unix2dos.c,v $ */
```

The changes to this module can be summarized as follows:

1. Files errno.h and string.h are included to provide the necessary declarations for `errno` and `strerror()`, respectively (lines 19 and 20).
2. A new return code variable `rc` is declared and initialized to `0` (line 30). It will be used as the `unix2dos()` function return code.
3. The value of `rc` is altered when errors occur (lines 42, 46, and 57).
4. One function exit point is declared at label `xit` (line 60). The one exception to this rule occurs when the `fopen()` call fails, causing a return (line 36). The point of having the common exit is to make sure that the file `in` is closed and make the code easier to understand by having one exit point at the bottom.
5. The success of the `fopen()` call is tested (line 33). If the call fails, the reason for the failure and the pathname of the file being opened are reported to `stderr` (lines 34 to 36). Note that you describe to the user that you are attempting to open the file for read. This information helps when the problem is related to lack of permissions.
6. The `putchar()` calls are replaced by a function `put_ch()` that you provide to encapsulate the `putchar()` and the error reporting functionality (lines 41 and 45). Using this function saves a lot of duplication of code. The function `put_ch()` returns a nonzero value when it reports an error (this function is illustrated later). The error is handled by setting variable `rc` (lines 42 and 46) and transferring control to `xit` (line 60).

7. You test for read errors on `FILE` stream `in` (line 54). Note that the `fgetc()` call (line 39) returns `EOF` if an error occurs in addition to the normal end-of-file condition. The error is reported to `stderr` (lines 55 to 58).

> Test and reference the `errno` value as close to the source of the error as possible. For example, if an `fopen()` call fails, be sure to report that error before other functions that set `errno` are called. Functions such as `printf()` and `fprintf()` may change the value of `errno`, even when no error is returned by them.
>
> If you need to defer reporting an error, copy the integer value `errno` to a local `int` type variable. Then reference that value when you are ready to test and report it.

Enhancing Module dos2unix.c

The changes you need to make to the dos2unix.c source module (see Listing 7.4) are similar to those made to the unix2dos.c module.

LISTING 7.4 07LST04.C—DOS2UNIX.C WITH ERROR CHECKING ADDED

```
/* $Header: /home/student1/dos_cvrt/RCS/dos2unix.c,v 1.2 ...
 * Basil Fawlty     $Date: 1998/12/06 21:33:38 $
 *
 * The DOS to UNIX text conversion:
 *
 * $Log: dos2unix.c,v $
 * Revision 1.2  1998/12/06 21:33:38  student1
 * Added error checking.
 *
 * Revision 1.1  1998/11/27 02:29:37  student1
 * Initial revision
 */
static const char rcsid[] =
    "$Id: dos2unix.c,v 1.2 1998/12/06 21:33:38 student1 Exp $";

#include <stdio.h>
#include <stdlib.h>
#include <unistd.h>
#include <errno.h>
#include <string.h>
#include "dos_cvrt.h"

/*
 * Convert file named by pathname, to
```


continues

LISTING 7.4 CONTINUED

```
 * UNIX text file format on standard output:
 */
int
dos2unix(const char *pathname) {
    int rc = 0;                 /* Return code */
    int ch;                     /* Current input character */
    int cr_flag;                /* True when CR prev. encountered */
    FILE *in = 0;               /* Input file */

    if ( !(in = fopen(pathname,"r")) ) {
        fprintf(stderr,"%s: opening %s for read.\n",
            strerror(errno),pathname);
        return RC_OPENERR;  /* Open failure */
    }

    cr_flag = 0;   /* No CR encountered yet */
    while ( (ch = fgetc(in)) != EOF ) {
        if ( cr_flag && ch != '\n' ) {
            /* This CR did not precede LF */
            if ( put_ch('\r') ) {
                rc = RC_WRITERR;    /* Write failed */
                goto xit;
            }
        }
        if ( !(cr_flag = ch == '\r') )
            if ( put_ch(ch) ) {
                rc = RC_WRITERR;    /* Write failed */
                goto xit;
            }
    }

    /*
     * Check for read errors:
     */
    if ( ferror(in) ) {
        fprintf(stderr,"%s: reading %s\n",
            strerror(errno),pathname);
        rc = RC_READERR;
    }

xit:fclose(in);
    return rc;
}

/* End $Source: /home/student1/dos_cvrt/RCS/dos2unix.c,v $ */
```

From the error testing and reporting point of view, the highlights in Listing 7.4 are as follows:

1. The `fopen()` call is tested for failure (line 34). If the open fails, a message is formatted to `stderr` (line 35).
2. The new `put_ch()` function is called, and its return value is tested for the presence of an error (lines 44 and 50). If an error occurs, you know that `put_ch()` has already reported it, and you transfer control to `xit` (line 65).
3. You test for a read error (line 59). If an error occurs, you format a message to `stderr` (line 60).
4. The success or failure of the function is returned (line 66) after you make sure that the input file has been closed (line 65).

Creating Module putch.c

Listing 7.5 shows the new source module putch.c, which defines the new external function `put_ch()`.

LISTING 7.5 07LST05.C—THE NEW `put_ch()` FUNCTION

```
/* $Header: /home/student1/dos_cvrt/RCS/putch.c,v ...
 *
 * Put characters to stdout with error checking:
 *
 * $Log: putch.c,v $
 * Revision 1.1  1998/12/06 21:32:49  student1
 * Initial revision
 *
 */
static const char rcsid[] =
    "$Id: putch.c,v 1.1 1998/12/06 21:32:49 student1 Exp $";

#include <stdio.h>
#include <stdlib.h>
#include <unistd.h>
#include <errno.h>
#include <string.h>

/*
 * Put a character to stdout, with proper
 * error checking:
 *
 * RETURNS: 0 == success
 *         -1 == Failed
 */
```

continues

LISTING 7.5 CONTINUED

```
26:  int
27:  put_ch(int ch) {
28:
29:      putchar(ch);
30:      if ( ferror(stdout) ) {
31:          fprintf(stderr,"%s: writing to stdout\n",
32:              strerror(errno));
33:          return -1;          /* Failed write */
34:      }
35:      return 0;               /* Successful write */
36:  }
37:
38:  /* End $Source: /home/student1/dos_cvrt/RCS/putch.c,v $ */
```

The program in Listing 7.5 is structured as follows:

1. Function `put_ch()` accepts one ASCII character as input in argument `ch`. The returned result is `0` if the character is written successfully or `-1` if an error occurs (line 27).
2. The character is written to `stdout` (line 29).
3. The `ferror()` function is called to test for the presence of a registered error in the `stdout` stream.
4. If an output error occurs, the error is reported to `stderr` (lines 31 and 32). When this happens, `-1` is returned to indicate that an error has been reported (line 33).
5. If no error is detected, `0` is returned (line 35).

Changing Include File dos_cvrt.h

The addition of a new source module requires you to change both the Makefile and the dos_cvrt.h header file. Listing 7.6 shows the new dos_cvrt.h file.

LISTING 7.6 07LST06.H—THE MODIFIED DOS_CVRT.H WITH THE `put_ch()` FUNCTION PROTOTYPE

```
/* $Header: /home/student1/dos_cvrt/RCS/dos_cvrt.h,v ...
 * Basil Fawlty      $Date: 1998/12/06 21:30:53 $
 *
 * Header File for the dos_cvrt utility program:
 *
 * $Log: dos_cvrt.h,v $
 * Revision 1.2  1998/12/06 21:30:53  student1
 * Added put_ch() and defined RC_* macros
 *
 * Revision 1.1  1998/11/27 02:28:57  student1
```

```
11:   * Initial revision
12:   */
13:  #ifndef _dos_cvrt_h_
14:  #define _dos_cvrt_h_ "@(#)dos_cvrt.h $Revision: 1.2 $"
15:
16:  /*
17:   * Command exit codes :
18:   */
19:  #define RC_CMDOPTS 1       /* Options usage error */
20:  #define RC_OPENERR 2       /* File open failure */
21:  #define RC_READERR 3       /* File read error */
22:  #define RC_WRITERR 4       /* File write error */
23:
24:  extern int unix2dos(const char *pathname);
25:  extern int dos2unix(const char *pathname);
26:  extern int put_ch(int ch);
27:
28:  #endif /* _dos_cvrt_h_ */
29:
30:  /* $Source: /home/student1/dos_cvrt/RCS/dos_cvrt.h,v $ */
```

The changes to Listing 7.6 are as follows:

1. The new function prototype for `put_ch()` is added (line 26). It is required by modules unix2dos.c and dos2unix.c.
2. Macros are defined to give symbolic names to the utility exit codes (lines 19 to 22). When used with `exit()` and returned from the `main()` program, these values provide information to a shell script about the general nature of the failure.

Enhancing the Makefile

Listing 7.7 shows the new Makefile for the project. Line 7 shows how you add the new module putch.o.

LISTING 7.7 07LST07.MK—THE NEW MAKEFILE FOR DOS_CVRT

```
1:   # $Source: /home/student1/dos_cvrt/RCS/Makefile,v $
2:   # $Revision: 1.2 $
3:   # $Date: 1998/12/06 21:34:26 $
4:
5:   CC=         gcc
6:   STD=        _GNU_SOURCE
7:   OBJS=       dos_cvrt.o unix2dos.o dos2unix.o putch.o
8:
9:   .c.o:
10:     $(CC) -c -Wall $(CFLAGS) -D$(STD) $<
```


continues

LISTING 7.7 CONTINUED

```

all:      dos_cvrt unix_cvrt

dos_cvrt: $(OBJS)
	$(CC) $(OBJS) -o dos_cvrt

unix_cvrt: dos_cvrt
	rm -f unix_cvrt
	ln dos_cvrt unix_cvrt

clean:
	rm -f *.o core

clobber: clean
	rm -f dos_cvrt unix_cvrt

# End Makefile
```

Enhancing Module dos_cvrt.c

Listing 7.8 shows the new and improved dos_cvrt.c program.

LISTING 7.8 07LST08.C—THE DOS_CVRT.C MODULE WITH ERROR CHECKING ADDED

```
/* dos_cvrt.c */

static const char rcsid[] =
    "$Id: dos_cvrt.c,v 1.11 1998/12/06 21:29:58 student1 Exp $";

/* REVISION HISTORY:
 * $Log: dos_cvrt.c,v $
 * Revision 1.11  1998/12/06 21:29:58  student1
 * Added error checking.
 *
 * Revision 1.10  1998/12/04 04:43:10  student1
 * Added GNU long options.
 */
#include <stdio.h>
#include <stdlib.h>
#include <unistd.h>
#include <errno.h>
#include <string.h>
#include <getopt.h>
#include "dos_cvrt.h"

extern char *optarg;    /* Option argument */
extern int optind;      /* Option/arg index */
extern int opterr;      /* Error handling flg */
```

```

/*
 * Show brief command usage help:
 */
static void
usage(const char *cmd) {

    fprintf(stderr,"Usage: %s [-h | --help] [--version] "
        "[-u] infile..\n",cmd);
    fputs("\t-h (or --help)\tGives this help display.\n",
    ➥stderr);
    fputs("\t--version\tDisplays program version.\n",stderr);
    fputs("\t-u\t\tSpecifies UNIX to DOS conversion.\n\n",
    ➥stderr);
    fputs("Command unix_cvrt converts UNIX to DOS text.\n",
    ➥stderr);
    fputs("while dos_cvrt converts DOS to UNIX, except "
        "when -u is used.\n\n",stderr);
}

/*
 * Return the pointer to the basename component
 * of a pathname:
 */
static char *
Basename(const char *path) {
    char *base_name = 0;

    if ( ( base_name = strrchr(path,'/') ) != 0 )
        ++base_name;                         /* Skip over '/' */
    else
        base_name = (char *) path;           /* No dir. */
    return base_name;
}

int
main(int argc,char **argv) {
    char *base_name = 0;    /* Basename of command */
    int rc = 0;             /* Command return code */
    int (*conv)(const char *pathname); /* Conv. Func. Ptr */
    int x;
    int cmdopt_u = 0;       /* -u ; True if UNIX -> DOS */
    static int cmdopt_v = 0;/* --version */
    int cmdx = 0;           /* lopts[] index */
    int optch;              /* Current option character */
    static char stropts[] = "hu"; /* Supported options */
    static struct option lopts[] = {
        { "help", 0, 0, 'h' },  /* --help */
        { "version", 0, &cmdopt_v, 1 }, /* --version */
        { 0, 0, 0, 0 }          /* No more options */
    };
```


continues

LISTING 7.8 CONTINUED

```
    /*
     * Determine the basename of the command name. This
     * is necessary since this command could be invoked
     * with a pathname. For example, argv[0] could be
     * "/usr/local/bin/unix_cvrt" if it was installed
     * in the system that way.
     */
    base_name = Basename(argv[0]);
    if ( !strcmp(base_name,"unix_cvrt") )
        cmdopt_u = 1;       /* Pretend that -u was given */

    /*
     * Process all command line options :
     */
    while ( (optch = getopt_long(argc,argv,stropts,
      lopts,&cmdx)) != EOF )

        switch ( optch ) {
        case 0 :            /* Processed lopts[cmdx] */
            break;
        case 'h' :          /* -h or --help */
            usage(base_name);
            return 0;
        case 'u' :          /* -u ; Specifies UNIX -> DOS */
            cmdopt_u = 1;
            break;
        default :           /* Unsupported option */
            fputs("Use --help for help.\n",stderr);
            return 1;
        }

    if ( cmdopt_v != 0 ) {
        fprintf(stderr,"Version 1.0\n");
        return 0;
    }

    /*
     * Check for missing input file:
     */
    if ( argc - optind < 1 ) {
        fprintf(stderr,"Missing input file(s).\n");
        fputs("Use --help for help.\n",stderr);
        return RC_CMDOPTS;
    }

    /*
     * -u determines the direction of conversion :
     */
    if ( cmdopt_u != 0 )
```

```
123:         conv = unix2dos;
124:     else
125:         conv = dos2unix;
126:
127:     /*
128:      * Perform a text conversion
129:      */
130:     for ( x=optind; x<argc; ++x )
131:         if ( (rc = conv(argv[x])) != 0 )
132:             break;      /* An error occured */
133:
134:     /*
135:      * Check that our possibly buffered stdout
136:      * gets flushed without errors:
137:      */
138:     fflush(stdout);
139:     if ( ferror(stdout) ) {
140:         fprintf(stderr,"%s: writing standard output.\n",
141:             strerror(errno));
142:         rc = RC_WRITERR;
143:     }
144:
145:     return rc;
146: }
```

The following changes have been made to Listing 7.8:

1. The `include` of errno.h is added (line 17).
2. When no input files are provided on the command line, you now return the symbolic value `RC_CMDOPTS` (line 116).
3. The return value from the conversion is tested (line 131). The first input file to report an error here causes all processing to cease (line 132).
4. The standard output `FILE` stream is flushed (line 138). This action forces any buffered data to be written at this point.
5. The result of the `fflush()` is tested (line 139). Because a write operation to standard output may be forced, it may also fail (due to lack of disk space and so on). If an error is detected, you report this fact to `stderr` (lines 140 to 143).
6. The return code in `rc` is provided as the exit code (line 145). If any command exit code is recorded in `rc`, it is passed back to the Linux kernel here.

Testing for All Errors

You might have noticed that you do not test for all possible errors in this program. It is true that you don't test whether all the writes to the standard error stream succeed

(Line 140 in Listing 7.8, for example). Some of these matters come down to a judgment call. What do you do in a program like this if you cannot write an error message?

In my opinion, because the program reports its success or failure by exit code, you can safely ignore a failure to write an error message to `stderr`. If this utility is used by a shell script, for example, the shell knows about this program's failure, regardless of error messages. If, on the other hand, you are using Linux for a military grade application, you might not be as tolerant about this situation.

Summary

In this lesson, you studied the general philosophy behind the Linux C library method of reporting success and failure. You learned how the reasons for failure are made available to the programmer in variable `errno`. You also looked at the old `errno` definition and learned the rules for using the new `errno`, as it is defined in the include file errno.h.

You also learned about the different ways that an error code can be changed into a user-friendly message. You examined some of the pitfalls, like that of using the `errno` value after `printf()` has been called.

Q&A

Q Why has the declaration of `errno` changed from an external integer to some "black box" definition?

A The implementation of threads forced a change in the way `errno` values were posted. Sharing a single `errno` value causes one thread to corrupt the `errno` value of the other thread.

Q Why is it a good idea to report the error message as soon after the error as possible?

A Many other functions can post errors to `errno`. For example, a formatted print with `printf()` may change your `errno` value, even if the function returns successfully because the function may produce errors internally that are dealt with successfully.

Q How do I declare the `errno` variable?

A You include file errno.h.

Q Where are the macros defined for the `errno` (error) code values?

A They are defined by including file errno.h.

Q Why must I not save string pointers from `strerror()` for long-term use?

A The returned pointer from `strerror()` is valid only until the next call to this function.

Workshop

You are encouraged to complete the quiz and the exercises to practice what you have learned before proceeding to the next chapter.

Quiz

1. How do you turn an error code from `errno` into a C message string for long-term use? (Two answers are acceptable.)
2. How do you find out what the highest numbered error code is?
3. How do you know when to consult `errno` after an `fopen()` call is made?
4. Why is it sometimes necessary to call upon `fflush()` and then `ferror()`?
5. When should `ferror()` be called when doing `FILE` I/O? Should it be immediately after each failure point, or can it be deferred until a more convenient point in the program, and why? (The answer must take into account the determination of the cause of error.)
6. Why is the function `perror()` not in widespread use?
7. Should `strerror()` ever be used more than once in a `printf()` call? Why or why not?

Exercises

1. Using a simple main program like the one shown in Listing 7.1, construct a program that includes the following statement:

   ```
   printf("sys_nerr=%d, msg1='%s', msg2='%s'\n",
       sys_nerr,
       strerror(sys_nerr),strerror(sys_nerr+1));
   ```

   Make sure you declare the external for variable `sys_nerr`. Does this `print` statement work correctly? Why or why not?
2. Write a simple program that opens a file named test_file for reading. If the open succeeds, just print a simple "`OK`" message and exit. If the open fails, print a meaningful error message.

   Compile the program and run it without creating the file test_file. Do you get the correct error message?

3. Using the program you compiled in exercise 2, run the following two shell commands:

```
bash$ >test_file
bash$ chmod 0 test_file
```

The first command creates an empty file test_file. The second command takes all permissions away from that file. Now run your test program. Does your error message complain about access?

HOUR 8

The Linux main Program and Its Environment

The main Program Interface

The main() program is perhaps one of the most underappreciated functions in the C programming language. In this lesson, you will expand on your knowledge of the main() function interface and learn a little about how the shell interacts with your C program.

In addition, you will take a detailed look at the arguments passed to the main() function, including one that is often forgotten. Many people forget that main() is actually called with three arguments instead of two.

You'll also look at how the exported environment variables of the shell appear from the point of view of the C program. You will also learn about fetching environment values as well as ways to create or alter them. Finally, you will take a "black box" look at the address space of the C program.

Forming the argv[] Array

The dos_cvrt utility developed throughout the preceding lessons made use of command-line arguments. From a programmer's viewpoint, they entered the application program through the main() function argument argc and array argv[]. The argv[] array was neatly set up so that each array element pointed to a C string that represented each command-line argument. However, when you typed in the command, presumably the shell read it as one long line of text. Who and what was responsible for breaking up that line into argv[] array values? How did main() gain access to them in this form if the shell read in the command line?

To explain this scenario, you need to know a little bit about the shell. Although users can choose different shells under Linux, here you can assume that you will be using the GNU bash shell that is usually the default.

Understanding Linux Shell Processes

The bash shell looks to Linux just like any other Linux process. It's simply a UNIX program that has a process ID, reads from standard input, and writes to standard output and to standard error. Usually, all three of these I/O streams are the terminal device that the user is using, but it need not be. In short, bash is just another Linux program.

This bash program, however, is quite important to the user. It interprets command lines and starts commands. These commands may be built-in shell commands, but most of the time they are external programs. Commands that are not built in are programs that are started by invoking an executable file somewhere in the Linux file system. For example, the hello.c source file can be compiled into the default a.out executable file. When you type **a.out** into the shell, this executable file is loaded and run by the shell.

Parsing the Command Lines

As you probably expected, bash parses the command line after it is read in. The shell built-in variable IFS determines how this is done. Normally, IFS is set such that blanks separate the different command-line arguments. Argument parsing is more complicated than this, however, because the shell permits the user to use single or double quotation marks around sections of the command line to allow the inclusion of special characters such as blanks into an argument field. Furthermore, if wildcard expansion is enabled within bash, as it is by default, then any wildcard filenames must be expanded and substituted for, before any further command-line parsing occurs. As you can see, the shell does a lot of work before starting a command.

Starting Commands

After the shell has parsed out a list of arguments into its private copy of array `argv[]`, it is tasked with starting the command that is identified in `argv[0]`. If the command name represents a shell built-in command, it is carried out by the shell directly (probably through a function call). If, however, this command is not known by the shell, the shell starts looking for a matching executable file to load and execute. It does so by searching all directories listed in the exported `PATH` environment variable. Finally, it finds an executable file with the execute permission bit(s) set.

Through the magic of the Linux `fork()` and `exec()` kernel calls, the bash shell is able to start your program on its merry way. Although I'll save these particular details for Hour 18, "Forked Processes," I can say that the command-line arguments are passed through the function arguments of the `exec()` call. The bash shell passes its idea of `argc` and array `argv[]` to Linux via the `exec()` function, and from there the Linux kernel makes sure that your program is loaded and called with these values.

Summarizing Shell Command Startup

This summary has provided a simplified view of the entire command startup process. I didn't discuss the startup activities that are performed by a C startup module that calls the `main()` program. However, the important point to learn here is that the process that invokes your program is the one that determines what the arguments will be.

Using `argv[]` Without `argc`

It's commonly known that `argv[0]` contains a string that points to the command's name. It's also known that `argv[argc-1]` points to the C string that represents the last command-line argument. What you may not know is that `argv[argc]` is also valid and is a `null` pointer, which marks the end of the array.

The `null` pointer at the end of `argv[]` permits you to pass the array `argv[]` or its subset, without requiring a corresponding `argc` value to be supplied. For example, you could supply the pointer `argv+1` to a function to give it the list of command-line arguments (excluding the command name in `argv[0]`).

Declaring the Third `main()` Argument

Many people forget that `main()` is actually called with three arguments instead of two. The full interface definition for a `main` program is this:

```
int main(int argc,char const *argv[],char const *envp[]) {
```

If you ignore the `const` keyword for a moment, you can simplify the interface to look like this:

```
int main(int argc,char *argv[],char *envp[]) {
```

You are already well acquainted with `argv[]` as an array of string pointers, but what is this `envp[]` array argument?

Passing Shell Exported Variables

One of the other pieces of information that arrives at the `main` program's doorstep is the exported list of environment variables. These variables are provided to the programmer in the array `envp[]`. Like the `argv[]` array, the last entry is a `null` pointer. This fact is important because you don't pass a count for the `envp[]` array, like the `argc` value is for `argv[]`. Also like the `argv[]` array, the `envp[]` array comes to you from the shell program, via the calling arguments in the `exec()` call. The shell wields a lot of power over your program.

To find the value of the exported `PATH` variable, for example, you can scan the list in `envp[]` until you find a C string that starts with `"PATH="`. If you don't find that substring, then you can conclude that the shell variable `PATH` is not exported.

You will find out shortly that you can more easily look up a variable with the help of the `getenv()` function call. Sometimes the `envp[]` array is useful, but I will come back to this idea later.

Using the External Pointer `environ`

In addition to the environment being passed to `main()` in the third function argument, any function can also access the external environment by means of the following external declaration:

```
extern char **environ;
```

This external declaration allows a function that has not been passed the environment's array structure to gain access to the environment. You will find that the pointer value of variable `environ` is identical to `envp`. This means that `environ[x]` is the same as `envp[x]`.

The Linux Program Address Space

At this point, you have learned about the role that the bash shell plays in the startup of your program. You've also seen that the Linux kernel is involved in the startup and with the passing of command-line arguments and the exported environment. To fully make use of your program's operating environment, you might find it useful to learn a few more things about the memory address space in which the program operates.

Here, you will take a "black box" approach to your examination of the memory of the Linux program. You'll determine by experiment where the various program components are placed in memory. You will also note where the exported shell variables are placed and what happens to new and changed environment variables within your C program.

Probing the Linux Process Address Space

To study the operating environment, you can probe your Linux address space a little bit with a program fit for the job.

Programming the Probe

Listing 8.1 shows a program that you can run on your Linux platform to probe your address space a little bit. The example run discussed here was done on an Intel Linux platform. If you are running Linux on a Digital Dec Alpha or some other (non-Intel) platform, you might get some different results. Differences are to be expected on different hardware platforms, so they should not worry you.

LISTING 8.1 08LST01.C—LISTING OF AN ENVIRONMENT PROBE PROGRAM

```
#include <stdio.h>
#include <stdlib.h>
#include <unistd.h>
#include <string.h>
#include <errno.h>

static const int s = 23;     /* Static var */

extern int main              /* Main appears later */
    (int argc,char *const argv[],char *const envp[]);

/*
 * Dump item's address to be sorted :
 */
void                         /* This must be extern */
dumpAddr(FILE *p,const char *desc,const void *addr) {

    fprintf(p,"0x%08lX  %-32s\t%lu\n",
```

continues

LISTING 8.1 CONTINUED

```
        (long)addr, desc, (unsigned long)addr);
}

/*
 * Splat out unprintable characters :
 */
static void
mkPrintable(char *buf) {

    for ( ; *buf; ++buf )
        if ( *buf <= ' ' || *buf >= 0x7F )
            *buf = '@';
}

/*
 * Test (static) Function 2 :
 */
static void
fun2(FILE *p) {
    int f2;

    dumpAddr(p,"&f2",&f2);
}

/*
 * Test (extern) Function 1 :
 */
void
fun1(FILE *p) {
    int f1;

    dumpAddr(p,"&f1",&f1);
    fun2(p);
}

/*
 * Dump the environment + various selected
 * addresses :
 *
 * ARGUMENTS:
 *      envp        Pointer to the argument (from main)
 *      heading     Display heading comment
 */
void
dump(char * const envp[],const char *heading) {
    int x;          /* Indexes envp[x] */
    char *cp;       /* Work pointer */
    char buf[32];   /* Local buffer */
    FILE *p = 0;    /* Pipe FILE pointer */
```

```

    /*
     * Open a pipe to sort all address by
     * decreasing address, so that the last
     * displayed address will be the lowest
     * addressed item:
     */
    if ( !(p = popen("sort -n -r -k3","w")) ) {
        fprintf(stderr,"%s: popen('sort ...');\n",
            strerror(errno));
        exit(13);
    }

    /*
     * Display a heading:
     */
    printf("\n%s\n\n",heading);
    fflush(stdout);

    /*
     * Display environment variables:
     */
    for ( x=0; envp[x] != 0; ++x ) {
        buf[0] = '&';           /* Put '&' in 1st col. */
        strncpy(buf+1,envp[x],sizeof buf-2);
        buf[sizeof buf - 1] = 0;/* Make sure we have a nul */
        mkPrintable(buf);       /* Splat out special chars */
        dumpAddr(p,buf,envp[x]);/* Dump this var's address */

        /*
         * Special test for TERM variable:
         * Here we discard the '=' and what follows.
         */
        if ( (cp = strchr(buf,'=')) != 0 )
            *cp = 0;

        /*
         * Test if envp[x] is the "TERM" entry:
         */
        if ( !strcmp(buf+1,"TERM")      /* Got "TERM" ?    */
        &&   (cp = getenv("TERM")) != 0 /* "TERM" defined? */
        &&   cp != envp[x]+5 ) {        /* Ptrs mismatch?  */
            strcpy(buf,"@TERM=");       /* Yes, mark this. */
            strncpy(buf+6,cp,sizeof buf-7); /* Copy new val.*/
            buf[sizeof buf - 1] = 0;    /* Enforce nul byte */
            mkPrintable(buf);           /* Splat out        */
            dumpAddr(p,buf,cp);         /* Dump this entry */
        }
    }   /* End for () */

```

continues

Listing 8.1 continued

```
    dumpAddr(p,"&envp[0]",&envp[0]);    /* Start of envp[] */
    sprintf(buf,"&envp[%u]",x);
    dumpAddr(p,buf,&envp[x]);        /* Dump end of envp[] */

    dumpAddr(p,"&s",&s);             /* Dump static &s addr */
    dumpAddr(p,"&x",&x);             /* Dump auto &x addr   */

    fun1(p);                         /* Call upon fun1()    */

    dumpAddr(p,"stderr",stderr);     /* Dump stderr address */
    dumpAddr(p,"stdout",stdout);     /* Dump stdout address */
    dumpAddr(p,"stdin",stdin);       /* Dump stdin address  */

    dumpAddr(p,"fprintf",fprintf);   /* Dump fprintf addr.  */
    dumpAddr(p,"main",main);         /* Dump main's addr.   */
    dumpAddr(p,"dump",dump);         /* Dump dump's addr.   */
    dumpAddr(p,"fun1",fun1);         /* Dump fun1's addr.   */
    dumpAddr(p,"fun2",fun2);         /* Dump fun2's addr.   */

    if ( (cp = getenv("NVAR1")) != 0 ) /* Is NVAR1 defined?*/
        dumpAddr(p,"&NVAR1",cp);       /* Dump &NVAR1      */

    if ( (cp = getenv("NVAR2")) != 0 ) /* Is NVAR2 defined?*/
        dumpAddr(p,"&NVAR2",cp);       /* Dump &NVAR2      */

    /*
     * By closing this pipe now, we'll start sort on its
     * merry way, sorting our results. The sort output will
     * be sent to standard output.
     */
    pclose(p);
}

/*
 * The main program:
 */
int
main(int argc,char * const argv[],char * const envp[]) {

    /*
     * This dump() call will dump our unmodified environment:
     */
    dump(envp,"INITIAL ENVIRONMENT:");

    /*
     * Here we'll create two new environment variables
     * NVAR1 and NVAR2.
     */
```

```
166:     if ( putenv("NVAR1=New Variable") == -1 ) {
167:         fprintf(stderr,"%s: putenv()\n", strerror(errno));
168:         exit(13);
169:     }
170:     if ( putenv("NVAR2=New Variable 2") == -1 ) {
171:         fprintf(stderr,"%s: putenv()\n", strerror(errno));
172:         exit(13);
173:     }
174:
175:     /*
176:      * Here we change the value of our TERM variable, to
177:      * see what changes take place for an existing exported
178:      * environment variable here:
179:      */
180:     if ( putenv("TERM=oink-term") == -1 ) {
181:         fprintf(stderr,"%s: putenv()\n", strerror(errno));
182:         exit(13);
183:     }
184:
185:     /*
186:      * Now that we've modified our environment, let us
187:      * see what havoc we wreaked:
188:      */
189:     dump(envp,"MODIFIED ENVIRONMENT:");
190:     sleep(1);    /* This waits for the sort output */
191:
192:     /*
193:      * This simple test just proves that the new value
194:      * for TERM has been changed.
195:      */
196:     printf("\ngetenv('TERM') = '%s';\n",getenv("TERM"));
197:     return 0;
198: }
```

Understanding the Probe

The program in Listing 8.1 is a little bit different from an application program. A number of things are declared with no real useful purpose other than to show how things are placed in memory. The highlights of this program can be summarized as follows:

1. The static variable `s` is declared (line 7). You want to find out what address it gets in memory.
2. A forward declaration for `main()` is necessary (line 9). You want to refer to the address of `main` before it is declared.
3. Function `dumpAddr()` is declared as a convenience for the rest of the program (lines 15 to 20). It allows all addresses to be formatted in the same manner and written to the pipe `p`, which is a `FILE` pointer. I will explain the need for the pipe shortly.

4. Function `mkPrintable()` is another convenience function (lines 25 to 31). It allows you to dump environment variables without worrying about the possibility of non-printable characters that some variables might have.
5. Test function `fun2()` is defined (lines 36 to 41). The address of this function and its stack-based variable `f2` will be dumped.
6. Test function `fun1()` is defined (lines 46 to 52). Again, this function and its stack-based variable `f1` will have their addresses dumped. This function calls upon `fun2()` to allow you to detect which way the program stack is growing.
7. Function `dump()` is defined to perform the bulk of the work of the probe (lines 62 to 149). This code is made a function so that it can be invoked "before" and "after" a change is made.
8. The `main()` program is defined to control the whole process (lines 154 to 198).

Understanding the `dump()` Function

The `dump()` function is a large piece of the software probe. The probe is explained in the following points:

1. The `FILE` variable `p` is declared (line 67). It is used for a UNIX pipe.
2. A UNIX pipe is opened to the `sort` command (line 75). This pipe is opened for write so that what you write will be sorted by the `sort` command. The `sort` command writes its sorted results to standard output (`stdout`). This is done so that the dumped addresses are sorted and displayed from top to bottom.
3. A `for` loop is written to process all exported shell variables (line 90). The loop iterates through all values of `x` until it locates the `null` pointer at the end of `envp[x]`.
4. The character `'&'` is copied to the first byte of the buffer array `buf[]` (line 91). It is the "address of" operator that you want to show in your output.
5. The environment variable and its value string are copied from `envp[x]` into the buffer starting at `buf[1]` (line 92). Line 93 makes sure that you have a `NUL` terminating byte stored in `buf[]`.
6. Function `mkPrintable(buf)` is called (line 94). This function looks for any non-printing characters in `buf[]`, substituting the character `'@'` for them.
7. The function `dumpAddr()` is called, given the pipe pointer `p`, the buffer `buf[]` to use as its description, and the address to dump `envp[x]` (line 95).
8. You then scan `buf[]` for the `'='` character (line 101). If you find it in a string like `"TERM=vt100"`, for example, you stomp out the string starting at the `'='` character (to arrive at the string `"TERM"`).

9. You test whether you find the TERM variable in envp[x] (line 107). Note that the '&' character is in buf[0], so you compare starting at buf[1] in the strcmp() call.
10. You call getenv() to look up the TERM environment variable (line 108). If it is defined, this function call returns a non-null pointer.
11. You compare the pointer cp value from step 10 with the pointer returned by envp[x]+5 (line 109). Note that you add five to the envp[x] value to point to the first byte after the '=' in the string "TERM=vt100". You need to do so because the getenv() function returns the pointer to the value.
12. If the tests in steps 9, 10, and 11 are all true, you proceed to the code in the block starting on line 110.
13. If any of the tests fail in steps 9, 10, or 11, you simply continue the next iteration of the loop at step 3.
14. At the end of the for loop, you dump some fixed addresses (lines 118 to 120). Here, you dump the address of envp[0] and the last element envp[x].
15. You dump the address of the static variable s (line 122).
16. You dump the address of the local auto variable x (line 123).
17. You call fun1(), passing it the pipe pointer for its own address dumps (line 125). This function also calls fun2() and then returns.
18. You dump the address of FILE blocks stderr, stdout, and stdin (lines 127 to 129).
19. You dump the addresses of functions fprintf(), main(), dump(), fun1(), and fun2() (lines 131 to 135).
20. If the environment variable NVAR1 is defined, you note its address (line 137) and then dump its address (line 138).
21. You perform the same test for NVAR2 and dump it as you did in step 20 (lines 140 and 141).
22. Finally, you close the pipe p (line 148). This action closes the input to the sort command that you started in line 75, and its sorted results are written to the standard output.

I will explain the reasons for looking for the TERM, NVAR1, and NVAR2 variables later. All these steps serve to trace where everything is located in your address space. The sort command gives you a sorted list of addresses.

Understanding the `main()` Function

The `main()` function drives the probe. The basic procedure implemented is this:

1. The initial program environment is probed, sorted, and dumped by calling function `dump()` (line 160). This step is taken before the program has any opportunity to make any changes.
2. Two new environment variables `NVAR1` and `NVAR2` are created (lines 166 to 173). This code changes the collection of environment variables.
3. You change the value of the environment value `TERM` (line 180). If `TERM` does not exist, it is created here. The probe assumes, however, that this variable already exists, as it normally would for an interactive shell session.
4. You call upon `dump()` again to see what has changed in process memory (line 189).
5. You call `sleep()` to wait for one second. This way, you can leave ample time for the `sort` command called by `dump()` to sort and report its results to the standard output. You want the output from step 6 to appear as the last text line of output.
6. After the program wakes up from the sleep in step 5, you print the last line of the display by showing what `getenv()` returns for `"TERM"`. I will explain this step later.

Running the Probe

Running the probe program produces two outputs because `dump()` is called "before" and "after." The "before" dump of the environment is provided in Listing 8.2.

LISTING 8.2 INTEL LINUX INITIAL ENVIRONMENT DUMP

```
INITIAL ENVIRONMENT:

0xBFFFFFC9  &_=./a.out                            3221225417
0xBFFFFFC1  &TZ=EST5                              3221225409
0xBFFFFFB9  &SHLVL=1                              3221225401
0xBFFFFF53  &MANPATH=/usr/local/man:/usr/ma       3221225299
0xBFFFFF4C  &PS2=>@                               3221225292
0xBFFFFF41  &PS1=bash$@                           3221225281
0xBFFFFF31  &SHELL=/bin/bash                      3221225265
0xBFFFFF1D  &HOME=/home/student1                  3221225245
0xBFFFFEA2  &PATH=/usr/local/bin:/bin:/usr/       3221225122
0xBFFFFE94  &HOSTTYPE=i586                        3221225108
0xBFFFFE89  &TERM=vt100                           3221225097
0xBFFFFE6D  &MACHTYPE=i586-unknown-linux          3221225069
0xBFFFFDF5  &LD_LIBRARY_PATH=/lib:/usr/lib:       3221224949
0xBFFFFD78  &envp[13]                             3221224824
0xBFFFFD44  &envp[0]                              3221224772
0xBFFFFD0C  &x                                    3221224716
0xBFFFFCD4  &f1                                   3221224660
```

```
20: 0xBFFFFCC4  &f2                                3221224644
21: 0x0804A1E8  stdin                              134521320
22: 0x0804A188  stderr                             134521224
23: 0x0804A138  stdout                             134521144
24: 0x08048EEC  &s                                 134516460
25: 0x08048D40  main                               134516032
26: 0x080489E0  dump                               134515168
27: 0x080489B0  fun1                               134515120
28: 0x08048990  fun2                               134515088
29: 0x080487EC  fprintf                            134514668
```

Interpreting the "Before" Results

The Listing 8.2 output can be summarized as follows:

1. Line 1 confirms the environment dump that you are looking at (string `"INITIAL ENVIRONMENT"` is passed to `dump()` in line 160 of Listing 8.1). This step confirms that this result is the "before" picture.
2. Three columns are displayed (starting at line 3). The leftmost column is the hexadecimal address of the item being dumped. The middle column is a description of what is being reported. The last column is the unsigned value used by the `sort` command (you can ignore this column).
3. The display shows that the environment variable _ (underscore) is the highest addressed item dumped (line 3). In this case, the bash shell has chosen to put the executable filename used to run this test—namely, file a.out—in this variable.
4. Environment variable `TZ` is the second-highest addressed item dumped, with an address of `BFFFFFC1` (line 4).
5. The lowest addressed environment variable is `LD_LIBRARY_PATH` with an address of `BFFFFDF5` (line 15). So far, you can see that the environment variables are all grouped at the top of the address space.
6. The `envp[]` array sits there beneath the environment variables starting at address `BFFFFD44` (lines 16 and 17).
7. The automatic variables `x`, `f1`, and `f2` have decreasing addresses (lines 18 to 20). Because `x` is in the `dump()` function's stack frame and has a higher address than the address of `f1`, you can conclude that because `dump()` calls `fun1()`, the stack grows downward. This point is further proved by `f1` having a higher address than `f2`, which is `fun2`'s automatic variable. Because `fun2()` is called by `fun1()`, you have further proof that the stack grows downward in memory.
8. The `FILE` control blocks of `stdin`, `stderr`, and `stdout` are much lower in address (lines 21 to 23). This suggests that they are at the bottom of the stack.

9. The static variable `s` has an address somewhat near the `stdout` address (line 24).
10. Function addresses appear lower still (lines 25 to 29).

Arriving at Initial Conclusions

A few points are worth noting about Listing 8.2:

- All the environment variables that you inherited from the shell appear to be grouped at the top of memory (lines 3 to 15).
- The `envp[]` pointer array is located beneath the environment variables (lines 16 and 17).
- The stack is located beneath the environment variables and grows downward (lines 18 to 20).
- Global variables are located beneath the stack bottom (lines 21 to 24).
- The function code appears to be loaded starting at the bottom (lines 25 to 29). Furthermore, because you know that other library code is linked into the executable, it is quite likely that function code started loading at hexadecimal address `80000000`.

Determining Stack Growth Direction

Most of the time, a C program does not need to be concerned about whether the stack grows up or grows down. However, in some specialized cases, knowing this fact is important.

Early versions of MicroEMACS, for example, needed to be configured for the correct direction of stack growth before it was compiled. Failure to configure stack growth correctly would cause certain functions within it to fail. You might encounter other software like this for which you will need to determine the stack growth direction for the platform that you are compiling for.

Interpreting the "After" Results

You can defer analysis of the "after" results for the moment. This way, you will have time to learn about how to work with environment variables in your C program. After this break, you will return to the "after" results when you review them later in this lesson.

Working with the Environment

I promised to cover the details on how to get and set environment variable values. You have seen them in action already, but now you can take a closer look at these functions.

Fetching an Environment Variable

To obtain the current value for an environment variable, you use the library function `getenv()`:

```
#include <stdlib.h>

char *getenv(const char *name);
```

This function takes care of locating the value that you are looking for. Furthermore, if the value changes, this function knows where to locate the new value for the variable.

The `getenv()` function takes the string name of the variable being sought, and if the variable is defined, a pointer to its string value is returned. For example, the home directory can be fetched and displayed by doing the following:

```
char *home_dir;

if ( (home_dir = getenv("HOME")) != 0 )
    printf("HOME Directory: %s\n",home_dir);
```

Note that if the value cannot be found, a `null` pointer is returned.

Changing an Environment Variable

Sometimes you might want to change an environment variable from within a C program. For example, your program may have subtle problems with the `vt220` terminal emulation choice that the user made in the `TERM` variable. For the duration of your program, you can alter this `TERM` value to use the simpler `vt100` terminal emulation instead. You can make changes to environment variables by using the `putenv()` call:

```
#include <stdlib.h>

int putenv(const char *string);
```

Using the `putenv()` Function

To change from a `vt220` terminal emulation setting to a `vt100` setting, you might code the following:

```
char *term = 0;

term = getenv("TERM");
if ( term && !strcmp(term,"vt220") )
    putenv("TERM=vt100");
```

The steps taken here are these:

1. You declare the pointer variable `term`.

2. You call function `getenv()` to see whether `TERM` is defined and exported.
3. If `TERM` is located, you test its value to see whether it matches the string `"vt220"`.
4. If both steps 2 and 3 succeed, you call upon `putenv()` to change the terminal emulation to `"vt100"` instead.

Notice that with the `putenv()` function call you must supply the variable name, an equal sign, and its value in the same string.

Using the `setenv()` Function

Another function is available for setting variables:

```
#include <stdlib.h>

int setenv(const char *name, const char *value, int overwrite);
```

With this function, you can name the variable and its value separately. The third argument `overwrite` has no effect if the variable being defined is new. However, when the variable already exists, the value is changed only if the value of `overwrite` is `true` (that is, it is nonzero). Consider the `TERM` example again:

```
setenv("TERM","vt220",1);
```

This example creates `TERM` if it does not exist and changes the value of `TERM` if it exists already. The following call creates `TERM` only if it does not already exist:

```
setenv("TERM","vt220",0);
```

Removing an Environment Variable Definition

Sometimes you need to remove the definition of the variable itself. You do so with the help of the following function:

```
#include <stdlib.h>

void unsetenv(const char *name);
```

For example, if you don't like the influence that the variable `TZ` is having on your C program, you might code the following call:

```
unsetenv("TZ");
```

This function call eliminates the value of environment variable `TZ`. Any attempt to call `getenv()` to get the value of `TZ` after the `unsetenv()` call is performed causes it to return a `null` pointer.

Understanding the Impact of Environment Changes

Now that you have looked at the functions that can alter your environment, it is useful to see what happens to the landscape of your C program address space when some changes are made to environment variables. Listing 8.3 shows the "after" results of the probe that you ran.

LISTING 8.3 INTEL LINUX ENVIRONMENT AFTER ENVIRONMENTAL CHANGES WERE MADE

```
MODIFIED ENVIRONMENT:

0xBFFFFFC9  &_=./a.out                          3221225417
0xBFFFFFC1  &TZ=EST5                            3221225409
0xBFFFFFB9  &SHLVL=1                            3221225401
0xBFFFFF53  &MANPATH=/usr/local/man:/usr/ma     3221225299
0xBFFFFF4C  &PS2=>@                             3221225292
0xBFFFFF41  &PS1=bash$@                         3221225281
0xBFFFFF31  &SHELL=/bin/bash                    3221225265
0xBFFFFF1D  &HOME=/home/student1                3221225245
0xBFFFFEA2  &PATH=/usr/local/bin:/bin:/usr/     3221225122
0xBFFFFE94  &HOSTTYPE=i586                      3221225108
0xBFFFFE89  &TERM=vt100                         3221225097
0xBFFFFE6D  &MACHTYPE=i586-unknown-linux        3221225069
0xBFFFFDF5  &LD_LIBRARY_PATH=/lib:/usr/lib:     3221224949
0xBFFFFD78  &envp[13]                           3221224824
0xBFFFFD44  &envp[0]                            3221224772
0xBFFFFD0C  &x                                  3221224716
0xBFFFFCD4  &f1                                 3221224660
0xBFFFFCC4  &f2                                 3221224644
0x0804A47E  &NVAR1                              134521982
0x0804A45D  @TERM=oink-term                     134521949
0x0804A43E  &NVAR2                              134521918
0x0804A1E8  stdin                               134521320
0x0804A188  stderr                              134521224
0x0804A138  stdout                              134521144
0x08048EEC  &s                                  134516460
0x08048D40  main                                134516032
0x080489E0  dump                                134515168
0x080489B0  fun1                                134515120
0x08048990  fun2                                134515088
0x080487EC  fprintf                             134514668

getenv('TERM') = 'oink-term';
```

Analyzing the Impact on the TERM Variable

Remember that the test program in Listing 8.1 deliberately changed the environment variable TERM to see what would happen to it. You also created two new environment variables NVAR1 and NVAR2 to see where they might end up. You now can make the following observations about Listing 8.3:

- The environment values in lines 3 to 15 have not changed.
- Notice that the `TERM` value has not changed in line 13.
- You know that the value of `TERM` has changed (line 34).
- Note the entry `@TERM=oink-term` (line 22).

Remember that strange code in the `dump()` function in Listing 8.1 (lines 107 to 115)? This code was included to locate the changed value of `TERM`. Based on the "after" display, notice that the current value of `TERM` has moved to a new address (`0804A45D`, shown in line 22 in Listing 8.3).

You can now arrive at the following conclusion from this change: `getenv()` keeps track of new values that supercede the `envp[]` array values, but the environment pointed to by the `envp[]` array never actually changes. This knowledge can be useful when you need to know what the original values of `PATH` or `TZ` were, for example, before the environment was modified. With a little bit of effort, you can find these original values in the `envp[]` array in a loop.

Analyzing the Impact of Adding New Variables

If you stared at line 22 in Listing 8.3, then you have probably noticed the new environment variables `NVAR1` and `NVAR2` (lines 21 and 23). Remember that these variables were created in the source Listing 8.1 in lines 137 and 140. Again, they were not placed with the original environment variables at the top of memory, nor were they added to `envp[]`. It appears that new values are put into dynamically allocated chunks of memory. You can see this trend because the addresses of these new variables are above all code, all external variables, and above all global static variables, and using memory between the top of the code and the bottom of the stack.

Analyzing the Impact on the Invoking Shell

With all this talk about modifying your environment, you might be tempted to think that the exported environment variables of your shell were altered by your C program. This is simply not the case, and there is no way to perform this feat.

When you look at the probe program and its results, it should become apparent that the variables and values that you have tampered with are local to your process only. This statement is true simply because the environment variables and their values are stored in your program's address space. You cannot alter the shell's environment variables because the shell's variables are defined in the shell's own private memory.

Process Exit Values

Eventually, the fun must end, and the `main()` program must cease to function. The `main` program is defined as a function that returns the data type integer. Why then do you see calls to the function `exit()`? Can you return 32-bit values from the `main` program? When should you use the `return` statement, and when should `exit()` be called instead? Where does this return value get stored? I'll answer a few of these questions here.

Understanding Exit Code Processing

The `return` code or the `exit()` code is returned to the Linux kernel. The parent process of your process is able to inquire how your program (process) completed. Normally, the parent process is the shell. For most Linux users, it is the bash shell program.

When `main()` invokes a `return` statement or when any function calls the function `exit()`, a normal exit event is posted. This event and its exit code are posted in the Linux kernel process table for future reference. Then your process memory and other resources are freed. When the parent process inquires of the Linux kernel about your program's termination status, this process table entry is released by the kernel. For the curious, this inquiry is performed by using the `wait()` or `waitpid()` functions.

The shell places this posted exit code into its shell variable `$?` for shell programmers who need it. Remember, however, that this value changes with the completion of every built-in or external command that is carried out by the shell.

Returning a Value

Because the function `main()` is called, it must also be acceptable to return from the `main` program. The function interface defines it as returning an integer, which for Linux on Intel means a 32-bit integer value.

```
int main(int argc,char *argv[],char *envp[] ) {
    return 13; /* Return 13 to indicate error */
}
```

The function interface definition might tempt you to think that a 32-bit value can be returned because that is the size of the `int` data type. This is not the case under Linux, and the values that you can return range from 0 to 255, inclusive. In other words, the return value must fit into one byte (8 bits). If you compile and run the preceding `main` program, you get the following value in the shell:

```
bash$ ./a.out
bash$ echo $?
13
bash$
```

If the program returns -1, note that the shell sees the value 255 because the -1 integer value is chopped to the eight least significant bits (which are 1-bits) and returned as an unsigned byte. Sometimes this is done intentionally to return the most nonzero value as possible.

> The accepted value for normal termination status is the value 0. Usually, nonzero values indicate an error has occurred. Some programs, however, specialize in different return codes that reflect the results of a test. These programs are usually shell programming aids.

Using the exit() Function

An alternative to the return statement in the main() program is to call the function exit() instead. The argument value passed to exit() becomes the return value for main. The synopsis for exit is as follows:

```
#include <stdlib.h>

void exit(int status);
```

Sometimes when you're performing some operation within a function, an unrecoverable error occurs. Sometimes the most appropriate action is to issue a message and exit the program. If you are buried four function calls deep, then a simple return statement is not going to terminate the program, and thus the need for exit() becomes apparent.

```
void myFunc(void) {
    if ( someOperation() != 0 ) {
        perror("Program choked!");
        exit(13); /* Indicate "no luck" */
    }
}
```

Although the exit() function accepts an integer valued argument, only the values 0 to 255 inclusive are meaningful. Other values are truncated to eight bits, just as they are for the main() program's return statement.

Choosing Between return and exit()

For most C programs, the difference between returning from main() or calling exit() is purely academic. In a few situations, you might want to unwind the stack by having all your functions return all the way back to main() and have main() use the return statement.

This difference is important if the various functions that have been called must "clean up." Calling the `exit()` function prevents any cleanup that might happen after a function return is performed. If functions have created files or use shared memory resources, for example, you might want to have those resources cleaned up before exiting the program. When no cleanup is required, then the choice becomes a matter of preference.

When you use object-oriented techniques within the confines of the C programming language, you will be concerned about object cleanup because objects may need to release resources as well.

The C++ language has made this whole area of cleanup much simpler for the programmer; this area is known as *object destruction*. As a C programmer, you should at least consider these issues when designing a new program or a C library function.

Using Compiler Warnings About `return` Statements

Sometimes you forget to return a value from the `main()` program. The side effect is that your bash shell reports random values for `$?` after your program's completion (or the value might be consistently wrong).

You get this result usually because your compiler failed to warn you about a missing `return` statement in the `main()` program. If you choose not to use the `gcc -Wall` option, then at least use the `gcc compile` option `-Wreturn-type` to allow the compiler to warn you about any missing or mismatched `return` statements. Doing so might save you a lot of debugging time.

> If you choose not to use the maximum `gcc` warning level `-Wall` for your compiles, then add the `-Wreturn-type` option to allow the compiler to report missing or mismatched return values. The default `gcc` warning setting is to silently ignore these problems.

Summary

In this lesson, you reviewed the `main()` program interface and learned about the `main` program's third argument. You also learned how you can gain access to the environment variables from the `environ` external pointer variable and the various library functions. This lesson also covered the methods for changing and unsetting an environment variable.

You now understand from the probe experiment approximately where the different components of your program reside in its process memory. Finally, you reviewed some of the finer points about process exit codes and how they are handled by the Linux kernel.

Q&A

Q Why is the external variable `environ` provided when `main()` is supplied with the third argument `envp[]`?

A Inside a function that is called by `main()` or some other function, you might not be given the pointer to the array `envp[]`. This allows the function to access that environment array.

Q The `argv[]` array is provided with the count in `argc`. How do I know how many elements are held within the array `envp[]`?

A The last element in `envp[]` is a `null` pointer. A loop can be constructed to scan the array and count for itself how many elements are provided.

Q Why might returning from a function back to `main()` be preferable to calling `exit()`?

A If your program needs to perform cleanup prior to exit or must destroy objects in a controlled fashion, you might want to return control all the way back to `main()` and then return.

Workshop

To practice what you have learned, work through the quiz and the exercises before proceeding to the next lesson.

Quiz

1. Where is the program's return code posted?
2. What is the array size of `argv[]`? Is it `argc-1`, `argc`, or `argc+1`?
3. When you call `putenv()`, `setenv()`, or `unsetenv()`, does any part of the array `envp[]` change?
4. Which function can you use to set a default environment variable if it doesn't already exist?
5. How do you get rid of an environment variable?
6. If your program appears to work successfully, but the exit status returned to `bash` is 47, what should you look for? (**Hint:** The answer has nothing to do with the specific value 47.)

Exercises

1. Write a small program to locate the exported shell variable HOME in the array envp[]. Save its pointer value in a character pointer variable p1. Then call the function getenv(), and save its character pointer in p2. Compare the values of these two pointers, and print the results of the comparison. Are these pointers identical? Why or why not? Where does p1 point? Where does p2 point?
2. Write a small program to display all the exported variable names from the main() argument envp[]. Do not display the variable's values, however.
3. Write a small program that obtains the value of HOME using the function getenv(), and display its value. Then modify the value of HOME using the function setenv(), and display it again (set it to the string value of "/dev/null"). Finally, restore the value of HOME by using the combination of the external environ pointer and the putenv() function call. Obtain the value of HOME one last time using getenv(), and display it for verification.

Hour 9

Useful Debugging Techniques

Introducing Debugging Techniques

Debugging used to mean the process of removing insects. However, the word *bug* came to be used by people like Thomas Edison to describe technical flaws in equipment. The first actual evidence that bugs existed in computers was captured for the first time in 1947. Technicians were building the Mark II computer at Harvard, when they eventually tracked down a malfunction, which was caused by a moth stuck in a relay. It was not long afterward that the term *bug* and the process of *debugging* came into popular use.

In this lesson, you will examine some of the limitations of using debugging tools to analyze your software. You will develop other techniques that you can use to trace or log events within your software. This lesson will also cover the advantages and disadvantages of the techniques presented so that you will know which technique is best suited for your needs.

Understanding the Limitations of a Debugger

One software aid that is available for Linux is the `gdb` command. Debuggers like this work very well on smaller programming efforts. They are also wonderful for looking at "postmortems" of programs that have aborted. However, in a number of situations, debuggers are difficult to apply.

Some software is difficult to debug because of its sheer size. An example is the X Window server Xfree86 used on many Linux platforms. The size of the software makes it difficult to trap a specific event because it has so many events that you need to skip. This situation may further be complicated by the fact that you need to intercept an event under a complex set of conditions.

A Linux kernel module (device driver) that is installed as part of the kernel creates another situation in which a debugger cannot be used. The `gdb` command works only on an executable. Even if the `gdb` command were extended to work on kernel modules, it would not be able to cope with time-sensitive events such as the servicing of interrupts.

Other software problems caused by memory corruption often change or disappear when a debugger is invoked. The reason for this stems from the fact that the memory address space of the program being debugged is altered by the debugger, even if only slightly so.

Tracing with C Macros

One debugging technique is to log information to a log file, which you can scrutinize later. The disadvantage to this technique, however, is that writing the statements required is often tedious. For this reason, programmers use the technique sparingly. To reduce the size and the repetitious components of these C language statements, a macro can help.

Another disadvantage to logging a great deal of debugging detail is that it can add a lot of overhead to the compiled program in terms of both memory and in CPU time. Again, the intelligent use of macros and C programming techniques can help in these areas.

Defining a `TRACE` Macro

One of the simplest forms of debugging aids is a simple `TRACE` macro:

```
#define TRACE    printf("%s @ %u\n",__FILE__,__LINE__)
```

To use this macro, you simply invoke the macro and place a semicolon after it:

```
#include <stdio.h>
#define TRACE    printf("%s @ %u\n",_ _FILE_ _,_ _LINE_ _)

int main(int argc,char **argv) {

    TRACE;
    return 0;
}
```


If the C language source code is compiled from file main.c, for example, then running this program yields the following results:

```
bash$ ./a.out
main.c @ 6
bash$
```

The `TRACE` macro prints to standard output showing that statement line 6 in main.c is executed.

Understanding the TRACE Macro

Your C compiler provides two built-in macros that are quite useful:

- `_ _FILE_ _`
- `_ _LINE_ _`

The C preprocessor substitutes a C string constant for every place that the `_ _FILE_ _` macro is invoked. This string represents the source filename being compiled. In the example shown earlier where main.c was compiled, the macro `_ _FILE_ _` is replaced by the string `"main.c"`.

In a similar fashion, the C preprocessor substitutes the line number of the source file for the `_ _LINE_ _` macro. This value is provided as an integer constant, not as a string.

The combination of the `_ _FILE_ _` and `_ _LINE_ _` macros allow the reader of the `TRACE` output to pinpoint the source module and the statement number of the statement that is traced.

Applying the TRACE Macro

After the `TRACE` macro has been defined, you can sprinkle the use of the macro around, as shown in Listing 9.1.

LISTING 9.1 09LST.01.C—A SIMPLE EXAMPLE OF USING THE TRACE MACRO

```
#include <stdio.h>

#define TRACE    printf("%s @ %u\n",_ _FILE_ _,_ _LINE_ _)

int main(int argc,char *argv[]) {
    int x;

    TRACE;
    for ( x=0; x<argc; ++x ) {
        TRACE;
        printf("argv[%d] = '%s'\n",x,argv[x]);
    }
    TRACE;
    return 0;
}
```

After the program in Listing 9.1 is compiled and run, you get output that looks like this:

```
bash$ ./a.out a b
09LST01.c @ 8
09LST01.c @ 10
argv[0] = './a.out'
09LST01.c @ 10
argv[1] = 'a'
09LST01.c @ 10
argv[2] = 'b'
09LST01.c @ 13
bash$
```

Improving the TRACE Macro

The `TRACE` macro used in Listing 9.1 shows where the program code is each step of the way. If the program aborts, and you have redirected the output to a file, some of that output might be lost in a buffer. You have this problem because of the way the standard I/O library buffers its output data. To prevent this problem, you can enhance the macro slightly to force the flushing of the buffer:

```
#define TRACE { printf("%s @ %u\n",_ _FILE_ _,_ _LINE_ _); \
                fflush(stdout); }
```

Notice that you have to place the pair of statements between braces. Using braces is important so that when you use the `TRACE` macro as part of an `if` statement, the macro is treated as one statement. Consider this example:

```
if ( expression )
    TRACE
else
    /* Something else here... */
```

If you omit the braces in this macro, the `fprintf()` is the singular statement following the `if` statement. Then the compiler produces an error about the `fflush()` call when the `else` statement is expected to follow instead.

The `TRACE` macro as it stands now provides a source file and source line trace of your code. However, you often need to know more than just where the control is passed. You often need to see values of things.

Defining TRACEF with a Variable Number of Arguments

Using the `printf()` statement is a convenient way to format and display C variables and values. However, within the infrastructure of a C macro, you have a problem. C preprocessor macros work only with predefined numbers of arguments, which are defined by the macro definition.

You can circumvent this problem by passing the whole argument list in the one macro argument position. To do so, define a `TRACEF` macro like this:

```
#define TRACEF(a) { \
    printf("%s @ %u : ",_ _FILE_ _,_ _LINE_ _); \
    printf a; \
    fflush(stdout); \
    }
```

This definition might appear strange, but it does allow you to do `printf()`-styled debugging now:

```
TRACEF(("argv[x=%d] = '%s'\n",x,argv[x]));
```

To pass all the `printf()`-styled arguments in macro argument `'a'` of `TRACEF`, you must enclose the list in an additional layer of brackets. This way, you can pass any number of arguments necessary to carry out your `printf()` mission.

The most difficult thing to get used to with this type of macro is to remember to supply the additional brackets—especially the closing ones. Usually, the first compile or two after liberally using these macros in a source file are spent looking for those missing closing brackets.

Defining Conditional Debugging Macros

Sometimes you must debug a difficult segment that must remain highly efficient. The `TRACE`- and `TRACEF`-styled macros provide a lot of assistance when it is needed. However, to regain the original efficiency after the problems have been fixed, you are left with the choice of disabling the macro or removing the macro calls entirely.

The macros you defined earlier could have been defined conditionally so that the compiler -D option could be used to select whether you included these debug facilities.

Here, you define the TRACE and TRACEF macros only when the macro value USE_TRACE is defined. When the USE_TRACE macro value is not defined, the TRACE and TRACEF macros become defined as null macros that expand into no code at all:

```
#ifdef USE_TRACE
# define TRACE { \
      printf("%s @ %u\n",__FILE__,__LINE__); \
      fflush(stdout); \
  }
# define TRACEF(a) { \
    printf("%s @ %u : ",__FILE__,__LINE__); \
    printf a; \
    fflush(stdout); \
  }
#else
# define TRACE
# define TRACEF(a)
#endif
```

With this type of definition for the TRACE macros, you obtain compiled-in debug code only if your make file supplies the compiler option -DUSE_TRACE.

Working with Runtime Debug Trace Facilities

The conditional compilation technique is effective for those debug macros that you want to compile in or compile out of a program. However, the disadvantage with this approach is that you must recompile the program to change this behavior.

Sometimes you might want to keep your debugging code in a complex program or library but not incur the overhead of having it there. This way, you can quickly turn on the debug facility when you need it and keep the application efficient when it is not required.

Controlling TRACE with Command Options

One way to control TRACE is to use the traditional -x option on a command line:

```
int cmdopt_x = 0;
int optch;

while ( (optch = getopt(argc,argv,"x")) != -1 )
    switch ( optch ) {
    case 'x' :
        cmdopt_x = 1;
        break;
```

The preceding code snippet shows how the variable cmdopt_x is set to true when the option -x appears on the command line. Now you can define macros like this:

```
# define TRACEF(a) { \
    if ( cmdopt_x != 0 ) { \
        printf("%s @ %u : ",_ _FILE_ _,_ _LINE_ _); \
        printf a; \
        fflush(stdout); \
    } \
  }
```


This macro definition uses a simple test of the variable cmdopt_x to determine whether any trace output should be produced. If no trace is required, only the cheap integer comparison costs in overhead CPU cycles.

Using Debug Levels

In larger programs, debug levels have proven useful. Instead of simply turning on all debug statements or none at all, you can code the debug statements with a debug level:

```
# define TRACEF(level,a) { \
    if ( cmdopt_x >= level ) { \
        printf("%s @ %u : ",_ _FILE_ _,_ _LINE_ _); \
        printf a; \
        fflush(stdout); \
    } \
  }
```

Note that the macro now has two arguments instead of one. The first is a *debug level* that must be supplied. In the program, you invoke the macro as follows:

```
TRACEF(5,("HOME='%s'\n",getenv("HOME")));
```

Argument one is the value 5, which is a medium debug level if your debug levels go from 0 to 9. Usually, 9 represents the most detailed debugging level, whereas 1 is the lowest level. Using 0 means that the debug statement will always print. Note how the brackets must be used for the macro's second argument.

To set the debugging level, usually -x takes a numeric debug level:

```
int cmdopt_x = 0;
int optch;

while ( (optch = getopt(argc,argv,"x:")) != -1 )
    switch ( optch ) {
    case 'x' :
        cmdopt_x = atoi(optarg);
        break;
```

Setting Debug Levels by Environment

Another way debug levels can be triggered is through an environment variable setting. Sometimes triggering them this way is easier because the source modules that you want to trace might be in a shared library for general use and may not have access to a debug value from the command line.

A shared library might do something like this:

```
static int cmdopt_x = -1;   /* Force first time check */
char *cp = 0;

if ( cmdopt_x < 0 ) {
    if ( (cp = getenv("TRACE_LEVEL")) != 0 )
        cmdopt_x = atoi(cp); /* Set trace level */
    else
        cmdopt_x = 0;        /* No debugging */
}
```

Code like this in a shared library looks up the environment variable `TRACE_LEVEL` only the first time through this code (this helps to keep it efficient). Having reached this code, you either set the trace level to `0` (no trace) or set it according to the integer value found in the variable `TRACE_LEVEL`. From the bash shell, you simply set the trace level for the entire session:

```
bash$ export TRACE_LEVEL=6
```

From this point on, your programs and shared libraries can test this value as required.

Designing Subsystem Trace Facilities

In larger programming efforts, a number of subsystems may participate. The idea of shared libraries having activated debug code by the use of an environment variable comes close to serving your needs in these larger projects. However, if several shared libraries are involved, you probably do not want the trace information for all of them, especially if you know the problem is specific to one particular module.

Writing the Subsystem Trace Facility

Listing 9.2 shows an example of how you can combine a C macro and a support C function to minimize the overhead and yet provide a flexible support system for debugging.

LISTING 9.2 09LST02.C—AN EXAMPLE OF SUBSYSTEM DEBUGGING

```
#include <stdio.h>
#include <stdlib.h>
#include <unistd.h>
#include <string.h>

/*
 * Trace by TRACE_LEVEL & TRACE_SUBSYS macro :
 */
#define TRACE_SUBSYSF(level,subsys,msg) { \
    if ( testSubsystem(level,subsys) ) { \
        printf("%s @ %u : ",__FILE__,__LINE__); \
        printf msg; \
        fflush(stdout); \
    } \
}

/*
 * Support function for TRACE_SUBSYSF() macro :
 *
 * Environment variables :
 *  TRACE_LEVEL=n           Sets debug level
 *  TRACE_SUBSYS=sys1,sys2  Defines which subsystems will
 *                          be traced.
 *
 * If TRACE_LEVEL is defined, but TRACE_SUBSYS is not, then
 * all subsystems will be traced at the appropriate level.
 */
static int
testSubsystem(short level,const char *subsys) {
    char *cp;                       /* Work pointer */
    char vbuf[128];                 /* Buffer for variable */
    static short trace_level = -1;/* Trace level after init */
    static char *trace_subsys = 0;/* Pointer to environment val*/

    /*
     * One time initialization : Test for the presence
     * of the environment variables TRACE_LEVEL and
     * TRACE_SUBSYS.
     */
    if ( trace_level == -1 ) {
        trace_subsys = getenv("TRACE_SUBSYS"); /* Get variable */
        if ( (cp = getenv("TRACE_LEVEL")) != 0 )
            trace_level = atoi(cp);         /* Trace level */
        else
            trace_level = 0;                /* No trace */
    }
```

continues

LISTING 9.2 CONTINUED

```
47:
48:     /*
49:      * If the TRACE_LEVEL is lower than this macro
50:      * call, then return false :
51:      */
52:     if ( trace_level < level )      /* Tracing at lower lvl? */
53:         return 0;                   /* Yes, No trace required */
54:
55:     /*
56:      * Return TRUE if no TRACE_SUBSYS environment
57:      * value is defined :
58:      */
59:     if ( !trace_subsys )            /* TRACE_SUBSYS defined? */
60:         return 1;                   /* No, Trace ALL subsystems */
61:
62:     /*
63:      * Copy string so we don't modify env. variable :
64:      */
65:     strncpy(vbuf,trace_subsys,sizeof vbuf);
66:     vbuf[sizeof vbuf - 1] = 0;      /* Enforce nul byte */
67:
68:     /*
69:      * Scan if we have a matching subsystem token :
70:      */
71:     for ( cp=strtok(vbuf,","); cp != 0; cp=strtok(NULL,",") )
72:         if ( !strcmp(subsys,cp) ) /* Compare strings? */
73:             return 1;               /* Yes, trace this call */
74:     return 0;                       /* Not in trace list */
75: }
76:
77: int main(int argc,char *argv[]) {
78:
79:     TRACE_SUBSYSF(5,"SYSA",("argv[0]='%s'\n",argv[0]));
80:     puts("Program 09LST02.c");
81:     TRACE_SUBSYSF(3,"SYSB",("argc=%d\n",argc));
82:     return 0;
83: }
```

Understanding Subsystem TRACE Design

The basic design principles behind the macro and the support function in Listing 9.2 are as follows:

A new TRACE macro `TRACE_SUBSYSF()` is defined (lines 9 to 15).

- To minimize the amount of expanded code where the macro is invoked and to keep the initialization centralized, you draw upon the function `testSubsystem()` (line 10).
- This function returns `true` (nonzero) if you need to print debugging information (lines 11 to 13).

The new support function `testSubsystem()` is defined (lines 28 to 75).

- The first argument `level` is supplied by the macro and is used to determine the first level need whether or not to trace.
- The second argument `subsys` is the string argument that is also supplied by the macro. It identifies what subsystem the macro call considers itself to be a part of.
- The variable `trace_level` is declared static and is initialized with `-1` (line 32).
- The function tests whether `trace_level` has been initialized yet (line 40). If not, then you enter lines 41 to 46 to perform the one-time initialization. You do so once to save CPU cycles later when this function is called from many places.
    - The environment value for `TRACE_SUBSYS` is saved if it is defined (line 41).
    - If `TRACE_SUBSYS` is not defined, the C variable `trace_subsys` is `null` in value when you test it in line 59.
    - You obtain the value of `TRACE_LEVEL` and put the integer value of it in the C variable `trace_level` (lines 42 and 43).
    - If the environment variable is not defined, you make the `trace_level 0` (line 45) to prevent the initialization code from being called more than once.
- You test whether you need to trace based on the level first because it is the cheapest test you can do (line 52).
    - If the `TRACE_LEVEL` is lower than what this macro is coded for, then you can simply return `false` to indicate no trace is required (line 53).
- You know that the `TRACE_LEVEL` supports doing a trace when line 59 is reached.
- You test whether environment variable `TRACE_SUBSYS` is not defined (line 59). If not, then you assume all subsystems are to be traced and return `true` (line 60).
- Control at line 65 means that environment variable `TRACE_SUBSYS` does in fact exist, and its value must be scanned.
- Because the `strtok()` function (line 71) is destructive, you must copy the string to a buffer `vbuf[]` first (lines 65 and 66). The string function `strtok()` will be covered in Hour 11, "Advanced String Functions."
- The `for` loop (lines 71 to 73) looks for each comma-separated string in `vbuf[]`. This string is copied from the environment variable `TRACE_SUBSYS`.

  - If you find a string match between the function's argument `subsys` and a token in this environment variable, you return `true` (line 73) to indicate that you should trace this call.
- If you fall through (line 74), then you know this subsystem is not being traced.

Lines 77 to 83 form a short test program for your tracing facility. Consider the following points:

- Line 79 traces only if the current `TRACE_LEVEL` is greater than or equal to the value `5` and the subsystem trace includes a subsystem arbitrarily named `SYSA`.
- Line 81 traces only if the current `TRACE_LEVEL` is `3` or better and the subsystem trace parameters include subsystem `SYSB`.

Running with Subsystem TRACE Facilities

Now you can compile and execute the example in Listing 9.2:

```
bash$ ./a.out
Program 09LST02.c
bash$
```

This run is normal. By *normal*, I mean that no trace facilities are activated for this run. In this manner, the program executes as efficiently as it can without invoking the overhead of the trace code.

Using TRACE_LEVEL=5 and No TRACE_SUBSYS

Now set the trace level to `5`, and report on all subsystems by leaving out environment variable `TRACE_SUBSYS`:

```
bash$ TRACE_LEVEL=5 ./a.out
09LST02.c @ 79 : argv[0]='./a.out'
Program 09LST02.c
09LST02.c @ 81 : argc=1
bash$
```

In this example, you set the environment variable by doing the assignment left of the command itself. When you use this approach, the shell exports the value automatically, and the assignment applies only to the command's execution. It does not affect the current session.

Looking at the trace output, you can see that all is reported.

Using TRACE_LEVEL=3 and No TRACE_SUBSYS

Dropping the TRACE_LEVEL down to the value 3 should eliminate the "09LST02.c @ 79" trace:

```
bash$ export TRACE_LEVEL=3
bash$ ./a.out
Program 09LST02.c
09LST02.c @ 81 : argc=1
bash$
```

This example shows an alternative way to export and set an environment variable. Here, you set the value for the current session and for the command's execution. The trace output is as you expect it.

Using TRACE_LEVEL=5 and TRACE_SUBSYS Defined

In the next two sessions, you will set the TRACE_LEVEL=5 and vary the TRACE_SUBSYS environment variable.

Using TRACE_LEVEL=5, you can specify the TRACE_SUBSYS variable to make sure that the subsystem facility works:

```
bash$ TRACE_LEVEL=5 TRACE_SUBSYS=SYSZ,SYSX,SYSA ./a.out
09LST02.c @ 79 : argv[0]='./a.out'
Program 09LST02.c
bash$
```

Here, you include a number of subsystems such as SYSZ and SYSX, but the only one that you actually code for in this list is SYSA. Nevertheless, the trace statement for line 79 of Listing 9.2 works. Note that because SYSB is not selected, you do not see its trace output here.

In the following session, you can include subsystem SYSB but exclude SYSA:

```
bash$ TRACE_LEVEL=5 TRACE_SUBSYS=SYSZ,SYSB,SYSQ ./a.out
Program 09LST02.c
09LST02.c @ 81 : argc=1
bash$
```

Subsystem TRACE Summary

The examples in this section have demonstrated the usefulness of the subsystem trace facility. This technique works well with a large set of C modules, particularly if they are partitioned in separate libraries, or when you have different people working on various components.

The subsystem names are completely arbitrary and are chosen simply to suit tracing needs. Sometimes two or more facets to a module may warrant different consideration. By the careful use of different subsystem names, you can selectively trace those features in which you are most interested.

Summary

In this lesson, you examined some of the limitations of using a debugger. You saw how C macros can make trace facilities more convenient to add to your source code. You also learned about the efficiency benefits of conditionally compiled macros and the advantages of runtime trace facilities.

Q&A

Q Why not just remove all the debug statements when the program has been debugged?

A Some programs are so complex that they never get fully debugged. Another reason to leave them in is to allow debugging of enhancements to the program that may follow later. Finally, if a business production process starts to act up, you can quickly and easily trace it with the appropriate debugging options activated.

Q Do subsystems have to match the names of their enclosing functions?

A No. They are arbitrary subsystem names that you devise to allow you to trace different facets of a program.

Q What is the valid range for debug level numbers?

A There is no hard rule for this numbering system. However, many software packages use `0` for no debug information to `9` as the maximum debug level (most detail).

Workshop

To practice what you have learned, work through the quiz and the exercises before proceeding to the next lesson.

Quiz

1. Why is a variable number of arguments a problem for macros?
2. How do macros get around the variable number of arguments problem?
3. What is the debugging or trace level used for?

4. Do debug and trace levels have to range between `0` and `9`? Why or why not?
5. Does the debug or trace command-line option have to be `-x`? If not, what examples of commands do not use this convention?

Exercises

> When you're working on these exercises, make sure that the environment variables are exported. Doing so is especially important if you set environment values on lines separate from the actual command line that follows (use the shell `export` keyword).
>
> If the variable is set on the same line as the command (left of the command name), the shell automatically exports the values.

1. Add another `TRACE_SUBSYSF()` macro call to the program in 09LST02.c, using subsystem name `SYSC` and trace level `6`. Set the environment variable `TRACE_LEVEL=7` and the variable `TRACE_SUBSYS=SYSA,SYSB,SYSC`. Compile and run the program. Do all the trace statements come out?
2. Run the program from exercise 1 again, but this time set the environment variable `TRACE_SUBSYS=SYSC,SYSA,SYSB`. Run the program. Does the order of these subsystems in the variable `TRACE_SUBSYS` make any difference? Why or why not?
3. Using the program from exercise 1, unset the variable `TRACE_LEVEL` (or don't define it), but set the variable `TRACE_SUBSYS=SYSA,SYSB,SYSC`. Run the program again. Is it the trace information reported? Why or why not?

Hour 10

Static and Shared Libraries

Introduction to C Libraries

In the earliest days of computer programming, a program was written completely from scratch because no code was available for reuse. Each program was new and unique. Since that time, however, programmers have recognized the value of subroutines and functions and have collected them into libraries of one form or another.

Linux C programming libraries come in two particular flavors:

- The static library
- The shared library

Each of these two library forms has its own advantages and disadvantages, but these libraries have one thing in common: They are collections of C functions that C programmers can reuse.

In this lesson, you will look at how to use static and shared libraries. You'll also learn how to create and manage these libraries.

The Static Library

A static library is a collection of object modules that are collected together into an archive file. In short, a library is a collection. In the following sections, you will examine how a static library is used and what archive files are all about.

Reviewing the Process Memory Image

In Hour 8, "The Linux `main` Program and Its Environment," you examined the memory addresses of various program components and developed a sense of where everything was placed into the final process memory image. Figure 10.1 shows a diagram of how that memory image might look for the `dos_cvrt` utility program. At the left of the diagram, the four compiled object modules `dos_cvrt.o`, `unix2dos.o`, `dos2unix.o`, and `putch.o` are installed into the memory image starting above address 080048990 by the linker (the addresses are only approximate). The environment variables are up high in memory, and the stack area is immediately below that. In between the stack and the top of the "text" (the function "instruction code") is the free memory area from which the function `malloc()` obtains its memory. Finally, at the bottom of memory, starting at address 080000000, is something labeled as "library code." There, you find that the function `fprintf()` is loaded.

FIGURE 10.1

Composition of a memory image.

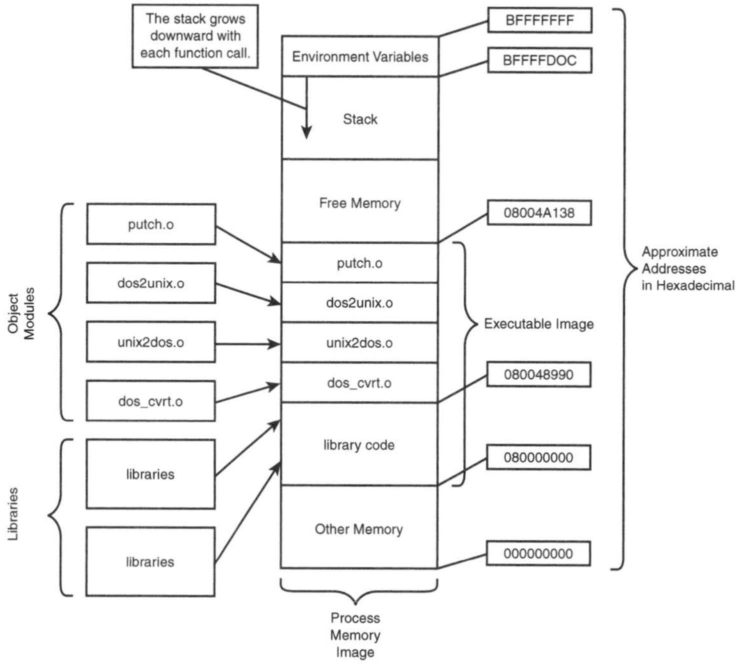

In Hour 8, you noted that the function `fprintf()` was installed down at the bottom of memory. You did not write the function `fprintf()`, so it must have been provided for you in some manner. This function was supplied automatically by a C library that is always searched at link time for C programs.

Understanding the Executable Image

At the right side of the process memory image in Figure 10.1, notice the annotation "Executable Image." This image data is loaded from the executable file `dos_cvrt`. Notice that this image does not include the memory image where the environment variables are stored, the stack, or the free memory areas. They are determined and initialized at the time the program is loaded.

Looking again at the executable image, you can see that the library code near the bottom and the object modules that you compiled are brought into memory from the executable image file.

Implementing a Static Library

Now say that you want to use those same functions in `unix2dos.o`, `dos2unix.o`, and `putch.o` in other programs in addition to the utility program `dos_cvrt`. What you want to accomplish, then, is to put these three object modules into a library of your own.

Remember that a static library is simply a collection of object modules that are collected together into an archive file.

Using the `ar` Command to Create an Archive

To create an archive, you use the `ar` archive command. Because a static library is a special form of an archive, you can use the `ar` command to create a static library.

To create a static library named libdoscvt.a, which contains your code in object modules `unix2dos.o`, `dos2unix.o`, and `putch.o`, enter the following:

```
bash$ ar r libdoscvt.a unix2dos.o dos2unix.o putch.o
```

The `r` that follows the command name is an option letter (it is one of those UNIX commands that break from the traditional `getopt()` processing standards). The `r` says to create the archive libdoscvt.a if necessary and replace the listed object modules in that archive if they already exist. If the object modules do not yet exist in the archive, they are added to it.

The normal convention for a library is that its name begins with the first three letters *lib*. An archive uses the suffix *.a*. Accordingly, you end up with a static library named libdoscvt.a.

Archives can be updated after their initial creation. If you discover that your `dos2unix.o` module has bugs in it, you can replace it with the fixed and recompiled version this way:

```
bash$ ar r libdoscvt.a dos2unix.o
```

You generally perform this type of updating only for large libraries. For smaller archives, you usually set up the make file to create the archive file from scratch.

Listing the Contents of an Archive

You can list the contents of an existing archive by performing the following:

```
bash$ ar t libdoscvt.a
unix2dos.o
dos2unix.o
putch.o
bash$
```

The option letter `t` here causes `ar` to list a table of contents for the archive libdoscvt.a.

Obtaining a Verbose Listing of an Archive

You can display more information by adding a second option letter `v` for a verbose table of contents:

```
bash$ ar tv libdoscvt.a
rw-r--r-- 507/104   1628 Dec  6 16:35 1998 unix2dos.o
rw-r--r-- 507/104   1660 Dec  6 16:35 1998 dos2unix.o
rw-r--r-- 507/104   1288 Dec  6 16:35 1998 putch.o
bash$
```

The leftmost column shows the permission bits that were present when the module was added to the archive. They are displayed in the same form as the `ls` command. The numbers `507/104` in the example are the user ID and group numbers for the corresponding user ID and group names. Finally, the date and time are shown just left of the module filename.

Linking with Static Libraries

So far in this book, you have relied on the `gcc` command to perform the linking for you. The traditional link command looks like this:

```
bash$ gcc dos_cvrt.o unix2dos.o dos2unix.o putch.o -o dos_cvrt
```

This command causes all the listed object modules to be loaded by the linker, the functions linked together, and an executable file written out.

When you want to link with your home-brewed library libdoscvt.a, you can do so this way:

```
bash$ gcc dos_cvrt.o libdoscvt.a -o dos_cvrt
```

Understanding Static Linking

The highlights of this static linking process are shown in Figure 10.2.

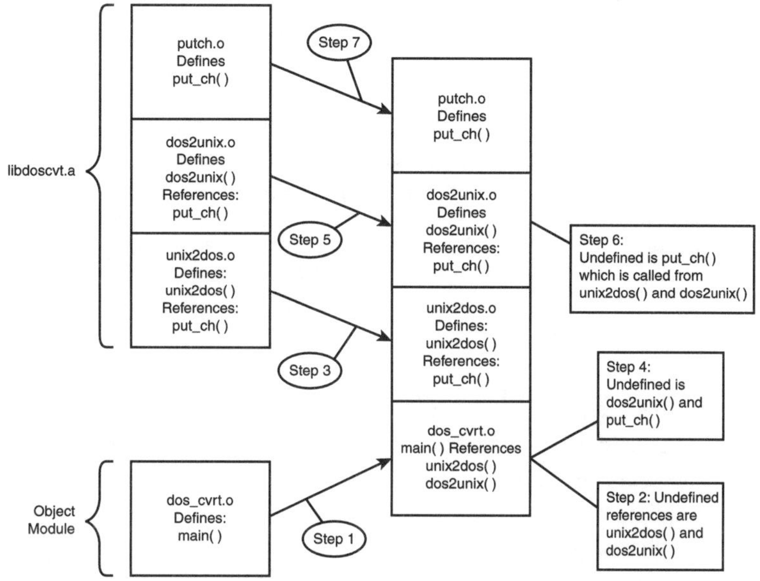

FIGURE 10.2
The static library linking process.

The steps used in the linking process are as follows:

1. The linking process begins with the loading of the singular object module `dos_cvrt`.o for this example.
2. After this step has been accomplished, the linker notes undefined references to symbols `unix2dos` and `dos2unix` referenced by the `main()` function.
3. Because a library named libdoscvt.a has been provided, this archive file is searched for an object module that defines the symbol `unix2dos`. The linker locates a function named `unix2dos()` in the object module `unix2dos.o`, which is contained within the archive file. The linker then extracts module `unix2dos.o` from the archive file and loads it.
4. The linker reviews its list of unresolved symbols. The symbol `dos2unix` is still unresolved, and now the new symbol `put_ch` is unresolved. This new reference comes from the object module `unix2dos.o`, which the linker just loaded.
5. Working from the top of the list, the linker searches the archive libdoscvt.a again and determines that it must extract and load module `dos2unix.o`. This load now satisfies the symbol `dos2unix`.

6. The remaining unresolved symbol in the linker's list is the symbol `put_ch`. This symbol is now needed by both of the object modules `unix2dos.o` and `dos2unix.o`, which were just loaded.
7. The linker extracts `putch.o` from libdoscvt.a because the linker can satisfy the remaining unresolved symbol `put_ch` in this manner. Now the load is complete, and no unresolved references remain on the linker's list.

This procedure is an oversimplification of the linking process because the references to the C library functions for standard I/O are ignored, for example. However, this procedure illustrates what happens when a static library is involved in the linking process.

From this process, you learn that the object modules are brought in by the linker only as required. This knowledge bodes well for you if you want to use only a few functions in a large collection of functions. After all, you do not want to link with every object module if you need only a small part of the library.

Linking with Dependencies

Another concept that should be clear from the example in the preceding section is that all the necessary support modules are automatically determined by the linker and loaded as required. When the module `unix2dos.o` is loaded in Figure 10.2, the linker determines that it also needs a module that defines a function named `put_ch()`. The linker then automatically extracts and loads `putch.o` so that the link is successful.

The Shared Library

In the following sections, you will learn about shared libraries and how they differ from static libraries. In addition, you will learn how to create and use shared libraries.

Understanding the Limitations of Static Libraries

Figure 10.2 shows how the linker can automatically extract object modules from an archive (static library) and load them as required. That figure shows the linking process for the utility program `dos_cvrt`. If you were to use the library libdoscvt.a for another program, you might use only the object modules `dos2unix.o` and `putch.o` from the library if the calling program required only DOS-to-UNIX text conversions.

Although the idea of linking only what you need with your program provides a certain amount of economy, some duplication still remains when you're looking at the systemwide picture. Imagine a huge hypothetical static library that contains 90 percent of the functions used by the Netscape Web browser. Netscape is then linked with this library and produces a 5MB executable file. Approximately 90 percent of this executable file is a copy of what is contained in the static library.

Now assume that you want to build a Web-enabled program that puts up a Netscape-like window in X Window fashion from within your application. Your 200KB program links with this Netscape static library, and your executable program is written out at about 4.5MB. Now you have a 5MB Netscape executable and a 4.5MB program of your own. Yet 90 percent of both are identical sets of functions and code.

If that were not enough, imagine further that you have five more unique programs that link with this static mode library. You would start to accumulate some large systemwide RAM requirements if all these programs were to run concurrently! Most of that memory requirement is from duplicated code.

Shared libraries provide a mechanism that allows a single copy of code to be shared among several instances of programs in the system. You will examine shared libraries and learn how to apply them next.

Creating a Shared Library

Linux makes creating a shared library as simple as creating an executable file. In times past, shared library creation and maintenance required some real hand waving by UNIX system administration wizards. To create a shared library for your own use, you can use the simple `gcc` command:

```
bash$ gcc unix2dos.o dos2unix.o putch.o -shared -o libdoscvt.so
bash$ ls -l libdoscvt.so
-rwxr-xr-x   1 student1 user        6008 Dec 26 21:23 libdoscvt.so
bash$
```

Here, you can see that the `gcc` command with the `-shared` option causes the output file to be written as a shared library rather than an executable file. In this case, you create file libdoscvt.so. The suffix .so is used to indicate shared library files.

Linking with a Shared Library

Using the shared library is a straightforward process, but it can pose some complications. First, note how you can link to a shared library:

```
bash$ gcc dos_cvrt.o -L. -ldoscvt -o dos_cvrt
```

Using the `-L` and `-l` gcc Linking Options

In the link step shown, the library options `-L` and `-l` (big and little "el") are used. I could have used these options for the static library examples earlier, but I chose to explain them here instead.

The `-L` option allows you to indicate to the linker the directories where additional libraries can be found. Normally, only certain default directories are searched for libraries (static and shared alike). In this example, you tell the linker that your current directory (directory `.`) has a library in it. The option `-ldoscvt` causes the linker to search for a static library libdoscvt.a or a shared library libdoscvt.so. Notice that *lib* is prefixed to the name given in the `-l` option, and the suffixes *.a* and *.so* are appended to determine whether a library by that name exists. The linker searches all the standard library directories and all your `-L` specified directories.

Choosing Static or Dynamic Libraries

When both a shared and a static library are available, normally `gcc` chooses the shared library. If, however, you specify the option `-static` on the `gcc` command line, the link phase uses static libraries instead.

Understanding the Shared Linking Process

Based on the command lines used, the linking process appears to be similar to the static library case. However, the implications for the size of your executable file and the amount of systemwide memory required are quite different.

The shared library is needed at link time so that the loader can make notes. It notes which shared library filenames can provide satisfaction of the unresolved symbols it has in its list. No code is loaded from the shared libraries at this time; however, that process is performed at runtime.

Listing Shared Library References

To see whether the new executable `dos_cvrt` is using the new shared library, you can use the `ldd` command:

```
bash$ ldd dos_cvrt
        libdoscvt.so => not found
        libc.so.6 => /lib/libc.so.6 (0x40003000)
        /lib/ld-linux.so.2 => /lib/ld-linux.so.2 (0x00000000)
bash$
```

From the output, you can conclude that the `dos_cvrt` program is indeed looking for a shared library named libdoscvt.so. The `not found` message indicates that the program cannot find the library. If you were to execute this program, you would likely run into a little trouble:

```
bash$ ./dos_cvrt --help
./dos_cvrt: error in loading shared libraries
libdoscvt.so: cannot open shared object file: No such file or
➥ directory
bash$
```

Indeed, the error messages show that you do get into trouble. Why doesn't the dynamic loader find the shared library? To find out why, you need to understand more about the dynamic loader.

Working with the Dynamic Loader

Shared libraries require a bit more fussing with than static libraries do because the shared libraries must be searched for and loaded on demand.

When you used the `ldd` command earlier, you saw in the display that another shared library was used; it was named something like /lib/ld-linux.so.2 (this name is version dependent, so yours may differ). This library code is used to facilitate the loading and dynamic linking of other shared libraries. It is known as the *dynamic loader*.

Searching for Shared Libraries

For the shared library to be loaded at runtime, the dynamic loader must know where to locate it at runtime. Just as the shell must have a search path for commands, the dynamic loader needs a search mechanism for its libraries.

You can locate a shared library under Linux in a number of ways. I will discuss two of them here and leave the other techniques for the more adventurous readers out there. The two normal ways to specify the location of shared libraries for Linux are to use the following:

- The /etc/ld.so.conf file
- The `LD_LIBRARY_PATH` environment variable

I will discuss each of these methods in the sections that follow.

Understanding the /etc/ld.so.conf File

To aid in the management of shared library searches, you can use a file named /etc/ld.so.conf. If you do not have root access to the Linux host that you are using, then you will likely have to resort to using the `LD_LIBRARY_PATH` approach instead.

The ld.so.conf file is a regular text file and can be listed as follows:

```
bash$ cat /etc/ld.so.conf
/usr/local/lesstif/lib
/usr/local/lib
/usr/X11R6/lib
/usr/openwin/lib
/usr/local/pgsql/lib
/usr/local/lib/rutabaga
bash$
```

Here, you can see several nonstandard library directories listed (one per line on my system).

Updating the /etc/ld.so.cache File

Whenever the file /etc/ld.so.conf is updated, you must run the program /sbin/ldconfig as shown:

```
bash$ su -
Password:

bash-2.00# /sbin/ldconfig
bash-2.00# exit
logout
bash$
```

Because the `ldconfig` command must be run as root, you enter the `su` command and the root password. Then the `/sbin/ldconfig` command is run. The `ldconfig` command reads in the /etc/ld.so.conf file and then updates its cache file /etc/ld.so.cache, which is used by the dynamic loader.

Installing Shared Libraries

If you set up a special shared library directory like /opt/custom/lib for your custom shared libraries, you simply add this pathname as another text line to the file /etc/ld.so.conf. After installing your library in the custom directory, you rerun the `/sbin/ldconfig` command as root.

Alternatively, you can just install the shared library in one of the directories already configured in the /etc/ld.so.conf file, such as the directory /usr/local/lib. Then you should rerun the `/sbin/ldconfig` command as root to update the cache file.

> The file /etc/ld.so.cache contains more than directory names. It also contains information about libraries contained within those directories.
>
> When the `/sbin/ldconfig` command is run, all appropriate libraries discovered in the configured list of directories from the file /etc/ld.so.conf are noted in the /etc/ld.so.cache file.
>
> This leads to the rule that whenever a change occurs in shared libraries in any configured directory, you must run the `/sbin/ldconfig` command to update its cache file /etc/ld.so.cache.

Using the LD_LIBRARY_PATH Variable

If you are testing, or you simply lack the necessary permissions to modify the /etc/ld.so.conf file, then you must take another approach. You can define and export environment variable LD_LIBRARY_PATH to be searched by the dynamic loader.

To satisfy the experiment where you got into trouble earlier, you can simply try this:

```
bash$ export LD_LIBRARY_PATH="$LD_LIBRARY_PATH:."
```

This variable works much like the shell PATH variable, except that it represents a set of search paths for shared libraries instead. Here, you simply add the current directory (.) to the existing set of paths (if any). As with the shell PATH variable, a colon separates each directory.

Testing the LD_LIBRARY_PATH Variable

Now you should be able to test your new dos_cvrt to see whether it works with the shared library:

```
bash$ ./dos_cvrt --help
Usage: dos_cvrt [-h ¦ --help] [--version] [-u] infile..
        -h (or --help)  Gives this help display.
        --version       Displays program version.
        -u              Specifies UNIX to DOS conversion.

Command unix_cvrt converts UNIX to DOS text.
while dos_cvrt converts DOS to UNIX, except when -u is used.

bash$
```

The program starts and displays its usage information now. The fact that the program runs successfully shows that the dynamic loader is able to locate and load the shared library.

Compiling Position Independent Code

I have not yet covered one small matter that is important to the subject of shared libraries. For the shared libraries to be most effective at sharing their code among several different programs, that code should be compiled in *position independent code* form.

When a program is compiled in *position independent* form, it can be executed from any memory location without regard to its starting address. As a result, the same physical memory segments can be shared virtually at different relative positions in each process that references them.

Figure 10.3 shows two programs—Program_A and Program_B—that call upon the same shared library. The shaded areas in the memory images show where in the address space the shared code appears. In Program_A, notice that the shared library functions are lower in address than they are in Program_B. Keep in mind that only one physical copy of this code occurs in the system's physical memory that is managed by the Linux kernel. The shaded areas represent virtual memory mappings of the same shared library code in both processes.

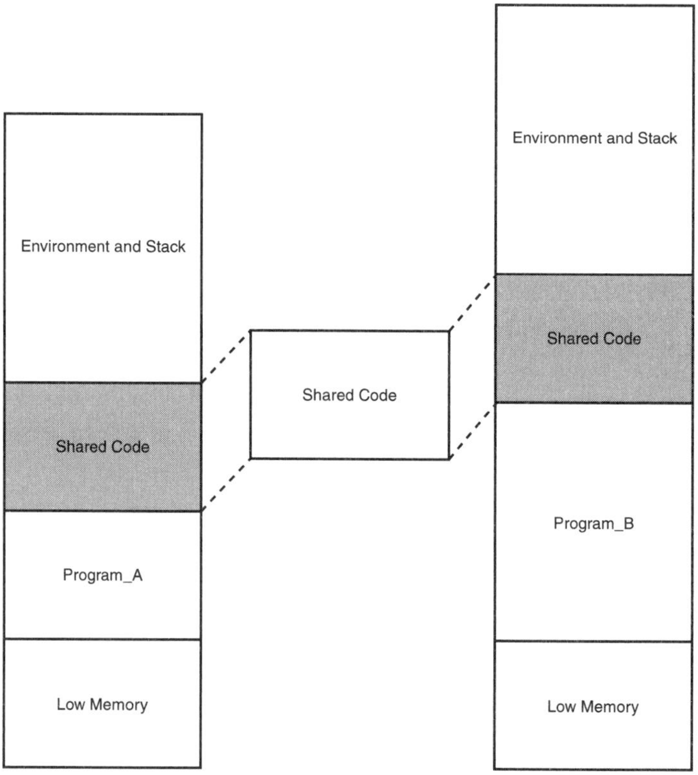

FIGURE 10.3
A shared library compiled as position independent code.

For shared library code to execute successfully in the way that Figure 10.3 shows, the library code must be compiled using position independent code. If the shared libraries are not compiled this way, the dynamic loader must create multiple copies of the library in memory, unless by chance the starting address happens to coincide with a currently shared copy of it.

To compile position independent code, you must use the `gcc` compile option `-fPIC`:

```
bash$ gcc -c -Wall -fPIC -D_GNU_SOURCE unix2dos.c
```

This command compiles module unix2dos.c into a position independent object module `unix2dos.o`.

Controlling What Is Shared

When you make a Linux shared library, you may be asking yourself, "How do I control what is externally visible to the user of my library?"

By default, whatever remains external in the normal sense of executables is also externally visible to the user of your shared library. If you have functions internal to your library, you would be wise to define them as static functions wherever possible to keep them private. Likewise, it is a good practice to have no unnecessary global variables or storage because they too will be visible from your shared library. Sloppiness in this area can cause programs to invoke functions or global variables in your shared library that you did not intend to release to the general public.

Now you have learned the mechanics of using static and shared libraries. It is time to step back and review the advantages and disadvantages of each approach with the understanding that you now have.

The Implications for Libraries

Now take the time to review the tools at your disposal. Although a shared library might seem to be the best library tool to use, it is not always the best choice.

Understanding the Benefits of Static Libraries

Although static libraries cannot eliminate duplicated code in the system, other benefits for using static libraries weigh in their favor. Some of these benefits are as follows:

- Static libraries are simpler to use.
- The executable does not depend on related external components (shared libraries). The executable contains everything it needs within it.
- Static libraries have no environmental or administration issues.
- The static library code does not need to be position independent code.

Enjoying the Ease of Static Linking

Ease of use is often the reason for choosing static linking in the early stages of development of a project. Later when the project is reviewed, you can make the change to shared libraries if this approach makes sense.

Utilizing the Independence of Static Linking

Utilizing the independence of static linking is probably the strongest point in favor of using static libraries. After an executable is linked statically, the program has everything it needs in its own executable file. This fact is important when you want to install a program on other systems where the versions of shared libraries that you need may or may not be present.

Installing Made Simpler

Statically linked programs do not require you to set up any environment variables such as `LD_LIBRARY_PATH`. No dynamic loader configuration adjustment is required. This helps when you don't have confidence in the ability of the administrators of those sites to manage the shared libraries well enough. Statically linked programs save you from having to deal with those types of problems.

Linking When Shared Libraries Are Not Supported

Statically linking a program is important if you are running Linux on a platform that does not yet support shared libraries. Another reason to revert to a static link is that the `gcc` option `-fPIC` is not supported, or it has bugs (as I have found in times past). Any time that a shared library cannot be used, you can depend on a static library instead.

Avoiding Licensing Restrictions

Sometimes static libraries are used only to avoid licensing issues. You can release a large office suite of programs that is statically linked to a MOTIF library that you have licensed and paid for. However, if the suite were to be released using the shared library mechanism, each site installing this software would have to choose between buying a MOTIF library or not using the software.

Understanding the Benefits of Shared Libraries

Shared libraries, on the other hand, have advantages of their own:

- Code sharing saves system resources.
- Several programs that depend on a common shared library can be fixed all at once by replacing the common shared library. Only the shared library that is fixed needs to be recompiled.

- The environment can be modified to cause a substitute shared library to be used.
- Programs can be written to load dynamic libraries without any prior arrangement at link time. Netscape, for example, can be told about a plug-in and is immediately able to load and execute it without any recompiling or linking.

Enjoying the Savings with Shared Memory

Code sharing is the shared library's main reason for being. A properly implemented shared library means that you have only a small amount of real memory assigned in the system to the library code being used. The number of programs using the shared library requires little or no additional memory from the system. The benefit is greatest for large libraries.

Centralizing Code in a Shared Library

Centralizing code in a shared library is both a pro and a con.

On the positive side, if you are running production-level code in several executables, and you discover a bug in the common shared library that they use, fixing that library instantly fixes all programs that use it. None of the executables that use that common shared library require recompiling or relinking.

At the same time, on the negative side, a working set of production-level executable programs can be busted by a single change in the common shared library.

Redirecting Shared Libraries

By using shared libraries, you can control which library gets used by a program. Reconfiguring the dynamic loader or changing the `LD_LIBRARY_PATH` variable allows you to determine which shared library is used by the program.

This feature means that you can substitute libraries without recompiling and linking the executable. You might, for example, try different versions of commercial MOTIF libraries and compare them against the behavior you get from the free LessTif library. This type of substitution requires relinking the executables if you are using static libraries.

Linking Dynamically at Runtime

Linking dynamically at runtime is simply something you cannot do with a static library. Your program can indicate a shared library filename and function entry point name, and the dynamic loader takes care of loading the shared library module and passes control to it. This way, your program can call on library modules without any prior arrangement.

Knowing When to Use Static or Shared Libraries

In some projects, such as the `dos_cvrt` project, the collection of modules is so small that using a shared library really does not make any sense. The administration of the library is probably more effort than it's worth. However, having a static library within the project directory does tend to make it tidier to use as the project gets larger. A static library makes it easy to determine which object modules are needed because the linker does all the work searching out dependencies.

Licensing Issues

Licensing issues can form a strong argument for using static libraries. You may own a MOTIF library, but you are not licensed to make your shared MOTIF library available to others. Furthermore, the license does not let you ship the static libraries themselves either (that would be giving the licensed product away). However, the license may permit you to ship statically linked executables to whomever you please.

Installing Made Foolproof

Logistics may force you to use statically linked programs. With a statically linked executable, you know that the user need only copy it to his or her system, and it will run. With shared libraries, the user has to make certain that the shared libraries are all properly installed first. Dealing with unknowledgeable users is not always something you want to do, especially if you are providing your product free.

Sharing for Savings

Generally, a shared library is used when the amount of the code to be shared is large and two or more different programs use this code.

Loading Dynamically

Anything that must be dynamically loaded, such as a Netscape plug-in, must be a shared library. Static library methods simply do not support this functionality.

Summary

In this lesson, you learned about static libraries and saw how they were created and used. You looked at creating shared libraries, linking against them, and using them at runtime. You also learned two ways that shared libraries can be configured on your system and found out why position independent code is important. The last part of the lesson reviewed of some of the strengths and weaknesses of these two library methods and provided guidance on how to choose between them.

Q&A

Q How does the format of the static library differ from that of the shared library?

A The static library is an archive file, which has object modules as its members. The shared library is very nearly the same as an executable file, and as such, it represents a loadable "code" image.

Q What if I don't have root access to configure the /etc/ld.so.conf file? Can I still reconfigure for shared libraries in my own home account directory?

A Yes. The exported shell variable `LD_LIBRARY_PATH` allows you to override the default settings that are configured for you in the /etc/ld.so.conf file. With appropriate changes to the `LD_LIBRARY_PATH` variable, you can have directories of your choice searched for shared libraries.

Q Are shared libraries slower than static libraries?

A They vary. A static library increases the load time of the executable programs because the static library increases the size of the executable files. On the other hand, the shared library requires a directory search, a load, and a number of other things at runtime to make the code available. If the library is very large, and the library is already in the Linux system memory, then it becomes faster for other programs to use the shared library. The first program that forces the load of the library into memory, however, experiences a delay.

Q Does using position independent code for static libraries present an advantage?

A No. In fact, in some computer architectures, position independent code may result in slightly larger code. Position independent code aids only in the library sharing because it allows the code to function correctly at any starting address within a process memory image.

Workshop

To acquire some practice with the knowledge that you have gained, you are encouraged to work through the quiz and the exercises before proceeding to the next lesson.

Quiz

1. Are all modules loaded from a static library (archive) file or just the modules that are required?
2. Assume that one particular object module within a static library defines three functions: `funa()`, `funb()`, and `func()`. If a program that needs `funb()` is linked against this library, are `funa()` and `func()` also included in the linked program? Why or why not?
3. What `gcc` option do you use to specify that the output is a shared library?
4. Which members of the shared library are visible to the program that uses it?
5. What environment variable is used to control the search order of the shared libraries?
6. What `gcc` option do you use to produce position independent code?

Exercises

1. Using the project `dos_cvrt` from earlier lessons, modify the make file to create a static library libdoscvt.a as required. Assume that the library is deleted and rebuilt from scratch whenever any of its object file members change. Make sure that the final link step uses only the `dos_cvrt.o` object module and the libdoscvt.a library as input.
2. Using the project `dos_cvrt` from earlier lessons, modify the make file to create a shared library libdoscvt.so (exclude main module `dos_cvrt.o` from the library). Then set up your `LD_LIBRARY_PATH` environment variable, and invoke your new `dos_cvrt` program to prove that it works.
3. Using the results from exercise 2, use `unset` on the `LD_LIBRARY_PATH` environment variable and invoke `dos_cvrt` again to further prove that the executable depends on your new shared library by provoking the `not found` error.
4. Using the executable from exercise 2 and the `LD_LIBRARY_PATH` variable properly set up, invoke the `ldd` command on `dos_cvrt`. Explain the display.

HOUR 11

Advanced String Functions

Introducing Advanced String Functions

If you have already started programming in C, then you probably know about some of the basic string functions such as `strcpy()` and `strlen()`. Maybe you are an experienced C programmer but find yourself being introduced to Linux. In either case, you may be unfamiliar with a few useful string functions.

In this lesson, I will introduce you to some useful string functions for programming under Linux. Although you might not use all these functions all the time, just knowing about them can save you a lot of time when the occasion arises.

Including the String Function Declarations

Unless otherwise indicated in this lesson, the functions discussed require the inclusion of the file string.h:

```
#include <string.h>
```

Including this header file is essential in order to define the correct function prototype for the string functions referenced.

With that information out of the way, you can begin to examine some of the string functions that Linux has available for you to use.

Functions `strcasecmp()` and `strncasecmp()`

The functions `strcasecmp()` and `strncasecmp()`, which follow, compare two strings such as the standard string functions `strcmp()` and `strncmp()`, except that they ignore the case of the strings. These functions can provide a great deal of convenience when the case of the string is to be ignored.

```
int strcasecmp(const char *s1, const char *s2);

int strncasecmp(const char *s1, const char *s2, size_t n);
```

Testing for a Command Name Match Example

A program written to accept commands may not care if the command name is capitalized. For example, to test whether a command in a character array `buf[]` contains the word *exit* (in any case), you can simply test it as follows:

```
if ( !strcasecmp(buf,"exit") ) {
    /* Got one of 'exit','Exit', 'eXit', ..., 'EXIT' */
    exit(0);
}
```

Comparing the First `n` Characters

The function `strncasecmp()` is identical in function to the `strcasecmp()` function, except that it compares only the first `n` characters (maximum). The strings compare shorter if a `NUL` byte is encountered before reaching the specified `n` count.

Interpreting the Return Value

The functions `strcasecmp()` and `strncasecmp()` return a value, which is similar to what the normal `strcmp()` function returns:

- The value returned is negative if the first string is considered less than the second string.
- Zero is returned if the strings match.
- A positive integer result is returned if the first string is considered to sort greater than the second string.

Function strdup()

The string function `strdup()` provides a compact way to duplicate a string and have the new string pointer returned, as you can see in the following example. The `strdup()` function calls on `malloc()` to allocate `strlen(s)+1` bytes of storage and then copies the argument string into this newly allocated string. One extra byte is allocated to store the terminating `NUL` byte.

```
char *strdup(const char *s);
```

Freeing the String

The pointer that is returned should be freed when the program has no more use for the new string. You can free `string` by passing this pointer to the `free()` function:


```
char *new_string = 0;

new_string = strdup("Copy this string!");

free(new_string);
new_string = 0;    /* Forget this pointer now */
```

In this example, you duplicate the string constant `"Copy this string!"`. Later, the storage is released by calling the function `free(new_string)`.

Notice that the pointer variable `new_string` is set to `null` (`0`) after `free()` is called. Setting the pointer to `null` is a good practice because in a large program, you might end up accidentally using this pointer again. Because this string has already been released by calling `free()`, it should not be used.

Testing for Errors

The `strdup()` function has the potential to return a `null` pointer if insufficient memory is available. This situation occurs when `malloc()` fails to allocate memory. In turn, it forces `strdup()` to return a `NULL` pointer. When this pointer is returned, the value of `errno` is set to `ENOMEM`.

Remember from Hour 7, "Error Handling and Reporting," that values for `errno` are defined in the errno.h include file. If you need access to these defined macro values or the `errno` variable, then you can include the following statement in your program:

```
#include <errno.h>
```

> How you choose to deal with insufficient memory in your programming is largely determined by how memory intensive your application is. In general, small to medium-sized applications can ignore the issue because it is highly unlikely that the system will deny moderate-sized memory requirements.
>
> On the other hand, because they are short of available RAM and swap space on a given Linux system, reasonable programs could encounter this shortage on rare occasions. Another source of potential memory shortage might be a user-imposed resource limit that restricts the amount of memory available for that session (see the `ulimit` command for more details).
>
> If you are writing for a library, however, you should always program for the worst case scenario because you do not know the needs of the calling application.

Functions `strchr()` and `strrchr()`

The `strchr()` and `strrchr()` string functions shown here locate the first or last occurrence of a character `c` within a string `s`, respectively. `strchr()` starts to scan at location `s` and stops when either a match is found or the `NUL` byte is encountered. The `strrchr()` function starts at the end of the string where the `NUL` byte is found and works its way back to location `s` (and includes the location `s`).

```
char *strchr(const char *s, int c);

char *strrchr(const char *s, int c);
```

The way to remember these functions is that `strchr()` locates the character normally and `strrchr()` does a "reverse" character scan.

Figure 11.1 shows that the pointer returned for `strchr()` is the leftmost slash character (address `s+1`) in the example, although the `strrchr()` function call returns the pointer to the rightmost slash character (address `s+5`).

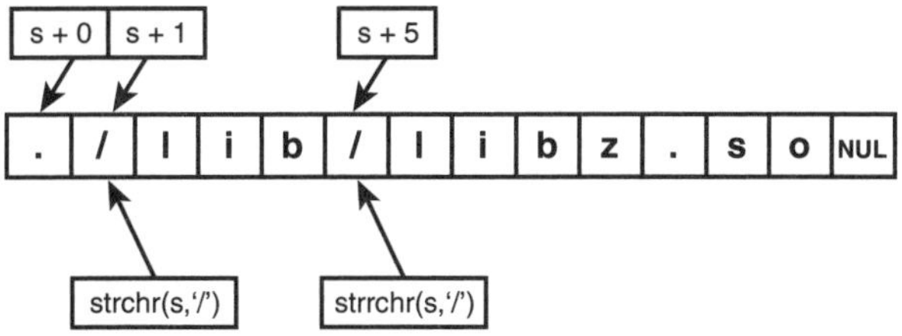

FIGURE 11.1

`strchr()` *and* `strrchr()`.

Interpreting the Return Value

If the character is not found in the string, then a `null` pointer is returned. The value of `errno` is not set by the `strchr()` function.

Function `strpbrk()`

The `strpbrk()` function is similar to the `strchr()` function, except that it is a bit more powerful. Instead of searching the string `s` for a single matching character, the `strpbrk()` function shown here searches for the first in a set of characters:

```
char *strpbrk(const char *s, const char *accept);
```

Scanning occurs from left to right, starting at location `s`. Each character encountered in string `s` is searched in the `accept` string. If the character is found in the `accept` string, then the pointer to that character within string `s` is returned. If a `NUL` byte is encountered before a match is found, a `null` pointer is returned.

Figure 11.2 shows how `strpbrk()` scans the date string `s` for any of the usual date delimiters: a slash, hyphen, or decimal point. The pointer returned by `strpbrk()` is the pointer value `s+2` because it points to a hyphen, which is one of the characters in the `accept` string.

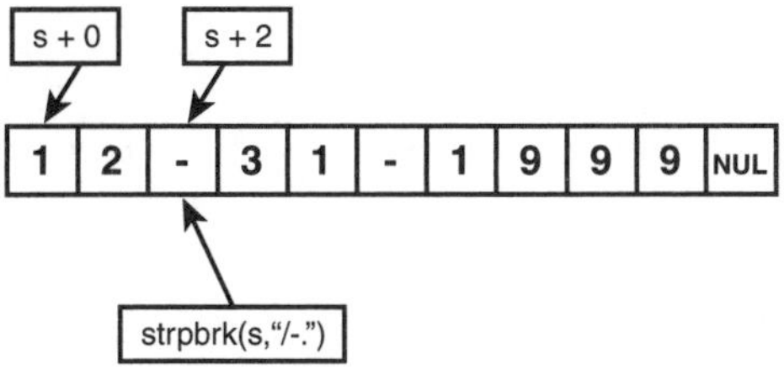

FIGURE 11.2

`strpbrk()`.

To remember how the `strpbrk()` function works, remember that `brk` tells you that the scan "breaks" when a match is found, leaving the pointer `p` pointing at the spot.

Functions strspn() and strcspn()

The `strspn()` and `strcspn()` functions shown here differ from the previous functions in that their return value is a numerical offset value instead of a string pointer:

```
size_t strspn(const char *s, const char *accept);

size_t strcspn(const char *s, const char *reject);
```

The function `strspn()` determines how many characters it can skip over (span). It uses the `accept` string as a list of acceptable characters that can be spanned. Any character not in this set causes the scan to stop, and the current span count is returned.

The `strcspn()` function uses a `reject` string instead. It skips over each character in string `s` until a character matches a character in the `reject` string. The number of characters spanned is returned.

Figure 11.3 shows a `strspn()` call that is given an `accept` string of the numeric digits `0` through `9`. This causes it to pass over the first two digits in the string `s` and to stop at the first nondigit character. This character is a slash at address `s+2`. However, because the function skips two characters, the value `2` is its return value.

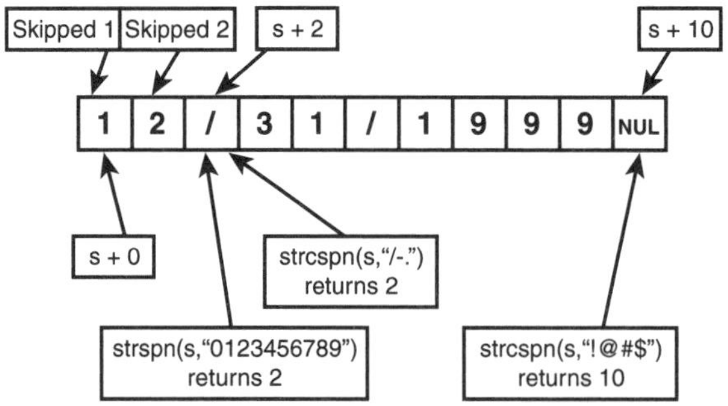

FIGURE 11.3
`strspn()` *and* `strcspn()`.

The `strcspn()` function call in Figure 11.3 also returns the value `2`, but for a different reason. Instead of skipping acceptable characters, it is told to stop on any of the three `reject` characters: a slash, hyphen, or decimal point. Because the slash at `s+2` is in that `reject` string, the function stops and returns the count of the characters it has managed to skip.

The rightmost `strcspn()` call in Figure 11.3 uses the reject string `"!@#$"`. Because none of these characters occur in string `s`, the value `10` is returned to indicate that the function is able to skip over 10 characters without encountering a `reject` character. This scan has to stop when it reaches the `NUL` byte at address `s+10`.

Interpreting the Return Value

If the search criterion is not met by the `strspn()` and `strcspn()` functions before the `NUL` byte is encountered in string `s`, the span count to the `NUL` byte is returned (that is, the length of the string).

Function `strstr()`

As the function prototype suggests, the `strstr()` function helps you to locate a needle in a haystack (this is how the Linux man page describes the function prototype):

```
char *strstr(const char *haystack, const char *needle);
```

Here, the string `haystack` is searched for any occurrence of the string `needle`. If substring `needle` is found in `haystack`, then the pointer to the substring is returned. If substring `needle` does not occur anywhere in `haystack`, then a `null` pointer is returned instead.

Figure 11.4 shows how `strstr()` locates the string `"needle"` in the string `s`. The substring `"needle"` is located at address `s+3`, so this pointer value is returned.

FIGURE 11.4

`strstr()`.

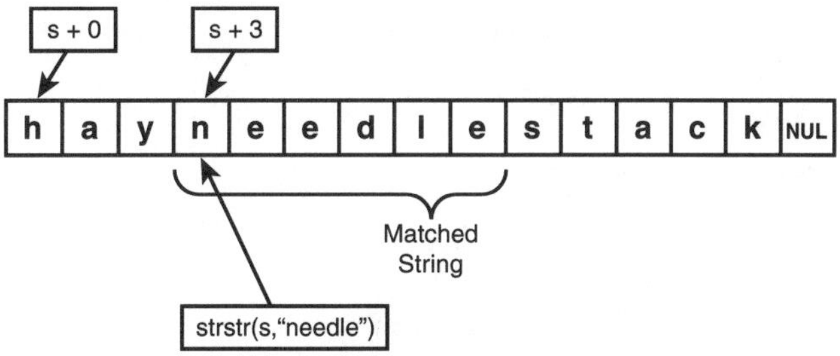

Functions `strtok()` and `strtok_r()`

`strtok()` and `strtok_r()` are simple but powerful string-scanning functions. Their use is more complex than the other functions because state information is involved. Their general purpose is to split a string into tokens based on a delimiter set. For example, a command line can be split into arguments if the space and tab characters are used as delimiters.

In the following sections, I will discuss the function `strtok()` in detail. When you have gained an understanding of this function, you can look at its limitations and then examine the more recent function `strtok_r()`.

Understanding the Function `strtok()`

In simple terms, you can think of `strtok()`, shown here, as a function that splits a C string into *tokens*.

```
char *strtok(char *s, const char *delim);
```

Generally, using `strtok()` is a two-step process:

1. Initially, you call `strtok()` with a non-`null` value for argument string `s` (argument one).
2. You call `strtok()` until it returns a `null` pointer or until the caller has finished processing tokens. In this step, the first argument is supplied as a `null` pointer.

Parsing a Command Line

To help see how this function works, assume a simple mission. Assume that you have been handed a command line, complete with the terminating `newline` (linefeed) character. Your job is to parse it into separate strings that can be placed into an `argv[]` character string array.

Reviewing the Initial State Before Calling `strtok()`

Figure 11.5 shows how the initial string looks before you call on `strtok()`. Pay close attention to this initial string because it is about to be modified.

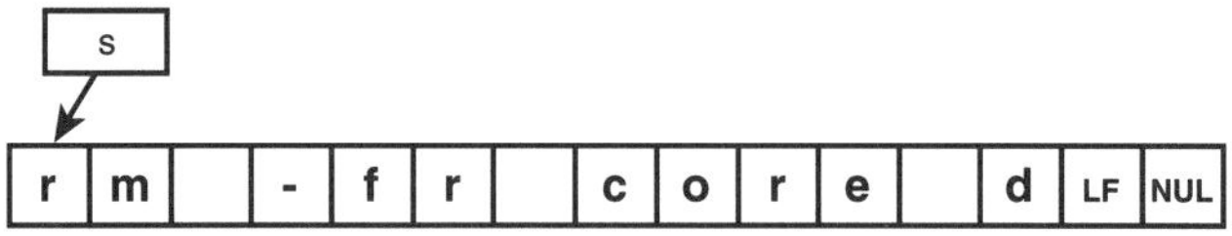

FIGURE 11.5
Initial string `s` *prior to calling* `strtok()`.

Because each command-line token can be separated by blanks, tabs, or newline characters, you can use these characters as your delimiter string as the second argument to the `strtok()` function call.

Understanding State After the First Call

Figure 11.6 shows the state of the string after the first call to `strtok()`. Argument one is the string value `s` that contains the command that you are parsing. Argument two is the delimiter string that contains the three characters blank, tab, and newline. This first call returns the same value `s`, which points to the first character of the command string. The side effect of the call, however, is to stomp out the blank byte at address `s+2` with a `NUL` byte. This action causes the returned pointer `s` to point to a substring containing `"rm"` instead of the entire command string.

FIGURE 11.6
First call to `strtok()`.

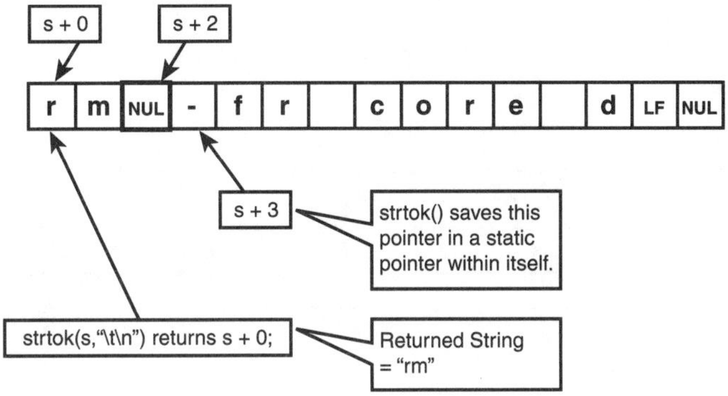

Note that the `strtok()` function saves the address (`s+3`) of the byte following the delimiter byte for the next function call. This is done in a static variable, hidden within the `strtok()` function code. If argument one is `NUL` in a future `strtok()` call, this value will be used for the next string to be parsed.

11

Understanding State After the Second Call

Figure 11.7 shows the state of the string after the second call to the `strtok()` function.

FIGURE 11.7
Second call to `strtok()`.

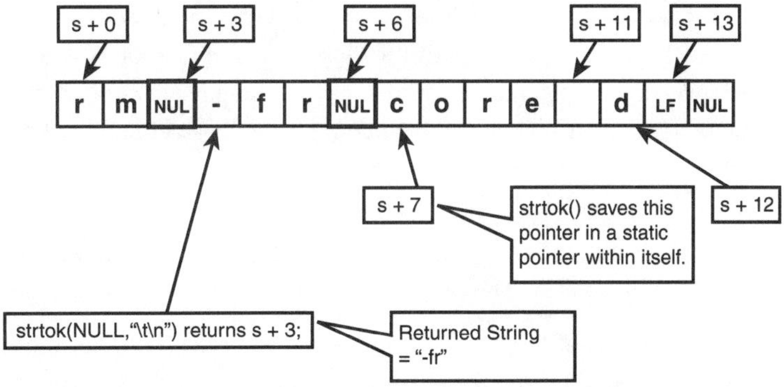

The pointer returned is address `s+3` because this string has no leading delimiter characters to skip. A delimiter character (blank) is found at `s+6`, and this character is stomped out with another `NUL` byte. This causes the returned string to appear as the C string `"-fr"`—the next string token. Now `strtok()` saves the address `s+7` for the next call in its hidden static variable.

Understanding the Final State

For each successive `strtok()` call in which argument one is a `null` pointer, function `strtok()` resumes with the last saved address (at this point `s+7`). The parsing continues until the `strtok()` encounters the `NUL` byte at address `s+14`.

Figure 11.8 shows the final state of the string `s` and the collected `argv[]` array of string pointers.

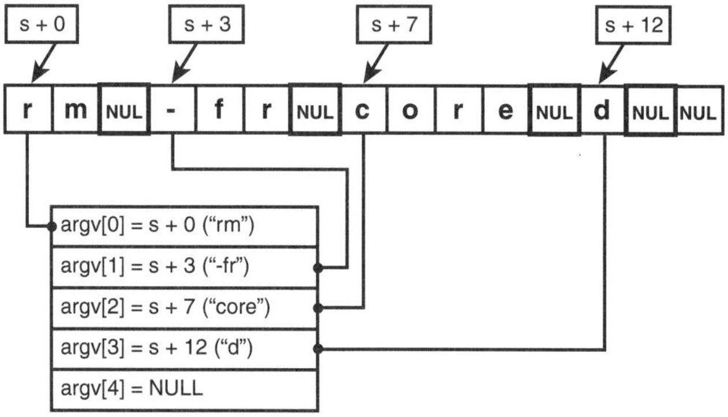

FIGURE 11.8
`strtok()` *values collected into* `argv[]`.

Figure 11.8 shows that `strtok()` returns two more pointers to tokens `"core"` and `"d"`. The final call returns a `null` pointer, which is saved in `argv[4]`.

Applying `strtok()` Correctly

In Figure 11.8, notice that the string `s` has been modified by stuffing it with `NUL` bytes to allow the return of tokenized substrings. The implication is that you must never pass the address of a string constant to `strtok()` to be parsed. Failure to heed this advice will result in a modified string constant that could have far-reaching consequences for your program.

Function `strtok_r()`

The original function `strtok()` might seem elegant at first sight, but your love affair with it will not last. The problem with this relationship is the secrets that it keeps.

The weakness of this function is the secretly saved pointer that is used between calls. You saw that after the first call to `strtok()`, it secretly saved the pointer value `s+3` (refer to Figure 11.6). After the second call, the function `strtok()` saved the value `s+7` (refer to Figure 11.7). It uses this secretly saved pointer when argument one is supplied as a `null` value.

Understanding the Limitation of `strtok()`

The "saved pointer" creates two severe limitations that prevent `strtok()` from being widely used:

- No nested `strtok()` parsing can occur on different strings.
- The `strtok()` function is not suitable for threaded programs.

Although you might not worry about threaded programs yet, the first problem is a serious limitation for all users. The problem develops when you are parsing one string, such as the command line in Figure 11.8, and you want to call a C function that might also make use of `strtok()` for its own internal purposes. The problem is that when that function returns after having used `strtok()`, the saved state of your string parsing is lost.

Saving State

The way to avoid this problem is to save the state information in the caller's data variable. You then can have any number of nested or pending parsing calls in progress because each has its state saved in its own unique location. The function `strtok_r()` accomplishes this task.

Introducing the `strtok_r()` Function

The function prototype for `strtok_r()` is as follows:

```
char *strtok_r(char *s,const char *delim,char **_save_ptr);
```

Note that argument three is new. Instead of `strtok()` saving its pointer in an internal static pointer variable, the `strtok_r()` function saves that pointer in the variable instead. You supply the address of that variable on each successive call in argument three. Listing 11.1 shows an example of how you can use `strtok_r()`.

LISTING 11.1 11LST01.C—EXAMPLE OF `strtok_r()` USE

```
#include <stdio.h>
#include <string.h>

int
main(int argc,char **argv) {
    char *my_argv[64];  /* Collected argv[] array */
    int my_argc;        /* My argc value */
    char *svptr;        /* strtok_r() updates this */
    char *s;            /* Returned strtok_r() pointer */
    char buf[256];      /* Command buffer */
```

continues

LISTING 11.1 CONTINUED

```
11:      int x;                /* Work index */
12:      static const char delim[] = " \t\n"; /* Delimiters */
13:
14:      strcpy(buf,"rm -fr core d\n");  /* Fake a command */
15:
16:      s = strtok_r(buf,delim,&svptr); /* First call */
17:      my_argc = 0;                    /* Start on my_argv[0] */
18:
19:      while ( s != 0 ) {
20:          my_argv[my_argc++] = s;     /* Save argv[] value */
21:          s = strtok_r(NULL,delim,&svptr); /* Parse next tkn */
22:      }
23:
24:      my_argv[my_argc] = 0;           /* null in last entry */
25:
26:      /*
27:       * Print out collected values:
28:       */
29:      for ( x=0; x<=my_argc; ++x )
30:          if ( my_argv[x] != 0 )
31:              printf("argv[%d] = '%s';\n",x,my_argv[x]);
32:          else
33:              printf("argv[%d] = NULL;\n",x);
34:
35:      return 0;
36:  }
```

This program performs the same procedure traced through in Figures 11.5 to 11.8. The only difference is that you are now using the more advanced `strtok_r()` function, which saves its state information external to the function itself.

The variables used in Listing 11.1 can be described as follows:

- Array `my_argv[]` is the one that you want to populate with tokens (line 6).
- The argument count is left in `int` variable `my_argc` (line 7).
- Character pointer `svptr` is declared (line 8) to be used as the variable that you will allow the function `strtok_r()` to update with its "state pointer."
- Character pointer `s` is declared to receive the return value of each `strtok_r()` call (line 9).
- Buffer `buf[]` holds the hypothetical command string (line 10).
- Working index variable `x` is used to display the collected array `my_argv[]` (line 11).
- String constant `delim[]` contains the three delimiters blank, tab, and newline (line 12).

The basic steps used in the program are as follows:

1. Fake the command by copying a string constant into the character array `buf[]` (line 14). Remember, you never want to work on a string constant directly because `strtok()` and `strtok_r()` will stuff `NUL` bytes into it.
2. Call `strtok_r()` for the first time, supplying the input string `buf[]` as argument one and array `delim[]` as the delimiters in argument two. Argument three points to the variable `svptr`, which the function call will update.
3. Initialize variable `my_argc` to `0` (line 17).
4. Begin a parsing loop (line 19). You exit this loop when `strtok_r()` returns a `null` pointer. The `null` pointer indicates that you have reached the end of the input string.
5. Save the non-`null` pointer `s` to array `my_argv[my_argc++]`. Note that the value of `my_argc` is autoincremented here.
6. Call `strtok_r()` within the loop, with argument one supplied as a `null` pointer (line 21). Doing so causes `strtok_r()` to inspect the third argument to determine where to continue parsing from.
7. Repeat step 4 (line 19) until no more tokens exist.
8. Store a `null` pointer in the last array element of `my_argv[]` (line 24).
9. The `for` loop dumps out your array `my_argv[]` to standard output (lines 29 to 33).

When Listing 11.1 is compiled and run, you obtain the following results:

```
bash$ ./a.out
argv[0] = 'rm';
argv[1] = '-fr';
argv[2] = 'core';
argv[3] = 'd';
argv[4] = NULL;
bash$
```

The session output shows that the `strtok_r()` function has successfully produced an `argv[]` array, like the one supplied to every `main()` program.

Having Fun with Strings

Programming should be fun, so in the same vein as David Letterman's "Stupid Pet Tricks," let me entertain you with the idea of "Stupid String Tricks."

In this section, you will learn some unconventional but legal C methods of working with strings. Two of the methods merely make use of the function return values that are usually ignored by programmers. The last technique simply applies the ubiquitous `strlen()` function in a manner that is sometimes overlooked.

The purpose of this section is primarily to get you to stretch your thinking beyond textbook examples. Doing so will help you to unleash the genius that is eager to attack the next challenge that awaits you.

Optimizing `strcat()` and `strcpy()` Calls

In the good old days, when everyone counted bytes of code generated, and when compilers were not very smart, the following was a common optimization:

```
strcat(strcpy(buf,"My dog")," has fleas!");
```

This simple trick generates the string `"My dog has fleas!"` in the character buffer `buf[]` (with no bounds checking, of course).

You can expand on this simple and probably well-known method of using the return values of these functions, as shown here:

```
strcat(strcat(strcpy(buf,"My dog")," bites "),
    "cats with fleas!");
```

This trick produces the string `"My dog bites cats with fleas!"` Both of these examples work because these string functions return pointers that can be reused.

These examples used string constants, but this technique works with any combination of string constants and variables as source strings.

Using the `strncpy()` Return Value Effectively

Using the `strncpy()` return value is one of my personal favorites because of the reaction it gets when inexperienced C programmers see it for the first time. They are surprised because they have a preconception that the square bracket operators can be used only on pointer variables and arrays. Here is the code:

```
void fun_a(const char *s) {
    char buf[64];

    strncpy(buf,s,sizeof buf-1)[sizeof buf-1] = 0;
```

This trick works because `strncpy()` returns the address of a string. This returned string pointer is naturally just as equally valid for use with subscripting as any pointer variable's value. Why should pointer variables have all the fun?

I developed this strncpy()[] trick when I got annoyed with the shortcomings of the strncpy() function. The problem is that strncpy() does not put a NUL byte at the end of the string if it runs out of space.

Traditionally, the NUL byte is forced at the end of the string with a second statement. However, this operation just seemed too trivial to justify a complete new line of source code to stare at every time this operation was needed.

With this simple technique, you can truncate the string if necessary and still have it terminated as NUL in one statement. Just make sure you allocate one extra byte to allow for the NUL byte in addition to your truncation length.

Improvising a sprintfcat() Function

How many times have you wanted to perform the equivalent of a strcat() but needed a formatted result? If you were to write such a function, you might name it sprintfcat(). You don't need to write such a function, however, because it can be improvised on the spot:

```
char buf[256];

strcpy(buf,"Do I have a process ID?");
sprintf(buf+strlen(buf),
    " Yes its PID=%ld;",
    (long)getpid());
```

11

The sprintf() function call shown here starts formatting at the tail end of the string because you pass it the starting address of the string's tail. If you compute the byte address buf + strlen(buf), then it points to the NUL byte at the end of the array buf[]. Because the sprintf() function always terminates its results with a NUL byte, you have accomplished what the mythical sprintfcat() function would have done for you.

Summary

In this lesson, you learned about a few string functions that you may not have taken the time to become familiar with. You looked at the simple but convenient string functions strcasecmp(), strncasecmp(), and strdup(). You also looked at the simple character-scanning functions strchr() and strrchr() in detail.

You also learned about the string-spanning functions strpbrk(), strspn(), and strcspn() and noted the differences in return values for these functions.

You discovered how to find a needle in a haystack with the strstr() function. Then you examined the intricacies of the strtok() and the newer strtok_r() functions.

Q&A

Q Why must I not pass a string constant to the `strtok()` or `strtok_r()` functions?

A These functions create tokens by writing `NUL` bytes into the strings to be parsed. If a string constant is passed in argument one, then these string constants may get modified or create an access violation if the CPU architecture forbids this modification.

Q Of the functions covered in this lesson, which function sets the `errno` value when an error return is made?

A The `strdup()` sets `errno` to the value `ENOMEM` if it cannot allocate enough memory to contain the string. The function returns a `null` pointer when this situation occurs.

Q What is the difference between function return values for `strpbrk()` and `strspn()`?

A The function `strpbrk()` returns a pointer, and `strspn()` returns the number of characters spanned.

Q How does the scan differ between `strpbrk()` and `strspn()`?

A The function `strpbrk()` stops scanning ("breaks") when a character is found matching a character in the `accept` set argument. The `strspn()` function, on the other hand, spans characters as long as each character scanned is in the `accept` set string argument.

Q Why is the function `strtok_r()` preferred over the older `strtok()` function?

A The new function allows several pending token parsing operations to exist because the state of the parse is saved in a user-provided variable. The older `strtok()` function relies on the bad practice of a hidden static variable, which prevents nesting or recursion.

Workshop

Before proceeding to the next lesson, you are encouraged to work through the quiz and the exercises.

Quiz

1. Which function duplicates a string for you?
2. If `strrchr()` returns the rightmost matching character in a string, what is the name of the companion function returning the leftmost character in the string?

3. Does string function `strcspn()` return a pointer or a `size_t` numeric offset value?
4. What is the second argument in the `strtok_r()` call used for?
5. When is the first argument of `strtok_r()` not null and why?

Exercise

Copy the program from Listing 11.1 (11LST01.c) into a work area for your work. Modify the program so that it is able to parse out quoted arguments. It should be able to parse the following command:

```
rm -fr 'Filename with blanks' core d
```

The value collected in `my_argv[2]` should be the string `Filename with blanks`. Use your choice of string functions discussed in this lesson to accomplish this task.

Copy the program from Listing 11.1 (11LST01.c) into a work area for your work. Using any string function except `strtok()` and `strtok_r()`, write your own version of the `strtok_r()` function as a static function, inserted above the `main()` program. Use the functions discussed in this lesson as much as possible to accomplish this task. Compile, link, and test your work.

Hour 12

Conversion Functions

Introduction to Conversion Functions

Any time a conversion is performed, trouble arrives on the scene. This situation necessarily occurs because data conversion implies data types with different data set domains. To get a better understanding, look at Figure 12.1.

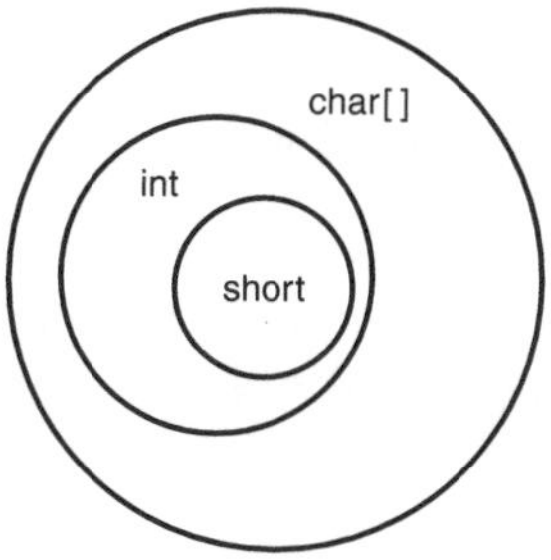

FIGURE 12.1
Data property sets of `char[]`, `short`, *and* `int`.

Figure 12.1 shows three basic C data types and their domains. The `short` data type has the smallest domain in the diagram because its range of values is the most limited. The `int` data type's domain completely encloses the `short` data type's domain because any value that a `short` data type can represent, the `int` data type can represent also. However, because the `int` data type can represent a larger range of integer values than a `short` can, its domain circle is larger.

The outer domain circle represents the set of data values that a `char[]` array can represent. This circle is necessarily much larger than both of the `int` and the `short` data domains because a `char[]` array can represent an unlimited number of digits. In addition, the `char[]` array can hold textual information such as letters and punctuation. The `char[]` array therefore has the most encompassing domain in the diagram.

If you start to convert among these various domains, you start to run into trouble. All `short` values can be converted to a `char[]` array representation as a string of numeric digits and a sign. However, not all `char[]` array strings can be converted to a `short` integer value. For example, how do you convert the text string `"penguin"` to a `short` integer?

You have a similar problem converting between the `short` and the `int` data types. The conversion always succeeds from `short` to `int`, but many `int` values are out of range of the `short` data type.

You can leave the domain of the abstract for now and get your hands dirty with real examples of data conversion. The purpose of this lesson is to prepare you for the various data conversions that you will frequently perform in your C programming life under Linux.

The `atoi()`, `atol()`, and `atof()` Family of Functions

The `atoi()`, `atol()`, and `atof()` functions are the easiest functions for a C programmer to use because they require no preparation or subsequent tests for conversion errors. The entire issue of conversion errors is ignored.

Every introductory text on C programming teaches the reader how to use these functions. However, they are frequently not the best choice of conversion functions available. Before you explore the alternatives, take some time to scrutinize these functions more closely.

Scrutinizing the Functions `atoi()` and `atol()`

The `atoi()` and `atol()` functions shown here simply take the starting address of a C string and return the result as an `integer` or a `long` data type value. Any leading white-space characters as defined by the C library function `isspace()` are skipped over before starting the conversion.

```
#include <stdlib.h>

int atoi(const char *nptr);
long atol(const char *nptr);
```

Using the `atoi()` Function

The following is a sample conversion using the `atoi()` function:

```
char buf[32];
int i;

strcpy(buf,"23");
i = atoi(buf);
```

In this example, the string `"23"` is converted to an integer value `23`. There's nothing hard about this procedure, is there? In fact, it is so easy that many C programmers are numbed into thinking that this is the only way that it can be done.

Understanding the Conversion Error Problem

Consider an everyday problem in which the function `atoi()` is used. Assume that you have a debug command-line option of the form `-x n`, where `n` is the debug level from `0` to `9`. Within your `getopt()` processing loop, you must now convert that `optarg` value to an integer value:

```
switch( optch ) {
case 'x' :
    cmdopt_x = atoi(optarg); /* Get debug level */
    break;
```

Converting Nonnumeric Data

12

Now assume that a user supplies the option `-x high` because he or she doesn't know any better. Your `atoi()` function glibly returns the value `0` in this case because it cannot convert `high` to an integer value. Your program is unaware that a debug level should be set because the value returned is `0` (due to the conversion error). As a result, the program runs without any debug level at all. This procedure is not user friendly, is it?

Converting Garbled Data

Another similar problem occurs when the user supplies the debug option as `-x 5oops` because he or she is all thumbs on the keyboard. Your program glibly accepts the value `5`, which `atoi()` is able to convert successfully. Then, quietly, the trailing `oops+` part is ignored. This is definitely not a "mil-spec." program!

The functions `atoi()`, `atol()`, and `atof()` all lack error return information. Consequently, you need a better sense of when the conversion succeeds and when it fails.

Knowing Where the Conversion Ends

Another limitation of the `atoi()` family of functions is that the caller is not given information about where the conversion ends in the input string. If you had to write a function to extract the month, day, and year from a date string, for example, then you would have some problems using the `atoi()` function. Consider the following variations in input date string formats that might be thrown at you:

- `"01/01/2000"`
- `"1/2/2000"`
- `"12/1/2000"`
- `" 1/ 9/2000"`
- `"   1  / 31   /   2000 "`

You can see that these variations can lead to a data conversion challenge. Fixed-column offsets are not any help here. The `atoi()` function can help only with the month extraction. After you have extracted the month, you are left with a bunch of questions: How many blanks were skipped over? How many digits were there? Were there trailing blanks? Because no scan information is returned by `atoi()`, you don't know where to start the extraction for the following day or year fields.

Using the `atof()` Function

The `atof()` function is similar to the `atoi()` function, as you can see here, except that it converts string values into floating-point values:

```
#include <stdlib.h>

double atof(const char *nptr);
```

Here is an example of its use:

```
char buf[32];
double f;

strcpy(buf,"  -467.01E+02");
f = atof(buf);
```

This example shows some leading whitespace, a sign character, and a decimal number followed by a signed exponent. The `atof()` function skips over the whitespace and converts the remaining characters into a `double` type value `f`.

Again, the simplicity of it all woos many C programmers into using this form of conversion. Yet all the attendant problems that exist for `atoi()` and `atol()` also apply to the use of the `atof()` function.

In the next section, you will look at an improved way to perform data conversions. This method can provide some error detection and location information.

Using `sscanf()` for Conversion and Validation

The function `sscanf()` is sort of a Swiss army knife for C input and conversion. Although the mechanism is not a perfect solution for all seasons, it still provides simplicity of use and yet provides some measure of error detection.

Applying `sscanf()` to Numeric Conversion

Listing 12.1 shows a simple program that extracts the month, day, and year from a string. I have deliberately made the date as messy as possible (line 10) with lots of whitespace.

LISTING 12.1 12LST01.C—EXTRACTING DATE FIELDS FROM A STRING

```
1:   #include <stdio.h>
2:   #include <stdlib.h>
3:   #include <string.h>
4:
5:   int
6:   main(int argc,char *argv[]) {
7:       int nf;             /* Number of fields converted */
8:       int n;              /* # of characters scanned */
9:       int mm, dd, yyyy;   /* Month, day and year */
10:      static char sdate[] = "   1 /  2  /  2000  ";
11:
12:      printf("Extracting from '%s'\n",sdate);
13:
14:      nf = sscanf(sdate,"%d /%d /%d%n",
15:          &mm, &dd, &yyyy, &n);
16:
17:      printf("%02d/%02d/%04d nf=%d, n=%d\n",
18:          mm, dd, yyyy, nf, n);
19:
20:      if ( nf >= 3 )
21:          printf("Remainder = '%s'\n",&sdate[n]);
22:
23:      return 0;
24:  }
```

The variables used in this program are as follows:

- Variable `nf` receives the number of the conversions that `sscanf()` successfully accomplishes (line 7).
- Variable `n` receives the number of characters scanned so far (line 8).
- Variables `mm`, `dd`, and `yyyy` are the month, day, and year extracted values respectively (line 9).
- The character array `sdate[]` is the string from which you are going to extract the date components (line 10).

The steps used in this program are as follows:

1. `sscanf()` is called using the input string `sdate[]` (line 14).
2. The first component of the format string is a `%d`. It causes `sscanf()` to skip any leading blanks. Then it converts an optional sign (if present) and one or more following digits into an integer. The converted result is passed back to the variable `mm` (note the `&mm` argument that supplies its address).
3. After the first `%d` component, you see two characters (`/`)—a space and a slash. The space tells `sscanf()` to skip over zero, one, or more blanks. The slash tells `sscanf()` to skip over the one slash also. Note the following:
   - Input blanks are optional here.
   - One slash is mandatory in the input string at this point.
4. After the `%d /` part of the format string, the `sscanf()` function encounters another `%d`. It causes the function to skip any blanks that might follow the slash and then convert a possibly signed integer into variable `dd` (in the same manner as step 2).
5. As in step 3, the `sscanf()` now must skip more optional blanks and yet another slash.
6. As in steps 2 and 4, another `%d` is encountered by `sscanf()` in the format string, so more optional blanks are bypassed, and another possibly signed integer is stored in variable `yyyy`.
7. The `sscanf()` now encounters the `%n` format specification. The corresponding address argument `&n` tells `sscanf()` to store the current character scan count into variable `n`. This value tells you how many characters you consumed from the input string.
8. The function `sscanf()` now forms its return value. The value returned represents the number of successful conversions that have been performed. In this example, that count is three because of the three `%d` (integer) conversions. The `%n` operation is not counted as a conversion. As a result, the function `sscanf()` returns the value `3`, which is stored in variable `nf` (line 14).

9. The program reports the extracted date field components mm, dd, and yyyy (lines 17 and 18). In addition, the values for nf and n are also reported.
10. The value of nf is tested (line 20). This step is necessary because the value of n is not defined (in line 21) if the sscanf() function is not able to work its way to the %n specification in the format string.
11. The unprocessed part of the input string is reported (line 21). This statement can be performed only if you know that sscanf() updated variable n (this is tested in step 10).

Remember that only three conversions are present in the sscanf() call coded here because the %n specification does not count as a conversion. This quirk of sscanf() is often the source of problems in new code.

Testing Numeric Conversions Using sscanf()

Compiling and running the program in Listing 12.1 yields the following results:

```
bash$ gcc -D_GNU_SOURCE 12LST01.c
bash$ ./a.out
Extracting from '   1 /  2  /  2000   '
01/02/2000 nf=3, n=18
Remainder = '   '
bash$
```

You can make the following observations from the results:

- The messy input date is successfully extracted and reformatted into the string "01/02/2000".
- Function sscanf() returns a value nf=3. This value confirms that the function counts only the three %d operations as conversions; that is, the %n operation is not counted as a conversion.
- Because nf returns 3 as you expected, you can be certain that the value n=18 is valid.
- Because n=18, you know that sscanf() processes the first 18 characters of the input string. Using n as a subscript into this string, you can print out the remaining unprocessed tail of the string (which are blanks).

Improving the sscanf() Conversion

One irritation that remains in the example in Listing 12.1 is that it does not skip over the trailing whitespace. Testing whether you consume the entire input to get the date is therefore difficult. If you have leftover parts, they indicate that you didn't put things together correctly.

You can quickly remedy this problem by fixing the `sscanf()` statement in line 14 of Listing 12.1 to read as follows:

```
nf = sscanf(sdate,"%d /%d /%d %n",
    &mm, &dd, &yyyy, &n);
```

If you look carefully at the format string, you will notice that one space is inserted before the `%n` specifier. This space coaxes `sscanf()` into skipping over more whitespace before reporting how many characters are scanned. With the whitespace skipped over, you can test for leftovers as follows:

```
if ( sdate[n] != 0 ) {
    printf("EEK! Leftovers = '%s'\n",&sdate[n]);
```

If no leftovers exist, then `sdate[n]` points to the trailing `NUL` byte in the string. If `n` does not point to the `NUL` byte after the conversion, then you know that the conversion is incomplete.

Pondering the Limitations of `sscanf()`

To conclude this discussion, note that the `sscanf()` return value indicates whether the conversion(s) is successful. When the `%n` specifier is processed by `sscanf()`, you can also determine where the scanning ends. One limitation remains, however: How do you determine the point in the string where the error occurred when the conversions are not successful? You need to look at other methods to solve this problem.

The `strtol()` and `strtoul()` Functions

The `sscanf()` solution still presents one problem: It is the "retail solution." Why pay retail prices when you can buy at wholesale prices instead? The `sscanf()` function must do a lot of additional overhead work just to parse the format string argument. After it determines what to do, it then calls on some other library functions to do all the dirty work. In the following sections, you will go directly to the source.

`sscanf()` calls on the functions `strtol()` and `strtoul()`. Their function prototypes are as follows:

```
#include <stdlib.h>

long strtol(const char *nptr, char **endptr, int base);

unsigned long strtoul(const char *nptr, char **endptr,
    int base);
```

The function `strtol()` converts a possibly signed integer within a character array to a `long` integer data type value. The function `strtoul()` is functionally identical, except that no sign is permitted, and the returned conversion value is an unsigned long integer.

In the following sections, you will examine only the `strtol()` function in detail, with the understanding that the same principles can be applied to the `strtoul()` function.

Using the Function `strtol()`

Listing 12.2 shows a short program that tries to convert the first signed value in a character array named `snum[]`. Not only does it extract the integer value, but it also indicates where the conversion ends.

LISTING 12.2 12LST02.C—THE `strtol()` CONVERSION FUNCTION EXAMPLE

```
1:   #include <stdio.h>
2:   #include <stdlib.h>
3:
4:   int
5:   main(int argc,char *argv[]) {
6:       long lval;
7:       char *ep;
8:       static char snum[] = "  -2567,45,39";
9:
10:      lval = strtol(snum,&ep,10);
11:
12:      printf("lval = %ld, ep = '%s'\n",
13:          lval, ep ? ep : "<NULL>");
14:      return 0;
15:  }
```


The highlights of the program can be described as follows:

- The function `strtol()` is called (line 10). It is given the input string `snum[]` as its first argument.
- The second argument tells `strtol()` to update the pointer variable `ep` before it returns. This variable will be updated with the address of the next unprocessed character in the input string.
- The third argument indicates that you are doing a decimal integer conversion.
- The value returned is assigned to `long` integer value `lval` (still line 10).
- The results of the conversion are reported (lines 12 and 13).

Testing the `strtol()` Function

When you compile and run the program in Listing 12.2, you get the following results:

```
bash$ gcc -D_GNU_SOURCE 12LST02.c
bash$ ./a.out
lval = -2567, ep = ',45,39'
bash$
```

From this session output, you can make the following observations:

- The value is converted to a long integer successfully (line 10), as shown by the display (lines 12 and 13).
- The pointer `ep` is updated and is left pointing at the substring `",45,39"`.
- If you need to extract the remaining values, you can use `ep` to verify and skip the comma, and proceed to extract the next number.

Testing for Errors

The `strtol()` and `strtoul()` functions return the value `0` if the conversion fails completely. However, `0` is a valid conversion value, so you should not use it as a basis for concluding that an error took place.

Setting the return pointer to the same value as the starting string indicates that a conversion error took place. This value indicates that the conversion function made no progress at all within the string. In Listing 12.2, you would test for the error in this manner:

```
if ( ep == snum ) {
    printf("Cannot convert value '%s'\n",snum);
```

In Listing 12.2, string snum is the string that is to be converted, and the return pointer `ep` points to where the conversion ends. If the conversion ends where the conversion starts then no conversion actually occurs.

Testing the Conversion Pointer

You have already seen in Listing 12.2 that the return pointer `ep` shows where the conversion ends. This allows a great deal of flexibility in your code in determining the success of the conversion. If the string to be converted is purely a number with no trailing blanks or trailing data, then the `ep` value should point to the string's trailing `NUL` byte. You can test for this value as follows:

```
if ( *ep != 0 ) {
    printf("Conversion of '%s' failed near '%s'\n",
        snum, ep);
```

This example not only tests that the conversion ate all the input, but it also shows the point of failure if it should occur.

Performing Multiple Conversions

In Listing 12.2, you saw three values separated by commas. You can test for a successful field parse by testing for the delimiting comma:

```
if ( *ep != ',' )
    printf("Failed near '%s'\n",ep);
else {
    ++ep;     /* Skip comma */
    /* Parse next field */
```

In this example, you know that the next character should be a comma. If it is not, then you have encountered an error. If the expected comma is encountered, however, you can simply skip over that character and convert the next numeric value using `strtol()` again.

Understanding Radix Conversions

When you were learning C (or perhaps even before that), you learned about different number systems. You should already be familiar with the number systems shown in Table 12.1.

TABLE 12.1 COMMON NUMBER SYSTEMS

Number System	*Radix*	*Description*
binary	2	The binary number system, consisting of the digits 1 and 0.
octal	8	The octal number system, consisting of digits 0 to 7.
decimal	10	The decimal number system, consisting of digits 0 to 9.
hexadecimal	16	The hexadecimal number system, consisting of the decimal digits 0 to 9, and the letters A to F.

The radix value is the "base" of the number system. For this familiar decimal system, the radix is 10.

Using the `base` Argument

Remember the `base` argument for `strtol()` that you so quickly dismissed? This parameter allows a number of other flexible numeric conversions to be performed. The man pages for these functions are a little obscure about what really happens when the `base` argument is `0` or when it is `16`. The best way to find out is to run some tests with the help of the program shown in Listing 12.3.

LISTING 12.3 12LST03.C—TESTING THE RADIX FEATURE OF `strtol()`

```
#include <stdio.h>
#include <stdlib.h>
#include <errno.h>

int
main(int argc,char *argv[]) {
    int i;          /* Iterator variable */
    char *ep;       /* End scan pointer */
    long base;      /* Conversion base */
    long lval;      /* Converted long value */

    /*
     * Test for arguments :
     */
    if ( argc < 2 ) {
        printf("Usage: %s base 'string' [base 'string]...\n",
            argv[0]);
        return 1;
    }

    /*
     * Process arguments :
     */
    for ( i=1; i<argc; ++i ) {
        /*
         * Get conversion base :
         */
        base = strtol(argv[i],&ep,10);
        if ( *ep != 0 ) {
            printf("Base error in '%s' near '%s'\n",
                argv[i], ep);
            return 1;
        } else if ( base > 36 || base < 0 ) {
            printf("Invalid base: %ld\n",base);
            return 1;
        }
        /*
         * Get conversion string :
         */
        if ( ++i >= argc ) {
            printf("Missing conversion string! Arg # %d\n",
                i);
            return 1;
        }
        errno = 0;  /* Clear prior errors, if any */
        lval = strtol(argv[i],&ep,(int)base);
        printf("strtol('%s',&ep,%ld) => %ld; ep='%s',
        ➥ errno=%d\n",
```

```
48:              argv[i], base, lval, ep, errno);
49:      }
50:
51:      return 0;
52:  }
53:   bash$
```

The following points can be made about the program:

- This program uses command-line arguments in pairs (loop in lines 24 to 49).
- The radix value (number `base`) is supplied in the first of the paired command-line arguments.
- The string to be converted is supplied in the second of the paired command-line arguments.
- To include whitespace and special characters, be sure to quote the arguments where needed on the command line.

Running the Radix Tests

Now you can compile and perform an initial checkout of the program:

```
bash$ gcc -D_GNU_SOURCE 12LST03.c
bash$ ./a.out 10 '   +2345' 10 -456 10 '123   '
strtol('   +2345',&ep,10) => 2345; ep='', errno=0
strtol('-456',&ep,10) => -456; ep='', errno=0
strtol('123   ',&ep,10) => 123; ep='   ', errno=0
bash$
```


After a successful compile, look at the three decimal conversions. The first shows that it successfully skips the whitespace. The second shows that it is successful at converting a negative value. The third shows how the variable `ep` points to the trailing whitespace.

Running Hexadecimal Tests

Setting the base to `16` should allow you to do some hexadecimal conversions:

```
bash$ ./a.out 16 012 16 0x12 16 FFx
strtol('012',&ep,16) => 18; ep='', errno=0
strtol('0x12',&ep,16) => 18; ep='', errno=0
strtol('FFx',&ep,16) => 255; ep='x', errno=0
bash$
```

The first conversion converts the string `'012'` to `18` decimal—clearly a hexadecimal conversion. The second conversion shows that the `strtol()` function skips over the leading `'0x'` characters when the base is `16`. The third case shows how `'FFx'` is properly converted, leaving a trailing unprocessed `'x'`.

Testing a Radix of `0`

The situation gets very interesting when the base is set to `0`. When this is done, numbers are considered decimal unless they are prefixed by a leading `0` or a leading `0` and letter `X`. The leading `0` and `X` represent a hexadecimal number, so the conversion proceeds as base 16. If the leading `0` is present but not `X`, then the base is set to `8` for an octal conversion. Now try the following examples:

```
bash$ ./a.out 0 '012' 0 '0x12' 0 '12'
strtol('012',&ep,0) => 10; ep='', errno=0
strtol('0x12',&ep,0) => 18; ep='', errno=0
strtol('12',&ep,0) => 12; ep='', errno=0
bash$
```

The first conversion of `'012'` does indeed convert as an octal number, leaving the integer value of `10`. The second conversion of `'0x12'` converts to the integer value of `18`--clearly a hexadecimal conversion. Finally, the plain `'12'` is converted as a decimal integer value of `12`. All work as advertised.

Testing Binary Conversions

Even more radix conversions are possible. How about binary bit strings?

```
bash$ ./a.out 2 '00001010' 2 '00010110'
strtol('00001010',&ep,2) => 10; ep='', errno=0
strtol('00010110',&ep,2) => 22; ep='', errno=0
bash$
```

Testing Radixes Above 16

Numbers can be represented in radixes above `16`. They are not used very often, but they are available for use if you have the application for it:

```
bash$ ./a.out 36 'A9BC;' 36 'Z005?' 36 'Linux!'
strtol('A9BC;',&ep,36) => 478632; ep=';', errno=0
strtol('Z005?',&ep,36) => 1632965; ep='?', errno=0
strtol('Linux!',&ep,36) => 36142665; ep='!', errno=0
bash$
```

Above base 10, the conversion routines consider the letter `A` as the digit `10`, `B` as the digit `11`, and so on. Lowercase letters are treated the same as their uppercase counterparts. Radix `36` is the highest base supported, and it has the letter `Z` defined as the value `35`.

The radix `36` value of Linux in decimal is `36142665`. Is this magic number used anywhere in the kernel, Linus?

Testing for Overflows and Underflows

Remember the abstract discussion about the character array data domains versus the `int` data domains? Clearly, a string can hold more digits than a `long` or an `unsigned long` data type can hold. This situation might lead you to worry about things like overflows and underflows.

If you try to convert a very large value into `lval` in the test program, you can see that it fails:

```
bash$ ./a.out 10 '99999999999999999999'
strtol('99999999999999999999',&ep,10) => 2147483647; ep='', errno=34
bash$
```

Notice how the conversion yields the result `2147483647` instead of the correct decimal value of `99999999999999999999`. Yet the `ep` variable shows that the scan makes it to the end of the string. Has `strtol()` let you down after all?

Interpreting LONG_MAX and ERANGE

The overflows are handled by a special return value `LONG_MAX`. You can check this result by using `grep` on the limits.h file:

```
bash$ grep 2147483647 /usr/include/limits.h
#  define INT_MAX       2147483647
#   define LONG_MAX     2147483647L
bash$
```

When `strtol()` returns the value `LONG_MAX`, you must consult the oracle according to `errno`. If it has the value `ERANGE` posted to it, then you can conclude that an overflow has indeed occurred. So do you get `ERANGE`?

```
bash$ grep 34 /usr/include/asm/errno.h
#define ERANGE   34    /* Math result not representable */
bash$
```

Sure enough, the `errno` value of `34` that was reported is confirmed as the `ERANGE` error.

Understanding the Overflow Test Procedure

Having `strtol()` return `2147483647` (`LONG_MAX`) whenever an overflow occurs would seem to preclude the function from ever being able to return this value normally. However, the overflow is further indicated by setting `errno` to `ERANGE`. This leads to the procedure for testing for overflows and underflows:

1. Clear variable `errno` to `0`. This step is necessary because `strtol()` does not zero it.
2. Call `strtol()` to perform the conversion.

3. If the value returned is not LONG_MAX, then no overflow has occurred and you are finished. Otherwise, proceed to step 4.
4. Test the value of errno. If it is still cleared to 0 from step 1, then no overflow occurred during the conversion, and the value returned truly represents the converted input value.
5. If the errno value is ERANGE instead, then an overflow occurred during the conversion, and the returned value LONG_MAX is not representative of the input value.

The same logic can be applied to testing for underflows when the value LONG_MIN is returned.

Proving the Overflow Test Procedure

You can prove this procedure with the test program from Listing 12.3:

```
bash$ ./a.out 10 '99999999999999999999' 10 2147483647
strtol('99999999999999999999',&ep,10) => 2147483647; ep='', errno=34
strtol('2147483647',&ep,10) => 2147483647; ep='', errno=0
bash$
```

The first conversion fails and returns LONG_MAX (value 2147483647). It shows an errno value of 34, which you now know to be the value ERANGE.

Notice that the second decimal conversion uses as input the maximum long value of 2147483647, and it converts successfully and returns LONG_MAX. This time, however, errno is not the value of ERANGE but is left as 0 instead. This result is thanks to line 45 in Listing 12.3, which reads as follows:

```
errno = 0;   /* Clear prior errors, if any */
```

Remember that the errno value is never cleared by a successful operation. It is used only to post errors to. To allow you to differentiate between a successful conversion and an overflow, you must clear errno before calling strtol(). Otherwise, you will be testing a leftover error code if the conversion is successful.

Coding an Overflow/Underflow Test

If lval is assigned the strtol() return value, the overflow/underflow test should be written like this:

```
if ( lval == LONG_MAX || lval == LONG_MIN ) {
    /* Test for over / under flow */
    if ( errno == ERANGE ) {
        puts("Over/Under-flow occurred!");
```

This test works only if you clear errno to 0 before calling the conversion function.

Testing for `strtoul()` Overflows

Function `strtoul()` converts unsigned integers. The maximum unsigned value is not the same as the maximum signed value. Consequently, the maximum value returned is `ULONG_MAX` instead. However, the general test procedure for overflow is quite similar to the `strtol()` procedure:

1. Clear variable `errno` to `0`.
2. Call `strtoul()` to perform the conversion.
3. If the value returned is not `ULONG_MAX`, then no overflow has occurred and you are finished. Otherwise, proceed to step 4.
4. Test the value of `errno`. If it is still cleared to `0` from step 1, then no overflow occurred during the conversion, and the value returned truly represents the input value.
5. If the `errno` value is `ERANGE` instead, then an overflow occurred during conversion, and the returned value `ULONG_MAX` is not truly representative of the input value.

That completes the tour of the integer conversion functions. In the following sections, you will look at how you can perform floating-point conversions from a string.

The `strtod()` Function

The `strtod()` function is used to perform string[nd]to[nd]floating-point conversions. This function is quite similar in operation to the integer conversion functions, but it has a few new wrinkles. The function prototype is as follows:

```
#include <stdlib.h>

double strtod(const char *nptr, char **endptr);
```


One difference is that it has no `base` argument. The implication is that no radix conversions are available for floating-point conversions.

The input string `nptr` and the second argument `endptr` are used in precisely the same way they are used in the `strtol()` function, however.

Using the `strtod()` Function

The following example shows how you can use the `strtod()` function to convert a floating-point value in a string buffer to the C `double` type:

```
static char buf[] = "-32000.009E+01";
char *ep;               /* Returned pointer */
double dval;            /* Converted value */

dval = strtod(buf,&ep); /* Convert buf to double */
```

The input string is converted character by character, and the floating-point result is returned and assigned to the variable `dval`. The point where the conversion ends is passed back to the caller by storing the pointer into pointer variable `ep`. In this example, `ep` should end up pointing to the `NUL` byte at the end of the `buf[]` array. This happens because all the input is used in this conversion.

Testing for Math Errors

The `strtod()` function adds a new twist for overflow and underflow detection. To test for overflows and underflows, you must include the file math.h:

```
#include <math.h>
```

This include file defines the special macro `HUGE_VAL`, which you need to use in your tests. Three return values from `strtod()` require you to do further investigation:

- `+HUGE_VAL`
- `0` (or `0.0`)
- `-HUGE_VAL`

The test procedure relies on the fact that the `errno` value is cleared before calling `strtod()`. Clearing this value is essential to the procedure.

Testing for Overflow

You can think of the value `+HUGE_VAL` as a huge positive number. When this value is returned, you must check `errno` to see whether the value `ERANGE` is posted there. If `errno` is set to `ERANGE`, then the conversion process has an overflow. If not, then the return value is still a valid number.

Testing for Underflow

The value `-HUGE_VAL` represents a huge but negative number. When this value is returned, you must also check `errno` to see whether the error `ERANGE` is posted there. If not, then the returned value is still a valid number.

Testing for Exponent Underflow

Why do you need to check `errno` when `strtod()` returns `0`? Floating-point numbers can be extremely small in value. They can be so small, in fact, that the underlying data type cannot represent it. When `0` is returned, and `ERANGE` is posted to the `errno` variable, then you know that the conversion failed because the input value is too small a fraction to represent. Another way to explain this event is that the exponent value underflows.

Handling Exponent Underflow

In many cases, you might be happy just to round that small fractional value to `0` and move on. However, this approach may not be suitable for all applications, especially scientific ones.

A scientific model may depend on the precision of that variable to represent a very small value. If the precision is maintained, then that value might be later multiplied by a large value to compute a reasonable result (according to the model).

However, if you simply allow the value to round to `0`, then the multiplied result is `0` also—leading to an incorrect answer. A better approach would be to abort the computation and point out that the value could not be contained with the necessary precision.

The entire procedure for math error testing is shown in Figure 12.2 as a flowchart. This flowchart should help summarize the overflow and underflow detection logic that should be used.

FIGURE 12.2

Testing for overflow and underflow after a `strtod()` *call.*

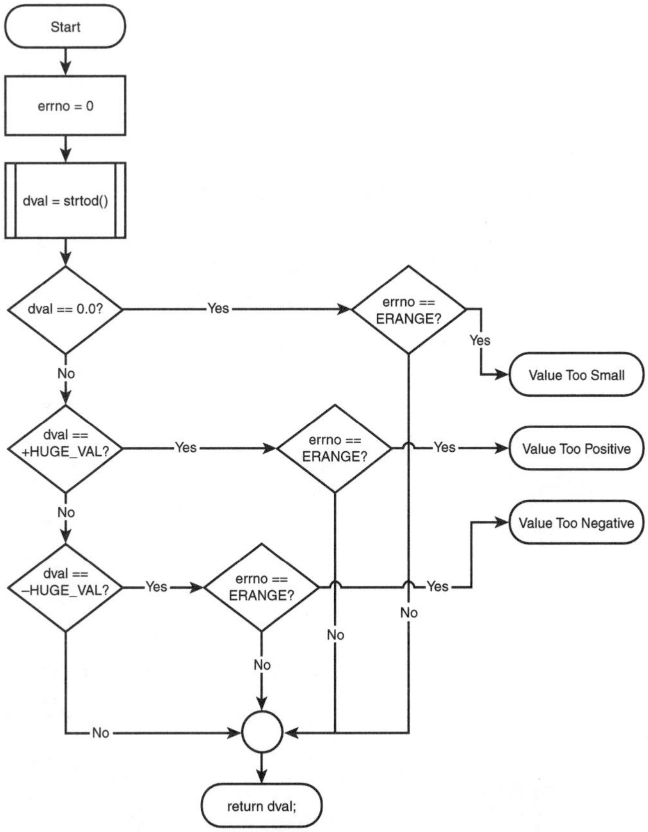

Summary

In this lesson, you learned about the limitations of the simple `atoi()` family of functions. I discussed the `sscanf()` function as a better replacement but noted some other limitations of this approach.

Then I covered the functions `strtol()`, `strtoul()`, and `strtod()`. You saw how they not only returned information about where the conversion ended, but they also properly reported all necessary types of conversion errors. You learned about overflows and underflows. You also saw that floating-point values can also have exponent underflows when a fractional value is too small to represent.

Q&A

Q What is the precondition necessary before testing for overflows and underflows?

A You must clear the `errno` value before calling your conversion routine. Otherwise, you end up testing a previously posted error code even when the conversion succeeds. The `errno` value is not cleared by the conversion function.

Q When does the `strtol()` function heed the octal and hexadecimal prefixing rules?

A When the base is set to `16`, the prefix `0x` is accepted and skipped over. When the base is set to `0`, the zero prefix rule causes the number to be interpreted as an octal value. The `0x` prefix rule causes the value to be interpreted as hexadecimal value. All other numbers are treated as decimal values.

Q Can the hexadecimal prefix be uppercase `0X`?

A Yes.

Workshop

The functions covered in this lesson are important to your programming skill-set. You are encouraged to complete the quiz and the exercises before proceeding to the next lesson.

Quiz

1. Can `sscanf()` tell you precisely where the conversion failed in the input string?
2. When `strtod()` returns a `0.0`, and `errno` is holding the value `ERANGE`, what does this tell you?

3. When `strtoul()` returns the value `ULONG_MAX`, and `errno` does not contain the value `ERANGE`, what does this tell you?
4. How do you test when the `strtol()` conversion failed completely?

Exercises

1. Copy the program from Listing 12.3 (13LST03.c) to a private work area. Modify the program to test when the `base` argument is given the letter `D` instead of a numeric base value. When `D` is given, call on the function `strtod()` instead of `strtol()`. Report the results without worrying about overflow or underflow.
2. Using the modified program from exercise 1, modify the program further to test for overflow and underflow for the `strtol()` case only. Be sure to test your results with the values `LONG_MAX`, `LONG_MAX+1`, `LONG_MIN`, and `LONG_MIN-1` as appropriate for your Linux platform.
3. Further modify the program from exercise 2 to check for overflow, underflow, and exponent underflow conditions after the `strtod()` call. Report each of these conditions specifically (that is, do not lump these reports into one under/overflow message). Test with extremely large and extremely small values, in addition to `+HUGE_VAL` and `-HUGE_VAL` values.
4. Write a small program that reads one standard input line after another until it reaches the end of file. After the line is read into a buffer, the program should be able parse and store up to, but not necessarily, 16 long integer values. Each integer is separated by a comma in the input line. After the input line has been fully parsed, print out your array of converted values, and indicate the count of values converted. If an error is detected in your input line, display the whole line and display the point of error. Do not forget to test for overflow and underflow, and report it.

HOUR 13

Linux Date and Time Facilities

Introducing Date and Time Support

Date and time facilities are fundamental to nearly everything you do in Linux. When a process starts, the time of this event is recorded in a kernel table. When you create a new file, the creation date and time are recorded. Modification times are recorded when you edit a file. Even when you just view a file, its access time is updated.

Applications that you write for Linux will have their own requirements for date and time management. For example, if you write a program that manages stock market trades, you need to compute the *T+3 settlement date* for that trade. A T+3 date means that you compute the trade date plus three days to arrive at the time the trade will be settled. Furthermore, you might be required to compute this date in a different time zone for the stock exchange where the trade took place.

In this lesson, you will learn about date and time management functions that Linux makes available to you. With a complete and thorough understanding of these functions, you will be fully equipped for any date and time challenge that you might face writing an application.

Introducing Epoch Time

When reading the Linux man pages, you will frequently encounter the term *epoch time*. It is simply the date and time that UNIX considers to be the beginning of time. Epoch time for UNIX is the following specific time and date:

```
00:00:00 GMT, January 1, 1970
```

In other words, for Linux, time began on January 1, 1970, at midnight Greenwich mean time (GMT).

Understanding Time Zones

Because the Linux kernel bases its epoch time on the GMT time standard, I will quickly review time standards in general and then help you look at how your local time zone is related.

Introducing World Time Standards

In the following sections, I will discuss two world time standards. Originally, the GMT time standard was the accepted world standard. Since that time, however, a new world standard has emerged to help coordinate the precise synchronization needed for distributed computer systems.

UNIX had its beginnings before the world time standard was changed, so Linux inherits this heritage with references to both the old and the new. I will explain the details in the next few sections.

Understanding GMT

The Greenwich mean time, or GMT, is based on the prime meridian of the earth, which passed through Great Britain's Greenwich Observatory in 1884. Since that time, the observatory has moved and been renamed the Royal Greenwich Observatory. However, the original location is still used to define the prime meridian.

The precise GMT time is determined by observations of the sun. Due to variations in the earth's rotation and its orbit around the sun, small corrections are computed regularly and applied to arrive at the precise time.

Understanding UTC

UTC is the abbreviation for the time standard named Universelle Tempes Coordinaté in French, or Coordinated Universal Time in English. This standard is based on atomic clock measurements instead of solar observations. This new standard replaced GMT as the world time standard in 1986.

Choosing a World Time Standard

If a fraction of a second makes no difference to you, you can set your Linux system clock according to the GMT time standard or UTC time. They are so similar that they are sometimes used interchangeably.

The correct designation to use for this time zone today is UTC because it has been the accepted world standard since 1986. New software should be written accordingly.

For the remainder of this lesson, I will use the term *UTC* to refer to the central time zone, with the understanding that GMT could be applied equally.

Understanding Local Time Zones

Linux makes allowances for those who do not live in the UTC time zone. This is done by taking the local time zone and adding an offset in hours to arrive at UTC. For Eastern North America, the UTC time is local time plus five hours, for example. For much of Europe, it is the local time minus one hour.

Customizing Local Time Zones

Because Linux is a multiuser operating system, it is designed to permit its users to define their own concept of a local time. The `tzset()` function is used internally by a number of date and time functions to determine your local time zone. You will examine this function in more detail later in this lesson. The important point about this function, however, is that it looks for an exported environment variable `TZ` to define your preference for local time. This value may be different from what other users on your system are using.

Setting the `TZ` Variable

When the environment variable `TZ` is found and has a properly defined value, the `tzset()` function configures your local time zone. This configured time zone is used by the rest of the date and time functions where necessary. If the value `TZ` is not defined, or is incorrectly set, the `tzset()` function falls back on the following zone info file:

```
/usr/lib/zoneinfo/localtime
```

Failing this, the UTC time is assumed.

To configure your session for eastern standard time and no daylight saving time, you can use the following:

```
bash$ export TZ=EST05
```

This line sets the time zone name to `EST`, and because it is west of the prime meridian, the offset is a positive `05` hours (think of this as local time + five hours = UTC). You can configure eastern daylight saving time as follows:

```
bash$ export TZ=EST05EDT
```

If you need more information on time zone configuration, a good place to start is the man page for `tzset(3)`. You can find more advanced information in the `tzfile(5)` man pages.

Understanding the Current Linux Date and Time

The date and time under UNIX is computed as the number of seconds since epoch time. Because epoch time is a UTC time, all dates and times are managed in the UTC time zone. With the appropriate local time zone configured, however, you don't need to think about time zones. They are all managed for you.

Assume, for simplicity's sake, that you are in the UTC time zone and the date is January 2, 1970, at midnight; in this case, the clock value is calculated as follows:

$$1 \text{ day} \times 24 \text{ hours} \times 60 \text{ minutes} \times 60 \text{ seconds} = 86400$$

After the first day in England then, the Linux clock would show a value of `86400`. In one second, the clock would show the value `86401`.

Defining the Date and Time Data Type

Originally, this time and date value was stored in the C `long` integer data type. As time passed, and as standardization efforts got under way, it was recognized that storing the value here was not good for long-range planning. The capacity of the `long` integer was going to run out.

If the precision of the `long` integer were to be exceeded, a number of problems would develop. One problem is that through an overflow, the `signed long` integer would become a negative number (based on its 2's complement representation). Then any computation that involved adding or subtracting time would end up incorrect.

Understanding Why Time Is Running Out

As time marches on, second by second, the Linux clock time starts to accumulate. On January 1, 1999, the approximate clock time is 915208499 seconds since epoch time. Considering that the maximum positive value of a `long` data type is 2147483647, the clock is fast approaching its limit.

In fact, time runs out for the `long` data type on January 19, 2038, at 03:14:07 UTC. The very next second after that will cause the 31-bit positive number to roll over to a 32-bit value. In 2's complement form, this makes it a negative number because the most significant bit is changed to a 1-bit.

This change might not affect the system clock because it probably treats the time as a 32-bit unsigned value anyway. Therefore, the clock will continue to count. However, this change will break all the code that computes the difference in time between two different dates because the sign of the epoch time has become a negative number.

Just when everyone has forgotten the woes of Year 2000 testing, all the old UNIX systems will need to undergo Year 2038 testing. This fact has already become a problem for some types of businesses. Take today's current date and add 40 or 50 years to it to compute the maturity date of a long bond or a mortgage termination date, and you have already gone beyond the year 2038.

Discovering the `time_t` Data Type

Because it was recognized that the `long` integer data type was going to overflow in the near future, it was decided that the date and time deserved their own special data type: `time_t`. This way, the underlying data type could be changed at a future date. As long as the software used the data type correctly, a simple recompile would automatically take care of the rest.

On my Linux system, the `time_t` value is still a `long` integer data type. To check it on your system, look at the include file time.h. Provided it has not changed, you should find the following line within it:

13

```
typedef __time_t time_t;
```

Just above this `typedef` statement should be this line:

```
#include <gnu/types.h>
```

Checking in that include file, you'll discover that type `__time_t` is defined as follows:

```
typedef long int __time_t;
```

Tracing back the evidence should lead you to conclude that the GNU software used on a Linux platform has yet to change the definition of type `time_t` to address the Year 2038 problem.

A future definition for type `time_t` might be the `unsigned long` data type. It provides 32 bits and should at least see us all past retirement! Longer range planning, however, suggests that it might be changed to an `unsigned long long` integer, which is a 64-bit value.

> When you're writing new code, assume that the type of the `time_t` value will change in signed-ness and size. Never use `long` to store a time value, and never assume that the `time_t` value will always be 32 bits. This data type is subject to change.

Obtaining the Date and Time Using `time()`

To obtain the current system date and time from the Linux kernel, you call on the `time()` library function:

```
#include <time.h>

time_t time(time_t *t);
```

The single argument provided to the `time()` function is optional. When provided, it must point to a `time_t` variable that is to receive the current date and time in epoch time. It will be the same value returned by the function. Consider this example:

```
time_t cur_time;

time(&cur_time);
```

When you do not want to have the value passed back this way, simply provide a `null` pointer:

```
time_t cur_time;

cur_time = time(0);
```

The reason the `time()` argument is necessary might seem curious, but it does prove to be convenient at times.

Although the epoch time is useful to the Linux kernel, you must convert it into various other forms to display it or to work with its components. In the next section, you will examine the library functions that are available to perform such tasks.

Working with Time Conversion Functions

All date and time functions in the following sections require that you include the include file time.h, as follows. It defines the function prototypes and the associated data types that are needed.

```
#include <time.h>
```

In the following sections, you will look at ways to convert

- `time_t` values into ASCII date/time strings
- `time_t` values into the date/time components (such as hour, minute, second, month, day, year, and so on)
- date/time components into ASCII date/time strings
- date/time components into `time_t` values

The `ctime()` Function

The `ctime()` function shown here is perhaps the easiest and most well known of the date and time conversion functions to use. This function takes the `time_t` value as input and converts it into an ASCII string that can be displayed.

```
char *ctime(const time_t *timep);
```

The `ctime()` function requires a `time_t` pointer provided as the argument. This pointer points to the time variable that contains the time and date to be converted.

The following example obtains the current system date and passes it to `ctime()`. The string pointer returned is then displayed:

```
time_t td;     /* Time and Date */

time(&td);     /* Get current date */
printf("Today is %s", ctime(&td) );
```

The `printf()` function output is a date and time string of the following form:

```
Mon Jan 18 22:14:07 2038
```

The function `ctime()` returns a pointer to an internal static character buffer. The value returned is valid only until the next call to `ctime()` takes place. If you must save this return value, you should copy it to a buffer of your own.

One annoying aspect of this returned date string is that a `newline` character is placed at the end (in the sample `printf()` call, notice that you do not need to supply `\n`).

13

The `localtime()` and `gmtime()` Functions

Programmers often need direct access to the date and time components. The `time_t` data type may be a convenient container, but it is not always convenient to compute from. To extract the date components from the `time_t` value, you can call on the `localtime()` or `gmtime()` functions:

```
struct tm *localtime(const time_t *timep);

struct tm *gmtime(const time_t *timep);
```

The `localtime()` function returns time and date components according to the local time. To obtain time components according to the UTC time zone, use the `gmtime()` function instead (note that the function is named based on the older GMT standard). The use of these functions is otherwise identical, so I will focus on the use of `localtime()` in the following description.

The input argument is a pointer to a `time_t` value. The returned result is a pointer to a static structure within the function. This result is valid only until the next call to `localtime()`. If you need to save these values, you must copy them to your own private structure.

In the following example, you fetch the current date using `time()`. Then you supply the returned `time_t` value to the function `localtime()`. You will copy the returned results in this example, as if you need to keep the component values for a long period of time:

```
time_t dt;     /* Current date */
struct tm dc; /* Date components */

time(&td);     /* Get current date */
dc = *localtime(&dt);
```

Because the function returns a pointer, you use the asterisk to indirect through that pointer. This action causes the structure to be copied to the local `struct tm dc` in the assignment.

The `tm` Structure

In this section, you'll inspect the form and content of the C structure `tm`. This structure is used by the `localtime()`, `gmtime()`, and `mktime()` functions (you will look at `mktime()` later in this lesson). The structure is defined as follows:

```
struct tm {
    int   tm_sec;     /* seconds */
    int   tm_min;     /* minutes */
    int   tm_hour;    /* hours (0-23) */
    int   tm_mday;    /* day of the month (1-31) */
```

```
    int   tm_mon;     /* month (0-11) */
    int   tm_year;    /* year */
    int   tm_wday;    /* day of the week (0-6) */
    int   tm_yday;    /* day in the year (0-365) */
    int   tm_isdst;   /* daylight saving time */
};
```

This C structure is defined in the include file time.h. The individual members of this structure are documented in Table 13.1.

TABLE 13.1 THE `tm` STRUCTURE MEMBERS

Member	*Description*
`tm_sec`	The number of seconds after the minute. Normally, the range is `0` to `59`, but this value can be as high as `61` to allow for leap seconds.
`tm_min`	The number of minutes after each hour. It ranges in value from `0` to `59`.
`tm_hour`	The hour past midnight. It ranges from `0` to `23`.
`tm_mday`	The day of the month. It ranges from `1` to `31`.
`tm_mon`	The month of the year. It ranges from `0` to `11`.
`tm_year`	The year, expressed as years since 1900. This value is `100` for the year 2000.
`tm_wday`	The day of the week with the range of `0` to `6`. Day `0` is Sunday, day `1` is Monday, and so on.
`tm_yday`	The day of the year with the range of `0` to `365`.
`tm_isdst`	A tri-state flag. When positive, it indicates that daylight saving time is in effect at the time described. A `0` indicates that daylight saving time is not in effect. A negative value indicates that this information is not available.

The following are some common sources of errors when displaying information from this structure:

- Forgetting to add one to the `tm_mon` value to arrive at the month number `1` to `12`
- Forgetting that 1900 should be added to `tm_year` to obtain a year-2000–compliant date
- Forgetting to allow for the fact that `tm_isdst` is a tri-state flag (see the next section for details)

Using the `tm_isdst` Structure Member Correctly

The `tm_isdst` structure member is a tri-state flag. Being a tri-state flag, it has the following three states:

- `tm_isdst` is a positive (nonzero) value. This state indicates that daylight saving time is in effect.
- `tm_isdst` is `0`. This state indicates that daylight saving time is not in effect.
- `tm_isdst` is a negative value. This state indicates that daylight information is not known or not available.

Using the `struct tm` Date Components

The following example obtains the current time and then saves the pointer to the returned `struct tm` structure. Using the pointer returned from `localtime()`, you then print the date and time in a format of your own choosing.

```
time_t td;               /* Current Date */
struct tm *dcp;          /* Date components */

time(&td);
dcp = localtime(&td);

printf("%02d/%02d/%04d %02d:%02d:%02d\n",
    dcp->tm_mon + 1,     /* Month */
    dcp->tm_mday,        /* Day */
    dcp->tm_year + 1900, /* Year */
    dcp->tm_hour,        /* Hour */
    dcp->tm_min,         /* Minute */
    dcp->tm_sec);        /* Second */
```

When this example code is executed, you get the following output:

```
01/01/1999 13:32:17
```

The `asctime()` Function

The `asctime()` function can take the date and time components from the `struct tm` structure and compose an ASCII-formatted date. The function prototype is as follows:

```
char *asctime(const struct tm *timeptr);
```

The single argument is a pointer to a `struct tm` structure, which is used as input to format a date string. The returned pointer is to a static character buffer that is valid only until the next call to `asctime()`. You should copy it if you need the result for longer term use. The resulting output string is in the same format as the `ctime()` function.

The `tzset()` Function

Earlier, you learned that the `tzset()` function is responsible for establishing your definition of local time. This function looks for the exported `TZ` environment variable and falls back to the system-configured zoneinfo file if it is not defined.

The `tzset()` function is called on by any of the library date functions that need to know about the configured local time for this session. For example, after the function `localtime()` returns, you know that the function `tzset()` has been called because it must know about local time.

After the function `tzset()` has been called, it does not need to be called again. If, however, you cannot be certain that it has been called, you should call it when you need the local time zone information.

The side effect of calling function `tzset()` is that certain external variables are assigned values. These external variables indicate to the date library routines what the local time zone is.

Introducing the `tzset()` External Variables

The side effect of calling the function `tzset()` is to define values for the following external variables:

```
extern long int timezone;
extern char *tzname[2];
extern int daylight;
```

Understanding External Variable `timezone`

The value `timezone` is the number of seconds you must add to your local time to arrive at UTC time. If you are in the eastern standard time zone, you need to add five hours to the local time to arrive at UTC time. To configure the external variable `timezone` for plus five hours, the value `+18000` seconds is stored there.

Understanding External Variable `daylight`

The value of external variable `daylight` is a flag variable:

- When variable `daylight` is `true` (nonzero), daylight saving time is in effect.
- When variable `daylight` is `false` (`0`), daylight saving time is not in effect.

Understanding External Array `tzname[]`

The array of two character strings `tzname[]` provides the name strings of two time zones. The normal time zone string is provided in `tzname[0]`, and the daylight saving time zone is provided in `tzname[1]`. Examples might be `EST` and `EDT` for eastern standard time and eastern daylight saving time, respectively.

When daylight saving time is not in effect, then array elements `tzname[0]` and `tzname[1]` point to the same C string describing the time zone.

Using External Array tzname[]

To display the current time zone in effect, you use code like this:

```
int x;      /* Subscript variable */

tzset();    /* Make sure externs are set */
x = ( daylight != 0 ? 1 : 0 );

printf("Zone is '%s'\n", tzname[x]);
```

The procedure used in the sample code to determine the time zone name is as follows:

1. Call function `tzset()` unless you can be certain it has already been called.
2. Test the external variable `daylight` to see whether daylight saving time is in effect. If it is `true` (nonzero), set subscript `x` to `1`. Otherwise, set subscript `x` to `0`.
3. Using the subscript `x` from step 2, the time zone name is given by `tzname[x]`.

> Do not rely on the external variable daylight to be exactly the value 1 or 0. The documentation simply states that this value is nonzero if daylight saving time is in effect.

The mktime() Function

If you want to construct a `time_t` value based on a specific date, you need to use the `mktime()` function. The function prototype is as follows:

```
time_t mktime(struct tm *timeptr);
```

The `mktime()` function requires a pointer to the input/output `struct tm` structure. This structure contributes date and time components that are used to compute a `time_t` value. You will also see later that some values are returned in this structure.

Testing for Errors

If the values in the `struct tm` are such that a date cannot be computed, then the value

```
(time_t)(-1)
```

is returned (a `time_t` value with all one bits). You might get this result when the `tm_year` is set before 1970 or when nonexistent dates are used. Two examples of bad dates are February 30 and June 35. Because the underlying data type for the `time_t` data type may not always be signed, always compare with the `time_t` casted `-1` as shown.

Setting Input Members of `struct tm`

Not all the `struct tm` members are used for input when passed to the `mktime()` function. The following members, however, must be defined so that they can be used for input. These members are input only and are not altered:

- `tm_sec` (second: `0` to `61`)
- `tm_min` (minute: `0` to `59`)
- `tm_hour` (hour: `0` to `23`)
- `tm_mday` (day of month: `1` to `31`)
- `tm_mon` (month: `0` to `11`)
- `tm_year` (year: year 2000 is value `100`)
- `tm_isdst` (positive for daylight saving; `0` if no daylight saving in effect)

Be sure to make the `tm_mon` member a zero-based month value (`0` to `11`).

Altered Members of `struct tm`

The `struct tm` structure contains several members, and some of that information overlaps. For this reason, the `mktime()` function ignores some members as input data. Instead, these ignored entries are recomputed from the other input values and then stored in the structure that is passed.

The following members are ignored as input but are recomputed and altered before the function returns:

- `tm_wday` is ignored as input and is recomputed for output.
- `tm_yday` is ignored as input and is recomputed for output.

The fact that these two values are recomputed allows you to plug in a date and time and then call `mktime()`. The returned values in the structure tell you what weekday and what day of the year it is.

> Do not forget to set `tm_isdst` before calling `mktime()`. This input value determines whether daylight saving time is in effect for the local date and time specified in the other members. Failure to set this value correctly can cause the computed UTC `time_t` value to be incorrect by the amount of the daylight saving time difference.

> Because the `tm_wday` and `tm_yday` values are replaced by recomputed values, never pass a constant or read-only structure to `mktime()`.

Putting `mktime()` to Work

Listing 13.1 illustrates a small C program that computes a `time_t` value for January 1, 2000, at midnight.

LISTING 13.1 A SIMPLE `mktime()` EXAMPLE

```
1:  #include <stdio.h>
2:  #include <stdlib.h>
3:  #include <errno.h>
4:  #include <time.h>
5:
6:  int
7:  main(int argc,char *argv[]) {
8:      time_t td;          /* Current Date */
9:      struct tm dc;       /* Date components */
10:
11:     dc.tm_mon = 0;      /* January */
12:     dc.tm_mday = 1;     /* 1, */
13:     dc.tm_year = 100;   /* Year 2000 */
14:     dc.tm_hour = 0;     /* Midnight */
15:     dc.tm_min  = 0;
16:     dc.tm_sec  = 0;
17:     dc.tm_isdst= 0;     /* Not D.S.T. */
18:
19:     td = mktime(&dc);   /* Make time_t */
20:
21:     /* Verify : */
22:     printf("Date: %s",ctime(&td));
23:
24:     return 0;
25: }
```

The highlights of this program can be summarized as follows:

1. The `struct tm` value that you will fill in with the necessary input values for `mktime()` is declared (line 9).
2. The date and time of the event are defined (lines 11 to 16).
3. So that the time given is not daylight saving time, `dc.tm_isdst` is set to `false` (line 17).

4. The function mktime() is called; then it is passed input/output structure dc (line 19). The time_t value returned is assigned to variable td (declared in line 8).
5. The returned time_t value is converted back to an ASCII date string, which is displayed for verification (line 22).

When you compile the program and run it, you get the following output:

```
bash$ ./a.out
Date: Sat Jan  1 00:00:00 2000
bash$
```

Indeed, this program reports the date that you used as input to mktime().

You have now covered the details of converting a time_t value into strings and converting a time_t value into its individual date and time components. Now you also know how to convert those components back into a time_t value or directly into an ASCII string for display purposes.

Customizing Date and Time Formats

The string format of the date and time can vary considerably with the preference of the user. Because this issue is critical in the mind of some users, I will spend some time explaining how you can deal with this issue effectively.

You have already looked at the ctime() and asctime() functions, which format the provided time_t value into a string. These routines force a particular chosen date and time format on you.

Introducing Function strftime()

Different applications and people have varying requirements for how a date and its time should be displayed. For this reason, the function strftime() was made available to C programmers. Its function prototype is as follows:

```
size_t strftime(
    char *s,
    size_t max,
    const char *format,
    const struct tm *tm);
```

Table 13.2 explains the arguments for the strftime() function.

TABLE 13.2 FUNCTION `strftime()` ARGUMENTS

Argument	*Description*
`s`	This argument points to the receiving character array. Formatted characters are placed here up to `max` characters.
`max`	This value specifies the maximum number of characters to place into the receiving buffer `s`.
`format`	This argument is a `sprintf()`-styled format string, except that the format specifiers are unique to the `strftime()` function.
`tm`	This argument is a pointer to a `struct tm` structure that is inspected for date and time components. These values are used as required by the format string.

The `strftime()` function is quite a flexible formatting function. It is similar to the `sprintf()` function in the way that it is used. The first argument is the buffer address that receives the formatted result. However, unlike `sprintf()`, the `strftime()` function has the second argument `max` to prevent the result from overstepping the buffer's bounds.

Understanding the Return Values

The `strftime()` function returns the number of characters formatted into the receiving buffer. This count does not include the `NUL` byte, which is placed at the end, however.

If the buffer is not sufficiently large, the value `max` is returned, indicating that `max` characters were placed into the buffer. However, because no room is available for the `NUL` byte when this happens, do not expect it to be there.

Understanding the `strftime()` Format Specifiers

The `strftime()` format specifiers are quite different from the `sprintf()` variety. Table 13.3 lists the format specifiers that are available. Notice that each specifier starts with the percent character and is followed by a letter. All other text in the format string is copied verbatim. To include one percent character, use two successive percent characters.

TABLE 13.3 FORMAT SPECIFIERS FOR `strftime()`

Specifier	*Description*
%a	The abbreviated weekday name is substituted according to the locale.
%A	The full weekday name is substituted according to the locale.
%b	The abbreviated month name is substituted according to the locale.
%B	The full month name is substituted according to the locale.
%c	The preferred date and time representation for the current locale.

Specifier	*Description*
`%d`	The day of the month in decimal.
`%H`	The hour of the day in 24-hour form (`00` to `23`).
`%I`	The hour in 12-hour form (01 to 12).
`%j`	The day of the year as a decimal number (`001` to `365`).
`%m`	The month as a decimal number (`01` to `12`).
`%M`	The minute as a decimal number.
`%p`	The string `AM` or `PM` according to the time.
`%S`	The second as a decimal value.
`%U`	The week number of the current year expressed as a decimal number. The first Sunday is considered the first day of the first week.
`%W`	The week number of the current year expressed as a decimal number. The first Monday is considered the first day of the first week.
`%w`	The day of the week as a decimal number (`0` to `6`).
`%x`	The preferred date representation without time for the current locale.
`%X`	The preferred time representation without date for the current locale.
`%y`	The year without a century (`00` to `99`).
`%Y`	The year with the century.
`%Z`	The time zone or zone abbreviation.
`%%`	The single character `%` itself.

Testing the `strftime()` Function

So that you can test-drive this function, I've provided Listing 13.2. This program uses the `mktime()` function to fabricate the `time_t` value for the morning of April Fool's Day in the year 2000.

LISTING 13.2 A TEST PROGRAM FOR `strftime()`

```
#include <stdio.h>
#include <stdlib.h>
#include <string.h>
#include <errno.h>
#include <time.h>

int
main(int argc,char *argv[]) {
```

continues

LISTING 13.2 CONTINUED

```
9:      time_t td;          /* Current Date */
10:     struct tm dc;       /* Date components */
11:     char sdate[64];     /* Formatted date result */
12:     char fmt[128];      /* Input line/format string */
13:     char *cp;
14:
15:     dc.tm_mon = 3;      /* April */
16:     dc.tm_mday = 1;     /* 1, */
17:     dc.tm_year = 100;   /* Year 2000 */
18:     dc.tm_hour = 11;    /* Just before noon */
19:     dc.tm_min  = 59;
20:     dc.tm_sec  = 30;
21:     dc.tm_isdst= 0;     /* Not D.S.T. */
22:
23:     td = mktime(&dc);   /* Make time_t */
24:
25:     while ( fgets(fmt,sizeof fmt,stdin) ) {
26:         if ( (cp = strchr(fmt,'\n')) != 0 )
27:             *cp = 0;    /* Remove the newline */
28:         strftime(sdate,sizeof sdate,fmt,&dc);
29:         printf("Format='%s':\n%s\n\n", fmt,sdate);
30:     }
31:
32:     return 0;
33: }
```

The following summarizes the important points of this program:

1. The program reads from standard input until the end of file is reached (the `while` loop at line 25). Each input text line is read into character buffer `fmt[]`.
2. The newline character at the end of the input line in `fmt[]` is removed (lines 26 and 27).
3. The input line `fmt[]` is now passed to the `strftime()` function as the format argument (argument three, line 28).
4. The April Fool's date components have already been established (lines 15 to 21) and are used as input to the `strftime()` function (still line 28).
5. The formatted result is displayed (line 29).

Listing 13.3 shows the input data that you can use. You can find this file, 13LST03.txt, on the supplied CD. You should be able to duplicate the results by supplying it as the standard input file.

LISTING 13.3 TEST DATA FOR LISTING 13.2

```
%c
%a %b %d/%y  (Week %W)
%a %B %d, %Y TIME %X
%A %b %d, %Y Zone %Z
%A %B %d, %Y (weekday # %w)
%x  **  %X
%m/%d/%Y  %I:%M %p
%Y/%d/%m %H:%M:%S
%Y-%m-%d  (day %j of year)
```

Running the Test Program

Now you can run this data through the program. Listing 13.4 shows the session output.

LISTING 13.4 THE `strftime()` SESSION OUTPUT

```
bash$ gcc -Wall -D_GNU_SOURCE 13LST02.c
bash$ ./a.out <13LST03.txt
Format='%c':
Sat Apr  1 11:59:30 2000

Format='%a %b %d/%y  (Week %W)':
Sat Apr 01/00  (Week 13)

Format='%a %B %d, %Y TIME %X':
Sat April 01, 2000 TIME 11:59:30

Format='%A %b %d, %Y Zone %Z':
Saturday Apr 01, 2000 Zone EST

Format='%A %B %d, %Y (weekday # %w)':
Saturday April 01, 2000 (weekday # 6)

Format='%x  **  %X':
04/01/00  **  11:59:30

Format='%m/%d/%Y  %I:%M %p':
04/01/2000  11:59 AM

Format='%Y/%d/%m %H:%M:%S':
2000/01/04 11:59:30

Format='%Y-%m-%d  (day %j of year)':
2000-04-01  (day 092 of year)

bash$
bash$
```

Listing 13.4 shows the compile step (line 1) and how you run the test program using file 13LST03.txt as standard input. The following points can be made about the sample session:

1. The `%c` specifier is tried (line 3). The results on the following line (line 4) show what your current locale is configured to show.
2. The abbreviated weekday name `%a`, the noncentury year format `%y`, and the week number `%W` are tried (lines 6 and 7).
3. Nonspecial characters are shown to be formatted as is (string `"TIME"` in this case) (lines 9 and 10). The locale-specific `%X` is also tried.
4. The zone specifier `%Z` and the nonabbreviated weekday name `%A` are tested (lines 12 and 13).
5. The 12-hour time format is tried with the `%I` and the AM/PM indicator `%p` (lines 21 and 22).
6. The day of the year specifier `%j` is tried (lines 27 and 28).

Understanding the Effects of Locale

Some of the format specifiers that `strftime()` supports format according to a *locale*. An example is the `%A` specifier (the full weekday name).

In the Linux context, the locale represents the set of language and cultural rules that are used on a particular host system. The locale defines the language used for certain messages, lexicographic conventions (such as date and time format), and the character set that is to be used.

The locale setting determines whether your system uses the English names for the days of the week or French names, for example. The names of the months are another aspect affected by locale. Lexicographical conventions such as the `%X` specifier dictate whether the time should be shown in 12- or 24-hour format, for example.

For more information about locale, view the man page for `locale(7)` on your system. Examining and configuring the locale for your system are beyond the scope of this book, however.

Summary

In this lesson, you learned how Linux keeps and manages time using the time-since-epoch value in the `time_t` data type. You learned about time zones as they apply to Linux and how to configure the local time zone for your session.

You also examined a number of functions that convert times and dates between different forms. You learned how to generate a `time_t` value with the help of the `mktime()` function. Finally, you used the `strftime()` function to format custom date and time strings.

Q&A

Q Why is the `time_t` value called *seconds since epoch time*?

A The `time_t` value represents the seconds since a certain point in time—specifically January 1, 1970, at midnight UTC.

Q Why should I always use the date type `time_t` instead of the more traditional `long` integer type?

A The data type will likely change in the near future to avoid the problem of overflowing the 31-bit limit of a positive number.

Q How do I compute the difference in days between two dates?

A Subtract the earlier `time_t` value from the later `time_t` value. The result is the difference in seconds. Divide that difference by the 86400, which is the number of seconds per day.

Q How do I compute the time and date of an event that must occur five days, three hours, and five minutes from now?

A Obtain the current date and time in the `time_t` data type. Add to this the value 5 times 86400, to forward-date it by five days. Then add 3 times 3600 to forward the time by three hours. Finally, add 5 times 60 seconds to arrive at the final time of the event.

Q How do I know when `mktime()` cannot convert the given `struct tm` structure into a valid `time_t` value?

A The value `(time_t)(-1)` is returned.

Q What must I be sure of before using any of the external variables `tzname[]`, `timezone`, or `daylight`?

A You must be certain that those values have been initialized. You can be sure of this fact when functions such as `localtime()` that need the time zone information have been previously called. If you have any doubt, you must call the function `tzset()`.

13

Workshop

You are encouraged to work through the quiz and the exercises to practice what you have learned before proceeding to the next lesson.

Quiz

1. What function do you use to obtain the current system date and time?
2. What function do you use to convert the `time_t` value into its date and time components?
3. What function takes the date and time components and converts them back into the `time_t` data type?
4. What are the two functions that return an ASCII string format date?
5. What function can you use to format a custom date string?
6. How can you tell whether the current system date and time are under daylight saving time?
7. What environment variable overrides your session's time zone?

Exercises

1. Write a new program that uses `getopt()`-styled command-line options. Name this new command `maketime`. It must support a `-t epoch` option, where the option argument value is the `time_t` time value in decimal. Be sure to use function `strtoul()` to perform the string to `unsigned long` conversion.

   When no `-t` option is given, obtain the current system date and time in its place.

   Finally, after processing the command-line options, if any, report the `time_t` value to standard output as a decimal number.
2. Using the program started in exercise 1, add a new command-line option `-f format`. When this option is present, do not print the final `time_t` value as in exercise 1. Call `strftime()` instead, using the supplied format string, and display its results. Make sure, however, that the `time_t` value prints if the option `-f` is omitted from the command line.
3. Using the program developed in exercise 2, add a new command-line option `-a days`, where `days` is the positive or negative number of days. When this option is provided, the specified number of days is to be added to the date and time value. This date and time will be the date given by the option `-t` or the current system date and time if `-t` has not been provided. Be sure to use function `strtol()` to convert the `-a` option argument to a `long` data type value.

The program that is completed in exercise 3 is sufficient to be of assistance to the shell programmer. The `maketime` command can take the current date and time and convert it to a `time_t` value for further computations:

```
LTIME='maketime'
```

The shell programmer then can perform some computations on it and turn it into a new date:

```
LTIME=$((LTIME+86400))
```

The variable `LTIME` now contains tomorrow's date, which can be formatted as follows:

```
maketime -t $LTIME -f'%c'
```

The `-a` option from exercise 3 provides a more convenient way to add one day to the current date and time:

```
maketime -a1 -f'%c'
```

HOUR 14

Userid, Password, and Group Management

Introduction to Linux Management

When you log in to your Linux system, you provide a username and a password at the login prompt. The login program has to look up that username in a database and obtain your registered password. The login program then encrypts the password you supply and compares the two encrypted passwords. If they are the same, the login program lets you pass in peace.

After you are logged in, however, you become just a number to the Linux kernel. As such, the kernel can manage things more easily. To find out what number you are, you can use the `id` command:

```
bash$ id
uid=507(student1) gid=104(user) groups=104(user)
bash$
```

Here, the `id` command indicates that the user named `student1` is uid number `507` and is a member of group number `104`. You see the original user and group names in brackets, but believe it or not, they have to be looked up in databases. In this lesson, you will look at the facilities that Linux provides to look up user and group information.

Understanding Username and uid Numbers

The `id` command reports that user `student1` is uid `507`. Where does this number come from? What is a user ID? Is it the same as the username? I will answer these questions next.

The name that you supply when you log in to your system is the *username*. In the example given, the username used is `student1`. This name is the human-friendly identification of you as a user. The login program looks up this name in a database and determines that the user `student1` is uid number `507` in this case. Sometimes the username is just referred to as the *account* or *user*.

The *uid number* is what Linux uses to keep track of who you are and what permissions you have. The C data type used for this value is the type `uid_t`. This value is assigned to you by the administrator of the system. It is a unique number given to you when your login account is created.

Using the Term *User ID*

The term *user ID* gets used a lot in UNIX circles. Most of the time, it refers to the username of a user. Sometimes, however, it is loosely used to describe your identity as a user, whether that means your username or your uid number. In essence, they are equivalent, although they represent different manifestations of the same identity.

Understanding Username root

The uid number `0` is special under Linux. It is known as the *root username*, though it need not be called root. Another term used for this user account is *super user*. The uid number `0` enjoys unrestricted access to the Linux system as a whole. This is why this account is very strictly guarded.

If you set up and run your own Linux system, however, you are allowed to be root when you want to be. Although being root might be great fun, you should do most of your non-administration chores in a nonroot account. This way, your system can use the permission mechanisms present to protect itself from harm when accidents occur (and they will).

Understanding Group Name and gid Numbers

Like the uid number, the *gid number* is used by Linux to refer to a group. The C data type used for this value is `gid_t`. This number is defined by the administrator of the system who creates the group.

Externally, users like you and me refer to the *group name*. The group name is often just referred to as *group*. These terms are the user-friendly equivalents of the gid values that are used internally.

The group database permits one user to be a member of multiple groups. This is why the `id` command lists the last field as `groups=104(user)` in the earlier example. If `student1` had been a member of other groups, those other group names and gid numbers would have been listed there also.

Understanding gid `0`

Like the uid value of `0`, the gid value of `0` grants unrestricted access to resources at the group level. Although this is not the same as being the super user, it still grants a lot of access. Consequently, this group is usually granted only to the root account or a special administration account.

The Identity Functions

Before you can look up anything, you need to be able to determine just who you are. When the `id` command runs, it has to find out what uid number and gid number it is running under. To get this information, it has to call on some information retrieval functions.

The `getuid()` and `geteuid()` Functions

The `getuid()` and `geteuid()` functions shown here allow the process to determine what real uid number it is operating under and which effective uid number it is operating under, respectively. Both of these functions return the id number in the data type `uid_t`.

```
#include <unistd.h>

uid_t getuid(void);
uid_t geteuid(void);
```

The `geteuid()` function returns the effective uid number. A UNIX process, through special arrangements, can become another uid number temporarily. For example, the `mailx` program temporarily switches to the `mail` uid number so that it can access directories and files that can be accessed only by the `mail` user account. The `geteuid()` function returns the current uid number in effect at the time of the call.

The `getuid()` function, on the other hand, returns the real uid number. Even if the process has temporarily switched to another user such as `mail`, the `getuid()` function returns your real uid number.

There are no errors to test for because these functions always succeed.

The `getgid()` and `getegid()` Functions

The `id` command must also find out about the gid number it is operating as. Two companion functions—`getgid()` and `getegid()`—are provided for this purpose:

```
#include <unistd.h>

gid_t getgid(void);
gid_t getegid(void);
```

Just as with the uid number, real and effective gid values can be obtained. The function `getgid()` returns the real gid, whereas the function `getegid()` returns the effective gid. Both functions return the id number in the data type `gid_t`.

There are no errors to test for because these functions always succeed.

uid and gid Numbers Examples

You can write a simple equivalent of the `id` command in C as follows:

```
printf("Real userid:  %ld\n",(long)getuid());
printf("Real groupid: %ld\n",(long)getgid());
```

You also can display the effective uid and gid numbers by using the `geteuid()` and `getegid()` functions instead:

```
printf("Effective userid:  %ld\n",(long)geteuid());
printf("Effective groupid: %ld\n",(long)getegid());
```

Understanding the /etc/passwd File

The information database for usernames and passwords has to be stored somewhere on the Linux system. The database used is actually a simple text file named /etc/passwd. This file is formatted as a number of different colon-separated fields. The following is an example of a small /etc/passwd file:

```
root:bbCsSRB7BZfM.:0:0:root:/root:/bin/bash
bin:*:1:1:bin:/bin:
daemon:*:2:2:daemon:/sbin:
adm:*:3:4:adm:/var/adm:
lp:*:4:7:lp:/var/spool/lpd:
mail:*:8:12:mail:/var/spool/mail:
news:*:9:13:news:/var/lib/news:
uucp:*:10:14:uucp:/var/spool/uucppublic:
man:*:13:15:man:/usr/man:
postmaster:*:14:12:postmaster:/var/spool/mail:/bin/bash
www:*:99:103:web server:/etc/httpd:/bin/bash
nobody:*:-1:100:nobody:/dev/null:
ftp:*:404:1::/home/ftp:/bin/bash
```

```
jan:/WzbqfJwMa/pA:503:100:Jan Hassebroek:/home/jhassebr:/bin/bash
postgres:gXQrO/hNwy5IQ:506:102:Postgres SQL:/usr/local/postgres:
➥/bin/bash
student1:6YNV6cIZxiM2E:507:104:Student 01:/home/student1:/bin/bash
bash$
```

Table 14.1 describes the fields using user `jhassebr` as an example.

TABLE 14.1 THE /ETC/PASSWD FIELDS

Field Number	*Value Shown*	*Description*
1	`jan`	The username
2	`/WzbqfJwMa/pA`	The encrypted password for this user
3	`503`	The uid number for this user
4	`100`	The gid number for this user
5	`Jan Hassebroek`	The name of the user. This Comment field is also known as the GECOS field
6	`/home/jhassebr`	The home directory for this user
7	`/bin/bash`	The shell program for this user

Notice that field 5 contains the user's full name.

Understanding the Comment Field

The Comment field is also known as the GECOS field, presumably due to an influence from the Honeywell GECOS operating system in times past. This field can be subdivided into comma-delimited subfields, as explained in Table 14.2.

TABLE 14.2 THE COMMENT/GECOS FIELD AS SUBFIELDS

Field	*Sample Data*	*Description*
1	`Jan Hassebroek`	The user's full name
2	`3rd Floor`	Office location
3	`x5823`	Office telephone or extension number
4	`905-555-1212`	Home phone number

In the /etc/passwd field, this data would appear as follows:

```
...:Jan Hassebroek,3rd Floor,x5823,905-555-1212:...
```

These extra subfields are optional.

Using the & Feature of the Comment Field

The Comment field also supports a substitution character: the ampersand (`&`). When this character appears, the username from field 1 is substituted, and the first letter is capitalized. The Comment field could have taken advantage of this feature as follows:

```
...:& Hassebroek,3rd Floor,x5823,905-555-1212:...
```

When this is done, the username `jan` is substituted for the ampersand character, and the *j* is capitalized. After the substitution is complete, the first subfield would have the name `Jan Hassebroek`.

Searching the Password Database

When you type the `id` command, this command must obtain the username from scanning the /etc/passwd file. What would you do if you had to write the `id` command? Here are the basic steps involved:

1. Obtain the effective uid value from `geteuid()`.
2. Open the /etc/passwd file.
3. Read a text line.
4. Parse the text line into fields.
5. Compare the uid value against the uid value in field 3. If they do not match, go back to step 3.
6. Report the username from field 1 and the uid value from step 1.

You would have to do more than this to handle the gid value and group membership as well.

The problem with this approach is that every program would have its own rendition of this type of code. It also ties the software to a particular implementation of the /etc/passwd file.

This type of lookup is performed so frequently that the system provides its own set of library functions for you to use. They provide the following benefits:

- You are freed from the implementation details of the password database.
- You are saved from having to write and test frequently required code.

> Newer distributions of Linux are configured to use *shadow password* files. This feature improves your system security by keeping the encrypted passwords hidden. The passwords are stored in a secured, separate file that cannot be read by normal users.
>
> If your Linux system uses a shadow password file, then you might see only an asterisk (*) or an x in the password field.

The Password Database Routines

To ease the burden of searching the /etc/passwd file, you can use the `getpwent()` function:

```
#include <pwd.h>
#include <sys/types.h>

struct passwd *getpwent(void);

void setpwent(void);

void endpwent(void);
```

The idea of these routines is that you call `getpwent()` to automatically open the /etc/passwd file. Then the first database entry with the fields already parsed and converted for you is returned. This return value is a pointer to a static structure, which is valid only until the next call to `getpwent()` is made.

If the first entry is not the one you want, you can continue to call `getpwent()` for more password file entries until it returns a `null` pointer. The `null` pointer indicates that it reached the end of the database (or an error occurred).

If you are done processing password file entries, you can then call on `endpwent()` to close the implicitly opened password database file. Otherwise, if you need to scan the database again, you can call `setpwent()` to rewind to the start of the database. Calling the function `setpwent()` should be considered more efficient than calling `endpwent()` because using the latter function would require another file open the next time `getpwent()` is called.

Understanding the `passwd` Structure

The function `getpwent()` returns a pointer to a static structure. Its contents are valid only until the next call to `getpwent()`. The `passwd` structure definition looks like this:

```
struct passwd {
    char    *pw_name;    /* user name */
    char    *pw_passwd;  /* user password */
```

```
    uid_t   pw_uid;      /* user id */
    gid_t   pw_gid;      /* group id */
    char    *pw_gecos;   /* comment field */
    char    *pw_dir;     /* home directory */
    char    *pw_shell;   /* shell program */
};
```

If you review the layout of the /etc/passwd fields, you can see a one-to-one correspondence between them and this structure. The nice thing is that all the grunt work has been done for you, including the numeric conversions of the uid and gid numbers into the `uid_t` and `gid_t` data types, respectively.

With the password database routines and this structure made available, you are now free to forget about the implementation of the password database. Furthermore, the library routines themselves perform all the data conversions for you. This way, you can focus on application tasks instead.

Handling Errors for `getpwent()`

When the `getpwent()` function returns a `null` pointer, it can indicate that the end of the password database was reached, or that an error occurred. You must check the `errno` value to distinguish between the end of file and an error.

The `ENOMEM` error can be posted to `errno` if some internal structures could not be allocated. However, note that success is never posted to `errno`. This requires that you clear the `errno` value before calling `getpwent()`. The following example shows how you might test for an error:

```
struct passwd *pwp;

errno = 0;          /* Clear error */
pwp = getpwent(); /* Get passwd entry */
if ( !pwp ) {
    if ( errno != 0 ) {
        perror("getpwent() failed!");
        abort();
    }
    /* Else end of password database */
}
```

The important point to remember is that you must clear the `errno` value before making the function call.

The `fgetpwent()` Function

Sometimes you might want to maintain a password file separately from the system password file. A private password file can protect access to certain server resources. To keep things simple and consistent, you can use the `fgetpwent()` function:

```
#include <stdio.h>
#include <pwd.h>
#include <sys/types.h>

struct passwd *fgetpwent(FILE *stream);
```

Notice that this function requires that you provide a `FILE` stream pointer. This use implies that you have opened the stream yourself and that the pointer represents a valid open `FILE`. Using this pointer also means that you are responsible for opening, rewinding, and closing the file.

The `fgetpwent()` file otherwise performs precisely the same as the `getpwent()` function. Each successive password entry is returned by a pointer to a `passwd` structure.

Note again that you should clear the `errno` value before calling `fgetpwent()` so that you can test for errors after the call. A returned `null` pointer can indicate that you reached the end or that an error occurred. The only currently documented error is `ENOMEM`.

If you supply a `null` or invalid pointer for the `stream` pointer argument, you experience a *Segmentation fault*. It might be changed to return the error `EINVAL` when the pointer is `null` (the reasoning is based on the fact that the `putpwent()` function currently checks for and posts this error).

The provision of this library function allows application designers to free themselves from the implementation details of using an application password database.

The `putpwent()` Function

The naming of the `putpwent()` function is not quite consistent with the `fgetpwent()` function, but the `putpwent()` function is indeed its counterpart. Whereas the `fgetpwent()` function lets you scan a password database of your choice, the `putpwent()` function shown here allows you to write a password database of your choice:

```
#include <stdio.h>
#include <pwd.h>
#include <sys/types.h>

int putpwent(const struct passwd *p, FILE *stream);
```

The input consists of the filled-in `passwd` structure passed in argument one by the pointer. The second argument must be an open `FILE` stream that is capable of writing.

The function returns the integer value `0` if the function succeeds. If an error occurs, `-1` is returned. The only documented error code is `EINVAL`, which is returned when an argument is provided with a `null` pointer.

Presumably, any I/O error could also be returned by the function, which has not been documented. Some possibilities include

- ENOSPC—When the disk being written to has run out of disk space.
- EIO—When the disk has developed an I/O error and cannot successfully write out its data. This might also apply to network errors for NFS-mounted files.
- EPIPE—If the opened stream is a pipe and is closed at the other end.

Note that you are not required to clear the errno value for this function because you always get a clear indication when an error occurs in the return value.

The getpwuid() Function

Recall that the id command has to take the uid number and convert it back to a username? Although the getpwent() function gives you the tool to do the lookup, it is not convenient. Because this need frequently arises, another convenience function—getpwuid()—has been provided for the purpose:

```
#include <pwd.h>
#include <sys/types.h>

struct passwd *getpwuid(uid_t uid);
```

To obtain the password entry for the current real uid, you can code something like this:

```
struct passwd *pwp;

if ( !(pwp = getpwuid(getgid())) )
    puts("No password entry found!");
else
    printf("user name %s\n",pwp->pw_name);
```

A uid being looked up might not have a password entry, so you should test for it this way.

To test for errors, you should clear errno first and then test errno if a null pointer is returned. The one documented error possibility for getpwuid() is ENOMEM.

The getpwnam() Function

Sometimes you need to look up the password entry by username. The login program needs to perform this task, for example. A convenience function—getpwnam()—has been provided for the occasion:

```
#include <pwd.h>
#include <sys/types.h>

struct passwd *getpwnam(const char * name);
```

The `getpwnam()` function simply takes a C string that contains the username and does the lookup for you. If a match is found in the password database, the pointer to the `passwd` structure is returned. If no match is found, or an error occurs, a `null` pointer is returned.

To display the home directory of the `mail` username, you might try the following:

```
struct passwd *pwp;

if ( (pwp = getpwnam("mail")) != 0 )
    printf("mail HOME=%s\n",pwp->pw_dir);
```

Because a `null` pointer returned may indicate an error, you should clear `errno` before calling `getpwnam()` and test for errors following the call. The only documented error for this function is `ENOMEM`.

The Group Database

The preceding sections covered the library functions that are available for managing the user and password database. Linux also supports the concept of groups and group membership. In the following sections, you will look at the facilities that are available to search and maintain the group database.

Introducing the /etc/group File

The group database has traditionally been a simple text file /etc/group. Its format is similar to the password database, as you can see in the small sample group file shown here:

```
root::0:root
bin::1:root,bin,daemon
daemon::2:root,bin,daemon
sys::3:root,bin,adm
adm::4:root,adm,daemon,wwg
lp::7:lp
mem::8:
kmem::9:
mail::12:mail
news::13:news
uucp::14:uucp
man::15:man
users::100:student1,jan
postgres::102:wwg
nogroup::-1:
nobody::-1:
```


The format of the group database is illustrated in Table 14.3.

TABLE 14.3 THE GROUP DATABASE FIELDS

Field Number	*Sample Data*	*Description*
1	`users`	The group name
2	`''`	The group password (if any; none is shown here)
3	`100`	The group id number
4	`student1,jan`	The list of usernames that belong to this group

Each text line in the /etc/group database is composed of colon-separated fields. The fourth field is a list of comma-separated usernames that belong to this group.

Working with the `getgrent()`, `setgrent()`, and `endgrent()` Functions

Just like the password database, the group database has its own set of functions for lookups—`getgrent()`, `setgrent()`, and `endgrent()`—as shown here:

```
#include <grp.h>
#include <sys/types.h>

struct group *getgrent(void);

void setgrent(void);

void endgrent(void);
```

The function `getgrent()` automatically opens the group database the first time it is called, or reopens it if it has been closed by the calling of the `endgrent()` function. To scan the database, you call the `getgrent()` function until a `null` pointer is returned. You can then rewind the database by calling `setgrent()` or simply close the database by calling `endgrent()`.

When `getgrent()` returns a `null` pointer, this result can indicate that an error occurred. To distinguish between the end of file and an error, you must test `errno`. You therefore must first clear `errno` before the call and then test `errno` after the call has returned a `null` pointer.

Understanding the `group` Structure

You should be able to see the correspondence between the group structure members and the group database file fields, as shown in the following. The `gr_name` entry points to a C string that contains the group name. The `gr_passwd` entry points to a C string containing the group's password, if any. If no password is configured, then it points to an empty string. It will not be a `null` pointer. The `gr_gid` member holds the `groupid` value in the data type `gid_t`.

```
struct group {
    char    *gr_name;   /* group name */
    char    *gr_passwd; /* group password */
    gid_t   gr_gid;     /* group id */
    char    **gr_mem;   /* group members */
};
```

The last structure member `gr_mem` points to a list of C strings. The last string pointer in this list is a `null` pointer to mark the end of the list. Each string in this list is the username that is a member of the group.

The following code shows how the entire group database can be scanned, with the group and member usernames listed as shown:

```
struct group *gp;
int x;

while ( (gp = getgrent()) != 0 ) {
    printf("gr_name='%s', gr_passwd='%s'\n",
        gp->gr_name,
        gp->gr_passwd);
    for ( x=0; gp->gr_mem[x] != 0; ++x )
        printf("  member='%s'\n",gp->gr_mem[x]);
}

endgrent(); /* Close the database */
```

Notice how the `for` loop tests for the `null` pointer in `gp->gr_mem[x]`.

The `fgetgrent()` Function

To process private copies of a group-formatted database, you can use the `fgetgrent()` function:

```
#include <stdio.h>
#include <grp.h>
#include <sys/types.h>

struct group *fgetgrent(FILE *stream);
```

The input argument requires an open `FILE` stream. The caller is responsible for all opens, rewinds, and closes on this `FILE` stream. The function `fgetgrent()` returns `null` if no more entries exist on the stream or an error occurs.

To test for the error, clear the errno value before making the call. The only documented error for this function is ENOMEM, but presumably, any other I/O error could also be posted.

Note that no putgrent() function or equivalent is available. If you need to write group database records, you have to write the code yourself.

The getgrgid() Function

Scanning the entire group database is not the most user-friendly way to convert the gid number into a group name. As a result, the getgrgid() convenience function has been provided:

```
#include <grp.h>
#include <sys/types.h>

struct group *getgrgid(gid_t gid);
```

The input argument is the gid number that might be obtained from getgid(), for example. The returned pointer is to a group structure. This pointer is valid until the next call to getgrgid(). If the returned pointer is null, then no matching gid was found, or an error occurred.

To determine whether an error occurred, the caller must clear errno before calling getgrgid(). The only documented error is ENOMEM.

The getgrnam() Function

The getgrnam() convenience function allows the caller to look up a group database record by group name:

```
#include <grp.h>
#include <sys/types.h>

struct group *getgrnam(const char *name);
```

The input argument to getgrnam() is a C string holding the group name to look up. The returned pointer result points to a static structure within the function. It is valid only until the next call to this function. If no match to the name can be made or an error occurs, the returned pointer is null.

To distinguish between a failed lookup and an error, you must clear the errno value before calling the function. The only documented error code for this function is ENOMEM.

Summary

In this lesson, you learned about usernames, uid numbers, group names, and gid numbers. The password and group database access routines were covered. Now you can convert a username into a uid value or perform the reverse lookup. You also have the knowledge to determine what a user's shell is and where the user's home directory is. You should now be fully prepared to deal with any user or group identification task in Linux.

Q&A

Q Can the `getuid()`, `geteuid()`, `getgid()`, or `getegid()` functions ever fail?

A Never.

Q Why must the `errno` value be cleared to `0` before calling `getpwent()` or `getgrent()`?

A To distinguish between the end of file, which is not an error, and the error `ENOMEM` if it arises. The `errno` value is never cleared to `0` by a successful operation.

Q What is another name for the Comments field in the password database?

A The GECOS field.

Q How long is the returned pointer from `getpwent()` valid?

A The pointer and the values that it points to are valid only until the next call to `getpwent()`.

Q Must the `endpwent()` function be called before the program terminates?

A Not necessarily. Generally, you should call it to close the open database file. This is especially true when you know that you do not need the password database open any longer, or it will not be required for quite some time. A process has a limit on the number of files it can have open at any one time. Consequently, to conserve open file descriptors, you should call this function to close the password database and make one more file descriptor available for other uses.

Q Is the first entry in the password database always the entry for the root userid?

A Not necessarily!

Workshop

You are encouraged to work through the quiz and the exercises to practice what you have learned before proceeding to the next lesson.

Quiz

1. Name the subfields of the GECOS field.
2. What are the first, second, third, and fourth fields of the password database?
3. What is the pathname of the group database?
4. Which fields contain the group name and the group number in the group database?
5. What is the delimiter character in the user list field of the group database?
6. What function do you call to rewind the password database so that `getpwent()` returns the first entry?
7. What function do you call to look up the username directly?
8. What function do you call to look up the gid number directly?

Exercises

1. Write your own `id` command so that it reports your current effective uid number and name in brackets, and your current effective group id number and its name in brackets.
2. Modify the program from exercise 1 to display all the supplementary groups of which the current effective uid is a member. By this, I mean that your current effective uid may be a member of more than one group, but only one of these groups can be current. Display all other groups of which your effective uid is a member (if any), excluding the current group which you have already displayed.
3. Add a `-r` option to the program developed in exercise 2 to display the real uid and group instead of the effective uid and group.
4. Write a command that takes a list of usernames on the command line. For each name listed, collect and report on all available information from the password and group database that applies to the named user. This information should include the list of all groups of which the username is a member. Additionally, the information displayed should include the encrypted form of the password, the user and group numbers, the GECOS subfields, the home directory, and the shell.

HOUR 15

File System Information and Management

Performing Basic File Operations

When you first started using Linux, the first interaction you had with the system was through the auspices of the bash shell. With the help of the shell, you created and changed directories. You listed, copied, linked, moved, and even removed files. All these routine tasks, you performed with the help of the shell.

During these early beginnings, you probably were not concerned with how these tasks were being accomplished—only that they were. Now, however, it is time to learn how these tasks are performed in C code.

The purpose of this lesson is to introduce to you the C library functions that permit you to delete, link, and move files. You will also learn how you can create and delete directories as well as change and obtain a current directory. Finally, you will learn how to obtain system information about files and directories.

Removing Files

C programs often create temporary files to hold results temporarily. When those temporary files are no longer required, they must be deleted. To delete files under Linux, you call on the `unlink()` function:

```
#include <unistd.h>

int unlink(const char *pathname);
```

Remember that on a UNIX file system, you can have more than one name linked to a physical copy of a file. Only when the last link is removed is the file itself deleted by the kernel.

Assuming that the name /tmp/12345.tmp is the only link to a temporary file, you can remove it with the following code fragment:

```
if ( unlink("/tmp/12345.tmp") != 0 ) {
    fprintf(stderr,"%s: removing /tmp/12345.tmp\n",
        strerror(errno));
    abort();
}
```

The general procedure for unlinking a file is this:

1. Call `unlink()` with the pathname to remove.
2. Check the return results. If `0` is returned, then the unlink is successful.
3. Otherwise, `-1` is returned, and the error code is posted to `errno`.

Linking Files

The opposite of unlinking a file is linking a file. If a file already exists under one name, you can create another link to the same file with another name. The function you use to do so is `link()`:

```
#include <unistd.h>

int link(const char *oldpath, const char *newpath);
```

Assume that you have a file dos_cvrt and that you want to link this file to the name unix_cvrt. Here is the C code that shows how to accomplish this task:

```
if ( link("dos_cvrt","unix_cvrt") != 0 ) {
    fprintf(stderr,"%s: link()\n",strerror(errno));
    abort();
}
```

The procedure you use for linking a file is this:

1. Call `link()` with the existing pathname in argument one and the new link pathname in argument two.
2. Check the return value. If the value is `0`, the link is established.
3. Otherwise, `-1` is returned indicating an error has occurred. The error code is posted to the external variable `errno`.

Moving Files

Have you wondered how the `mv` command works? In reality, it is simply a combination of the `link()` and `unlink()` calls. Assume that you want to move the file a.out to a subdirectory and rename it bin/dos_cvrt in the process. From bash, you simply do the following:

```
bash$ mv ./a.out ./bin/dos_cvrt
```

You also could have made this change from the shell as follows:

```
bash$ ln ./a.out ./bin/dos_cvrt
bash$ rm ./a.out
bash$
```

The following code essentially illustrates what the `mv` command does internally. In C terms, it is done like this:

```
if ( link("./a.out","./bin/dos_cvrt") != 0 ) {
    fprintf(stderr,"%s: link()\n",strerror(errno));
    abort();
}
if ( unlink("./a.out") ) {
    fprintf(stderr,"%s: unlink()\n",strerror(errno));
    abort();
}
```

The basic move procedure is this:

1. Call the `link()` function to link the existing name to the new name (arguments one and two, respectively).
2. Check the return results. If `-1` (nonzero) is returned, then report the error that is posted to external variable `errno` and stop.
3. If the results of the `link()` call are `0`, continue to step 4.
4. Call the `unlink()` function to remove the old pathname (a.out).
5. Check the return results. If `-1` (nonzero) is returned, report the error that is posted to the external variable `errno` and stop.
6. If the results of the `unlink()` call are `0`, then the unlink operation is successful.

The idea behind moving a file is to create a new link and then remove the old link. This procedure gives the illusion of moving the file from one path to another.

Performing Directory Operations

Just as the shell can obtain its current directory, change it, create a directory, or remove a directory, your C program is also able to do so. After all, the shell itself is just a C program. In the following sections, you will look at the functions you need to perform these operations.

Getting the Current Working Directory

The shell allows you to issue the `pwd` command to print the current working directory. From a C program, you must call on a library function to get this information:

```
#include <unistd.h>

char *getcwd(char *buf, size_t size);
```

You provide a pointer to the buffer that receives the absolute pathname in argument one. The second argument indicates the size in bytes of that buffer.

```
char buf[256]; /* Buffer to hold pathname */

if ( !getcwd(buf,sizeof buf) ) {
    perror("getcwd()");
    abort();
} else
    printf("cwd = '%s'\n",buf);
```

The general procedure for using the `getcwd()` is this:

1. Call `getcwd()` with the buffer's pointer in argument one and the size in bytes of that buffer in argument two.
2. Check the return value. If the returned pointer is `null`, then an error has occurred. The error code is posted to external variable `errno`.
3. If the returned pointer is non-`null`, then the operation is successful, and the buffer provided in argument one is now holding the current working directory.

One particular error is worth extra attention here. When the buffer is too small to receive the pathname and the terminating `NUL` byte, the error posted to `errno` is `ERANGE`. Don't forget to allow space for the `NUL` byte when you're specifying the buffer size in your code.

Specifying a `null` Buffer Argument

If the argument `buf` is provided as a `null` pointer under Linux, a buffer is allocated by `malloc()`, and the storage with the directory name in it is returned. When this is done, you are responsible for calling the function `free()` when you are finished with its contents.

```
char *buf; /* Allocated buffer */

buf = getcwd(0,-1);
if ( !buf ) {
    perror("getcwd()");
    abort();
} else {
    printf("cwd = '%s'\n",buf);
    free(buf);
}
```

The procedure used to obtain the current directory is this:

1. Call `getcwd()` with argument one supplied with a `null` pointer. Argument two is supplied with a negative value (`-1` is recommended).
2. Check the return value. If the returned pointer is `null`, then an error has occurred. The error code is posted to external variable `errno`.
3. If a non-`null` pointer is returned, then it points to the allocated storage that holds the `NUL`-terminated pathname. This pathname represents the current working directory.
4. Use the returned pointer.
5. Free the returned pointer. Because this storage is allocated by a call to `malloc()`, you should free this storage when you are finished with it. Use the function `free()` for this purpose.

> If you call `getcwd()` with a `null` first argument, the second argument must be negative according to the GNU documentation. You should not use `0` or positive values when argument one is `null`.
>
> Note also that `null` in argument one is not portable to other UNIX platforms.

Changing Directory

Your program can change its current directory by calling on the `chdir()` function:

```
#include <unistd.h>

int chdir(const char *path);
```

The function `chdir()` changes your current directory to the pathname given as the argument in the call:

```
if ( chdir("/usr/tmp") != 0 ) {
    perror("Cannot cd /usr/tmp");
    abort();
}
```

The procedure for changing directories is this:

1. Call `chdir()` with the new directory pathname to change to.
2. Check the returned result. If it is `0`, the operation is successful.
3. If the returned value is `-1` (nonzero), an error has occurred. The reason for the error is posted to external variable `errno`.

Making a New Directory

In days of old, under UNIX, you had to call on the shell to create a new directory. All modern UNIX platforms, including Linux, support a function to make a new directory. The following is the function prototype information for the `mkdir()` function:

```
#include <sys/types.h>
#include <fcntl.h>
#include <unistd.h>

int mkdir(const char *pathname, mode_t mode);
```

This function takes the pathname of the directory to be created as argument one. The second argument contains the permission bits to use as the new directory's permission bits.

Using the `mode_t` Data Type

Creating a directory requires that you specify permission bits. Other file functions require the use of this data type as well. Let's spend a little time now looking at what these permission bits are all about.

As a user of Linux from the command line, you should already be familiar with permissions. The `ls` command shows permission bits in its long display:

```
bash$ ls -l
total 1
-rw-r--r--   1 student1 user        110 Nov 21 00:37 dos_cvrt.c
```

After the first character at the left (the hyphen), you see three repeating groups. If full permissions were granted in each group, you would have seen `rwxrwxrwx`. Instead, hyphens are shown where the permissions are lacking. The meanings of the `r`, `w`, and `x` are outlined in Table 15.1. The meanings of the octal values will be explained shortly.

TABLE 15.1 THE PERMISSION BITS

Permission	*Octal*	*Meaning*
`r`	4	Permission to read. For files, this permission allows the user to read file information. For directories, this permission allows the user to search the directory.
`w`	2	Permission to write. For files, this permission allows the user to write over or change its content. For directories, this permission allows the user to create new files, delete old ones, or create subdirectories.
`x`	1	Permission to execute. For files, this permission means that the file can be loaded as a process and have control passed to it. For directories, this permission means that the user can set this directory as its current directory.

The three groups indicate permissions that apply to different groups of users. From left to right, these user groups are as follows:

- The owner of the file or directory. The owner is the uid of the user who "owns" the object.
- The group of the file or directory. The gid specifies a group ownership of the object.
- Everyone else. This is often referred to as *other* or *world* access.

Traditionally, permissions for these groups have been represented as three octal digits. Each octal digit represents the bits for read, write, and execute permission (review the octal values in Table 15.1). Three digits then represent the permissions for the user, the group, and everyone else.

Expressing the permission bits from the `ls` example earlier, you would arrive at an octal value of `0644` to indicate read and write for the owner, read for the group, and read for all others.

More recently, there has been a movement away from using the octal values directly. As a result, programmers can write code that is more portable. C macros representing permission bits would ideally allow the permission scheme to change at some future date without requiring any programming changes. To use the C macros, you should include the following additional include file:

```
#include <sys/stat.h>
```

Table 15.2 shows a list of C macros for the corresponding permission bit. To arrive at a combination of permissions, you use the logical `or` operator (¦) to combine these various bits. The Octal Value column shows how the C macro translates into an octal bit pattern.

TABLE 15.2 SYMBOLIC PERMISSION BITS

C Macro	*Octal Value*	*Description*
`S_IRUSR`	`0400`	The owner is granted read permission.
`S_IWUSR`	`0200`	The owner is granted write permission.
`S_IXUSR`	`0100`	The owner is granted execute permission.
`S_IRGRP`	`0040`	The group is granted read permission.
`S_IWGRP`	`0020`	The group is granted write permission.
`S_IXGRP`	`0010`	The group is granted execute permission.
`S_IROTH`	`0004`	All others are granted read permission.
`S_IWOTH`	`0002`	All others are granted write permission.
`S_IXOTH`	`0001`	All others are granted execute permission.

Using the `mkdir()` Function

The next example shows how to create a subdirectory my_subdir with a `mode_t` value of `0770` octal. It defines read, write, and execute permission for the owner and read, write, and execute permission for the group. The last octal digit is `0` so that no one else gets any permissions on the new directory being created.

The following is the call to `mkdir()` that creates the subdirectory ./my_subdir:

```
if ( mkdir("./my_subdir",0770) != 0 ) {
    perror("mkdir ./my_subdir failed.");
    abort();
}
```

> Unless otherwise noted, the examples assume that the session is using a `umask` value of `0`. To change your `umask` to `0`, enter this command:
>
> ```
> bash$ umask 0
> ```
>
> To check your current `umask` setting, enter the following command:
>
> ```
> bash$ umask
> ```

The procedure used by the code is as follows:

1. Call `mkdir()` with the pathname of the new directory given as a C string in argument one. The second argument specifies the permission bits to create this new directory with.
2. Check the return value. If `0` is returned, the new directory has been created successfully.
3. If `-1` (nonzero) is returned, then an error has occurred. Check the posted error code in external variable `errno`. Here, the error is reported, and `abort()` is called.

To perform the same operation using the C macros for the permission bits, you code it like this:

```
if ( mkdir("./my_subdir",S_IRUSR|S_IWUSR|S_IXUSR
     |S_IRGRP|S_IWGRP|S_IXGRP) != 0 ) {
    perror("mkdir ./my_subdir failed.");
    abort();
}
```

Removing a Directory

A directory is a bit different from a file. A directory contains references to other subdirectories and files within it. Consequently, it must not be removed until all the files and directories that it references are removed first. For this reason, Linux does not let `unlink()` remove a directory. Instead, you use the function `rmdir()` to make sure that the directory is empty before it is successfully removed.

The function prototype information is as follows for `rmdir()`:

```
#include <unistd.h>

int rmdir(const char *pathname);
```

To remove the sample subdirectory, you might code the following:

```
if ( rmdir("./my_subdir") != 0 ) {
    perror("rmdir() failed.");
    abort();
}
```

The procedure employed to remove a directory is as follows:

1. Call `rmdir()` with the pathname of the directory to be deleted.
2. Check the return value. If it is `0`, the directory indicated is removed without error.
3. If the return value is `-1` (nonzero), then the directory is not removed successfully. Check the posted error code in external variable `errno` for the cause.

> Note that the `rmdir()` function insists that the directory named must be empty before it can be removed. If it is not empty, then it is the programmer's responsibility to remove the directory's content before calling `rmdir()`.

You have now covered how a C program can change, create, and remove directories. You looked at permission bits and got a hint of this thing called `umask`. I will now introduce the `umask` setting.

Setting Your `umask` Value

When you create new files and directories, as the designer of the program, you must decide which permissions to use. They are usually specified as quite liberal permissions. Sometimes greater security is required when you do not want to give certain permissions away to the group or to the world.

Understanding the Need for `umask`

Consider a situation in which you are working in a student environment with a number of other students on the same machine. You create a program to hand in as an assignment and save it. The vi editor creates the text file with read and write permissions for the owner, the group, and the world. Another enterprising student copies your assignment to his home directory and later hands it in. He can do so because he can read your saved assignment. Now because he also has write permission on your text file, he overwrites your file with something else so that you have nothing to hand in. This whole mess happened because vi gave permissions to read and write the file to the owner, the group, and the world.

The way the designers of UNIX have chosen to deal with this problem is to allow program designers to specify the most liberal permissions that they dare to for the application involved. Then a mask is applied on a process-level basis to exclude permission rights that the user does not want to give away. In the example, the student (in this case, you) would have been prudent to exclude group and world access to his new files.

Your Linux process maintains a `umask` value to allow you to have control over the permissions being handed out. It is a mask value because it is used to mask out certain permission bits that you do not want to give away. To prevent the group or the world from being granted any permission on your top-secret set of new files, you could set the `umask` value to octal `077`. This value would allow the `umask` value to remove any permission at the group and world (other) levels.

Understanding the Scope of umask

The umask value is maintained by the Linux kernel at the process level. The umask built-in command for the bash shell sets the umask value for that shell process (that is, its own process). Whenever the shell creates a new process, however, that new process inherits the shell's umask setting. In this manner, setting the umask value in the shell causes the umask value to be set for the entire user session, even new shell processes.

The scope of the umask value is also limited to file system objects. This means that it applies to files and directories, but it does not apply to semaphores, message queues, and shared memory, for example (these topics will be covered later).

Using the umask() Function

The umask value applies to file system objects. Therefore, whenever your current process creates a new directory or file, the umask value is applied before the final permission bits are established.

In C language terms, the umask value is computed like this:

```
actual_permissions = requested_permissions & ( ~umask );
```

The value requested_permissions represents the liberal set of permissions that might be given in the mkdir() call covered earlier. Note the use of the unary ~ (tilde) operator to invert the umask bits before using the binary & (and) operator. The resulting actual_permissions bits are the ones that are actually applied when the file or directory is created.

Using umask Value

If the vi editor creates a new text file requesting permission bits 0666 (read and write for everyone), for example, and the current umask value is 0077 (exclude group and others), then the following computations would occur (successively simplifying):

1. actual_permissions = requested_permissions & (~umask)
2. actual_permissions = 0666 & (~0077)
3. actual_permissions = 0666 & 0700
4. actual_permissions = 0600

The final permission bits would be computed as 0600, which represents read and write for the owner of the file, but no permission for the group or for the others.

Defining `umask()`

The `umask` setting is queried and set by the function `umask()`. The function prototype is as follows:

```
#include <sys/stat.h>

int umask(int mask);
```

The value provided in the argument is the new `umask` value that you want to assert. The value returned is the `umask` value that was in effect before the current call.

In the following code, a new `umask` value of `077` is being established. At the same time, the original `umask` setting in the variable `old_mask` is being saved:

```
int old_mask;

old_mask = umask(0077);
```

Setting the `umask`

The procedure for setting the `umask` value is as follows:

1. Call `umask()` with the new mask value.
2. Save the old `umask` value if you might need to restore the present `umask` setting.

You save the original `umask` value frequently because you might want to restore the original value later. This is often done in a library function, where the `umask` value may need to be temporarily changed. The original `umask` value is restored before returning to the calling application.

Note that `umask()` never returns an error.

Querying the `umask`

There is no function to inquire about the `umask()` value. For this reason, you must inquire using a procedure that sets one `umask` value and then restores the original. The inquiry procedure is as follows:

1. Call `umask()` with a new mask value; `0` will do.
2. Save the returned value as the present `umask` value in a variable. Call it `orig_umask`.
3. Call `umask()` again, with the value of `orig_umask` to restore it to its original value.

This procedure may seem awkward, but it does not usually present a hardship. Normally, you simply want to establish a `umask` value, as you did in the preceding section, rather than query it.

Understanding File System Information

A large part of working with files and directories has to do with managing various properties of these files and directories. One side of this management is obtaining file system information about the file or directory.

In the following sections, I will introduce you to the `stat()` function and the information that it provides. I will also demonstrate how you can apply some of this information in your applications.

Introducing the `stat()` Function

Linux maintains a lot of detail about every file system object. This is true whether the object is a file, a directory, a special device node, or a named pipe. Whatever the file system object is, Linux maintains information about it.

To obtain information about a file, you can use the Linux library function `stat()`. This function provides you with all the details about the file. The following shows the function prototype for this function:

```
#include <sys/stat.h>
#include <unistd.h>

int stat(const char *file_name, struct stat *buf);
```

Using the `stat()` Function

To find out information about the executable file bin/dos_cvrt, you could code the following function call:

```
struct stat sbuf;

if ( stat("bin/dos_cvrt",&sbuf) != 0 ) {
    fprintf(stderr,"%s: stat()\n",strerror(errno));
    abort();
}
```

The procedure used to inquire about this file is this:

1. The `stat()` function is called with the pathname of the executable file that you want information about in argument one. Argument two provides the address of the structure `sbuf`, which is going to receive information if this call is successful.
2. Check the returned value. If the value is `0`, then the structure `sbuf` contains the information you want to know.
3. If the returned value is `-1` (nonzero), then an error has occurred, and the error code has been posted to the external variable `errno`. In the example, the cause of the error is printed, and the procedure is then aborted.

The sample code shows how you get the information into this C structure named `stat` (variable `sbuf`). In the next section, I will explain what jewels of information are present within that structure.

Understanding the `stat` Structure

The function `stat()` returns information in a structure provided in argument two. The `stat` structure is defined as follows:

```
struct stat {
    dev_t         st_dev;     /* device */
    ino_t         st_ino;     /* inode */
    umode_t       st_mode;    /* protection */
    nlink_t       st_nlink;   /* number of hard links */
    uid_t         st_uid;     /* user ID of owner */
    gid_t         st_gid;     /* group ID of owner */
    dev_t         st_rdev;    /* device type (if inode dev) */
    off_t         st_size;    /* total size, in bytes */
    unsigned long st_blksize;/* blksize for filesystem I/O */
    unsigned long st_blocks; /* number of blocks allocated */
    time_t        st_atime;   /* time of last access */
    time_t        st_mtime;   /* time of last modification */
    time_t        st_ctime;   /* time of last change */
};
```

Table 15.3 describes the `stat` structure members in detail.

TABLE 15.3 THE `stat` STRUCTURE

Data Type	*Member Name*	*Description*
`dev_t`	`st_dev`	The device number for this file system
`ino_t`	`st_ino`	The i-node number for this file system entry
`umode_t`	`st_mode`	File system object permission bits
`nlink_t`	`st_nlink`	The number of hard links to this file
`uid_t`	`st_uid`	The uid number of the owning user for this file system object
`gid_t`	`st_gid`	The gid number of the group for this file system object
`dev_t`	`st_rdev`	The device type, if the device is an i-node device
`off_t`	`st_size`	The total size in bytes for this file system object
`unsigned long`	`st_blksize`	The block size for file system I/O
`unsigned long` object	`st_blocks`	The number of blocks allocated to this file system
`time_t`	`st_atime`	The last time of access to this file system object
`time_t`	`st_mtime`	The last time of modification to this file system object
`time_t`	`st_ctime`	The time of creation for this file system object

A full treatment of all these structure members would require a few lessons on file system design. However, I will focus on the most useful information for application programming use.

Testing Links for the Same File System

Remember the example you did using `link()` and `unlink()` to move a file from one path to another? This procedure works only if the old and the new paths are on the same file system device because the links are *hard links*. They are known as hard links because each link to the file must reside on the same hardware (same disk).

Because you cannot create a new hard link if the new pathname is on a different disk from the original link, it is useful to determine this fact in advance. If the `mv` command can determine that the destination path is a different disk device, then the command can copy the file instead of attempting to link to it (which is what the modern `mv` command does).

Understanding File System Devices

Every Linux file system has a root file system. This file system is formatted on one disk (or partition) and contains essential directories and files. Each directory and file in that partition is identified to the Linux kernel as an i-node number.

Many Linux file systems have more than just the root file system, however. To extend the root file system, other file systems can be "mounted" logically on directories in the root file system. These additional file systems themselves exist on other disks (or partitions). Their files and directories are identified by i-node numbers as well.

To keep multiple partitions containing file systems organized within the kernel, each file system (partition or disk) has its own unique device number. Therefore, to uniquely identify a file, the kernel must have the following:

- The device number
- The i-node number

The device number is necessary because the i-node number is unique only to the device that it is contained within. Remember that the device number identifies the specific disk (or partition).

These concepts are important to grasp if you are to take full advantage of the information that the `stat()` function has to offer.

Performing a Test

In the following sample code, you perform a `stat()` operation on two different pathnames: path1 and path2. The information returned is placed into two different `stat` structures, and you then determine whether they are on the same file system.

```
struct stat link1_sbuf;
struct stat link2_sbuf;

if ( stat(path1,&link1_sbuf) != 0
||   stat(path2,&link2_sbuf) != 0 ) {
    /* Process error(s) */
}

if ( link1_sbuf.st_dev != link2_sbuf.st_dev ) ) {
    fprintf(stderr,"Sorry but %s is not on the same "
        "device as %s; Cannot mv!\n",
        path1, path2);
    return -1;
}
```

You use the following procedure to test two pathnames to see whether they are on the same file system:

1. Call `stat()` for pathname 1. Save the information in `stat` structure `link1_sbuf`.
2. If the return status is `-1`, then go no further. The error prevents testing any further.
3. Call `stat()` for pathname 2. Save the information in `stat` structure `link2_sbuf`.
4. If the return status from this call is `-1`, then go no further. The error prevents continuing this test.
5. Compare the `link1_sbuf.st_dev` value against the `link2_sbuf.st_dev` value. If they differ, then the two pathnames are on different file systems.
6. Otherwise, if the device numbers match, the two pathnames are on the same file system.

If you make it to step 6, then you know that a simple `mv` type of operation will succeed.

> When the `st_dev` number is the same for two different pathnames, you know that these two file system objects reside on the same device (disk or partition).

Testing Links If They Are the Same

The `stat` member `st_ino` is another useful piece of information. It is the unique i-node number that uniquely identifies the file system object on a particular device. Have you ever wondered how you would test if the links dos_cvrt and unix_cvrt were actually links to the same file? Here is the procedure for testing if two pathnames are hard links to the same object:

1. Call `stat()` for object 1. Make sure that it succeeds; otherwise, go no further.
2. Call `stat()` for object 2. Make sure that it succeeds; otherwise, go no further.
3. Test that the `st_dev` values match for objects 1 and 2. If they do not match, then conclude that pathname 1 is not linked to pathname 2. Go no further because these pathnames are on different devices.
4. Test that the `st_ino` values match for objects 1 and 2. If they do not match, then conclude that pathname 1 is not linked to pathname 2. Go no further because they refer to two different objects on the same disk device.
5. If you get to this point, then both the `st_dev` and the `st_ino` values match for both pathnames. They therefore are linked to the same physical file system object.

> Two pathnames are links to the same object if the `st_dev` and `st_ino` values match for both objects. If either of these values differs, then they are not linked to each other.

Obtaining Permission Bits

The `stat` structure `st_mode` member contains the UNIX permission bits for the owner, group, and others for this file system object. I covered permission bits earlier in this lesson.

Testing for File Type

The `st_mode` member also holds information about the type of file system object. To determine the object type, use one of the following macros, where `m` is the `st_mode` value to be tested:

- `S_ISLNK(m)` is `true` when the object is a symlink.
- `S_ISREG(m)` is `true` when the object is a regular file.
- `S_ISDIR(m)` is `true` when the object is a directory.

A few other types can be tested, but I will stick to the basics here. The `S_ISREG(m)` and `S_ISDIR(m)` are the most important tests that you can apply because these macros let you determine whether the pathname represents a file or a directory.

Obtaining the Number of Links

The `stat` structure member `st_nlink` contains the count of the hard links to this file. If this count is greater than `1`, then you have more than one link to this file system object. When this count is reduced to `0` by the `unlink()` function, the file is removed from the file system.

Obtaining the Owner and Group

The structure `stat` members `st_uid` and `st_gid` are the uid (owner) and gid (group) values for this file system object. You can use the routines covered in Hour 14, "Userid, Password, and Group Management," to convert these numbers into user and group names, respectively.

Obtaining the File Size

The `stat` structure `st_size` member contains the size of the file in bytes.

Obtaining Modification, Access, and Creation Times

The time values `st_atime`, `st_mtime`, and `st_ctime` are sometimes valuable assets to programmers. Most of the time, you look at the `st_mtime` value, which is the last time of modification. However, the time of last access (`st_atime`) can be extremely useful if you need to see whether the object has been recently accessed. The creation time (`st_ctime`) tells you when the object was created. Because these values are stored in the `time_t` data type, you can apply your knowledge gained from Hour 13, "Linux Date and Time Facilities," to work with these values.

Note that using `stat()` to query a file system object does not alter its date and time accessed. Opening the file or directory, however, is considered accessing the object, causing the time last accessed to be updated.

Summary

In this lesson, you learned about manipulating files. You learned how to delete files, link them together, and move them around under new names. You also learned how to perform a number of directory operations such as change directory, get the current directory, create a directory, and remove a directory.

You also looked at permission bits in this lesson. You saw how the `umask` value overrides permission bits in your current process when a file system object is created.

Finally, you found a wealth of information that is returned by the `stat()` function. You learned how to apply some of this information to determine whether the links are on the same file system or whether they are links to each other.

Q&A

Q If a particular file has two links, when is the file itself deleted?

A The first `unlink()` operation leaves one surviving link. Only when this surviving link is removed is the file itself deleted.

Q What is the condition that must be met before the `link()` function can succeed?

A The new pathname to be linked to the existing pathname must be on the same device (file system).

Q What is the function call that the C programmer must make to duplicate the functionality of the `pwd` command of the bash shell?

A The `getcwd()` function returns the pathname of the current directory.

Q Why are the symbolic permission macros such as `S_IRUSR` being encouraged for use in new programs?

A These macros allow the program to become more portable to new platforms. They also allow for the possibility of some future change to the permission bit scheme.

Q Why is the `umask` setting useful for a user's session?

A The `umask` setting allows the user to control the permissions being handed out on new files and directories being created.

Q How does a programmer obtain the `umask` value without changing the current `umask` value?

A He or she can't. The programmer must first change it to obtain the current `umask` setting. Then he or she must restore that setting with a second call to `umask()` if the present `umask` value is to be preserved.

Q Does the `rmdir()` function remove files and subdirectories beneath the named directory?

A No. It is the programmer's responsibility to remove all members of the directory that is being deleted.

Workshop

To practice what you have learned in this lesson, you are encouraged to answer the quiz and work through the exercises.

Quiz

1. How does the `unlink()` command indicate that it is successful?
2. How do you perform the equivalent of an `mv` command from one location to another on the same file system?
3. Is the practice of passing a `null` pointer in argument one of the `getcwd()` function portable? Why or why not?

4. Does the second argument of the `getcwd()` call include the size of the buffer including the terminating `NUL` byte, or not?
5. What type of data is stored in the `mode_t` data type?
6. Which include file should you use if you plan to use the C macros for the permission bits such as `S_IRUSR`?
7. What permission does the C macro `S_IXGRP` represent?
8. How do you specify multiple permission bits when using the C macros? For example, how do you specify that you want both `S_IRUSR` and `S_IRGRP`?
9. What affects the final permission bits used for the directory created by the `mkdir()` function?
10. Which `stat` structure member holds the last date and time that a file or directory was last modified?
11. Which `stat` structure member contains the size in bytes of a file?

Exercises

1. Write a small program that accepts two or more arguments on the command line. Argument one must represent a pathname of a file that already exists. The remaining arguments represent new pathnames that are to become links to the first argument. Use the `link()` function to establish the links.
2. Write a small program that accepts two arguments on the command line. Your program should move the file from the pathname in argument one to the new pathname in argument two, like the `mv` command does. If it cannot, then provide a meaningful error message for the user.
3. Enhance the program in exercise 2 to allow more than two arguments. When more than two arguments are supplied, make certain with the help of the `stat()` function that the last argument is a directory. All but the last pathname should be moved into the directory, if possible. Stop on the first error, providing a meaningful error message.
4. Enhance the program in exercise 3 to use `stat()` to test for the possibility that the source and destination pathnames are actually links to the same object. If they are, then report a meaningful message to the user.
5. Write your own `umask` command. When no command-line argument is supplied, it simply reports the current `umask` setting, without changing the setting. When one argument is supplied, then use `strtoul()` to convert the argument to a `mode_t` data type, and make the appropriate `umask` change.

HOUR 16

Temporary Files and Process Cleanup

Generating Temporary Filenames

A program occasionally requires temporary storage to contain unknown quantities of data. Sometimes this temporary data is passed to another process for sorting and later is read back in. At other times, some other type of filtering is applied. In all cases, the temporary file is discarded later to allow the system to reclaim the disk space.

The temporary file functions that are discussed in this lesson are all capable of returning errors. When an error occurs, the reason for the error is posted to the external integer `errno`. Table 16.1 summarizes these documented error codes. You can find Table 16.1 in the section "Interpreting Temporary File Function Errors" within this lesson. Refer to this table when you need to know what error codes are returned by a particular function.

In this lesson, you will look at the different ways C programmers can create temporary files. You will also look at some of the issues related to cleaning up temporary files and some of their solutions.

Using the `tmpnam()` Function

One of the functions available to Linux programmers is the `tmpnam()` function, shown here. The purpose of this function is to generate a pathname for a new temporary file that does not yet exist.

```
#include <stdio.h>

char *tmpnam(char *s);
```

Using `tmpnam()` with a `null` Argument

The one argument to `tmpnam()` is a C string pointer. However, this argument can be supplied as `null`, as shown in the sample program in Listing 16.1.

LISTING 16.1 16LST01.C—SAMPLE PROGRAM USING `tmpnam()`

```
#include <stdio.h>
#include <string.h>
#include <errno.h>

int
main(int argc,char *argv[]) {
    char *tmp_pathname; /* Temp. File Pathname */
    FILE *tmpf = 0;     /* Opened temp. file */

    if ( !(tmp_pathname = tmpnam(0)) ) {
        fprintf(stderr,"%s: generating a temp file name.\n",
            strerror(errno));
        abort();
    }

    printf("Using temp file: %s\n",tmp_pathname);

    if ( !(tmpf = fopen(tmp_pathname,"w")) ) {
        fprintf(stderr,"%s: creating temp file %s\n",
            strerror(errno), tmp_pathname);
        abort();
    }

    return 0;
}
```

The procedure used in this program for creating and opening the temporary file is as follows:

1. The function `tmpnam()` is called with a `null` argument (line 10). This action causes the function to return a pointer to a static buffer internal to the function.
2. If the returned character pointer is a `null` pointer, then you know an error has occurred. The `tmpnam()` function posts errors to the external variable `errno` (line 12). Refer to Table 16.1 for a list of possible errors.
3. Otherwise, variable `tmp_pathname` contains a pointer to a temporary file pathname. For this example, you display it (line 16).
4. The function `fopen()` is called to open it for write (line 18). Calling this function automatically creates the file.
5. If the `fopen()` call returns a `null` `FILE` pointer, then you know that the open has failed. The reason for the failure is posted to the external variable `errno` (line 20).
6. Otherwise, `FILE` variable `tmpf` is available for write operations (line 23).

If you compile and run Listing 16.1, you get a display like this:

```
Using temp file: /tmp/01060aaa
```

If you check the pathname by using `ls -l` on it, you should see that you indeed did create the temporary file. The time stamp should show that it was just created.

> To keep the examples short, some of the programs in this section do not call `fclose()` to close the file properly. Furthermore, most of these programs do not release the temporary file that is created by them (these files are actually permanent until they are removed). These are not normally acceptable programming practices.
>
> Be sure to release the temporary files manually where necessary with the `rm` command if you run the sample programs. By doing so, you can free disk space and keep your /tmp directory tidy.
>
> I will cover automatic temporary file removal in detail later in this lesson.

Using `tmpnam()` with a Buffer

A better way to use the `tmpnam()` function is to supply your own buffer so that the pathname can be stored there. This way, you can keep the pathname of the temporary file for as long as you need. Previously, the pathname was valid only until the next call to `tmpnam()`. Listing 16.2 shows a sample program that supplies its own buffer.

LISTING 16.2 16LST02.C—SAMPLE USE OF `tmpnam()` WITH SUPPLIED BUFFER

```
#include <stdio.h>
#include <string.h>
#include <errno.h>

int
main(int argc,char *argv[]) {
    char tmp_pathname[L_tmpnam];     /* Temp. File Pathname */
    FILE *tmpf = 0;                  /* Opened temp. file */

    if ( !tmpnam(tmp_pathname) ) {
        fprintf(stderr,"%s: generating a temp file name.\n",
            strerror(errno));
        abort();
    }

    printf("Using temp file: %s\n",tmp_pathname);

    if ( !(tmpf = fopen(tmp_pathname,"w")) ) {
        fprintf(stderr,"%s: creating temp file %s\n",
            strerror(errno), tmp_pathname);
        abort();
    }

    return 0;
}
```

The procedure used in Listing 16.2 is the same as before. However, a buffer is supplied this time; it must be at least `L_tmpnam` bytes in length. The C macro `L_tmpnam` is defined in the include file stdio.h.

Using the `mkstemp()` Function

Another library function that is available to Linux C programmers is the `mkstemp()` function, shown here. Note that this function requires that the include file stdlib.h be included.

```
#include <stdlib.h>

int mkstemp(char *template);
```

This function is called with a C string pointer argument, which points to a `NULL`-terminated string. This string acts like a template for the function, and a `null` pointer is not permitted.

The template string is used as a "form" for the temporary pathname to be generated within. It can be a file or pathname of your choice, but the last six characters must be the capital letter *X*. The following example shows how you can establish a template in a character array:

```
char buf[64];

strcpy(buf,"/tmp/01-XXXXXX");
```

You must always copy the template to a buffer because the last six capital *X* letters are overwritten with generated temporary filename characters that make the pathname unique.

The program in Listing 16.3 demonstrates how to use the `mkstemp()` function.

LISTING 16.3 16LST03.C—EXAMPLE USING THE `mkstemp()` FUNCTION

```
1:  #include <stdio.h>
2:  #include <stdlib.h>
3:  #include <unistd.h>
4:  #include <string.h>
5:  #include <errno.h>
6:
7:  int
8:  main(int argc,char *argv[]) {
9:      char tf_path[64];    /* Temp. File Pathname */
10:     int tfd = -1;        /* UNIX File Descriptor */
11:     FILE *tmpf = 0;      /* Opened temporary FILE */
12:
13:     strcpy(tf_path,"/tmp/01-XXXXXX"); /* Init template */
14:
15:     if ( (tfd = mkstemp(tf_path)) < 0 ) {
16:         fprintf(stderr,"%s: generating a temp file name.\n",
17:             strerror(errno));
18:         abort();
19:     }
20:
21:     printf("Using temp file: %s\n",tf_path);
22:
23:     tmpf = fdopen(tfd,"w+");         /* Use FILE I/O */
24:     fprintf(tmpf,"Written by PID=%ld\n", (long)getpid());
25:     fclose(tmpf);
26:
27:     return 0;
28: }
```

The steps used in Listing 16.3 are as follows:

1. A buffer of suitable size for the temporary file's pathname is defined (line 9). Here, I arbitrarily chose 64 bytes.

2. A template string is copied into the pathname buffer (line 13). This step is required because the pathname template will be modified by the `mkstemp()` function call. Make sure that the last six characters of this string are capital *X* characters.
3. The function `mkstemp()` is called, supplying it with the pathname template as input argument one (line 15). The function will modify the contents of this buffer, replacing the last six *X* characters with something unique.
4. The returned integer result `tfd` is checked (line 15). If this value is `-1`, then an error has occurred. The error posted in the external integer `errno` is then checked (line 17).
5. If the returned result is `0` or positive, then an opened UNIX file descriptor has been returned in variable `tfd`. It will be the created and opened temporary file. Line 21 shows how you display the generated temporary filename.
6. To use stream I/O, the UNIX file descriptor is opened with `fdopen()` in line 23. No error check is performed here to keep the example short.
7. One text line is formatted and written to the temporary file (line 24).
8. The temporary file is closed to make sure that the buffered data is properly written (line 25).

The program in Listing 16.3 makes use of the `fdopen()` function, which you may not have used before. It accepts an open UNIX file descriptor and creates a `FILE` stream that uses it. The mode parameter in argument two is the same as the familiar `fopen()` argument two. However, you must be careful to match the `fdopen()` mode with the mode that the UNIX file descriptor is opened with. Otherwise, I/O errors occur. Temporary files are opened for reading and writing, so the sample program in Listing 16.3 opens it with `w+` to allow both reading and writing to this stream.

> The man page for the `mkstemp()` function dated April 3, 1993, has a number of errors in it. It indicates that the include file should be unistd.h. The correct include file is stdlib.h, according to recent include file content.
>
> Some man pages with the same date also indicate that the function returns an `int *` (integer pointer), which is incorrect. The `mkstemp()` function returns an `int` (integer), representing the opened UNIX file descriptor, or `-1` if it fails.
>
> If your manual page is newer than April 3, 1993, then one or both of these errors may have been corrected by the volunteers of the Linux Documentation Project (LDP).

Using Multiple Temporary Files

The program in Listing 16.3 uses a temporary filename template, as shown here:

```
strcpy(tf_path,"/tmp/01-XXXXXX");
```

Adding the leading prefix `01-` is a technique you might want to use if you open more than one temporary file in your program. For example, the second temporary file might use the following template:

```
strcpy(tf_path,"/tmp/02-XXXXXX");
```

This technique is not necessary for using multiple temporary files, but it can be helpful when you're debugging your program. When you see temporary files named this way in the /tmp directory, you immediately know which of the many temporary files they are.

> One temptation that often arises is placing the six *X* letters at the beginning or middle of the filename. This technique does not work because `mkstemp()` insists that they be the last six letters of the template.

Using the `tmpfile()` Function

There is no shortage of temporary file functions for Linux C programmers. The `tmpfile()` function shown here creates and opens a temporary file for you, returning a `FILE` stream pointer.

```
#include <stdio.h>

FILE *tmpfile (void);
```

See the example using `tmpfile()` in Listing 16.4.

LISTING 16.4 16LST04.C—EXAMPLE USING `tmpfile()`

```
#include <stdio.h>
#include <unistd.h>
#include <string.h>
#include <errno.h>

int
main(int argc,char *argv[]) {
    FILE *tmpf = 0;         /* Opened temp. file */
    char buf[128];          /* Input buffer */

```

continues

LISTING 16.4 CONTINUED

```
11:     if ( !(tmpf = tmpfile()) ) {
12:         fprintf(stderr,"%s: generating a temp file name.\n",
13:             strerror(errno));
14:         abort();
15:     }
16:
17:     fprintf(tmpf,"PID %ld was here.\n",(long)getpid());
18:     fflush(tmpf);
19:
20:     rewind(tmpf);
21:     fgets(buf,sizeof buf,tmpf);
22:     printf("GOT: '%s';\n",buf);
23:
24:     return 0;
25: }
```

The short program in Listing 16.4 uses the following procedure:

1. The function `tmpfile()` is called to generate, create, and open a temporary file. The result is a `FILE` stream pointer (line 11).
2. The returned `FILE` pointer is checked. If it is a `null` pointer, then an error has occurred. The error code is posted to external integer `errno`. This error is reported in lines 12 and 13.
3. When a `FILE` pointer is returned, you know that a temporary file has been created. The `FILE` pointer `tmpf` is open for reading and writing. Line 17 shows a formatted print to the temporary file.
4. The buffers are flushed to force a physical write to the temporary file (line 18).
5. The temporary file's offset is rewound to the start of the file (line 20).
6. The text line that you wrote in step 3 is read back (line 21).
7. The text line that was read back is displayed to standard output (line 22).

You may have noticed that the pathname of the temporary file is not displayed this time. There is a good reason for it: There is no filename! "How'd they do that?" you might ask. I will save that topic for later in the section titled "Using `unlink()` to Make Files Temporary."

Note that because this temporary file has no filename, there is no file to remove later. When the temporary file is closed, the system automatically deletes it and reclaims the disk space.

Using the `tempnam()` Function

The last temporary file function I will cover here is the `tempnam()` function:

```
#include <stdio.h>

char *tempnam(const char *dir, const char *pfx);
```

This function accepts two arguments. The second argument, `pfx`, is optional and can be supplied as a `null` pointer. However, when it is not `null`, it points to a C string that specifies up to five characters that can be used as a prefix to the generated temporary filename.

The first argument, `dir`, is more complicated. It can be specified as a `null` pointer, or it can point to a string specifying a directory that the programmer has chosen. Whether or not `dir` is `null`, the following procedure determines the final directory chosen for the temporary filename:

1. The function tries to obtain exported environment variable `TMPDIR`. If this variable is defined, and it specifies a directory that is writable to the current process, then this directory is used. In effect, the `TMPDIR` variable overrides the program's choice of directory.
2. When step 1 fails, the `dir` argument of the `tempnam()` call is examined. If this argument is not a `null` pointer, then this directory is used if the specified directory exists.
3. When step 2 is not satisfied, the directory specified by the stdio.h macro `P_tmpdir` is tried.
4. As a last resort, the directory /tmp is used.

Normally, steps 1 or 2 specify the directory. Steps 3 and 4 represent fallback directory names.

Listing 16.5 shows a short program that uses the `tempnam()` function.

Listing 16.5 16LST05.c—Example Using the `tempnam()` Function

```
#include <stdio.h>
#include <unistd.h>
#include <string.h>
#include <malloc.h>
#include <errno.h>

int
main(int argc,char *argv[]) {
```

continues

LISTING 16.5 CONTINUED

```
9:       char *tf_path = 0;       /* Temp. File Pathname */
10:      FILE *tmpf = 0;          /* Temp. File stream */
11:
12:      if ( !(tf_path = tempnam("./my_tmp","tmp-")) ) {
13:          fprintf(stderr,"%s: generating a temp file name.\n",
14:              strerror(errno));
15:          abort();
16:      }
17:
18:      printf("Temp. file name is %s\n",tf_path);
19:
20:      if ( !(tmpf = fopen(tf_path,"w+")) ) {
21:          fprintf(stderr,"%s: opening %s for I/O\n",
22:              strerror(errno),tf_path);
23:          abort();
24:      }
25:
26:      fprintf(tmpf,"PID %ld was here.\n",(long)getpid());
27:      fclose(tmpf);
28:
29:      free(tf_path);      /* Free malloc()'d string */
30:
31:      return 0;
32:  }
```

The steps used in Listing 16.5 are as follows:

1. The `tempnam()` function is called (line 12), with values defined in arguments one and two. The returned value is a C string pointer to a string allocated by `malloc()`.
2. The returned string pointer (`tf_path`) is tested. If the pointer is `null`, then an error has occurred, and the error code is found in external variable `errno`. This error is reported in line 14.
3. When `tempnam()` is successful, the name of the temporary file's pathname is reported (line 18).
4. The generated temporary file pathname `tf_path` is opened using `fopen()` for reading and writing (line 20).
5. If the `FILE` stream pointer `tmpf` from step 4 is `null`, then the error code found in `errno` is reported (line 22).
6. The program uses the opened `FILE` stream `tmpf` to write one text line containing the process ID (line 26).

7. The temporary file is closed (line 27).
8. The pathname of the temporary file is released by passing the pointer `tf_path` to `free()` (line 29). Remember that this string is created by `tempnam()` calling `malloc()`. Therefore, it is the caller's responsibility to free the allocated memory.

With the program in Listing 16.5 compiled, you are ready to run some tests. First, you can define the environment `TMPDIR` and verify where the temporary file is created:


```
bash$ TMPDIR=/var/tmp ./a.out
Temp. file name is /var/tmp/tmp-01544aaa
bash$
```

Here, you see that the `TMPDIR` variable is used as the directory. Now you can unset `TMPDIR` (to be certain it is not defined) and try the program again:

```
bash$ unset TMPDIR
bash$ ./a.out
Temp. file name is /tmp/tmp-01547aaa
bash$
```

Apparently, the directory `./my_tmp` as coded in line 12 of Listing 16.5 has had no effect because the directory does not exist, so the fallback of /tmp is used. Now you can create a subdirectory and see whether it gets used:

```
bash$ mkdir ./my_tmp
bash$ ./a.out
Temp. file name is ./my_tmp/tmp-01552aaa
bash$
```

Sure enough, the `tempnam()` function does find the subdirectory and use it.

One interesting experiment you can try is this: Remove all permissions from ./my_tmp and see whether the function `tempnam()` falls back to /tmp.

You can try this experiment to determine what the man pages mean by "fallback" here. Does it mean the function will fall back when the directory does not exist, or does it mean the function will fall back when it cannot use the directory (for example, when no permissions appear on it)? Try this example to see:

```
bash$ chmod 0 ./my_tmp
bash$ ls -l ./my_tmp
/bin/ls: ./my_tmp: Permission denied
bash$ ./a.out
CTRL+C
bash$
```

This test proves quite interesting indeed. Apparently, the fallback procedure applies only to the existence of the directory—not on its usability. The steps you use here are as follows:

1. Remove all permissions from ./my_tmp by using the `chmod` command.
2. Prove that you have no permissions by using `ls` on the directory ./my_tmp.
3. Run the program ./a.out.
4. Interrupt the program (Ctrl+C is the interrupt character for the session).

When I ran this example, the program hung, so I was forced to interrupt it (step 4). I suspect that the `tempnam()` function was trying different temporary filenames, assuming that the permission problem was at the file level instead of at the directory level. At the time of this writing, this was the errant behavior of this function.

Interpreting Temporary File Function Errors

Table 16.1 summarizes the documented error codes that the various temporary file functions can return. This list was compiled from the existing manual pages. Some undocumented error codes may be outstanding.

TABLE 16.1 SUMMARY OF DOCUMENTED TEMPORARY FUNCTION ERRORS

Error Code	*Functions*	*Description*
`EEXIST`	`tmpnam()`, `mkstemp()`, `tmpfile()`, `tempnam()`	Unable to generate a unique filename.
`EINVAL`	`mkstemp()`	The last six characters of the template name are not the letters *XXXXXX*.
`EACCES`	`tmpfile()`	Search permission denied for directory in file's path prefix.
`EMFILE`	`tmpfile()`	Too many file descriptors in use by process.
`ENFILE`	`tmpfile()`	Too many files open in system.
`EROFS`	`tmpfile()`	Read-only file system.

In the preceding sections, you looked at a few different ways to create temporary files. In the next section, you will address the issue of cleaning up temporary files.

Making Files Temporary

After a temporary file is created, a C program must remember to release that file when it is finished with the file. Otherwise, the /tmp directory (or similar directory) fills with many abandoned files over a period of time.

Writing a program segment that releases a file is quite simple. You can simply call the `unlink()` function, which was covered in Hour 15, "File System Information and Management." The problem occurs when these programs prematurely exit for some reason. When premature terminations occur, the temporary files that have been created usually are not cleaned up. Consequently, various techniques have been developed under UNIX to deal with this problem.

Using `unlink()` to Make Files Temporary

One way you can make sure that the temporary file is released is to release it immediately after it is created and opened. "What?" Yes, you read that sentence correctly. This statement looks inconceivable to those who are new to UNIX, but a file can exist after it has been deleted.

What precisely happens is that after you have opened a file under UNIX, the kernel maintains an open file table entry for it. This is true of any file, including temporary files. If you then call `unlink()` to delete this file, the kernel removes the link name of that file, but the physical file itself is not yet removed. The file actually becomes a file with no name at this point (with zero links).

The file contents are removed only after the process has closed that nameless file. Closing the file causes the kernel to free the file table entry for it. Because the file entry has zero links to it (no name), the kernel releases the contents of the file.

Remember that function `tmpfile()`, which creates temporary files that have no names? The following is the general procedure it uses:

1. A unique temporary filename is generated. This is done just like any of the other functions covered in this book.
2. The file is created, and an opened UNIX file descriptor is obtained for it. (UNIX allows the create and open to be performed in one step.)
3. The function `unlink()` is called on the temporary file. This step now makes the file nameless, but the file itself remains open.
4. The function `fdopen()` is called to open a `FILE` stream, using the open file descriptor.
5. The `FILE` stream pointer is returned to the caller.

The nameless temporary file has two advantages:

- The file has already been released. No cleanup is required.
- No other process can subsequently open and tamper with the temporary file. This also provides a measure of privacy.

The second point almost guarantees that no other process, even a root process, can tamper with or inspect your temporary file contents. This is not a 100 percent guarantee, however, because the file must be created and then passed to `unlink()`. A narrow window of opportunity is left for another process to open that same file.

Performing Exit Cleanup

Sometimes the `unlink()` approach is not appropriate. If the file must be closed and then at a later time reopened, you have no choice but to keep a name associated with the temporary file. You cannot put a name on a nameless file. This point raises the temporary file cleanup problem when a program exits prematurely.

Using the `atexit()` Function

A solution is provided by the C library `atexit()` function. In fact, you can use it for all forms of different cleanup tasks, including the removal of temporary files. The function prototype for the `atexit()` function is as follows:

```
#include <stdlib.h>

int atexit(void (*function)(void));
```

The function prototype might look a little confusing at first. This declaration tells you that the `atexit()` function wants a pointer to a function that takes no arguments (hence `(void)`) and returns no value (returns `void`). Your cleanup function is declared as follows:

```
extern void my_cleanup_func(void);
```

To register this function with `atexit()`, as shown here, you simply pass the function's pointer to it. Listing 16.6 shows a sample program that uses `atexit()` to cause a cleanup function to be called.

```
atexit(my_cleanup_func);
```

LISTING 16.6 16LST06.C—USING `atexit()` TO CLEAN UP

```
#include <stdio.h>
#include <stdlib.h>
#include <unistd.h>
#include <string.h>
```

```
5:  #include <malloc.h>
6:  #include <errno.h>
7:
8:  static char *tf_path = 0;      /* Temp. File Pathname */
9:
10: static void
11: myCleanup(void) {
12:     puts("myCleanup() called.");
13:     if ( tf_path != 0 ) {
14:         printf("Cleaning up temp. file %s\n",tf_path);
15:         unlink(tf_path);
16:         free(tf_path);
17:     }
18: }
19:
20: int
21: main(int argc,char *argv[]) {
22:     FILE *tmpf = 0;           /* Temp. File stream */
23:
24:     atexit(myCleanup);        /* Register our cleanup func */
25:
26:     if ( !(tf_path = tempnam("./my_tmp","tmp-")) ) {
27:         fprintf(stderr,"%s: generating a temp file name.\n",
28:             strerror(errno));
29:         abort();
30:     }
31:
32:     printf("Temp. file name is %s\n",tf_path);
33:
34:     if ( !(tmpf = fopen(tf_path,"w+")) ) {
35:         fprintf(stderr,"%s: opening %s for I/O\n",
36:             strerror(errno),tf_path);
37:         abort();
38:     }
39:
40:     fprintf(tmpf,"PID %ld was here.\n",(long)getpid());
41:     fclose(tmpf);
42:
43:     return 0;
44: }
```

The general steps taken in the program shown in Listing 16.6 are as follows:

1. The cleanup function `myCleanup()` is registered with the `atexit()` function (line 24). Registering this function ensures that `myCleanup()` is called before the program terminates.
2. The usual program processing is performed (lines 26 to 41).

3. The program exits (line 43) from `main()`. Alternatively, the program may invoke the `exit()` function from some other point of processing if this application is larger.
4. The termination logic of the C libraries notes that a function is registered with `atexit()`. The function `myCleanup()` is then called (line 11 gets control).
5. Function `myCleanup()` calls `unlink()` if the pathname is non-`null` (line 15). This step makes certain that the temporary file is removed.
6. Function `myCleanup()` returns (line 18).

More processing occurs within the C libraries after step 6. All open `FILE` streams are flushed and then closed, for example.

The `atexit()` function has a limit as to how many functions can be registered. The return value from `atexit()` is `0` when the registration is successful. If an error occurs, `-1` is returned, and the reason for the error is posted to the external variable `errno`. The only documented error for Linux is `ENOMEM`, which occurs if insufficient memory is available to log the request.

Functions registered with `atexit()` are called in the reverse order that they were registered. You should keep this point in mind if sequence is important.

Summary

In this lesson, you examined a number of functions that allow C programmers to generate temporary filenames and temporary files themselves. You learned about some of the issues for temporary files and finished by examining two ways that temporary files can be cleaned up automatically.

Q&A

Q Why is so much effort spent on generating a temporary filename? Why not just use a temporary filename named after the program?

A The problem is that a program can be used by more than one user at the same time. If both instances of that program try to use the same temporary filename, then they would each overwrite the other's data.

Q When I supply my own buffer to function `tmpnam()`, how large must that buffer be in bytes?

A The buffer must be a minimum of `L_tmpnam` bytes. It can be larger, but it must not be smaller!

Q Is the temporary filename template /tmp/XXXXXX.tmp valid for function `mkstemp()`?

A This template is not valid because the `mkstemp()` function insists that the last six characters must be the uppercase letter *X*.

Q Can `mkstemp()` be called with a string constant, such as `mkstemp("/tmp/01-XXXXXX")`?

A This example is not acceptable because the `mkstemp()` function modifies the string by replacing the last six *X* characters with the generated temporary filename characters that were selected. If this code were executed, your string constant would be corrupted (if alterable), or a memory fault would occur.

Q What is the valid range of file descriptors that `tmpfile()` can return when it is successful?

A Zero and up. Zero is normally open for standard input. However, if standard input is closed by your program, that file descriptor will be the first one to be used if another file is opened.

Workshop

To practice what you have learned in this lesson, you are encouraged to answer the quiz and work through the exercises.

Quiz

1. What function can be used to register a cleanup function before all file streams are closed?
2. What order are the cleanup functions called in?
3. When `tmpnam()` is called with a `null` argument, where does the returned string pointer point to? Is this string allocated by `malloc()`, or does it point to a static buffer?
4. When `tempnam()` returns a non-`null` pointer to a pathname, does this pointer point to space allocated by `malloc()` or to a static buffer?
5. What environment variable overrides the directory chosen for temporary files when `tempnam()` is used?
6. Where is the string `P_tmpdir` defined?
7. How do you create a nameless file?

Exercise

Write a simple program that takes one pathname argument on the command line. Open that pathname for reading, and convert all lowercase characters to uppercase. The output should be written to a temporary file until the end of the input file is reached.

Close the input file, and rewind the temporary file to its beginning.

Open the input file for writing, and copy the temporary file data back to the input file that is now open for write.

The end result of this program should appear as if the file were converted to uppercase "in place." Make certain that the temporary file is automatically removed.

HOUR 17

Pipes and Processes

Using External Processes

One of the strengths of UNIX that Linux inherits is its capability to reuse different commands and processes. The bash shell is an example, using pipes to connect the output of one process to the input of another. The `sort` command is one of these examples of reusable components that you used in Listing 8.1 in Hour 8, "The Linux `main` Program and Its Environment."

In this hour, you will fully explore the potential for your C programs to create pipes to other processes. In addition to pipes that can be read or written, this lesson will examine another way to run commands.

Introducing Pipes

A UNIX pipe between two processes is almost what it sounds like. It is logically a pipeline between one writing process and one reading process. Unlike with a physical pipe, however, in this pipe the data must flow in one direction only—from source to destination.

The type of pipe that I will talk about in this lesson is a *nameless* pipe. Just as with a temporary file that is open but has all its links removed, a nameless pipe does not exist in the file system. When all processes that had the pipe open have closed it, the pipe is destroyed.

Opening a Pipe

The C standard I/O library provides a convenient `popen()` function for application designers to use:

```
#include <stdio.h>

FILE *popen(const char *command, const char *type);
```

The `popen()` function arguments are similar to the `fopen()` function except that the first argument is a command rather than a pathname. The argument `command` must be a command that is acceptable to the shell.

The second argument `type` must be the string `"r"` for reading or `"w"` for writing. No other combination like `"w+"` is acceptable because the pipe must be opened for reading or writing, but never for both. Remember that the data travels in the pipe in one direction only.

Invoking a Command Through popen()

The string given as argument `command` must be acceptable to the shell because the `popen()` function invokes a shell process first (shell `sh`). The pipe creation process can be simply described as follows:

1. The `popen()` function is called.
2. The `popen()` function calls functions `fork()` and `exec()` to start the shell (`sh`). On Linux systems, `sh` is equivalent to `bash` by default.
3. The bash shell interprets the `command` string provided in argument one of the `popen()` call.
4. The shell starts your `command` if it is able to. If not, the shell returns an error to the `popen()` call.

Note that the process started by `popen()` can be referred to as a *child process*. The program calling the `popen()` function is known as the *parent process*. This terminology helps to identify the process and avoids confusion.

Strengths of the popen() Function

Because your command string is passed to the bash shell under Linux, you have considerable flexibility in the command features at your disposal. For example, you can use command lines that use wildcard filenames and so on.

You also can use the shell input or output redirection operators to redirect standard input and output from or to different files of your choosing.

> If you write programs that use the `popen()` function and that must be portable to other UNIX operating systems, keep in mind the limitations of the shell. Under many UNIX platforms, the Bourne shell is used; it supports a limited subset of the features that the bash shell supports.

Defining the Environment for popen()

The `popen()` function uses the shell to interpret and execute your command. This fact means that any commands that you expect it to invoke are subject to the usual directory searches, as controlled by the exported `PATH` variable. You might want to execute a special `sort` program, like this:

```
FILE *p;

p = popen("fast_sort >/tmp/sorted.tmp","w");
```

However, if this special `sort` command is available only in a special directory, and your `PATH` variable does not specify this directory, this `popen()` call fails to execute the command (the shell does not find it). You might want to specify the fully qualified pathname for the `fast_sort` command instead, or you can modify the `PATH` variable in your program before you call `popen()`.

Reading from Pipes

After you open a pipe for reading, your process can read from the pipe using the standard I/O functions. To illustrate how this is done, look at the sample program in Listing 17.1.

LISTING 17.1 17LST01.C—READING A PIPE

```
#include <stdio.h>
#include <stdlib.h>
#include <errno.h>
#include <string.h>

int
main(int argc,char **argv) {
    char *cp;                       /* Work ptr */
```

continues

LISTING 17.1 CONTINUED

```
9:       char buf[256];                 /* Input buffer */
10:      FILE *p = popen(cp="ps f","r"); /* Input pipe */
11:
12:      if ( !p ) {
13:          fprintf(stderr,
14:              "%s: Opening pipe(%s) for read.\n",
15:              strerror(errno),cp);
16:          return 13;
17:      }
18:
19:      /*
20:       * Read the output of the pipe:
21:       */
22:      while ( fgets(buf,sizeof buf,p) != 0 )
23:          fputs(buf,stdout);
24:
25:      if ( pclose(p) ) {
26:          fprintf(stderr,"%s: pclose()\n",
27:              strerror(errno));
28:          return 13;
29:      }
30:
31:      return 0;
32:  }
```

Originally, under Linux, the `ps` command optionally used a hyphen to introduce options on its command line. In newer Linux distributions, a hyphen on the `ps` command indicates that the options are Unix98 standard options and are interpreted differently from the GNU option letters.

Consequently, the examples in this lesson often use the command `"ps f"` without the hyphen. The `"f"` option letter invokes the GNU "forest" option when used without the hyphen.

In the program, notice that pipe `p` in line 22 is read as if the pipe were a file. The overall steps used by the program in Listing 17.1 are summarized as follows:

1. The `popen()` call is made, and the returned pointer is assigned to the declared `FILE` variable `p` (line 10). The command that you expect to execute is the `"ps f"` command to list the processes in GNU "forest" format.
2. A test is made to see whether the `popen()` call failed (line 12). If the call failed, the error is reported and the program terminates (lines 13 to 17).

3. Input is read into the buffer array `buf[]` until end-file is reached (line 22).
4. The text line just read is written to standard output (line 23). Note that the newline is provided by the line that is read.
5. Steps 3 and 4 are repeated until end-file is reached.
6. The `pclose()` function is called to close the pipe (line 25). Notice that you do not call `fclose()` for this stream.
7. The `main()` program returns (line 31), which causes all `FILE` streams including `stdout` to be flushed and closed.

When this program is compiled and executed, you obtain the following results:

```
bash$ ./a.out
  PID TTY STAT  TIME COMMAND
   71  a0 S     0:02 -bash
  238  a0 S     0:00  \_ ./a.out
  239  a0 R     0:00      \_ ps f
bash$
```


In the session output, you can note the following:

- The output is `ps` command output. So clearly, the program has successfully opened a pipe to the `ps` command and read its output.
- The `ps` command (process ID 239) is invoked by the program (`a.out`, process ID 238).
- No evidence of the shell that invoked the `ps` command remains (between the `a.out` process and the `ps` command) because the shell performs an `exec` of the `ps` command to save one process. (The `exec()` call is covered in Hour 18, "Forked Processes.")

Writing to Pipes

When the current process writes to a pipe, another process at the other end of the pipe reads that data from its standard input. To illustrate that procedure, look at the sample program provided in Listing 17.2.

LISTING 17.2 17LST02.C—WRITING TO A PIPE

```
#include <stdio.h>
#include <stdlib.h>
#include <unistd.h>
#include <errno.h>
```

continues

LISTING 17.2 CONTINUED

```
#include <string.h>
#include <pwd.h>
#include <sys/types.h>

int
main(int argc,char **argv) {
    struct passwd *pw = 0;        /* Password info */
    char cmd[256];                /* Command buffer */
    FILE *p = 0;                  /* mailx pipe */

    /*
     * Lookup our userid:
     */
    if ( !(pw = getpwuid(geteuid())) ) {
        fprintf(stderr,"%s: unknown userid\n",
            strerror(errno));
        return 13;
    }

    /*
     * Format command :
     */
    sprintf(cmd,
        "mailx -s 'A message from process ID %ld' %s",
        (long) getpid(),     /* Process ID */
        pw->pw_name);        /* User name */

    /*
     * Open a pipe to mailx:
     */
    if ( !(p = popen(cmd,"w")) ) {
        fprintf(stderr,
            "%s: popen(%s) for write.\n",
            strerror(errno),
            cmd);
        return 13;
    }

    /*
     * Now write our message:
     */
    fprintf(p,"This is command %s speaking.\n",argv[0]);
    fprintf(p,"I am operating in the account for %s\n",
        pw->pw_gecos);

    if ( getuid() != 0 ) {
        fprintf(p,"I'd like to operate in root instead.\n");
        fprintf(p,"I could do more damage there. :)\n\n");
```

```
53:        } else {
54:            fprintf(p,"I'd like to operate in a "
55:                "non-root ID instead.\n");
56:            fprintf(p,"I would be safer there.\n");
57:        }
58:        fprintf(p,"Sincerely,\n  Process ID %ld\n",
59:            (long)getpid());
60:
61:        if ( pclose(p) == -1 ) {
62:            fprintf(stderr,"%s: pclose(%s)\n",
63:                strerror(errno),cmd);
64:            return 13;
65:        } else
66:            printf("Message sent to %s\n",pw->pw_name);
67:
68:        return 0;
69:    }
```

Some Linux distributions may not provide the `mailx` command that is widely available under Linux, and UNIX in general. For the purposes of these illustrations, however, you can substitute the `mail` program instead. Change line 28 of Listing 17.2 to invoke `mail` instead of `mailx` if this applies to your situation.

Alternatively, if you have root privileges on your host, you might want to install a symlink for /bin/mailx to the existing program /bin/mail.

The overall design of the program can be summarized as follows:

1. The password entry is obtained from function `getpwuid()` based on the current effective user ID (line 18). If this step fails, a message and return code 13 are issued (line 21).
2. A command is formatted to invoke the `mailx` command, which mails a message (lines 27 to 30). The command is structured to provide a subject line and sends the message to the current effective user ID.
3. A pipe to the `mailx` command is opened for writing (line 35). The written data will be the input message to be sent. If the open fails, a message is displayed, and the program returns code 13 (lines 36 to 41).
4. The message to the pipe is written (lines 46 to 59). Note that line 50 tests to see whether the program is not running as root. If not, it requests root access in its message (lines 51 and 52). Otherwise, it makes another request instead (lines 54 to 56).

5. The pipe is closed (line 61). If an error occurs, a message is provided and the program returns exit code 13 (line 64).
6. If successful, the `Message sent` notice is given (line 66).

Running the program yields these results:

```
bash$ ./a.out
Message sent to student1
bash$ mailx
Mail version 5.5 6/1/90.  Type ? for help.
"/var/spool/mail/student1": 1 message 1 new
>N  1 student1@slug   Fri Jan 22 19:06  19/531 "A message from proces"
& 1
Message 1:
From student1  Fri Jan 22 19:06:36 1999
Date: Fri, 22 Jan 1999 19:06:35 -0500
From: Student 01 <student1@slug>
To: student1@slug
Subject: A message from process ID 497

This is command ./a.out speaking.
I am operating in the account for Student 01
I'd like to operate in root instead.
I could do more damage there. :)

Sincerely,
  Process ID 497

& d 1
& q
bash$
```

The preceding session employed the following steps to produce the session output shown:

1. The program `a.out` was invoked. Then a response came back saying `Message sent to student1`.
2. The `mailx` command was invoked to look at the mailbox (you can use `pine` or some other email program if you prefer).
3. The user typed **1** to read message number 1.
4. The user typed **d 1** to delete message number 1 from the mailbox.
5. The user typed **q** to quit the `mailx` command.

In this example, the program fed data to the command through the pipe.

Closing a Pipe

After a pipe is opened for reading or writing, you indicate that you have completed reading or writing by closing the pipe. A number of important concluding functions therefore can take place; I will discuss them in this section.

A pipe is closed using the following function:

```
#include <stdio.h>

int pclose(FILE *stream);
```

Because an opened pipe can be read or written using the standard I/O routines, you might be wondering why a pipe must be closed differently. Why not just use `fclose()`?

The `pclose()` function does more than close down the stream associated with the pipe. After closing the stream, the `pclose()` function calls the Linux function `wait4()` to wait for the child process at the other end of the pipe to terminate. In this manner, function `pclose()` can pass back the success or failure status of that child process. Furthermore, you know that the timing is such that the child process has completed.

If you call `fclose()` on a pipe (some UNIX implementations might not allow you to do so), then you close only the stream on the pipe. The other process sees the end-file as a result of closing the pipe, but it may continue to process long after your `fclose()` function has returned control to your calling process.

The other problem with using `fclose()` on a pipe stream is that it cannot know whether the command actually ran to completion. Because the `pclose()` command is able to perform a `wait4()` call, it knows when and how the process terminated. The `wait` family of functions is covered in Hour 18, "Forked Processes."

One final problem is that *zombie processes* are created when `pclose()` is not used. This can be a serious problem if this practice is exercised many times over the lifetime of your process. The topic of zombie processes is also covered in Hour 18.

> Always use function `pclose()` to close a pipe opened with `popen()`. Failure to obey this rule results in undetected process errors, possible memory leaks, and on some UNIX platforms, aborts.
>
> Furthermore, this practice results in zombie processes while your program continues to run. For more details about zombie processes, see Hour 18.

Handling a Broken Pipe

When a program opens a pipe to another process for writing, and that other process aborts and causes its end of the pipe to be closed, then what happens? It turns out that Linux causes the signal SIGPIPE to be raised in the process that is trying to write to the pipe, which is now half closed. This signal indicates that the pipe is "broken."

A signal is an asynchronous event that is generated by the Linux kernel. Every process has default actions available for each signal type, but these defaults can be altered by the program. I will cover only the basics about signal handling here—just enough to allow you to cope with broken pipes.

The program in Listing 17.2 writes a message to the mailx command. If, partway through its message, the mailx command is killed by a system administrator or the program aborts, Linux terminates that program and closes its read end of the pipe. The next time the program tries to write to that pipe, Linux raises the signal SIGPIPE in the process to notify you of the broken pipe. The default action registered to SIGPIPE causes the program to terminate.

To allow the program to retain control if this situation should occur, you must plan for the SIGPIPE signal. The simplest procedure is as follows:

1. Include the file signal.h.
2. Before you open the first pipe, call signal(SIGPIPE,SIG_IGN). This call tells the Linux kernel to ignore the signal SIGPIPE if it is raised.

To enhance the program in Listing 17.2, you could just add this call at the start of the main program (fragment shown):

```
int
main(int argc,char **argv) {
    struct passwd *pw = 0;      /* Password info */
    char cmd[256];              /* Command buffer */
    FILE *p = 0;                /* mailx pipe */

    signal(SIGPIPE,SIG_IGN);    /* Ignore SIGPIPE */
```

This method causes either your write calls to return an error (EPIPE) or the pclose() function to return an error when signal SIGPIPE is raised. This result is much preferred to the default action of terminating your process when SIGPIPE is raised.

In this section, you explored how to create a process with a data input pipe or a data output pipe to it. In the next section, you will examine another way to start processes without using a pipe.

Introducing the system() Function

In the preceding sections, you learned how one process can open a pipe to another. In this way, they can exchange data. However, sometimes a process simply wants to invoke another process, without exchanging data.

In the remainder of this lesson, you'll look at the `system()` function call, which accomplishes this task. This function is simple for programmers to use, but it suffers from a few drawbacks. I will describe the details behind this function's use and discuss its weaknesses.

The `system()` function has the following function prototype:

```
#include <stdlib.h>

int system(const char *command);
```


This function call uses the /bin/sh shell to interpret and execute the command string. For Linux, this shell is linked to the bash shell.

Interpreting system() Return Values

The return value for the `system()` function is tricky. It requires careful analysis if the correct conclusion is to be arrived at. Table 17.1 contains a summary of the return values from the `system()` function. Note that the `errno` value should be cleared to `0` before calling this function. This way, the caller can distinguish between a failure to start the command and a command returning a return value of `127`.

TABLE 17.1 THE `system()` FUNCTION RETURN VALUES

Return Value	*Check* `errno`	*Description*
`0`	No	The function call is successful launching the command, and the command exits with a zero exit status.
`-1`	Yes	An error has occurred. Check the value of `errno` to determine the reason for failure.
`127`	Maybe	If `errno` was cleared to `0` before calling `system()`, and it is not `0` after the call, then an error has occurred while starting the new process. Check `errno` for the reason that the process could not be started. Otherwise, if `errno` remains `0`, then the command is executed and returns exit code `127`.
`1 to 126`	No	These are return codes from the command that has executed.
`128 to 255`	No	These are return codes from the command that has executed.

Using the system() Function

To illustrate how you can use the `system()` function and test its confused return values, I've provided a program in Listing 17.3. (Change line 28 to invoke `mail` if your system does not include a `mailx` command.)

Listing 17.3 17LST03.c—Sample Program Using the `system()` Function

```
1:  #include <stdio.h>
2:  #include <stdlib.h>
3:  #include <unistd.h>
4:  #include <errno.h>
5:  #include <string.h>
6:  #include <pwd.h>
7:  #include <sys/types.h>
8:
9:  int
10: main(int argc,char **argv) {
11:     struct passwd *pw = 0;        /* Password info */
12:     char cmd[256];                /* Command buffer */
13:     int rc;                       /* Command return code */
14:
15:     /*
16:      * Lookup our userid:
17:      */
18:     if ( !(pw = getpwuid(geteuid())) ) {
19:         fprintf(stderr,"%s: unknown userid\n",
20:             strerror(errno));
21:         return 13;
22:     }
23:
24:     /*
25:      * Format command :
26:      */
27:     sprintf(cmd,
28:         "ps f | mailx -s 'PID %ld' %s",
29:         (long) getpid(),      /* Process ID */
30:         pw->pw_name);         /* User name */
31:
32:     /*
33:      * Run the command :
34:      */
35:     errno = 0;                /* Clear errno */
36:     rc = system(cmd);         /* Execute the command */
37:
38:     if ( rc == 127 && errno != 0 ) {
39:         /* Command failed to start */
40:         fprintf(stderr,
41:             "%s: starting system(%s)\n",
```

```
42:             strerror(errno),cmd);
43:     } else if ( rc == -1 ) {
44:         /* Other errors occurred */
45:         fprintf(stderr,
46:             "%s: system(%s)\n",
47:             strerror(errno),cmd);
48:     } else {
49:         printf("Command '%s'\n  returned code %d\n",cmd,rc);
50:         puts("Check your mail.");
51:     }
52:
53:     return 0;
54: }
```


The steps used in Listing 17.3 can be summarized as follows:

1. The effective user ID of this process is looked up. The pointer `pw` to the `passwd` entry is set (line 18).
2. A command is formatted to send the `ps` command output to the `mailx` command (lines 27 to 30). This step causes email to be mailed to the current user when this command is executed.
3. The `errno` value is cleared (line 35). This step is necessary to distinguish between a returned error and a command returning the value `127`.
4. The `system()` function is called to execute the command formatted in buffer array `cmd[]` (line 36). The return code is stored in variable `rc` for analysis later.
5. A test is performed to check if `rc` is the value `127` and if `errno` holds a nonzero error code. If so, then the program knows that one or more of the commands in `cmd[]` never got started. The value `errno` holds the reason, and it is reported (lines 39 to 42).
6. A test is performed to check whether `rc` is `-1`. This result is an obvious indication that an error occurred. If `true`, the error is reported (lines 44 to 47).
7. If control passes to line 49, then you know that the command that was passed to the `system()` function is executed. However, one or more of the commands may have failed. All you can check at this point is the returned exit code in `rc` here (lines 49 and 50).

Running the Sample Program

When you compile and execute the program in Listing 17.3, you obtain the following results:

```
bash$ ./a.out
Command 'ps f | mailx -s 'PID 847' student1'
```

```
  returned code 0
Check your mail.
bash$
```

This session tells you that the command was carried out successfully. You can check your mail now:

```
bash$ mailx
Mail version 5.5 6/1/90.  Type ? for help.
"/var/spool/mail/student1": 1 message 1 unread
>U  1 student1@slug  Fri Jan 22 21:08  19/615   "PID 847"
& 1
Message 1:
From student1  Fri Jan 22 21:08:49 1999
Date: Fri, 22 Jan 1999 21:08:48 -0500
From: Student 01 <student1@slug>
To: student1@slug
Subject: PID 847

  PID TTY STAT  TIME COMMAND
   71  a0 S    0:06 -bash
  847  a0 S    0:00  \_ ./a.out
  848  a0 S    0:00      \_ sh -c ps f ¦ mailx -s 'PID 847' student1
  849  a0 R    0:00          \_ ps f
  850  a0 R    0:00          \_ mailx -s 'PID 847' student1

& d 1
& q
bash$
```

In the email message, you can see an interesting list of processes. Note the following points (PID is an abbreviation for Process ID):

- PID 71 (bash) is the shell used to start the program `a.out`.
- The process `a.out` (PID 847) invokes an `sh` (shell) process (PID 848). Listed there is the full command that the `system()` command fabricates from the input.
- The shell forks a process `ps` (PID 849). This process writes to a pipe to PID 850.
- The `mailx` process (PID 850) reads from the pipe that PID 850 is writing to. Notice how this process has the `ps` process as its parent.

In this example, you can see that the `system()` call creates three different processes: the shell and the two processes at each end of the pipe.

Understanding Different Results

If you run the program as shown in the preceding section, you might experience different results occasionally. The normal result in the email is as follows:

```
PID TTY STAT  TIME COMMAND
   71  a0 S    0:06 -bash
  847  a0 S    0:00  \_ ./a.out
  848  a0 S    0:00      \_ sh -c ps f ¦ mailx -s 'PID 847' student1
  849  a0 R    0:00          \_ ps f
  850  a0 R    0:00          \_ mailx -s 'PID 847' student1
```

However, you might have seen something like this instead:

```
PID TTY STAT  TIME COMMAND
   71  a0 S    0:06 -bash
  847  a0 S    0:00  \_ ./a.out
  848  a0 S    0:00      \_ sh -c ps f ¦ mailx -s 'PID 847' student1
  849  a0 R    0:00          \_ ps f
  850  a0 R    0:00          \_ sh -c ps f ¦ mailx -s 'PID 847'
➥ student1
```


Can you explain the line for PID 850? Why does it not just show the `mailx` command instead of the shell?

The answer is that this is simply a matter of timing. This display shows that the `ps` command starts before the shell (PID 850) has a chance to run `exec()` on the `mailx` command. These points will be clearer after you study `fork()` and `exec()` in Hour 18.

Evaluating the `system()` Function

Although the `system()` function is quite easy to use, it does have its drawbacks. One of them is the muddled set of return values that the `system()` call returns (review Table 17.1).

The `system()` call is also considered a security leak and should not be used by programs that are run with `setuid` permissions (these programs can temporarily change to another user ID or group).

Many of the objections to the `system()` function will become clearer when you finish Hour 18. In that lesson, you will learn how the `system()` function actually accomplishes its task.

Summary

In this lesson, you focused on the creation of other processes from within your process—with and without pipes. You learned how pipes can be read and how pipes can be written. You also learned that pipes need to use a special close function. Finally, you explored the `system()` function and learned how to interpret its returned results.

Q&A

Q Can a `popen()` call open a pipe to a command that redirects I/O?

A Yes, but be careful. Because the shell starts the command, the facilities of the shell are available, including I/O redirection. However, if you open the pipe for reading, make sure that the process at the other end of the pipe will be sending you data. The reverse also applies when you are writing to a pipe: Make sure that process will read your data as input.

Q Is the command given in the `popen()` call affected by your current `PATH` environment variable?

A Yes. The `popen()` call uses the shell to start your command, and the shell searches according to the `PATH` variable it inherits from your present process.

Q Can the `popen()` command specify piped commands?

A Yes. Because the shell is used to initiate your command, all the facilities of the shell are available to you in the `popen()` call. You therefore can specify a command that pipes its output to yet another command.

Q Can the opened `FILE` stream for a pipe be rewound to reread the data from a pipe?

A No. Pipes cannot be rewound like a regular file can be. No seek operations are permitted on a pipe.

Workshop

You are encouraged to work through the quiz and the exercises to practice what you have learned. Working through them will help you to retain what you have just learned.

Quiz

1. If you use `popen()` to open a pipe to the command `"ps lax ¦ sort"` for reading, which command is attached to the other end of your pipe?
2. If you use `popen()` to open a pipe to the command `"sort ¦ mailx -s 'Test Run' root"` for writing, which command is reading the data at the other end of the pipe?
3. What step should you perform before calling `system()`?
4. When `system()` returns `3`, what does this value mean?
5. Should you use `fclose()` on a `FILE` opened by `popen()`? Why or why not?

Exercises

1. Write a program that uses `popen()` for reading the results of a `"ps laxu"` command and displays them on standard output.
2. Using the program in exercise 1, pipe the `ps` command to sort so that the `sort` process sorts the processes in decreasing `CPU` utilization order. The `%CPU` utilization is the third column when `"ps laxu"` is used.
3. Write a function that can be given the subject line as an argument and the user ID as the recipient argument. Within the function, open a pipe to the `mailx` (or `mail`) command, and return that opened `FILE` pointer to the caller. From your test `main()` program, call this function and format a short message to yourself to prove that it works.
4. Write a small program that calls `system()` to perform a `who` command, and email it to yourself.

Hour 18

Forked Processes

Introduction to Processes

As a user of Linux, you are already probably quite familiar with UNIX processes and process IDs. This lesson begins with a review to make certain that you understand process ID numbers and the difference between the parent and child processes. These concepts are important to understand when you're dealing with forked processes.

In this lesson, you will learn what Linux does when it forks a new process. You will also see how to use the `fork()` and `exec()` system calls together. These functions are very important because they allow the Linux system to create new processes and to execute new programs.

Understanding Process ID Numbers

Every executing program under Linux is known as a *process*. You can think of a process as a unit of work or simply a running program. Each process has a number, which is known as the *process ID* (or *PID*). Numbering processes makes it convenient for both the kernel and application to keep track of tasks running in the system.

Process ID numbers are positive numbers. The process ID number 1 is special and refers to the `init` process. If a parent no longer exists for a given process because it has terminated, the `init` process adopts that existing child process. The `init` process becomes the parent of all orphaned processes.

Other process ID numbers are special. For example, under Linux, process ID 2 is the daemon `kflushd`, which flushes out the disk cache. Process ID 3 is `kswapd`, which is used for swapping virtual memory to the swap file. Because they are reserved process ID numbers, your process will never have an ID number of 1, 2, or 3.

Process ID numbers increment up to a high value and then start over (process ID numbers are limited to the maximum precision of the C data type `pid_t`). However, two processes can never have the same ID number. The Linux kernel makes certain that the new process gets its own unique ID number that is not in use.

Understanding Parent and Child Processes

Every process running under Linux has been created from another process (with the exception of system startup). This means that every process has a parent process. If the parent process exits, then the parent becomes the `init` process, as noted in the preceding section.

When a new process is *forked* under Linux, the parent process is the original process that you started with. The child process is the new process that is created.

Creating a Process

Every process under Linux is created using the `fork()` call. I will discuss how to use this function later in the lesson, but for now, let me make sure you understand the concept behind it. The `fork()` function creates a new process with the following steps:

1. The parent process calls the function `fork()`, expecting a new process ID value to be returned.
2. The Linux kernel "virtually" copies all the parent's process memory into the memory address space of the new child process. In this manner, the child process is, byte for byte, identical to the parent process.
3. Certain kernel entities such as open file descriptors, the current working directory, the `umask` value, and resource limits are copied from the parent process and established for the child process.
4. Certain kernel entities unique to the child process are established. The child process gets its own unique process ID, and its parent PID is set to that of the process that forked to create this process.

5. The `fork()` function establishes the value it is going to return. For the parent process, the return value becomes the child process ID that was created. For the child process, the `fork()` function returns `0`.
6. Upon returning from `fork()`, two nearly identical processes are now running: a parent process and its child process.

This procedure might seem a bit confusing to the novice, but you will see in the sample programs presented later that it is easier than it sounds.

You have now completed your review of processes, process IDs, and the parent/child relationship. Now that you understand the procedure that the Linux `fork()` is going to use, it is time to introduce the `fork()` function and put it to use.

The `fork()` Function

One of the outstanding differences between UNIX and other operating systems is the way a new process is created. Other operating systems create a process from scratch, complete with memory, and then load a program into that memory. UNIX, on the other hand, never creates a process from scratch (the `init` process at boot time is the only exception). Every process is created by cloning the existing process at the point of the `fork()` function call.

In Hour 17, "Pipes and Processes," you learned that `fork()` and `exec()` work behind the scenes when you call on `popen()` and `system()`. In this section, you will see how they create a new process.

The synopsis for the `fork()` function is as follows:

```
#include <unistd.h>
#include <sys/types.h>

pid_t fork(void);
```

The Linux man page for `fork(2)` does not mention the need for the include file sys/types.h, but you do need that include file for the type definition `pid_t`. The `pid_t` data type holds a process ID that is returned by the `fork()` function call.

If, however, the value `-1` is returned by the function, you should test the reason for the error held in the external integer `errno`. When `fork()` reports an error, no new process has been created.

As you can see, `fork()` takes no arguments. It simply returns a process ID to the caller. The child process is returned the value `0`. This way, the program can determine which of the two forks it is executing.

Using the `fork()` Function

The program in Listing 18.1 illustrates a simple example that creates one child process using the `fork()` function. It also illustrates how you should test for errors upon returning from `fork()`.

LISTING 18.1 18LST01.C—SAMPLE PROGRAM CALLING `fork()`

```
#include <stdio.h>
#include <unistd.h>
#include <string.h>
#include <errno.h>
#include <sys/types.h>

int
main(int argc,char **argv) {
    pid_t pid;          /* Process ID of the child process */

    pid = fork();       /* Create a new child process */

    if ( pid == -1 ) {
        fprintf(stderr,
            "%s: Failed to fork()\n",
            strerror(errno));
        exit(13);
    } else if ( pid == 0 ) {
        printf("PID %ld: Child started, parent is %ld.\n",
            (long)getpid(),     /* Our PID */
            (long)getppid());   /* Parent PID */
    } else  {
        printf("PID %ld: Started child PID %ld.\n",
            (long)getpid(),     /* Our PID */
            (long)pid);         /* Child's PID */
    }

    sleep(1);   /* Stick around a bit */
    return 0;
}
```

> When you're using the `printf()` family of functions to report data types like `pid_t`, always cast the variable to a fixed data type matching the format specifier. By doing so, you make the program more portable because it becomes independent of any change that might take place to the underlying data type. For example, data type `xyz_t` might change from a `short` integer value to a `long` integer value at a future date. Consider this example:
>
> ```
> pid_t pid = getpid();
>
> printf("PID is %ld\n",(long)pid);
> ```
>
> The casting of variable `pid` to a `(long)` forces the data type to match the format specifier `%ld`.

The program in Listing 18.1 uses the following steps:

1. Variable `pid` of type `pid_t` is declared to hold the process ID that will be returned by the `fork()` call (line 9).
2. Function `fork()` is called to create a new process (line 11). The returned process ID is stored in variable `pid`.
3. A test is performed to check for an error in the `fork()` call (line 13). If the variable `pid` is the value `-1`, then the error is reported and the program is exited (lines 14 to 17).
4. A test is performed to check for a process ID of `0` (line 18). If variable `pid` is `0`, then this process is a copy of the parent process. This value indicates that you are executing instructions for the child process. In this case, the child process message is reported (lines 19 to 21). Note how you use the function `getppid()` to obtain the process ID of the parent process.
5. Otherwise (line 22), you know that you are executing in the original parent process because the variable `pid` stores the child process ID from the `fork()` return value. The parent message is displayed (lines 23 to 25).
6. The `sleep()` function is called to pause the program for one second (line 28) so that the child process is not orphaned by a hasty exit of the parent process. If the parent process exits before the child process can report its message, the child process reports PID 1 as its parent (the `init` process).

Your process can call the function `getppid()` to obtain the process ID of the parent process. This function takes no arguments and generates no errors.

This capability is especially helpful to the child process after the `fork()` function returns. The child process is returned the value `0`, so it becomes necessary for the child process to call `getppid()` to determine its parent process ID.

Running the `fork()` Example

After compiling the program in Listing 18.1, you should be able to run it and get output similar to this (your process ID values will be different):

```
bash$ ./a.out
PID 310: Started child PID 311.
PID 311: Child started, parent is 310.
bash$
```

The session can be summarized as follows:

1. The compiled program `a.out` is started.
2. The parent process ID 310 starts a child process ID 311.
3. The child process ID 311 starts and reports its parent process ID to be 310.
4. Both processes are exited.

In this example, the parent process reports its message first. Sometimes, however, the child process may report its message first. This behavior occurs because the child process competes with its parent process for CPU resources after it is created.

Running the Modified Example

If you take the program in Listing 18.1 and add a `system()` call to it, you can display the process relationships more graphically. Look at Listing 18.2.

LISTING 18.2 18LST02.C—MODIFIED EXAMPLE OF THE `fork()` CALL

```
#include <stdio.h>
#include <stdlib.h>
#include <unistd.h>
#include <string.h>
#include <errno.h>
#include <sys/types.h>

int
main(int argc,char **argv) {
    pid_t pid;          /* Process ID of the child process */
```

```
11:
12:     pid = fork();       /* Create a new child process */
13:
14:     if ( pid == -1 ) {
15:         fprintf(stderr,
16:             "%s: Failed to fork()\n",
17:             strerror(errno));
18:         exit(13);
19:     } else if ( pid == 0 ) {
20:         printf("PID %ld: Child started, parent is %ld.\n",
21:             (long)getpid(),     /* Our PID */
22:             (long)getppid());   /* Parent PID */
23:         system("ps f");        /* Show processes */
24:     } else {
25:         printf("PID %ld: Started child PID %ld.\n",
26:             (long)getpid(),     /* Our PID */
27:             (long)pid);         /* Child's PID */
28:     }
29:
30:     sleep(1);   /* Stick around a bit */
31:     return 0;
32: }
```


The changes made to the program in Listing 18.1 to arrive at the program in Listing 18.2 are as follows:

1. The include file stdlib.h is required for the `system()` function (line 2).
2. The `system()` function is called by the child process to list the processes in GNU "forest" format (line 23).

Compiling this program and running it should yield results similar to this:

```
bash$ ./a.out
PID 336: Started child PID 337.
PID 337: Child started, parent is 336.
  PID TTY STAT  TIME COMMAND
   72  a0 S     0:03 -bash
  336  a0 S     0:00  \_ ./a.out
  337  a0 S     0:00      \_ ./a.out
  338  a0 R     0:00          \_ ps f
bash$
```

Notice the relationships between the processes in the following steps:

1. The bash shell in which you are conducting the session is PID 72.
2. The program `a.out` that you have started executing has as its parent the bash shell (PID 72). The program runs as PID 336 (reported as the parent process in the program output).

3. The child process (PID 337) is also the program `a.out` because it is simply a forked copy of the parent. The `ps` command output agrees with the child program's assertion that the parent of that process is PID 336.
4. The final child process is the `ps` command itself (PID 338).

Now you are armed with the ability to fork new processes from your C programs. In the following sections, you'll examine the `wait()` family of functions because parent processes need them to find out how a child process is terminated.

The `wait()` Family of Functions

In the sample `fork()` programs in the preceding sections, you simply called `sleep()` to wait for approximately one second. This way, the parent program was able to stick around long enough that the child could report on it. However, the program would actually perform better if the `main` program had a way to determine when the child process had completed.

Other questions that arise are as follows: How does a program determine how the child process completed? What was the exit code? Did it abort? Was it killed? Was a core file created?

Understanding the Importance of `wait()`

The `wait()` family of functions allows a parent process to inquire of its child processes. These functions are also important to the Linux kernel because they allow the kernel to know when the termination status is no longer required. When a child process terminates, the exit status is saved in the process table of that process, although most of the resources are released. That process table entry and its process ID cannot be reused until this table entry is freed.

Understanding Zombie Processes

Zombie processes are child processes that have terminated for one reason or another, while their parent process continues to execute without inquiring about their fate. You could almost say that the parent process is negligent about its children. The `wait()` functions are called by the parent process, allowing the kernel to remove these zombies from the system.

After the child process has terminated, the Linux kernel releases its memory and closes its files. Most of the process resources are freed, with the exception of the process table entry. The process table entry is identified by its process ID, and the termination status of the process is stored in the process table entry.

Until the parent process fetches this information, this table entry must remain in the Linux kernel. A process in this state is known as a *zombie*. The following is a sample session in which the child process has exited, but the parent process has not inquired yet of its termination status:

```
PID TTY STAT  TIME COMMAND
   72  a0 S    0:03 -bash
  379  a0 S    0:00  \_ ./a.out
  380  a0 Z    0:00      \_ (a.out <zombie>)
  381  a0 R    0:00      \_ ps f
```

This `ps` output shows that child process ID 380 has exited and that the `ps` command has labeled it as a zombie. However, the parent process (PID 379) of the child is still running. You therefore know that it has not inquired about its child process yet. For this reason, the Linux kernel keeps the process table entry around so that the process termination status of PID 380 will not be lost.

Using the `wait()` Function

The parent process can inquire about its child process by using the `wait()` function. The function prototype for it is as follows:

```
#include <sys/types.h>
#include <sys/wait.h>

pid_t wait(int *status)
```


This function accepts one argument, which must be a pointer to an integer data type to receive the return status information. The return value of the function is the data type `pid_t`. This return value indicates which child process is being reported by the call (some parent processes may have more than one child process outstanding).

The program shown in Listing 18.3 is similar to the original program in Listing 18.1. However, in this program, the `sleep()` call is replaced in favor of the `wait()` call.

LISTING 18.3 18LST03.C—EXAMPLE USING THE `wait()` FUNCTION

```
#include <stdio.h>
#include <unistd.h>
#include <string.h>
#include <errno.h>
#include <sys/types.h>
#include <sys/wait.h>

int
```

continues

LISTING 18.3 CONTINUED

```
9:   main(int argc,char **argv) {
10:      pid_t pid;           /* Process ID of the child process */
11:      pid_t wpid;          /* Process ID from wait() */
12:      int status;          /* Exit status from wait() */
13:
14:      pid = fork();        /* Create a new child process */
15:
16:      if ( pid == -1 ) {
17:          fprintf(stderr,
18:              "%s: Failed to fork()\n",
19:              strerror(errno));
20:          exit(13);
21:      } else if ( pid == 0 ) {
22:          printf("PID %ld: Child started, parent is %ld.\n",
23:              (long)getpid(),     /* Our PID */
24:              (long)getppid());   /* Parent PID */
25:      } else  {
26:          printf("PID %ld: Started child PID %ld.\n",
27:              (long)getpid(),     /* Our PID */
28:              (long)pid);         /* Child's PID */
29:          wpid = wait(&status);   /* Child's exit status */
30:          if ( wpid == -1 ) {
31:              fprintf(stderr,"%s: wait()\n",
32:                  strerror(errno));
33:              return 1;
34:          } else if ( wpid != pid )
35:              abort(); /* Should never happen in this prog. */
36:          else {
37:              printf("Child PID %ld exited status 0x%04X\n",
38:                  (long)pid,      /* Child PID */
39:                  status);        /* Exit status */
40:          }
41:      }
42:
43:      return 0;
44:  }
```

The following changes were applied to Listing 18.1 to arrive at the program in Listing 18.3:

1. Variable `wpid` of type `pid_t` is declared (line 11).
2. A variable `status` is declared to receive the child process exit status (line 12).
3. The `sleep()` call is removed. Neither parent nor child calls `sleep()` now.
4. Function `wait()` is called by the parent process (line 29). The returned value is placed in variable `wpid`. The status of the child program is stored by the `wait()` call in the variable `status`.
5. A test is performed to check `wpid` for the value `-1`. This value indicates that the function failed (line 30). The error is reported if an error occurs (lines 31 to 33).

6. A test is performed to check whether `wpid` matches the variable `pid` (line 34). They should never disagree in this program, so you code a call to `abort()` in line 35 if they should disagree.
7. The exit status is reported (lines 37 to 39). The exit status is reported in hexadecimal because there are subfields in this value (you will test this information with macros later).

If you compile and invoke the program in Listing 18.3 from the shell, you should get the following output:

```
bash$ ./a.out
PID 421: Started child PID 422.
PID 422: Child started, parent is 421.
Child PID 422 exited status 0x0000
bash$
```

If you run this demo, you will immediately notice how much faster it runs because you don't have a `sleep()` of one second involved. The output is similar to what you saw before, except that now you have the exit status of `0x0000` being reported by the parent process.

Interpreting the `wait()` Exit Status

The status returned by `wait()` has more in it than a program exit code. It records whether the program exited normally, was aborted, was killed (or signaled), or stopped. Programmers are expected to use macros to test for these differences in status because this is the only portable way to write code using this status information. Table 18.1 identifies macros that can be used.

TABLE 18.1 TABLE OF STATUS TEST MACROS

Macro	*Description*
`WIFEXITED(status)`	This macro returns `true` if the status indicates that the process exited normally. An exit code for this process is available using macro `WEXITSTATUS(status)`, which returns an 8-bit exit code.
`WIFSIGNALED(status)`	This macro returns `true` if the status indicates that the process received a signal that it did not catch and caused its termination. The macro `WTERMSIG(status)` is available to extract the signal number from status that caused the termination. The macro `WCOREDUMP(status)` is available; it indicates `true` if a core file was created.
`WIFSTOPPED(status)`	This macro returns `true` if the status indicates that the process is currently stopped. The macro `WSTOPSIG(status)` is available to extract the signal number of the signal that caused the process to stop.

Testing the `wait()` Status

To help illustrate the details in Table 18.1, I've supplied the following code, which shows how to test for a normal program termination and display the 8-bit exit code:

```
int status;

if ( WIFEXITED(status) ) {
    printf("Exited with return code %d;\n",
       (int)WEXITSTATUS(status));
}
```

The code tests for a normal exit with the `WIFEXITED()` macro. When this macro returns `true`, the value returned by `WEXITSTATUS()` provides the exit code from that process. This is the exit code that the bash shell reports with its built-in variable `$?`.

To test if your program aborted or was killed/signaled, you use the following tests:

```
int status;

if ( WIFSIGNALED(status) ) {
    printf("Terminated with signal %d;\n",
        (int)WTERMSIG(status));
    if ( WCOREDUMP(status) )
        printf("A core file was written.\n");
}
```

For the preceding code fragment, you follow these steps:

1. Use macro `WIFSIGNALED()` to test if the status indicates whether the process was terminated due to a signal. If the result is `true`, continue to step 2.
2. Extract the signal that caused the termination by using the macro `WTERMSIG()`.
3. Extract whether the core file was written by using the `WCOREDUMP()` macro.

Note that the macros `WTERMSIG()` and `WCOREDUMP()` are valid only if `WIFSIGNALED()` tests `true`.

Reviewing Other Members of the `wait` Family

Other members of the `wait()` function family provide some features that are not present in the standard `wait()` call. The function `waitpid()` can return with no data, if there is no data to report. The standard `wait()` function blocks the calling process until information is available to report.

Another advantage of the `waitpid()` function is that it can wait on a specific child process ID if the parent process has more than one child process outstanding.

Linux also makes the BSD UNIX calls `wait3()` and `wait4()` available. They allow the resource utilization of the exited process to be returned in addition to the status.

In the following sections of this lesson, I will just keep things simple and move on to the `exec()` family of functions. For the curious, check out the Linux man pages for `waitpid(2)`, `wait3(2)`, and `wait4(2)` for more details.

The `exec()` Family of Functions

If `fork()` were the only function available on your system for creating a new process, you would only be running several copies of the same program. The `exec()` family of functions allows you to run new programs.

In the following sections, you will look at what `exec()` does and how it is used. You'll also examine why `fork()` and `exec()` are used together.

Understanding the `exec()` Procedure

Table 18.2 shows the analogy I will use to illustrate the purpose of the `exec()` function. It compares the idea of a home to a process going through the `exec()` procedure.

18

TABLE 18.2 HOME AND PROCESS ANALOGY ACTORS/PROPS

Home Component	*Equivalent Process Component*
Street Address	Linux Process ID (PID)
Home (& lot)	Process memory address space
Tenants	The program instructions (code)

Using the actors and props from Table 18.2, Table 18.3 lists the steps that the `exec()` function performs.

TABLE 18.3 THE `exec()` STEPS PERFORMED

Step	*Home Equivalent*	*Equivalent* `exec()` *Procedure*
1.	Keep street address.	Keep process ID (PID).
2.	Keep the same home.	Keep the same addressable process memory.
3.	Serve eviction notice.	Stop the currently executing program.
4.	Evict the tenants.	The current program image is abandoned (it will be overwritten next).
5.	Bring in new tenants.	The existing memory address space is overwritten as the new program is loaded in from a file.
6.	Welcome the tenants.	The new program that was loaded is now given control. The new `main()` program starts to execute.

The overall effect of an `exec()` call is to replace the currently executing process with a new program within the same process memory. You also should note that if the `exec()` call is successful, it never returns control to the caller. The calling process is discarded (step 3 in Table 18.3).

Combining `fork()` and `exec()`

When the bash shell starts a new command, it uses both of the functions `fork()` and `exec()` to carry out this task. The reasons for this are as follows:

1. The `fork()` function creates a new child process.
2. The new child process uses `exec()` to load the command into its memory and execute it.

The general procedure just shown can be described in detail as follows:

1. The current shell process calls upon `fork()`. (Assume PID 100 for this process.)
2. The `fork()` call returns to the parent process (PID 100) with the process ID of the child process. (Assume PID 101 for the child process.)
3. The parent shell process (PID 100) calls `wait()` to wait for the child process to terminate.
4. The child process returns from `fork()` with a return value of `0`. This value indicates that it is the child process.
5. The child process (PID 101) now calls `exec()` to replace the shell program it is currently running with the command that is to be started.
6. The command executes as PID 101 (remember that `exec()` keeps the same process ID of the caller).
7. The command process (PID 101) terminates. The Linux kernel notes this fact in its process table.
8. The parent process (shell PID 100) now receives information from `wait()` that process ID 101 has terminated and receives the termination status of that child process.
9. The shell (PID 100) updates its shell variable `$?`.

Applying the `exec()` Function Call

Now that you understand how the `fork()` and `exec()` functions work together, it is time to look at the function prototype for the `exec()` function itself. You will look specifically at the `execve()` function, which is one of the family of `exec()` functions:

```
#include <unistd.h>

int execve(const char *filename,
    const char *argv[],
    const char *envp[]);
```

This function takes three arguments:

- The filename of the binary executable program or interpreter script
- The `argv[]` array to be passed to the program
- The `envp[]` array of environment variables to export

Starting Script Files from `exec()`

The filename argument can be the name of a script file. The script must begin with the first two bytes as `#!` and the remaining bytes specify the pathname of the interpreter to use. Most of the time, the first line of the script specifies a shell #!/bin/sh. If the script does not begin this way, however, it is up to the caller to invoke a shell to be used to interpret that script.

Understanding the Sample Program

To illustrate the use of the `execve()` call, I have created the program in Listing 18.4. In this example, you are going to start the `ps` command without any help from the shell whatsoever. In a limited sense, this program performs the same steps that a shell would use to start the `ps` command.

Listing 18.4 18LST04.c—Sample `exec()` Program

```
#include <stdio.h>
#include <unistd.h>
#include <string.h>
#include <errno.h>
#include <sys/types.h>
#include <sys/wait.h>

/*
 * If the ps command is not located at /bin/ps
 * on your system, then change the pathname
 * defined for PS_PATH below.
 */
#define PS_PATH "/bin/ps"

extern char **environ;   /* Our environment array */

/*
 * Replace this process with the ps command :
```

continues

LISTING 18.4 CONTINUED

```
 */
static void
exec_ps_cmd(void) {
    static char *argv[] =
        { "ps", "f", NULL };

    /*
     * Exec the ps command: ps f
     */
    execve(PS_PATH,argv,environ);

    /*
     * If control reaches here, then the execve()
     * call has failed!
     */
    fprintf(stderr,"%s: execve()\n",
        strerror(errno));
}

/*
 * Main program :
 */
int
main(int argc,char **argv) {
    pid_t pid;          /* Process ID of the child process */
    pid_t wpid;         /* Process ID from wait() */
    int status;         /* Exit status from wait() */

    /*
     * Create a new child process :
     */
    pid = fork();

    if ( pid == -1 ) {
        /*
         * Fork failed to create a process :
         */
        fprintf(stderr,
            "%s: Failed to fork()\n",
            strerror(errno));
        exit(13);

    } else if ( pid == 0 ) {
        /*
         * This is the child process running :
         */
        printf("PID %ld: Child started, parent is %ld.\n",
            (long)getpid(),     /* Our PID */
            (long)getppid());   /* Parent PID */
```

```
        exec_ps_cmd();          /* Start the ps command */

    } else  {
        /*
         * This is the parent process running :
         */
        printf("PID %ld: Started child PID %ld.\n",
            (long)getpid(),     /* Our PID */
            (long)pid);         /* Child's PID */

        /*
         * Wait for the child process to terminate :
         */
        wpid = wait(&status);   /* Child's exit status */
        if ( wpid == -1 ) {
            /*
             * The wait() call failed :
             */
            fprintf(stderr,"%s: wait()\n",
                strerror(errno));
            return 1;

        } else if ( wpid != pid )
            /* Should never happen in this program: */
            abort();

        else {
            /*
             * The child process has terminated:
             */
            if ( WIFEXITED(status) ) {
                /*
                 * Normal exit -- print status
                 */
                printf("Exited: $? = %d\n",
                    WEXITSTATUS(status));

            } else if ( WIFSIGNALED(status) ) {
                /*
                 * Process abort, kill or signal:
                 */
                printf("Signal: %d%s\n",
                    WTERMSIG(status),
                    WCOREDUMP(status)
                        ? " with core file."
                        : "");
            } else {
                /*
                 * Stopped child process:
```


continues

LISTING 18.4 CONTINUED

```
117:                      */
118:                      printf("Stopped.\n");
119:              }
120:          }
121:      }
122:
123:      return 0;
124: }
```

In the step-by-step description of the program that is being presented, the specific process ID numbers given in brackets can be matched with the sample run of the program that follows. Here is the systematic procedure:

1. The `a.out` process (PID 911) calls `fork()` (line 50).
2. A test is performed to check for a `fork()` error (line 52).
3. The parent process (PID 911) displays its process ID (line 74) and then calls the `wait()` function (line 81). This call blocks until the child process terminates.
4. The child process (PID 912) receives the value `pid` of `0`. It prints its process ID (line 65) and then calls the function named `exec_ps_cmd()`.
5. Within the function `exec_ps_cmd()`, the process calls on the function `execve()` (line 28).
6. If step 5 is successful, the program `/bin/ps` binary executable replaces the current process, and the function in line 28 never returns. Instead, the `ps` command runs now, with the `argv[]` array passed to it from line 28, defined in lines 22 to 23. The `ps` command receives the same exported environment you have because you pass it the pointer of the `environ` pointer.

Examining the Output from the Sample Program

When you compile and run the program from Listing 18.4, you should get results similar to this (the process ID numbers can be referenced back to the steps given in the preceding section):

```
bash$ ./a.out
PID 911: Started child PID 912.
PID 912: Child started, parent is 911.
  PID TTY STAT  TIME COMMAND
   72  a0 S    0:04 -bash
  911  a0 S    0:00  \_ ./a.out
  912  a0 R    0:00      \_ ps f
Exited: $? = 0
bash$
```

The program issues its parent and child messages immediately after the program is started. By the third output line, however, the `ps` binary executable replaces the child process and provides a process display. It shows that the `ps` command is still the child process to the `a.out` parent process, based on the process ID shown.

The line `Exited: $? = 0` is this little program's attempt to pretend it is a shell. It reports that the `ps` command exited normally and that it returned an exit code of `0`.

Reviewing Other Members of the `exec()` Family

Several other `exec()` family member functions act as front-end programs to the `execve()` function that you just used. I won't cover them here because they are all listed in your Linux man pages under `exec(2)`. I will just list the function prototypes for the curious:

```
#include <unistd.h>

int execl(const char *path,const char *arg,...);
int execlp(const char *file,const char *arg,...);
int execle(const char *path,const char *arg,...,
    char *const envp[]);
int exect(const char *path,char *const argv[]);
int execv(const char *path,char *const argv[]);
int execvp(const char *file,char *const argv[]);
```

These different functions are provided for programmer convenience. They each offer something different, but they all call `execve()` in the end. Some of these interfaces take a variable number of arguments. Others search all the paths listed in the `PATH` environment variable. The choice boils down to your preference and needs.

That concludes the discussion on `fork()` and `exec()`. In the next lesson, you'll look at semaphores so that you can learn how to synchronize separate processes.

Summary

In this lesson, you learned about Linux processes. You saw how `fork()` and `exec()` work together as a team to create a new process and execute a new program. You also learned how to use the `wait()` call to determine how your child process is terminated.

At the end of the lesson, you saw the entire process at work: how the shell determines the arguments and the environment of the new process. You saw the `fork()` and `exec()` process that the bash shell uses. You also saw the `wait()` function used and learned how its returned values could be used by a shell program to update its `$?` variable.

Q&A

Q Can a program using `waitpid()` obtain the termination status for a process that is not its child process?

A No. The Linux kernel permits only the parent process to obtain the termination status of a child process.

Q What happens if the parent process never calls `wait()` on a child process? How do zombies go away?

A Only a parent process can obtain child termination status information. If the parent process terminates, then its zombies (child processes) are automatically released by the Linux kernel.

Q What return code does `execve()` return when the call is successful? Zero?

A A successful call to `execve()` never returns. If the function does return, then an error has occurred.

Q How do you run `exec()` on a shell script that does not begin with the characters `#!`?

A You must run `exec()` on a shell of your choice to execute the script. Linux uses the bash shell by default because the `/bin/sh` path is linked to bash.

Workshop

To practice what you have learned in this lesson, answer the quiz and work through the exercises.

Quiz

1. What does `fork()` return for the child process?
2. What does `execve()` return for the parent process?
3. What are two limitations of the `wait()` function?
4. Is the child process ID number always greater than the parent process ID?
5. What is the parent process ID of the child process after the parent process is terminated?
6. What macro do you use on the `wait()` status to test whether the program terminated normally?
7. What two macros must you use to determine whether a core file was created by a process abort?

Exercises

1. Write a small program to act as a shell. It must prompt the user for a command with the prompt `$ `. After you obtain the input command, use `strtok()` to parse the command into tokens. Place the tokens into an `argv[]` array (be sure to make the last element of the array a `null` pointer). For this exercise, assume that the command name is the full pathname of the command to execute. Use the `fork()` and `exec()` functions to execute the command. Use the `wait()` command to block your program until the command terminates.
2. Using the program from exercise 1, enhance the program to use the information from the `wait()` function to report the exit status of the command.
3. Using the program from exercise 2, enhance the program to obtain the value of the `PATH` environment. If the command starts with a slash (`/`) or a dot (`.`), then pass that command path directly to `execve()` as you did before. Otherwise, using the `PATH` variable, parsed with the `strtok()` function and the help of the `stat()` function, locate the command to be executed. Then pass the final pathname to `execve()`.

HOUR 19

Semaphores

Introducing Semaphores

The semaphore is one of a few Linux resources that allow separate processes to communicate with each other. For this reason, the semaphore is considered a member of the *Inter-Process Communication* set (*IPC*). The role of a semaphore is to synchronize two or more processes while accessing a common set of resources.

A semaphore is a counter value that can be manipulated atomically as a set from several processes. An atomic operation can never partially succeed. It must fully succeed with all semaphores participating in the operation, or the operation must totally fail. The atomic nature of the operation is important when multiple processes, possibly running on multiple CPUs, are involved.

In this lesson, you will look at Linux functions that create and access semaphores and examine how they are used. After you have completed this lesson, you will be able to apply your knowledge to any application that must synchronize among different processes.

The Single Shower Analogy

To learn why synchronization is necessary and how semaphores accomplish this function, you can consider an everyday household example.

Think of a home that has only one shower. Assume that the household in question has three children, a mother, and a father, and that they all need to take a shower on a weekday morning before 8:30 a.m. Figure 19.1 illustrates the situation.

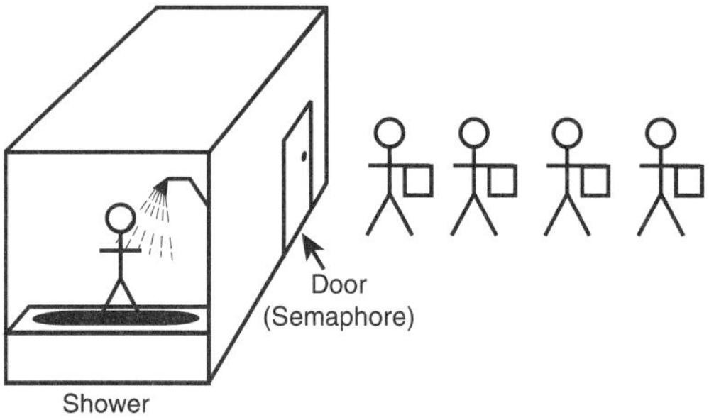

FIGURE 19.1
In this shower situation, only one person can be in the shower at one time.

The synchronizing component in Figure 19.1 is the door to the bathroom. After the occupant goes into the bathroom, he or she closes and locks the door to enforce some privacy. After the occupant is finished with his or her shower, he or she unlocks the door and leaves. Another person then can enter.

In this shower scenario, the door acting as the semaphore lets at most one person into the shower. However, later in the day, the shower can be found empty because no one wants to use the shower during that time. The door that is acting as a semaphore then enforces the rule that zero or one persons can occupy the shower at one time. The door is an example of a binary semaphore.

The Multiple Shower Analogy

This analogy can be extended to the boy's shower room at a school. In this scenario, there may be six showerheads, allowing at most six boys to shower at one time. When the six showerheads are in use, the remainder of the class lines up at the shower stall doorway (enforced by the teacher present). When one occupant leaves the shower, then another can go in to use the vacant showerhead.

After every boy has finished his shower and has left, zero showerheads are in use. In this manner, the doorway (or teacher) that is acting as the semaphore allows zero to six occupants to be present in the shower stall at one time. In this example, the semaphore represents the number of available showerheads. When no shower is in use, the semaphore count value is six. When all showerheads are in use, the semaphore count value has reached zero.

In the same fashion, you can initialize a Linux semaphore to specify `n` items to be available. You do so by setting the semaphore counter value to `n`. As each of those `n` resource items gets used, the counter is reduced. When the semaphore counter value reaches the value `0`, the semaphore prevents any process from proceeding further until the counter is increased again. This way, a semaphore controls access to `n` instances of a resource.

Applying Linux Semaphores

The counter value of the semaphore is what controls the access to the resource. To manipulate this counter value, semaphores employ two primary operations:

1. A user of the resource "waits" on a semaphore before the resource is used.
2. A user of the resource "notifies" the semaphore when the use of the resource is relinquished.

These operations are described in more detail in the sections that follow.

Waiting on a Semaphore

A binary semaphore is initialized to the count of one (for example). When the user waits on this semaphore, the following procedure takes place:

1. The semaphore count is examined. If the count is zero, the user must continue to wait indefinitely. If the current semaphore count is greater than zero, the user can proceed to the next step.
2. The semaphore count is decremented.
3. The user is allowed to proceed to use the resource.

When the semaphore contains the initial value `1`, the first user to wait on that semaphore changes that semaphore count to `0`. Because the value was initially greater than zero, that first user succeeds at waiting on the semaphore.

When the semaphore count is `0`, however, any subsequent users waiting on that semaphore must continue to wait indefinitely. They wait until that semaphore count is increased by a notify operation. This is done by the current user of the resource.

Notifying a Semaphore

After the user of the resource has finished with it, that user notifies the semaphore. The semaphore notification procedure consists of the following steps:

1. The user notifies the semaphore, indicating that the resource is no longer in use.
2. The semaphore value is incremented.

3. The semaphore waiting list is examined to see whether other users are waiting. If users are waiting, the semaphore wait procedure is applied.

Step 2 of this notification procedure allows the next user waiting for the resource to succeed at gaining access to it. This situation occurs because the notify operation increments the semaphore count from `0` to `1`.

Waiting for Multiple Instances

The preceding discussion of the semaphore wait and notify operations used a binary semaphore. However, if you must control access to `n` instances of a resource, you can simply initialize the semaphore value to `n` instead of the value `1`.

With the semaphore value initialized to `n`, `n` wait operations can take place successfully before a process is blocked indefinitely. After the notify operations begin to take place, then those blocked waiting on the semaphore will then succeed, according to the number of notify operations performed. In this manner, Linux semaphores can restrict access to `n` instances of a resource.

In the following sections, you will look at how semaphores are created, accessed, and used under Linux.

Creating and Accessing Semaphore Sets

Before an application is able to use a semaphore set, it must either access an existing semaphore set, or it must create a new set. The topic of this section is creating, accessing, and initializing semaphore sets.

In Hour 20, "Shared Memory," you will see that you frequently need to synchronize access to memory. The semaphore often fills this role. Learning how to use the semaphore facilities presented in this section therefore is important.

Identifying Existing Semaphore Sets

The IPC set of resources uses a C data type `key_t` to identify them. Consequently, existing semaphores can be accessed by a process when the `key_t` key value is known. The value chosen for the key is completely arbitrary and must be unique systemwide. The key value of `0` is reserved.

On many UNIX systems, you can discover which key values are currently in use by using the `ipcs` command. Unfortunately, older versions of the Linux `ipcs` command do not show the key values in its output.

Using `semget()` to Create and Access Semaphore Sets

To create a new semaphore set or to access an existing semaphore set, you use the `semget()` function. The following is the function synopsis for `semget()`:

```
#include <sys/types.h>
#include <sys/ipc.h>
#include <sys/sem.h>

int semget(key_t key,int nsems,int semflg)
```

The `semget()` function takes three arguments:

- `key`—The key value that identifies the semaphore set that you are creating or accessing in the local system
- `nsems`—The number of semaphores in the set that are being created or accessed
- `semflg`—A flag that specifies different options and permission bits

The key value is used to identify the semaphore set. After the semaphore set is created by one process, other processes can use this key value to locate the same semaphore set.

The argument `nsems` indicates to the function how many semaphores are in the set to be created. If you are accessing an existing set of semaphores, you can specify `0` to indicate that you want access to all the defined semaphores in its set.

The third argument, `semflg`, specifies certain option flags and permission bits if you are creating a new set. Table 19.1 shows the different values that are permitted in the `semflg` argument.

19

TABLE 19.1 THE `semflg` ARGUMENT OF `semget()`

Value	*Meaning*
`IPC_CREAT`	This value creates a semaphore set (without this option flag, an existing semaphore set is accessed if it exists).
`IPC_EXCL`	When used with `IPC_CREAT`, this option flag causes the `semget()` function to return error `EEXIST` if the semaphore set already exists.
`<lower-9-bits>`	The least value> significant nine bits represent the permission bits used to create the semaphore set. These bits apply to the user, the group, and others as they do for files and directories. However, with these permissions, unlike files and directories, no `umask` value is applied. These bits apply only if `IPC_CREAT` is used.

The function `semget()` returns the IPC ID of the semaphore set. It is an internal identifier that the Linux kernel uses to reference the semaphore set and should not be confused with the key value. Your application uses this IPC ID value when it performs other semaphore operations on the set. Note that `0` is a valid IPC ID.

If an error occurs, the value `-1` is returned, and `errno` contains the posted reason for the error.

Creating with the `IPC_EXCL` Flag

You should create semaphore sets using the `IPC_EXCL` flag. This is the only way that your code can be certain that it did indeed create the semaphore set. When your code knows that the set was created, it can proceed to initialize the counter values of the semaphore set. The following code shows how to create a semaphore set using the `IPC_EXCL` flag:

```
int semid;

semid = semget(0x1234,2,IPC_CREAT|IPC_EXCL|0600);
if ( semid < 0 ) {
    if ( errno == EEXIST ) {
        /* Action for pre-existing semaphore set */
    }
    fprintf(stderr,"%s: semget()\n",
        strerror(errno));
    abort();
} else {
    /* Initialize the semaphore set */
}
```

When this semaphore set creation code succeeds, you know that the set was created and that the semaphore values should be initialized. Semaphore initialization will be covered shortly.

If, however, the semaphore set already exists, the code returns the error `EEXIST`. This message may indicate that your current server process is a duplicate of another that is still running. Consequently, some sort of error procedure should normally be employed when this situation occurs.

Obtaining an Existing Semaphore Set

If one process is responsible for creating the semaphore set, then the other processes simply want access to the set. The way that you gain access to the set is to omit the `IPC_CREAT` flag as coded here:

```
int semid;

semid = semget(0x1234,0,0);
if ( semid < 0 ) {
```

```
    fprintf(stderr,"%s: semget()\n",
        strerror(errno));
    abort();
```

In this example, notice that the code specifies the number of semaphores in the set as `0`. Because you are not creating the set, you can give this value as `0` to access the entire existing set.

The `semflg` argument is also given as `0` because the `IPC_EXCL` flag has no meaning if `IPC_CREAT` is not used. Furthermore, you do not need to specify permission bits because they have already been established by the creator of the semaphore set.

Creating Private Semaphore Sets

Previously, you saw that an existing semaphore set could be identified and accessed by a key value. Because this key value is global to the system, a conflict can occur because of a collision of key values between two different applications. To avoid a collision, you must choose a different key value for one of the two applications.

You also can create a private set of semaphores. You do so by using the `IPC_PRIVATE` key as follows:

```
int semid;

semid = semget(IPC_PRIVATE,2,0600);
if ( semid < 0 ) {
    fprintf(stderr,"%s: semget()\n",
        strerror(errno));
    abort();
```


In this example, notice that specifying the flag `IPC_CREAT` is not necessary because a create operation is implied when you use a key value of `IPC_PRIVATE`. Note also that the flag `IPC_EXCL` has no meaning here either. Because `IPC_PRIVATE` always causes a new semaphore set to be created, it cannot previously exist. Note, however, you must supply the permission bits that you want to use.

Semaphore sets that are created this way are, in a sense, nameless. That is, they cannot be looked up by another process with a specific key value. This is why these semaphore sets are called *private*.

Privacy ends there, however. Any process that has the correct access permissions on the created set can use that set if it knows the value of `semid`.

Because of this feature, you will often find that semaphore sets are created with `IPC_PRIVATE`, and then the IPC ID of the created set is communicated somehow to the other process that needs to use it. This setup avoids any potential for conflict with existing key values that are in use on your system.

Understanding Semaphore Set Permissions

The permission bits for semaphores deserve special attention. The following points can be made about permission bits as they apply to semaphores:

- The read permission bit specifies that the value of a semaphore can be obtained or "read."
- The write permission bit means that the semaphore value can be "altered." This means the semaphore can be waited on or notified.
- The execute permission bit is not used.

Write permission is required if the process is ever to perform a wait or notify operation on the semaphore because these operations alter the semaphore count. Read permission allows a process to inquire of its current value.

Initializing Semaphore Sets

Immediately after creating a semaphore set, you should initialize the semaphore values. Two reasons for insisting on semaphore count initialization are as follows:

- The default initial value may not be the correct value for your particular application.
- The default value may change at a future release of the operating system software or may be different on other UNIX platforms that your code might be ported to.

For these reasons, you should always initialize the values for your semaphores. The function that you use to initialize your semaphore set is `semctl()`. The function synopsis is as follows:

```
#include <sys/types.h>
#include <sys/ipc.h>
#include <sys/sem.h>

int semctl(int semid,int semnun,int cmd,union semun arg)
```

This function performs many different control functions on semaphore sets. For this reason, some operations have a number of unused arguments. The `semctl()` function takes the following four arguments:

- The semaphore IPC ID that you obtained from the `semget()` function.
- The number of the semaphore that you want to perform this control operation on. When argument three is `SETALL`, this value is ignored.
- The operation that you want to perform. In this case, you specify the value `SETALL` to initialize all semaphores in the set.

- The C union data type arg. This argument supplies the initial values for the semaphores in the set.

The fourth argument is a C union type, which is defined as follows:

```
union semun {
    int     val;            /* used for SETVAL only */
    struct semid_ds *buf; /* for IPC_STAT and IPC_SET */
    ushort  *array;         /* used for GETALL and SETALL */
};
```

This union simply defines the different C data types that the fourth argument can pass. For the SETALL operation, you will be passing the array of initial values for all semaphores in the set. Hence, you need to use the array member of this union.

A return value of -1 indicates an error. You can find the reason for the error in the external integer errno. When the call is successful, 0 is returned.

The following short example illustrates how to initialize a semaphore set that consists of two semaphores in the set:

```
int semid;        /* Semaphore IPC ID */
int z;            /* Status return code */
union semun arg; /* arg.array is used */
ushort initv[] = { /* Initial values */
    4,             /* Semaphore #0 */
    2              /* Semaphore #1 */
};

arg.array = initv; /* Point to init values */
z = semctl(semid,2,SETALL,arg);
if ( z == -1 )
    perror("semctl(SETALL)");
```

Just before the call to setctl(), you assign the address of the initv[] array to the member arg.array. This action tells the semctl() function, through argument arg, where to locate the array of initial semaphore counts. The initial values are expected to be in semaphore sequence. The first semaphore is initialized from initv[0], the second is initialized from initv[1], and so on.

Now that you have learned how to access, create, and initialize semaphore sets, it is time to examine the wait and notify options.

Waiting on and Notifying Semaphore Sets

When a process needs to gain access to a resource, it voluntarily performs a wait operation on the controlling semaphore set. I stress the word *voluntarily* because the semaphore itself cannot enforce restrictions upon the access of a resource.

Each program you write will, by voluntary convention, perform the following:

1. Wait on the semaphore set before accessing the controlled resource
2. Notify the semaphore when releasing the controlled resource

Now take a look at the function calls that perform these operations.

Waiting on a Semaphore Set

The wait operation on the semaphore set has the effect of decrementing the affected semaphore counts. In a set, only the semaphores that are participating are affected.

You use the function `semop()` to wait on a semaphore set. The function synopsis is as follows:

```
#include <sys/types.h>
#include <sys/ipc.h>
#include <sys/sem.h>

int semop(int semid,struct sembuf *sops,unsigned nsops)
```

The function requires the semaphore IPC ID value in argument one. This ID value is returned by the `semget()` function. The second argument is a structure that describes the semaphore operations to be performed. You will look at that structure next. The last argument specifies the number of semaphore operation values present in argument two.

A return value of `-1` indicates an error. You can find the reason for the error in the external integer `errno`. When the call is successful, `0` is returned.

Understanding the `sembuf` Structure

The structure `sembuf`, which is used by `semop()`, is defined as follows:

```
struct sembuf {
    short    sem_num;    /* semaphore number */
    short    sem_op;     /* semaphore operation */
    short    sem_flg;    /* operation flag */
};
```

The structure member `sem_num` is a zero-based index value into the set of semaphores. If you have only one semaphore in the set, this value is always `0`. If you have two semaphores in the set, then you specify `0` to reference the first semaphore and `1` to reference the second in the set. Within the array of sembuf values, you are free to reference any semaphore in the set, in any order. As you will see in the sample program in Listing 19.1, semaphores can be referenced individually or as a group.

The sem_op value for a wait operation must be a negative value. For example, for a process to gain access to one resource instance, a value of -1 is used. If the waiting process needs two or three resource instances, a value of -2 or -3 is used, respectively.

The sem_flg member contains optional flag bits as follows:

- 0—No optional flags.
- IPC_NOWAIT—Do not wait if unsuccessful.
- SEM_UNDO—Adjust the "semaphore undo" value.

When IPC_NOWAIT is provided, the semop() function returns with an error if it cannot successfully gain access to the resource. The value provided in errno is the value EAGAIN to indicate this fact. This value is used by programs that cannot indefinitely wait for the resource to be freed. Instead, the program can supply IPC_NOWAIT and poll the readiness of the resource.

You use the SEM_UNDO flag to undo any pending modifications to the semaphore if your program terminates prematurely. This advanced topic is not covered here. You can find more information by reading the man pages for semop(2).

Using the sembuf Structure and semop()

To wait on two semaphores in a set, you can set up the sembuf structure and code the following semop() call:

```
int z;
static struct sembuf sops[] = {
    { 1, -1, 0 },   /* Wait on sem #1 */
    { 0, -1, 0 }    /* Wait on sem #0 */
};

z = semop(semid,sops,2);
if ( z == -1 ) {
    perror("semop(wait)");
```

In this example, I have purposely waited on the semaphores in reverse order to show you that order has no significance here (remember that semaphore operations are atomic). The sops[] array is initialized so that you specify the second semaphore first, and then the first. Both operations use a wait operation value of -1, and no flags are specified. Argument three in the semop() call specifies how many array elements are in the sops[] array. This example specifies two.

Notifying a Semaphore Set

Notifying the semaphore set is essentially the reverse of what you just did. You use the same `semop()` function and arguments. The only difference is in the value of the `sem_op` member of the `sembuf` structure. The following example performs a notify operation that undoes the wait operation you used previously:

```
int z;
static struct sembuf sops[] = {
    { 1, +1, 0 },  /* Notify on sem #1 */
    { 0, +1, 0 }   /* Notify on sem #0 */
};

z = semop(semid,sops,2);
if ( z == -1 ) {
    perror("semop(notify)");
```

Notice that the `sem_op` values are `+1` now instead of `-1`. Otherwise, all other aspects of the code remain the same.

You now know how to apply semaphore sets after they are created or accessed. One more subject area must be covered: the removal of semaphore sets. Semaphore sets should be removed when they are no longer required to free critical systemwide resources.

Releasing Semaphore System Resources

When files are opened, they are automatically closed when the process exits. This is not the case for semaphores or other resources in the IPC set. When a semaphore set is no longer required, it should be removed from the system to release its resources.

Removing a Semaphore Set

When the semaphore set no longer serves a purpose in the system, it should be removed to release memory occupied by kernel support tables and so on. Removing semaphores also releases the IPC ID value from the system so that it can be reused. You remove semaphores by using the `semctl()` function that you saw previously. The function synopsis is repeated here:

```
#include <sys/types.h>
#include <sys/ipc.h>
#include <sys/sem.h>

int semctl(int semid,int semnun,int cmd,union semun arg)
```

The four arguments to `semctl()` are as follows:

- The semaphore IPC ID obtained from the semget() function.
- The number of the semaphore that you want to perform this control operation on. When argument three is IPC_RMID, this value is ignored.
- The operation that you want to perform. In this case, you specify the value IPC_RMID to request that the semaphore set be destroyed.
- The C union data type arg. This argument is ignored when you use IPC_RMID in argument three.

To remove a semaphore set identified by a variable semid, you use the following code:

```
int semid;        /* Semaphore IPC ID */
int z;            /* Status return code */
union semun arg; /* Unused by semctl */

z = semctl(semid,0,IPC_RMID,arg);
if ( z == -1 )
    perror("semctl(IPC_RMID)");
```

Note that you have to define only the variable arg here. The IPC_RMID operation of the semctl() function does not require the use of the argument arg, but it must be supplied. Argument two is supplied as 0 because this value is not used by this particular control operation.

A return value of -1 indicates an error. You can find the reason for the error in the external integer errno. When the call is successful, 0 is returned.

When this function call is successful at removing the semaphore set, any other process that might attempt to use the semaphore set will have the error EIDRM returned. This message indicates that the semaphore set has been removed.

Using the ipcrm Command to Release Semaphores

Sometimes your program starts up and attempts to create an IPC resource like a semaphore set. However, if that resource already exists, then the program may report an error and exit if it uses the IPC_EXCL flag. This situation can occur when a program that uses semaphores was previously running and has aborted. The program abort operation prevented the semaphore set from being removed as it should have been. Consequently, you occasionally need to use the ipcrm command to remove the IPC resource manually before restarting the process.

I mentioned earlier that the ipcs command is able to display information about semaphores. This command is useful because it can show you what IPC resources have been created on your system. The following example shows how it can display existing semaphore sets (note that newer Linux distributions may show a column labeled key):

```
bash$ ipcs -s

------ Semaphore Arrays --------
semid     owner     perms     nsems     status
2         student1  666       2
3         student1  666       2

bash$
```

The sample command session shows two semaphore IPC ID (`semid`) values `2` and `3` that were created by `student1`. These semaphores were not automatically removed by the student's program. Rather than write a program to release them, you can just use the `ipcrm` command shown in the following:

```
bash$ ipcrm sem 2
resource deleted
bash$ ipcrm sem 3
resource deleted
bash$ ipcs -s

------ Semaphore Arrays --------
semid     owner     perms     nsems     status

bash$
```

Now you are prepared to put semaphores to work. The following sections introduce a simulation program that consists of one main process and four child processes. Together, they run a simulation using semaphores for synchronization.

Using Semaphores in a Simulation

To pull all the semaphore concepts together, I will now introduce a working sample program that models a simulation. In this simulation, you have the following three basic resources:

- Three hammers
- Two screwdrivers
- One chisel

You have four worker processes named as follows:

- Paul
- Alfred
- Robert
- Adam

Each of these worker processes will be assigned random tasks requiring various mixes of tools. You can let the simulation run for a short period and then let the workers quit. You should see all the tools return to the toolbox because workers must finish their current task before leaving the job site. Workers always return their tools when they complete their task.

The simulation program, shown in Listing 19.1, makes use of three semaphores in one set. Each of the semaphores in the set controls access to the specific tool it represents. Each semaphore is initialized with the number of tools of the types that are initially available.

LISTING 19.1 19LST01.c—SIMULATION PROGRAM FOR TOOLS AND WORKERS

```
/* 19LST01.c -- Workers/Tools Demo */

#include <stdio.h>
#include <stdlib.h>
#include <unistd.h>
#include <string.h>
#include <time.h>
#include <errno.h>
#include <sys/types.h>
#include <sys/ipc.h>
#include <sys/sem.h>
#include <sys/wait.h>

#define N_SEC   3        /* Run simulation for n seconds */

static int semid = -1;   /* Semaphore IPC ID */

/*
 * Worker List :
 */
static struct {
    char    *name;       /* Worker name */
    pid_t   PID;         /* Process ID */
} workers[] = {
    { "Paul", 0 },
    { "Alfred", 0 },
    { "Robert", 0 },
    { "Adam", 0 }
};

/*
 * Tool names :
 */
```


continues

LISTING 19.1 CONTINUED

```
static char *tools[] = {
    "Hammer",
    "Screwdriver",
    "Chisel"
};

/*
 * In this case we just want to notify the control
 * semaphore (#3). The control semaphore prevents
 * other processes from reporting something to
 * stdout until the present process is finished its
 * reporting to stdout. This keeps the report serialized.
 */
static void
notifyControl(void) {
    int z;
    static struct sembuf sops = { 3, 1, 0 };

    z = semop(semid,&sops,1);
    if ( z == -1 ) {
        perror("semop(notify ctl)");
        exit(13);
    }
}

/*
 * This function randomly selects 1 to 3 tools that
 * will be required. When hammers or chisels are
 * selected, only require one tool. For screwdrivers
 * allow one or two screwdrivers to be required.
 */
static struct sembuf *
identifyToolsNeeded(int *n) {
    int x, y, sem;
    static struct sembuf sops[3];

    /*
     * Determine the number of tools required:
     */
    *n = rand() % 3 + 1;    /* 1 to 3 */

    /*
     * Now uniquely define the tools needed:
     */
    for ( x=0; x<*n; ++x ) {
        do  {
            sem = rand() % 3;
            for ( y=0; y<x; ++y )
                if ( sops[y].sem_num == sem ) {
```

```
                        /* Already used */
                        sem = -1;
                        break;
                    }
            } while ( sem == -1 );
            sops[x].sem_num = sem;  /* Tool required */
            if ( sem == 1 ) /* Allow up to 2 screwdrivers */
                sops[x].sem_op = rand() % 2 + 1;
            else            /* All other tools, only one each */
                sops[x].sem_op = -1;
            sops[x].sem_flg = 0;    /* No flags */
        }

        /*
         * The control semaphore :
         */
        sops[*n].sem_num = 3;   /* Sem #3 controls stdout */
        sops[*n].sem_op = -1;   /* Wait operation */
        sops[*n].sem_flg = 0;   /* No flags */

        return sops;
    }

    /*
     * This function is used to report our tools & state:
     */
    void
    reportTools(int n,struct sembuf *sops,char *name,char flg) {
        int x;
        int nt;             /* Number of tools */
        char *oper;         /* Operation */
        char buf[1024];     /* Formatting buffer */

        if ( flg == 'W' )
            oper = "waiting for tools";
        else if ( flg == 'X' )
            oper = "using tools";
        else
            oper = "returning tools";

        sprintf(buf,"Worker %s is %s\n",
            name,oper);

        /*
         * Only report the tools for the "using"
         * status report:
         */
        if ( flg == 'X' ) {
            for ( x=0; x<n; ++x ) {
```

continues

19

LISTING 19.1 CONTINUED

```
            nt = abs(sops[x].sem_op);
            sprintf(buf+strlen(buf),
                "  %d %s%s\n",
                nt,
                tools[sops[x].sem_num],
                nt == 1 ? "" : "s");
        }
    }

    /*
     * Write all of our text lines atomically to
     * standard output :
     */
    write(1,buf,strlen(buf));
}

/*
 * This function is run by the child process to
 * simulate one worker needing and returning tools:
 */
static void
toolTime(int workerx,time_t t0) {
    char *name = workers[workerx].name;
    pid_t pid = getpid();    /* Get our process ID */
    int x;                   /* Work int */
    time_t tn;               /* Current time */
    int n_tools;             /* Number of tools required */
    struct sembuf *sops = 0;/* Tool list */

    /*
     * Start random number generator :
     */
    srand((unsigned)pid);

    /*
     * Loop for N_SEC seconds :
     */
    for (;;) {
        /*
         * Check for quitting time :
         */
        time(&tn);
        if ( tn - t0 >= N_SEC )
            return;          /* Quitting time! */

        /*
         * Identify the tools that we need:
         */
        sops = identifyToolsNeeded(&n_tools);
        reportTools(n_tools,sops,name,'W');
```

```
        /*
         * Wait for tools to become available:
         * Note: n_tools+1 includes ctl semaphore.
         */
        semop(semid,sops,n_tools+1);
        reportTools(n_tools,sops,name,'X');
        notifyControl();    /* Done with stdout */

        /*
         * Pretend to work :
         */
        sleep(1);

        /*
         * Turn wait sem_ops into notifies for
         * the tools only (we don't use the control
         * semaphore here):
         */
        for ( x=0; x<n_tools; ++x)
            sops[x].sem_op = -sops[x].sem_op;

        /*
         * Return the tools to the toolbox :
         * [Notify operation]
         */
        reportTools(n_tools,sops,name,'R');
        semop(semid,sops,n_tools);
    }
}

/*
 * Main program :
 */
int
main(int argc,char **argv) {
    int z;                      /* Return code */
    int x;                      /* Work index */
    time_t t0;                  /* Start time */
    union semun semarg;         /* semctl() arg */
    /* Initial counts of tools in toolbox: */
    static ushort icounts[] = {
        3,  /* Hammers */
        2,  /* Screwdrivers */
        1,  /* Chisel */
        1   /* Control semaphore */
    };
    ushort tcounts[4];          /* Final tool counts */
    int status;                 /* Termination status */
    pid_t chPID;                /* Child process ID */

```

continues

LISTING 19.1 CONTINUED

```
    /*
     * Get a private set of semaphores :
     */
    semid = semget(IPC_PRIVATE,4,0600);
    if ( semid == -1 ) {
        perror("semget()");
        exit(1);
    }

    /*
     * Initialize the semaphore counts :
     */
    semarg.array = icounts;
    z = semctl(semid,0,SETALL,semarg);
    if ( z == -1 ) {
        perror("semctl(SETALL)");
        exit(1);
    }

    /*
     * Record our start time :
     */
    time(&t0);

    /*
     * Now create four worker processes :
     */
    for ( x=0; x<4; ++x ) {
        fflush(stdout);
        fflush(stderr);

        if ( !(chPID = fork()) ) {
            /* Child process: */
            toolTime(x,t0);
            return 0;

        } else if ( chPID == (pid_t)(-1) ) {
            fprintf(stderr,"%s: fork(x=%d)\n",
                strerror(errno),x);
            return 13;
        }
        workers[x].PID = chPID;
    }

    /*
     * Now wait for all processes to end :
     */
    do  {
        chPID = wait(&status);
        for ( x=0; x<4; ++x )
```

```
            if ( workers[x].PID == chPID ) {
                workers[x].PID = 0;
                break;
               }
        /*
         * See if they have all terminated :
         */
        for ( x=0; x<4; ++x )
            if ( workers[x].PID != 0 )
                break;
    } while ( x < 4 );

    printf("All workers have quit.\n");

    /*
     * Obtain all semaphore counts :
     */
    semarg.array = tcounts;
    z = semctl(semid,0,GETALL,semarg);
    if ( z == -1 ) {
        perror("semctl(GETALL)");
        exit(1);
    }

    /*
     * Check our tool counts :
     */
    for ( x=0; x<3; ++x )
        if ( tcounts[x] != icounts[x] )
            printf("Now have %d %ss. Had initially %d.\n",
                tcounts[x], tools[x], icounts[x]);
        else
            printf("All %d %ss are accounted for.\n",
                tcounts[x], tools[x]);

    puts("Simulation Complete.");

    /*
     * Remove the semaphore set:
     */
    z = semctl(semid,0,IPC_RMID,semarg);
    if ( z == -1 ) {
        perror("semctl(IPC_RMID)");
        exit(1);
    }

    return 0;
}
```

Although the program in Listing 19.1 is quite long, you can easily understand it by looking at it in functional groups. To keep things brief, I will cover only the noteworthy aspects of the program here. Some points worth noting are as follows:

1. The `main` program creates a private set of semaphores (lines 236 to 240). Because all other processes are child processes, this operation works because they know what the value of `semid` is because of the `fork()` operation used.
2. The semaphore set is initialized with the various counts of tools (lines 245 to 250).
3. A start time is noted so that the child processes know when "quitting time" is (line 255).
4. The `for` loop starts all the worker child processes and keeps a table of their process IDs (lines 260 to 275).
5. The `main` program waits for the workers to quit (lines 280 to 293).
6. The `main` program obtains from the semaphore set the final semaphore values using the `GETALL semctl()` function. I did not cover this function, but you can see that it's almost identical to the way you use `SETALL`.
7. The `main` program does a final inventory check (lines 310 to 316). If any tools are missing, that fact is noted here.
8. The semaphore set is removed (lines 323 to 327).

Some notes about the worker (child) processes are summarized as follows:

1. Function `toolTime()` is called for each worker (child) process (line 266).
2. Function `srand()` initializes a random number generator with the process ID as a "seed" value (line 164).
3. The `for` loop is the worker loop. This loop continues until `N_SEC` seconds have elapsed, and then the child process returns and exits the `main` program (lines 169 to 210).
4. Function `identifyToolsNeeded()` is called to generate a `struct sembuf` structure to be used in a semaphore wait call (line 180 and lines 65 to 104). This semaphore wait simulates the borrowing of the randomly selected tools. Note that only one hammer or chisel can be borrowed, but one or two screwdrivers can be borrowed. The function `rand()` is used to generate random numbers, and the modulo operator (`%`) is used to limit the range of the generated number.
5. The `reportTools()` function reports the current state. To keep the output brief, the tools are shown only when they are "being used" (lines 181, 188, and 208).
6. Another `for` loop changes the semaphore wait operation into a notify operation for each of the tool semaphores (lines 201 and 202).

7. The semaphore notify operation is performed to return the tools (lines 208 and 209).

The first three semaphores represent the semaphores controlling access to each of the tools. Only these semaphores are required to manage the resources. However, to keep the output serialized in a manner that you can better interpret, you add a fourth semaphore.

The fourth semaphore is necessary to prevent the other worker processes from intermixing their output at a critical moment. The fourth semaphore locks out the other processes until you can report the tools taken out by the current working process. Then, by calling on function `notifyControl()`, you then release the lock and allow other worker processes to obtain tools. This example demonstrates how semaphores can be used individually and as a set.

The preceding description covers the functional aspects of the program. Now you can turn your attention to running the simulation and then examine the output that it produces. The output from a short simulation run is shown in Listing 19.2.

LISTING 19.2 WORKER/TOOL SIMULATION OUTPUT

```
Worker Paul is waiting for tools
Worker Paul is using tools
  1 Chisel
  1 Hammer
  1 Screwdriver
Worker Alfred is waiting for tools
Worker Robert is waiting for tools
Worker Adam is waiting for tools
Worker Adam is using tools
  1 Screwdriver
Worker Paul is returning tools
Worker Paul is waiting for tools
Worker Alfred is using tools
  1 Chisel
  1 Hammer
Worker Paul is using tools
  1 Hammer
Worker Adam is returning tools
Worker Adam is waiting for tools
Worker Paul is returning tools
Worker Paul is waiting for tools
Worker Alfred is returning tools
Worker Alfred is waiting for tools
Worker Robert is using tools
  1 Hammer
  1 Chisel
  2 Screwdrivers
```

LISTING 19.2 CONTINUED

```
28:  Worker Alfred is using tools
29:    1 Screwdriver
30:  Worker Robert is returning tools
31:  Worker Adam is using tools
32:    1 Chisel
33:  Worker Alfred is returning tools
34:  Worker Adam is returning tools
35:  Worker Paul is using tools
36:    2 Screwdrivers
37:    1 Chisel
38:  Worker Paul is returning tools
39:  All workers have quit.
40:  All 3 Hammers are accounted for.
41:  All 2 Screwdrivers are accounted for.
42:  All 1 Chisels are accounted for.
43:  Simulation Complete.
```

In line 27 of Listing 19.2, notice that Robert is using two screwdrivers. Line 29 shows that Alfred is using a screwdriver as well. This result might suggest that the semaphore is not working correctly. However, if you look at line 30, you will find that Robert returned his tools, making the screwdrivers available. Robert was simply late in reporting the fact that he had returned his tools. This example illustrates the problem with multiple processes competing to report to one standard output.

Although the control semaphore serializes the "getting" of the tools in its display, I chose to keep the program brief and not to apply corrective measures to the return side. You can easily identify this discrepancy in the output and resolve it by looking ahead a line or two. The semaphores are, in fact, doing their job well.

Space prevents a detailed analysis of the output. However, if you get out paper and a pencil to keep score of who has what tools, you will see that the semaphores are good managers. Line 39 shows when the workers quit, and lines 40 to 42 indicate that all the tools were returned. Dealing with honest workers is always a pleasure!

Summary

In this lesson, you looked at all the fundamental aspects of using semaphores under Linux. You now know how to access, create, and initialize semaphores. You can perform semaphore wait and semaphore notify operations. Finally, you learned how to remove a semaphore set from your program.

In the next lesson, you will look at shared memory. There, you will see that semaphores and shared memory are often used together.

Q&A

Q Why is it a good idea to use `IPC_EXCL` when using `IPC_CREAT` in a call to `semget()`?

A When you use `IPC_EXCL` successfully, you know that the semaphore set was just created and needs to be initialized. When the `semget()` call fails, you know that the set already exists. If the semaphore set already exists, this fact may indicate a conflict in semaphore key values.

Q Why is it desirable to use `IPC_PRIVATE` whenever possible?

A You avoid the whole issue of key conflicts because your semaphore set has no key.

Q What is a semaphore called when it can hold only the values `1` or `0`?

A This type of semaphore is known as a binary semaphore.

Workshop

To apply what you have learned to the concepts that will be covered in the next lesson, you are encouraged to work through the quiz and exercises in this lesson.

Quiz

1. What is the opposite of the notify operation?
2. What function is used to initialize semaphore values?
3. What is the implication of "atomic" semaphore operations?
4. What does the write permission bit imply for semaphore access?

Exercises

1. Write a small program that creates a single binary semaphore when the option `-k` key is provided. You can specify the key in octal, decimal, or hex. If the semaphore set already exists, access the set and report the IPC ID of that set.
2. Extend the program from exercise 1 to accept the option `-r` and the IPC ID as its argument to remove that semaphore set.
3. Further extend the program from exercise 2 to accept options `-w` to wait on the semaphore or option `-n` to notify the semaphore.

Hour 20

Shared Memory

Understanding the Need for Shared Memory

Before threads became available on UNIX platforms, the main recourse to higher performance from a server was to use multiple processes on a multi-CPU system. In this manner, a server could obtain results more quickly by executing code in parallel on different CPUs. Designing servers as multiple processes, however, required that a certain amount of information had to be shared between them efficiently. Shared memory provided an effective answer to the problem.

In this lesson, you will look at how shared memory is created, attached, and used. You will also look at why shared memory requires synchronization and how it can be achieved. Finally, you will demonstrate your knowledge of shared memory techniques by using a simple real-time Battleship game.

Identifying Shared Memory

Some of this lesson is going to feel like déjà vu because shared memory has a few things in common with semaphores, which were covered in the preceding lesson. These similarities exist because the original designers of the IPC group of communication facilities designed them to be created, accessed, controlled, and destroyed in a similar fashion. However, beyond the access of these resources, they are quite different.

Existing shared memory on a Linux system can be referenced by its key value. This key is specified in the C data type `key_t`, which you have seen before. This systemwide key value identifies the instance of shared memory being referenced. The advantages and disadvantages to using this key value are as follows:

- Advantage—It allows an unrelated process to look up a shared memory region by a prearranged key value.
- Disadvantage—The key value used for one application may conflict with a key value currently in use by another application.

You can also use `IPC_PRIVATE` as a key value to create "private shared memory." Sounds like an oxymoron, doesn't it? You will see that private shared memory is not that private.

Just like semaphores, when the shared memory region is located or created, Linux has you reference it with an IPC ID value. For the semaphore, it is often referred to as an `semid` value. For shared memory, an IPC ID is often called an `shmid` value. This IPC ID is `0` or a number that is positive in value.

Creating, Attaching, and Destroying Shared Memory

The following sections focus on the Linux system calls that you need to locate existing shared memory, create new shared memory, and attach the shared memory to your process.

Creating New Shared Memory

The procedure for creating new shared memory is similar to creating a new set of semaphores. The function that you use for creating shared memory is `shmget()`, and its synopsis is as follows:

```
#include <sys/types.h>
```

```
#include <sys/ipc.h>
#include <sys/shm.h>

int shmget(key_t key,int size,int shmflg);
```

The `shmget()` function requires the following three arguments:

- The key value that is used to identify this shared memory region. This key value must be unique to the local system if a new memory region is to be created. Alternatively, you can use the key value `IPC_PRIVATE` to create a keyless shared memory region.
- The minimum size in bytes of the memory region to be created. The kernel rounds this size up to the nearest virtual memory page size, for efficiency reasons.
- The flags argument. You can specify flag bits `IPC_CREAT` and `IPC_EXCL`, in addition to the nine least significant bits that specify the permissions when a memory region is being created.

The first argument, `key`, works in the same fashion as the `semget()` function covered in the preceding lesson. You can give a key value or use `IPC_PRIVATE` in the place of a key. Remember that when `IPC_PRIVATE` is used, flag bit `IPC_CREAT` is implied, and a shared memory region is always created (system resources permitting).

The IPC ID that is returned by `shmget()` is used to refer to the shared memory instance. Any process with the appropriate access rights can use the shared memory created by `IPC_PRIVATE` if it knows the IPC ID returned from `shmget()`. Because of this capability, no privacy is inferred by the `IPC_PRIVATE` key. The key value `IPC_PRIVATE` indicates only that the resource is keyless and distinct from a memory region accessed with a key.

The second argument specifies the size in bytes of the memory region being requested. It is the minimum size of the region because the Linux kernel rounds this size up to the nearest virtual memory page size.

You use the third argument, `shmflg`, to specify flag bits and permission bits. The least significant nine bits have the following permission semantics:

- The read permission bit grants the right to read information from the shared memory segment (that is, to inspect its contents).
- The write permission bit grants the right to alter the shared memory region (that is, to store or overwrite data there).
- The execute permission bit is currently not used. You probably should specify it as `0` when you're creating shared memory.

The following example shows how a shared memory region is created with a key value of `IPC_PRIVATE` that is 4096 bytes in size and permits the user and the group to read and write this memory region. Everyone else is denied access to this memory region.

```
int shmid;

shmid = shmget(IPC_PRIVATE,4096,IPC_CREAT¦IPC_EXCL¦0660);
if ( shmid == -1 ) {
    perror("shmget()");
```

The `shmget()` function returns `0` or a positive IPC ID if it successful. Otherwise, `-1` is returned, and you can find the reason for the error in external integer `errno`.

Attaching Shared Memory

Merely creating or locating existing shared memory with `shmget()` is not enough. This action only arranges that the shared memory instance is made available. To use the shared memory, you must have it attached to your process memory address space somewhere. The function for performing this duty is `shmat()`. Its function prototype is as follows:

```
#include <sys/types.h>
#include <sys/ipc.h>
#include <sys/shm.h>

char *shmat(int shmid,char *shmaddr,int shmflg)
```

The function `shmat()` has the following three calling arguments:

- The `shmid` (IPC ID) value that was obtained from the `shmget()` function. This value identifies the memory region that you want to attach.
- The `shmaddr` argument that specifies where in your memory address space you want to have this shared memory appear. The simplest way to use `shmat()` is to specify a `null` pointer here (`0`). Using the `null` pointer allows the Linux kernel to determine where to safely attach the memory for you.
- The `shmflg` argument that allows option bits to be provided. Supply `0` for this argument when no option flags are used.

The second argument allows a process to be specific about where you want to have the shared memory appear in your address space. You won't use this advanced feature here; note that you can design the need for it out of your program. I will discuss why programs might want to specify an address later in this section.

Currently, the `shmflg` argument has only these three acceptable values:

- `0`—No flag bits are specified.

- SHM_RDONLY—The flag attaches the shared memory to this process with read-only access to it.
- SHM_RND—When shmaddr is not null, this flag permits the shmat() function to round the given shmaddr down to the next multiple of SHMLBA. In other words, it rounds the shmaddr down to a virtual memory page boundary.

The SHM_RDONLY access flag is useful when one program needs access to shared memory for lookup purposes but never needs to alter it. With the SHM_RDONLY flag applied, a bug-ridden program attempting to overwrite the shared memory region causes the program to abort, thus preserving the integrity of the shared memory region.

The SHM_RND flag is useful when you don't want your program to be concerned about the virtual memory page size used on the machine it was compiled for. I will discuss this flag again in the next section.

The shmat() routine returns a character pointer to the location where the memory region is attached in your process address space. When an error occurs, the following special pointer value is returned:

```
(char *)(-1)
```

This pointer contains all 1-bits. You can find the reason for the error in the external variable errno. Assuming that the value shmid is defined, the following example shows how you can attach a shared memory segment to the current process:

```
int shmid;      /* Shared Memory ID */
char *shmp;     /* Pointer to shared memory */

shmp = shmat(shmid,0,0);
if ( shmp == (char *)(-1) ) {
    perror("shmat()");
    abort();
}
memset(shmp,0,4096);   /* Zero out shared memory region */
```

The preceding example assumes that the memory region being attached is 4096 bytes in size. The second argument is given as a null pointer, allowing the Linux kernel to determine where to attach the memory region. The address of this region is returned and stored in the pointer variable shmp. After it knows that the call is successful, the sample program shown here zeros out this shared memory region with the use of the memset() function.

When you're calling `shmat()`, always test for an error using a comparison to the pointer value:

```
(char *)(-1)
```

A common programming blunder is to assume that a `null` pointer represents an error return value.

Attaching at Specific Addresses

Previously, you saw that the easiest way to use `shmat()` is to specify a `null` pointer in argument two (`shmaddr`). In this manner, you allow the Linux kernel to look for a safe place to attach the shared memory for you. This, of course, begs the question, why specify an address at all in this function call?

The answer to this question lies in how shared memory is used. Consider Program-A, which attaches the shared memory at one location and builds a table in it. Assume that the table is attached at starting address 400C0000 in hexadecimal. Now assume that Program-A stores a pointer value in this shared table somewhere, which you can refer to as Pointer-1. This Pointer-1 value references another location within the same table that is 288 bytes from the beginning of that table. In other words, Pointer-1 has the address value of 400C0120. Now examine Figure 20.1.

FIGURE 20.1

Shared memory attached at different physical locations in process address space.

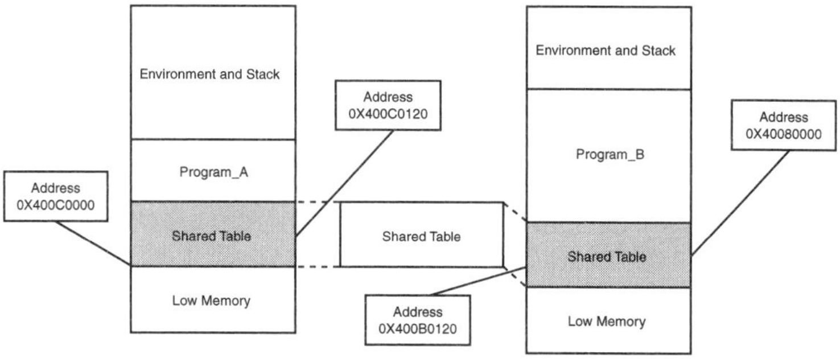

Now Program-B calls on `shmat()` to attach the same shared table to its address space. This program is different in size, with different memory requirements, and this difference causes the Linux kernel to attach the table at location 400B0000 instead. Program-B then retrieves the value of Pointer-1 that was stored in the table. However, the value of Pointer-1 is address 400C0120, which is 65,824 bytes away from the start of the table. The correct value should have been 400B0120 in the executing context of Program-B.

The basic problem is that the value of Pointer-1 is correct only if the table is attached at a starting address of 400C0000. If the table is located anywhere else in the address space, the pointer values will come out wrong. Had Program-B attached the table at the same location as Program-A, it would have had no difficulties with the pointer value.

Program-A and Program-B can force this location to be the same by providing the address to `shmat()` instead of using the `null` pointer value. This approach has a few disadvantages, however:

- The attach address usually must be arrived at by experiment.
- If the programs involved use shared libraries, and these shared libraries later change, previously working attach addresses may fail.
- The addresses found to be acceptable under Intel Linux, for example, are not likely to be acceptable for different hardware platforms.

If you are distributing source code for free and want to avoid email messages from troubled users, then you should avoid specifying fixed attach addresses for the reasons just listed.

When you're experimenting to find the correct address, you should use the flag `SHM_RND`. This flag permits the `shmat()` function to round down an address that would otherwise fail. The `SHM_RND` flag takes the system's virtual memory paging size into account and allows you to arrive at valid attach addresses.

> If you must use a fixed attach address, you need a good starting guess for an address. You can obtain it by simply specifying `null` as the attach address and printing it in hexadecimal:
>
> ```
> shmp = shmat(shmid,0,0);
> if ( shmp != (char *)(-1) )
>     printf("Try 0x%08lX\n",(long)shmp);
> ```
>
> This trick tells you where the Linux kernel felt it was safe to put the address. If multiple programs are involved, then you might need to apply this technique to all of them to find a common address that works.

In this section, I simply wanted to make you aware of the limitations of the practice of using pointers in shared memory tables. If you design your programs to use offsets instead of pointers, then it does not matter where your shared memory region is attached to your process.

Forked processes do not share this problem with pointers in shared tables because each fork inherits all currently attached shared memory at the same locations. However, your options will be limited if some different program must be designed to access this same shared region. Designing code that uses offsets instead of pointers within shared memory tables is usually best.

Detaching Shared Memory

A program can detach shared memory when it no longer needs that memory. This result is desirable because it frees some system resources that manage virtual memory. Another reason to detach shared memory is to allow it to be destroyed.

Detaching shared memory from your process means that the process no longer has access to it. The process loses its virtual memory descriptors that granted it access to that memory. After detachment, however, the shared memory continues to exist in the system until it is destroyed. (You'll learn how to destroy shared memory in the following section.)

You use the `shmdt()` function to detach shared memory. The function prototype is as follows:

```
#include <sys/types.h>
#include <sys/ipc.h>
#include <sys/shm.h>

int shmdt(char *shmaddr);
```

The attach address is passed to the `shmdt()` function to detach it. When the call is successful, the value `0` is returned. If an error occurred, the return value is `-1`, and you can find the reason for the failure in extern integer `errno`.

Destroying Shared Memory

After the shared memory instance is no longer serving a purpose, you should destroy it to free valuable systemwide resources. The destruction of shared memory is initiated by the `shmctl()` function. The synopsis for this shared memory control function is as follows:

```
#include <sys/types.h>
#include <sys/ipc.h>
#include <sys/shm.h>

int shmctl(int shmid,int cmd,struct shmid_ds *buf);
```

This function accepts the following three arguments:

- The argument `shmid` is the IPC ID value that was returned from a prior call to `shmget()`. It identifies the shared memory instance to be destroyed.
- The argument `cmd` is specified as the value `IPC_RMID`. It requests the destruction of the indicated shared memory instance.
- The argument `buf` is not used when argument two is the value `IPC_RMID`. Specify a `null` pointer (`0`).

Note that the shared memory is only marked for destruction by this call. Only after all the processes have detached the shared memory instance, however, does the Linux kernel destroy it.

Now you have learned how to create shared memory and attach it to your process. When your processes are finished with shared memory, you can have the memory detached and destroyed. What comes in between is the actual use of the shared memory resource. That is the next topic for discussion.

Using Shared Memory

When multiple processes access shared memory, a need for synchronization develops. If Program-A starts to update a linked list in a shared table, Program-B might access the same table when the job is only partly complete. This situation occurs because of the way programs can be preempted by the kernel to run other programs like Program-B.

For this reason, shared memory and a semaphore are often used together as a pair. Usually, a binary semaphore is used, providing access to at most one process at a time.

Applying Safe Shared Memory Access

When a shared memory region is established as a table, then a binary semaphore is also created, and the following voluntary convention is used:

- When access to the shared memory is required, the process waits on the semaphore. This process is often referred to as *locking the table*.
- When the process succeeds at waiting on the semaphore, it can read and modify the shared memory region. All other processes following this procedure are *locked out*, however.
- When the process using the shared table is finished, it notifies the semaphore and withdraws from using the table. This process is often referred to as *unlocking the table*.

The binary semaphore prevents more than one user of the table at one instant. In this manner, multiple processes can be synchronized in such a way that the table can be safely accessed and modified.

Referring to Shared Memory Without Semaphores

Often, you might have a strong temptation to reference a shared memory table in read-only terms without using the semaphore wait and notify procedure—but be careful. For example, often you might be tempted to pick up one integer value from the shared memory region without incurring the overhead of the semaphore wait and notify process. The reasoning often stated is that if this value is ever changed, it will be changed atomically. This assumption is not valid, however, and can vary widely from hardware platform to hardware platform.

> Do not make atomic change assumptions about small or large data types that are subject to change in shared memory. The atomic nature of values varies widely from hardware platform to hardware platform.

The only time skipping the semaphore locking procedure is considered safe is when reading values that are not subject to change after they are established. For example, at startup time, a transaction server may establish a table that contains IPC ID values of other associated semaphores, shared memory tables, and message queues. Because these values never change after the startup occurs, accessing these constant values without synchronization is safe. However, you must make certain that the startup initialization is complete.

Applying Shared Memory to a Game

To illustrate the use of shared memory in a real, live application, I will present a simple text-based version of the Battleship game. The Battleship game demonstrates the use of shared memory well for two reasons:

- The battle zone (the sea with the ships on it) is shared between two processes. The battle zone is implemented as a shared memory table within a C structure.
- Two processes access the shared table concurrently. For this reason, a semaphore protects access to the shared table.

The idea behind the game is that you and your enemy have ships at sea, but because of the fog, you know only where your own ships are located. It is your mission to seek out and destroy the enemy lurking in the sea around you.

Traditionally, the game is played with each player taking turns. In this rendition of the game, there are no turns to take. After the game begins, you and your enemy both attack each other as quickly and as smartly as you are able. The first one to annihilate the opponent wins.

Lack of space prevents me from printing all the game source code. You can, however, find the entire set of files, including a Makefile, on the accompanying CD-ROM. If your CD mounts on directory /cdrom under Linux, you can find the game files in the directory /cdrom/source/chap20.

If you are inspecting the CD from DOS or Windows, and D: is your CD-ROM drive, then you should find the necessary files in the path D:\source\chap20.

Some of the relevant source code modules will be listed and discussed in the sections that follow.

Overview of the Battleship Game

The basic design of the Battleship game is centered on two separate processes accessing one common instance of shared memory. As the first player (player one), you can start the program with no command-line arguments:

```
bash$ ./bttlship
```

This process creates the shared memory and its semaphore set using the key `IPC_PRIVATE`. Setting up the process this way avoids any clashes with any software that might be on the system (particularly in a classroom situation). The program announces to you that you have started game number `x`. The value `x` that is displayed is actually the IPC ID of the shared memory region created for the game.

The opposing player (player two) is simply another person using another terminal on the same host computer. Player two must know the game number `x` in order to join the game where you are currently waiting. Player two must run the same program, `bttlship`, and specify game number `x` as the command-line argument (`x=512` in this example):

```
bash$ ./bttlship 512
```

The command-line argument causes the program to link up with the existing game that you started as player one. After player two presses Return at the prompt, the battle begins in earnest with you and your opponent entering a Y and X letter coordinate pair in an attempt to bomb your enemy. The game completes when no more bomb-sites remain.

Playing Instructions

As player one, you can start a new battle by running the program with no command-line arguments:

```
bash$ ./bttlship
```

After doing so, you see the display illustrated in Listing 20.1.

LISTING 20.1 INITIAL BATTLE SCENE FOR PLAYER ONE

```
bash$ ./bttlship
   A B C D E F G H I J
A¦ . . . . . . . . . ! ¦
B¦ . . . . . . . . . ! ¦
C¦ . . . . . . . . . V ¦
D¦ . . . . . . . . . . ¦
E¦ . . ! . . . . . . . ¦
F¦ . . ! . . . . . . . ¦
G¦ . . V . . = = = > . ¦
H¦ . . . . . . . . . . ¦
I¦ . . . . . . . . . . ¦
J¦ . . . . . . . . . . ¦
   A B C D E F G H I J
ENEMY HAS 010 BOMB SITES LEFT
YOU HAVE  010 BOMB SITES LEFT

*** GAME # 2304 ***
Waiting for opponent...
```

The initial display in Listing 20.1 shows only the positions of your ships. Position EC is the stern of one ship, and position GC is the bow of that same ship. The Y coordinate is immediately followed by the X coordinate when entering bombing positions.

At the bottom of the display is the message `Waiting for opponent...`. It tells you that you are waiting for player two to join the battle. On the line above, a game number is reported (`2304` in Listing 20.1). This number is used by your opponent to challenge you at sea. The opponent then starts her game program as follows:

```
bash$ ./bttlship 2304
```

In a classroom situation, multiple pairs of challengers can run individual battles. Each shared memory instance is created with `IPC_PRIVATE`, so it is new and unique.

When the IPC ID is provided on the command line, the game program can attach to the existing shared memory instance that has a battle you prepared in it as the waiting player one. Listing 20.2 shows what player two's initial display looks like.

LISTING 20.2 PLAYER TWO'S INITIAL BATTLE SCENE

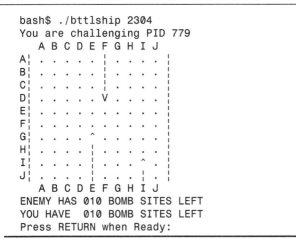

```
bash$ ./bttlship 2304
You are challenging PID 779
   A B C D E F G H I J
A¦ . . . . . ¦ . . . . ¦
B¦ . . . . . ¦ . . . . ¦
C¦ . . . . . ¦ . . . . ¦
D¦ . . . . . V . . . . ¦
E¦ . . . . . . . . . . ¦
F¦ . . . . . . . . . . ¦
G¦ . . . . ^ . . . . . ¦
H¦ . . . . ¦ . . . . . ¦
I¦ . . . . ¦ . . . ^ . ¦
J¦ . . . . ¦ . . . ¦ . ¦
   A B C D E F G H I J
ENEMY HAS 010 BOMB SITES LEFT
YOU HAVE  010 BOMB SITES LEFT
Press RETURN when Ready:
```

This display is similar to your display for player one, except that only player two's ships are displayed. At this point, the game is all ready to go. Player two now has a moment to study her positions. When she is ready, she must press Return at the prompt `Press RETURN when Ready:` to start the battle.

Table 20.1 lists the identification markings that are used in the game.

TABLE 20.1 BATTLESHIP IDENTIFICATION MARKINGS

Markings	*Identification*
`===>`	Identifies player one's ship heading in an easterly direction
`<-------`	Identifies player two's ship heading west (ships vary in length)
`^`	
`!`	Identifies player one's ship heading north
`¦`	
`V`	Identifies player two's ship heading south
`#`	Exploded bomb on player one's ship
`@`	Exploded bomb on player two's ship
`*`	Splash in the ocean where a bomb exploded
`.`	Empty ocean

Listing 20.3 shows the display after player two has started the battle by pressing Return. After she has done so, you both can feverishly enter bombing coordinates. Uppercase and lowercase are accepted, Y coordinate first, immediately followed by X coordinate and a Return. You cannot enter spaces.

Because player two peeked at your screen across the room, she is immediately attacking at position GF in Listing 20.3.

LISTING 20.3 PLAYER TWO'S FIRST ATTACK

```
Press RETURN when Ready:
: GF
   A B C D E F G H I J
A¦ . . . . . ¦ . . . . ¦
B¦ . . . . . ¦ . . . . ¦
C¦ . . . . . ¦ . . . . ¦
D¦ . . . . . V . . . . ¦
E¦ . . . . . . . . . . ¦
F¦ . . . . . . . . . . ¦
G¦ . . . . ^ @ . . . . ¦
H¦ . . . . ¦ . . . . . ¦
I¦ . . . . ¦ . . . ^ . ¦
J¦ . . . . ¦ . . . ¦ . ¦
   A B C D E F G H I J
ENEMY HAS 009 BOMB SITES LEFT
YOU HAVE  010 BOMB SITES LEFT
```

The @ character shows that player two has made a successful hit on part of your ship. Your ship is not sunk, however, until all that ship's bomb sites have been hit.

You can retaliate by bombing location CE where you think player two's ship is located, as shown in Listing 20.4.

LISTING 20.4 PLAYER ONE'S FIRST ATTACK

```
ENEMY HAS 010 BOMB SITES LEFT
YOU HAVE  009 BOMB SITES LEFT
: CE
   A B C D E F G H I J
A¦ . . . . . . . . . ! ¦
B¦ . . . . . . . . . ! ¦
C¦ . . . . * . . . . V ¦
D¦ . . . . . . . . . . ¦
E¦ . . ! . . . . . . . ¦
F¦ . . ! . . . . . . . ¦
G¦ . . V . . @ = = > . ¦
H¦ . . . . . . . . . . ¦
I¦ . . . . . . . . . . ¦
J¦ . . . . . . . . . . ¦
   A B C D E F G H I J
ENEMY HAS 010 BOMB SITES LEFT
YOU HAVE  009 BOMB SITES LEFT
:
```

Listing 20.4 shows that you have made only a splash in the ocean where the asterisk (*) is shown. The at (@) sign shows where you have been hit.

The play continues until either you or your opponent has no more bomb sites left to obliterate (a *bomb site* here means a portion of a ship).

If you just want an update on the battle scene without bombing, you can just press Return to get a new display. If you enter a bombing coordinate that the game cannot decode, it simply behaves as if you pressed a simple Return to update the battle display and let you try again.

Analyzing Player One's Code

The `main` program of the game is first shown in Listing 20.5.

LISTING 20.5 main.c—THE `main` PROGRAM FOR THE BATTLESHIP GAME

```
/* main.c */

#include "bttlship.h"

int shmid = -1;                 /* Shared Memory IPC ID */
int semid = -1;                 /* Table locking semaphore */
char *shmp = 0;                 /* Pointer to shared memory */
int us = 0;                     /* 0=starter / 1=challenger */
int them = 0;                   /* 1=challenger / 0=starter */
int flg_game_over = 0;          /* != 0 => game over */

struct S_TABLE *table = 0;  /* Shared Memory Table */

int
main(int argc,char **argv) {
    union semun semarg;             /* for semctl() */
    ushort seminit[] = { 1, 0 };/* Initial sem values */
    pid_t p1, p2;                   /* PID for player 1 & 2 */
    char buf[256];                  /* For fgets() */
    int x, y, z;                    /* move x,y and status z */

    srand(getpid());                /* Init random no.s */

    if ( argc == 1 ) {              /* No args? */
        /*
         * Create a new game :
```


continues

LISTING 20.5 CONTINUED

```
         */
        atexit(cleanup);

        /*
         * Create Shared Memory
         */
        shmid = shmget(IPC_PRIVATE,sizeof *table,0666);
        if ( shmid == -1 ) {
            perror("shmget()");
            return 13;
        }

        attachTable();          /* Attach new table */

        /*
         * Create a binary semaphore set :
         */
        semid = semget(IPC_PRIVATE,2,0666);
        if ( semid == -1 ) {
            perror("semget()");
            return 13;
        }

        /*
         * Initialize semaphores:
         */
        semarg.array = seminit;
        if ( semctl(semid,0,SETALL,semarg) == -1 ) {
            perror("semctl(SETALL)");
            return 13;
        }

        /*
         * Initialize & Generate Battle in shared
         * memory table :
         */
        LOCK;                         /* Wait on semaphore */
        table->semid = semid;         /* Make IPC ID public */
        table->player[0].pid = getpid();
        table->player[1].pid = 0;     /* No opponent yet */
        genBattle();                  /* Generate battle */

        us = 0;                       /* We're player [0]  */
        them = 1;                     /* They're player[1] */
```

```

        /*
         * Wait for challenger to notify us :
         */
        showBattle();
        UNLOCK;                         /* Notify semaphore */

        printf("\n*** GAME # %d ***\n",shmid);
        puts("Waiting for opponent...");
        WAIT2;
        puts("\nTHE BATTLE BEGINS!\n");
    } else {
        /*
         * Opponent is joining a game :
         */
        us = 1;                     /* We're player[1] */
        them = 0;                   /* They're player[0] */

        shmid = atoi(argv[1]);      /* Simple int conversion */
        attachTable();              /* Attach existing shm */

        /* No lock is required for this fetch: */
        semid = table->semid;       /* Locking semaphore ID */

        LOCK;                       /* Wait on semaphore */
        p1 = table->player[0].pid;
        p2 = table->player[1].pid;
        if ( p2 == 0 )              /* No opponent yet? */
            p2 = table->player[1].pid = getpid();
        UNLOCK;                     /* Notify semaphore */

        if ( p2 != getpid() ) {
            printf("Sorry: PID %ld and %ld are already "
                "playing.\n",(long)p1,(long)p2);
            return 1;
        }

        printf("You are battling PID %ld\n",(long)p1);

        LOCK;
        showBattle();
        UNLOCK;

        fputs("Press RETURN: ",stdout);
        fgets(buf,sizeof buf,stdin);

        NOTIFY2;                    /* Notify player1 */
    }

```


continues

LISTING 20.5 CONTINUED

```
120:     /*
121:      * The battle rages :
122:      */
123:     while ( !flg_game_over ) {
124:         if ( (z = getInput(&x,&y)) == INP_NONE ) {
125:             LOCK;               /* Lock semaphore */
126:             showBattle();       /* Display battle scene */
127:             UNLOCK;             /* Unlock semaphore */
128:             fflush(stdout);
129:         } else {  /* INP_YX */
130:             LOCK;               /* Lock semaphore */
131:             bomb(x,y);          /* Bomb this location */
132:             showBattle();       /* Now show results */
133:             UNLOCK;             /* Unlock semaphore */
134:         }
135:     }
136:
137:     /*
138:      * Battle is over:
139:      */
140:     LOCK;
141:     showBattle();
142:     UNLOCK;
143:     puts("GAME OVER!");
144:
145:     if ( !us )        /* Player1? */
146:         WAIT2;        /* Yes, Wait for opponent to finish */
147:     else
148:         NOTIFY2;      /* Notify player 1 that we're done */
149:
150:     return 0; /* Cleanup removes IPC resource for player1 */
151: }
```

The main program for you as player one uses the following steps:

1. If no command-line arguments are provided, then the program begins the creation of a new game. The first step is to register the function `cleanup()` that will be called if this program exits or returns from the `main` program. The cleanup function removes the IPC resources (line 28).
2. The shared memory region is created using `IPC_PRIVATE` by calling `shmget()` (lines 33 to 37). Notice that the permissions allow anyone to play (permissions 0666).
3. The shared memory is attached by calling the `attachTable()` function (line 39). This function initializes the `table` pointer variable to point to the shared memory region that is attached.

4. A semaphore set is created by calling `semget()` (lines 44 to 48).
5. The semaphores are initialized by calling `semctl()` (lines 53 to 57). The first semaphore is initialized to the value `1` (to make a binary semaphore), and the second semaphore is initialized to the value `0`.
6. The shared memory region is locked with the use of the macro `LOCK` (line 63). This makes sure that you have exclusive use of the shared memory. I will describe how this `LOCK` macro is defined later.
7. The shared memory table is initialized, an initial battle scene is displayed, and then the shared table lock is released (lines 64 to 76).
8. The game number and the message `Waiting for opponent...` are displayed. The program waits on the second semaphore for player two to notify you when she is ready to start (lines 78 to 80). Note that because the second semaphore is initialized to `0` (in step 5), the code is blocked here until player two notifies you.
9. The game then rages until the flag variable `flg_game_over` is nonzero (lines 123 to 135).
10. The final battle scene is displayed, and the `GAME OVER!` message is given (lines 140 and 143).
11. You then must wait for player two to notify you that she is ending the game (line 146).
12. Your player one code exits (line 150).

This program uses two semaphores in the set. The program itself never uses them together, only separately. Their functions are as follows:

- The binary semaphore locks access to the shared table. This semaphore is initialized to the value `1`.
- The second semaphore waits for a notify operation from player two for you. It is initialized to `0`.

The first semaphore simply acts as a lock for the shared table.

The second semaphore is new in its use here. Because the semaphore is initialized to `0`, any process that waits on it will wait. The game process for you uses this semaphore in two places:

- Waiting for you to start the game (line 80)
- Waiting for player two to end the game (line 146)

In this manner, your program can be synchronized with player two's. You wait at line 80 until player two presses Return to begin the game. After that event, both processes do battle on equal terms.

Because your `cleanup()` function is going to destroy the shared memory and the semaphore set, it must wait for player two to finish before it exits. For this reason, the game process for you waits at line 146 until player two notifies it by performing the notify operation at line 148.

If you (player one) interrupt out of the game, the shared memory and the semaphore are left in existence. After you read Hour 22, "Signals," you will be able to come back to this project and allow for this situation. In the meantime, use the `ipcs` and `ipcrm` commands to remove the lingering shared memory and semaphore set. This situation occurs, however, only when you interrupt out of the program.

Analyzing Player Two's Code

Player two's code is simpler to trace because it must attach only to the existing shared memory table. The important points to note for player two are as follows:

1. The IPC ID in `argv[1]` is used to attach to the shared table (lines 89 and 90).
2. The semaphore set's IPC ID is obtained by copying it directly out of the shared memory table (line 93). Note here that locking the table is not necessary because `table->semid` is never changed after it is established.
3. A test is performed to check whether someone else beat you to the game (lines 95 to 100). If so, a message is reported, and the program is exited (lines 102 to 106).
4. The battle scene is displayed, and a prompt `Press RETURN:` is provided (lines 108 to 115). After the user has complied, the program notifies you (player one) that the game has begun (line 117).

The remainder of the code was covered in the section "Analyzing Player One's Code."

Examining Other Key Source Modules

The include file used by the program modules is shown in Listing 20.6.

LISTING 20.6 BTTLESHIP.H—THE BTTLSHIP.H INCLUDE FILE

```
/* bttlship.h */
#ifndef _bttlship_h_
#define _bttlship_h_

#include <stdio.h>
#include <stdlib.h>
#include <unistd.h>
#include <string.h>
#include <ctype.h>
#include <errno.h>
```

```
#include <time.h>
#include <sys/types.h>
#include <sys/ipc.h>
#include <sys/sem.h>
#include <sys/shm.h>

#define N_X         10      /* X dimension */
#define N_Y         10      /* Y dimension */
#define N_Z         5       /* Max length of ship */
#define N_SHIPS     6       /* Max number of ships */

#define INP_NONE    0       /* No input / not recognizable */
#define INP_YX      1       /* YX was given */

#define LOCK        lockTable(0,1)  /* Lock Table */
#define UNLOCK      lockTable(0,0)  /* Unlock Table */

#define WAIT2       lockTable(1,1)  /* Wait for Notify */
#define NOTIFY2     lockTable(1,0)  /* Notify player 1 */

/*
 * Table flags :
 */
#define FLG_P1      001     /* Owned by player 1 */
#define FLG_P2      002     /* Owned by player 2 */
#define FLG_SEEN0   004     /* Seen by player 1 */
#define FLG_SEEN1   010     /* Seen by player 2 */
#define FLG_BOMBD   020     /* Bombed */
#define FLG_SPLSH   040     /* Splash */

/*
 * Shared Memory Table :
 */
struct S_TABLE {
    int     semid;          /* Locking sem IPC ID */
    struct  {
      pid_t pid;            /* Process ID of player */
      int   bsites;         /* Sites left for bombing */
    }       player[2];
    char    sea[N_X][N_Y];  /* Matrix of sea locations */
    char    flg[N_X][N_Y];  /* Flags */
};

extern struct S_TABLE *table;

extern int shmid;           /* Shared Memory IPC ID */
extern int semid;           /* Table locking semaphore */
extern char *shmp;          /* Pointer to shared memory */
extern int us;              /* 0=starter / 1=challenger */
extern int them;            /* 1=challenger / 0=starter */
```


continues

LISTING 20.6 CONTINUED

```
61:  extern int flg_game_over;    /* != 0 => game over */
62:
63:  extern void cleanup(void);
64:  extern void attachTable(void);
65:  extern void lockTable(int semx,int bLock);
66:
67:  extern void recount(void);
68:  extern void bomb(int x,int y);
69:  extern int getInput(int *px,int *py);
70:  extern int draw_hz(int sx,int sy,int z,int who);
71:  extern int draw_vt(int sx,int sy,int z,int who);
72:  extern void genBattle(void);
73:  extern void showRow(void);
74:  extern void showBattle(void);
75:
76:  #endif /* _bttlship_h_ */
```

The C macros `LOCK` and `UNLOCK` are defined in lines 25 and 26. They invoke another function `lockTable()` to perform the semaphore wait and notify operations. The C macros `WAIT2` and `NOTIFY2` also call on function `lockTable()`, except that they use semaphore one instead of zero.

The structure of the shared memory table is given in lines 44 to 52. Note that the semaphore IPC ID is stored in structure member `semid`. You can obtain this value safely without the semaphore because this value is constant after it is established during initialization.

Listing 20.7 shows the code used for the function `lockTable()`.

LISTING 20.7 SEMOP.C—THE `lockTable()` FUNCTION

```
/* semop.c */

#include "bttlship.h"

/*
 * Perform semaphore wait/notifies:
 * ARGUMENTS:
 *  semx    0 : table lock semaphore
 *          1 : opponent notify semaphore
 *  bLock   0 : perform notify
 *          1 : perform wait
 */
void
lockTable(int semx,int bLock) {
```

```
15:      int z;                           /* Return status */
16:      static struct sembuf sops = { 0, -1, 0 };
17:
18:      /*
19:       * Lock or unlock the semaphore
20:       */
21:      sops.sem_num = semx;             /* Select semaphore */
22:      sops.sem_op = bLock ? -1 : 1;    /* Wait / Notify */
23:      do  {
24:          z = semop(semid,&sops,1);    /* Semaphore operation */
25:      } while ( z == -1 && errno == EINTR );
26:
27:      if ( z == -1 ) {
28:          perror("semop()");           /* Should not happen */
29:          exit(13);
30:      }
31:  }
32:
33:  /* End semop.c */
```

The function `lockTable()` in Listing 20.7 takes two arguments. The first argument, `semx`, chooses the semaphore you are using. The `LOCK` and `UNLOCK` macros both use `0` for this argument. The `WAIT2` and `NOTIFY2` macros use the value `1`.

The second argument, `bLock`, is treated as a Boolean value. When it is `true`, a wait operation (lock) is performed. Otherwise, it performs a notify operation instead.

The code uses the following basic steps:

1. The semaphore is selected (line 21).
2. The wait or notify operation is selected (line 22).
3. The semaphore operation is performed (line 24).
4. The returned results are checked (line 25). Here, you loop back to line 24 and repeat the operation if an error `EINTR` is returned (more details on this operation shortly).
5. Outside the loop, a test is performed to check for non-`EINTR` errors (lines 27 to 30).

To explain the need for the `EINTR` test would require that I cover the topic of signals. I'll save that topic for Hour 22, "Signals." For now, let me just summarize by saying that when a signal occurs, a semaphore operation can be interrupted. This fact is indicated to the caller by returning the error code `EINTR`. Simply by repeating the semaphore operation, you can succeed eventually.

Listing 20.8 illustrates the shared memory attach code.

LISTING 20.8 ATTCH.C—THE `attachTable()` FUNCTION CODE

```
1:   /* attch.c */
2:
3:   #include "bttlship.h"
4:
5:   void
6:   attachTable(void) {
7:
8:       /*
9:        * Attach the shared memory :
10:       */
11:      shmp = shmat(shmid,0,0);
12:      if ( shmp == (char *)(-1) ) {
13:          perror("shmat()");
14:          exit(13);
15:      }
16:      table = (struct S_TABLE *)shmp;
17:  }
18:
19:  /* End attch.c */
```

The code in Listing 20.8 is put into its own module because it has to be performed from two different places in the `main` program. The attach operation is performed in lines 11 to 15. Note the unusual error test in line 12.

When the call is successful, the table pointer is pointed to the shared region by assigning the cast pointer value in line 16.

Listing 20.9 shows the cleanup procedure that is called on by the player one code.

LISTING 20.9 CLEANUP.C—THE `cleanup()` FUNCTION CODE

```
/* cleanup.c */

#include "bttlship.h"

/*
 * Cleanup procedure called by atexit processing:
 */
void
cleanup(void) {
    union semun semarg;

    /*
     * Detach shared memory if it is attached:
     */
    if ( shmp != 0 && shmp != (char *)(-1) )
```

```
16:         if ( shmdt(shmp) == -1 )
17:             perror("shmdt()");
18:
19:     /*
20:      * Destroy shared memory:
21:      */
22:     if ( shmid != -1 )
23:         if ( shmctl(shmid,IPC_RMID,0) == -1 )
24:             perror("shmctl(IPC_RMID)");
25:
26:     /*
27:      * Destroy semaphore:
28:      */
29:     if ( semid != -1 )
30:         if ( semctl(semid,0,IPC_RMID,semarg) == -1 )
31:             perror("semctl(IPC_RMID)");
32: }
33:
34: /* End cleanup.c */
```

The code shown in Listing 20.9 is called on by the `atexit()` processing that occurs when you (player one) exit the main program. The basic steps used are as follows:

1. If the shared memory pointer is not null and not the error pointer value `(char *)(-1)`, the memory is detached by calling `shmdt()` (lines 15 to 17).
2. If the shared memory IPC ID is not `-1`, then it is released by calling `shmctl()` (lines 22 to 24).
3. If the semaphore IPC ID in `semid` is not `-1`, the semaphore set is released by calling `semctl()` (lines 29 to 31).

When the cleanup function returns, the `atexit()` processing completes, and the program finally terminates.

At this point, you have looked at a simple game that shares memory between two processes. You've seen how a semaphore shared between two processes ensures that only one of the processes modifies the shared table at one time.

In addition, from this game, you learned that a semaphore can be initialized with a value of `0`. This use of the semaphore is different, though it still performs a synchronizing function. This semaphore allows your player one code to sit and wait for an event from player two.

You will find that the application of shared memory and semaphores in real Linux applications is generally very similar to what you have just seen in this lesson.

Summary

In this lesson, you examined how you can create, access, and use shared memory. You also saw how it is used with a semaphore to synchronize multiple accesses to the same shared table.

Q&A

Q Must semaphores always be used with shared memory?

A Not necessarily. However, synchronization often requires the use of semaphores, unless synchronization can be achieved by other means.

Q When is it possible to ignore synchronization when accessing shared memory?

A You can ignore synchronization issues if you are reading a value that is considered constant. However, you must be certain that you do not attempt to access that value before it has been established by initialization.

Workshop

To retain what you have learned, you are encouraged to work through the exercises and quiz before proceeding to the next lesson.

Quiz

1. What function is used to access existing shared memory or to create new shared memory?
2. What function do you use to attach shared memory to your process?
3. Why should pointer values be avoided in shared tables?
4. What function do you use to destroy shared memory from your process?
5. What value does function `shmat()` return when it returns an error?

Exercises

1. Write a small program that reads the `message of the day` from standard input, and copy it to a temporary file. Then call `stat()` to determine the size of that temporary file. Using the size of the temporary file, create a shared memory region large enough to contain the contents of that temporary file and one integer size variable. Read back the text from that temporary file, and place it into the shared memory region. Place the size of the text loaded into the integer size variable that is located at the start of the shared memory region. Use an arbitrary `key_t` value to identify the shared memory region for later use (do not use `IPC_PRIVATE`).

2. Write a small program that uses the same `key_t` key value that the program in exercise 1 used. This program should attach to the existing shared memory region, obtain the `message of the day` message from there, and write its contents to your standard output. The size of the text should be found in the integer size variable that is located at the start of the shared memory region.

HOUR 21

Message Queues

Introducing the Message Queue

The UNIX message queue is perhaps one of the most underappreciated gems in the IPC Communication set of facilities. In this lesson, you will learn that the message queue is an extremely flexible facility for communication.

You also will learn how to access existing message queues and create, read, write, and destroy message queues under Linux. Most important of all, you will learn when to apply message queues to the problem at hand. At the end of the lesson, you will work with a simple paging server that uses a message queue.

The Linux Message Queue

Many people imagine a line at the bank when they think of the word *queue*. Others might think of a long wait for a job in a print queue. Certainly, the Linux message queue facility does permit messages to queue one after another in this fashion. The design of this facility, however, goes way beyond a simple FIFO queue. Start by looking at some of its characteristics. The following data transfer characteristics apply to Linux message queues:

- A message can be written to the message queue by any process.
- A message, if one exists, can be read by any process.

The point made in this pair of statements is that no specific process is designated as a writer or a reader. Remember that the pipe has data flow in one direction only. With message queues, data can flow to a number of different destinations.

Message queues and pipes have a few things in common. Pipes are similar in the respect that they can queue up data at one end to be read by a process at the other end. However, note these major differences:

- Pipes transport a stream of bytes.
- Messages transport packets.

Pipes just pass a stream of bytes from one end to the other. No divisions or groupings of bytes are discernable at the receiving end.

Message queues, on the other hand, deliver packets in the same sizes as they were queued. The message boundaries are defined when a message is sent to the queue and are detected when the message is received. This is another factor that is often attractive to software engineers.

Applying Message Types

Messages that are sent through a message queue have a specific message type that is defined by the sender. The message type can be used in a number of ways:

- Not used at all. All messages sent use a constant value for the message type because the type value is ignored at the receiving end.
- As an address value to route the message to a specific receiver.
- As a classification value to route the message to a class of receivers.
- As a priority value to assign a specific priority to the message.

One of the marvelous aspects of the message queue facility is that it can be applied in these different ways. The use is primarily determined by the role of the message type and the manner in which the receiver is using this message type. This fact will become more evident when you examine the `msgrcv()` function later in this lesson.

The first points illustrate that the message type feature does not have to be put to use at all. In this case, the message queue behaves as a simple FIFO communication tool. However, it still enjoys advantages over the pipe, such as the transmission of message units instead of byte streams.

When the message type is used as an address, the message can be routed to one specific receiver out of several. For example, the process ID can be used to specify which of several receiving processes you want the message to be sent to.

Figure 21.1 illustrates how process ID (PID) 5823 can route a message to any one of the processes 735, 2039, or 12735. To do so, it simply uses the value 735, 2039, or 12735 as its message type. Each receiver takes off the queue only messages that match their respective process ID numbers.

FIGURE 21.1
Specific recipient processes.

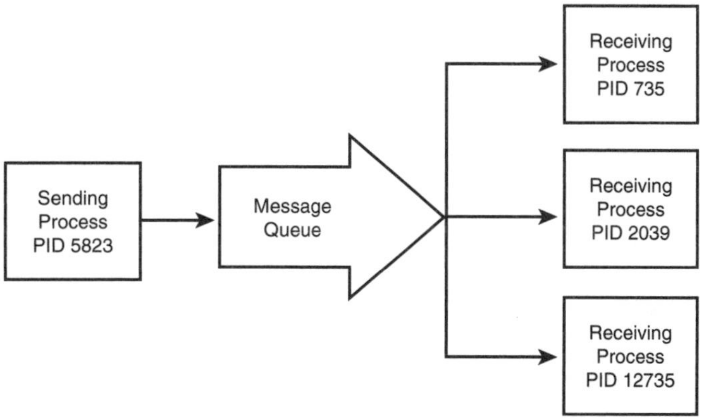

A variation on the addressing scheme is to use the message type as the message classification value. The message is therefore classified in such a way that it is delivered to a specific class of receivers. An example occurs when the classification (message type) identifies the transaction type, and one of a few transaction handling processes receives the message and acts on it. In effect, the message is routed to the first process in a class of processes that can receive the message first. I'll discuss this situation further in the next section.

The message type component can also be used as a priority indicator. The C data type used for the message type is a `long integer`. Furthermore, the value placed in the message type component of the message must be positive and nonzero. This leaves 31 bits of message priority values to choose from when assigning a priority to a message. The lowest message type values have the highest priority. If the receiver wants to receive messages in priority sequence, the receiver can take the lowest typed messages off the queue first.

These examples don't exhaust all the possibilities. The message type can sometimes be used in combination. The versatility of the message queue is quite amazing.

Competing Receivers

An attractive feature of the message queue is its capability to allow receiving processes to compete for the same message. I described this process earlier when the message type field was used to classify a message.

The following example demonstrates how a message queue can be applied to a transaction server:

1. Imagine three processes that are equally capable of carrying out a particular transaction. You can call them *transaction handlers*. All three of these transaction handlers are waiting to receive a message from the message queue.
2. Transactions arrive from PCs from various branch offices, and the transactions are read by a process that acts as a transaction concentrator. The function of this process is to funnel multiple input streams into one output.
3. The transaction concentrator queues its output to the message queue. It is the same queue from which the three transaction handlers are waiting to receive a message.
4. As the first message is queued, only one of the three transaction handlers succeeds at reading this message (transaction-1). That handler starts to process the lengthy transaction that is described by the message received.
5. While the transaction in step 4 is being processed, the next message queued is received by one of the remaining idle transaction handlers (transaction-2). The receiving transaction handler then begins to process this lengthy transaction (transaction-2) concurrently with the other.
6. The third remaining transaction handler remains idle, unless another message should arrive.

Figure 21.2 illustrates how this process works.

Designing your transaction server with parallel receiving processes allows you to achieve better response times. You can achieve this result by allowing processes to accept and process the transactions in parallel. Alternatively, you can cut back system utilization by reducing the number of serving processes. By doing so, you leave considerable latitude for tuning. The multiple process approach permits you to take better advantage of a multi-CPU system because more work is performed simultaneously.

Now that you understand the usefulness of message queues, it is time to look at the functions that Linux provides to work with them.

FIGURE 21.2

Processes competing for messages.

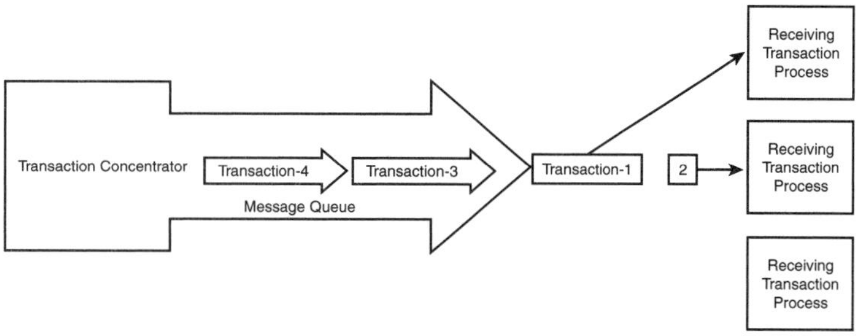

Working with Message Queues

In the following sections, you will learn how to create, access, and destroy message queues. Later in this lesson, you'll examine the process of sending and receiving a message.

Creating and Accessing a Message Queue

You create a message queue by calling on the services of the function `msgget()`. Just as you saw for semaphores and shared memory regions, you can request a new message queue to be associated with a specific key value or request a private message queue by using `IPC_PRIVATE`. The function prototype for `msgget()` is as follows:

```
#include <sys/types.h>
#include <sys/ipc.h>
#include <sys/msg.h>

int msgget(key_t key,int msgflg)
```

The key value is specified as `IPC_PRIVATE` or as a systemwide key value that identifies this message queue.

The `msgflg` argument specifies certain optional flag bits and the lower nine bits of permissions, as follows:

- `IPC_CREAT` indicates that the message queue should be created if necessary. This flag is implied if the key value `IPC_PRIVATE` is used.
- `IPC_EXCL` indicates that the `msgget()` function should return the error `EEXIST` if the message queue already exists (when used with `IPC_CREAT`).
- The lower nine bits of permissions are specified when `IPC_CREAT` is used or implied.

The least significant nine bits of permissions have the following permission semantics for the user, the group, and everyone else:

- The read permission bit allows the caller to receive messages from the queue.
- The write bit allows the caller to send messages to the queue.
- The execute bit is not used and should be specified as `0`.

When the `msgget()` function is successful, a message queue IPC ID is returned. It is `0` or positive in value and often referred to as the `msqid` in the documentation. If an error occurs, the value `-1` is returned, and the external integer `errno` contains the reason for the error.

The following example shows how to create a new message queue, with the key value of `DEADBEEF` in hexadecimal:

```
int msqid; /* Message Queue IPC ID */

msqid = msgget(0xDEADBEEF,IPC_CREAT|IPC_EXCL|0660);
if ( msqid == -1 ) {
    perror("msgget(create)");
    abort();
}
```

To access this same message queue after creation, from another program, you use this code:

```
int msqid;

msqid = msgget(0xDEADBEEF,0);
if ( msqid == -1 ) {
    perror("msgget(access)");
    abort();
}
```

In this example, no flag bits nor permission bits are provided. However, based on how the message queue was created earlier, this process must be running under the same user ID or be a member of the same group to have use of this message queue. The queue was created with owner read and write permissions, and group read and write permissions, but no other access was given.

Destroying a Message Queue

When the message queue is no longer required, it should be destroyed. Destroying it frees memory resources used by the queue within the Linux kernel. You can destroy a message queue by using the `msgctl()` function. The control function synopsis is as follows:

```
#include <sys/types.h>
#include <sys/ipc.h>
#include <sys/msg.h>
```

```
int msgctl(int msqid,int cmd,struct msqid_ds *buf);
```

The first argument, `msqid`, is the IPC ID that was returned earlier from a call to `msgget()`. This argument identifies the instance of the message queue that you want to destroy.

The second argument is the command for this control function. To destroy the message queue, you use the command `IPC_RMID`. When this command value is used, the third argument is ignored, and you can supply a `null` pointer for it.

If the call is successful, the function returns the value `0`. Otherwise, `-1` is returned, and the reason for the error is posted to external integer `errno`.

The following code shows how you can remove a message queue:

```
int msqid; /* Message Queue ID */

if ( msgctl(msgqid,IPC_RMID,0) == -1 ) {
    perror("msgctl(IPC_RMID)");
    abort();
}
```

After the message queue is removed, any other process attempting to use the same message queue obtains an error, and the posted reason for the error is `EIDRM`. This message simply means that the queue was destroyed. Unlike with shared memory, queue destruction is immediate.

Understanding the Message Structure

In the next section, you will learn how to send a message through the message queue. However, before you can do that, you need to learn about the structure of the message being sent. The general format of the message is listed in the man pages as follows:

```
struct msgbuf {
    long    mtype;     /* message type */
    char    mtext[1];  /* message data */
};
```

Obviously, sending a one-byte message is not always very useful. What the structure conveys, however, is that the first component of the message is the `long` integer data type, which holds the message type value. The next component is the first byte of the message that you want to send.

The messages themselves can vary in length. For example, if you want to send a message with a 47-byte pathname in it, your sending message might look like this:

```
struct S_MyMsg {
```

```
    long    mtype;
    char    pathname[47];
} msg_pathname;
```

The actual layout and use of the `mtext[]` component of the message are design aspects that are between you as the application developer and the process receiving the message. Another sample message might look like this:

```
struct S_PrintReq {
    long    mtype;          /* Print priority */
    pid_t   req_PID;        /* Requesting Process ID */
    uid_t   uid;            /* User requesting the print */
    gid_t   gid;            /* The group id of the user */
    char    path[128];      /* File to print */
} req_print;
```

This message contains a number of components. Note that it still begins with the mandatory `mtype` message type component.

Specifying the Size of a Message

The function used for sending a message requires that you specify the size of the message. Knowing what the size in bytes actually represents can be confusing. Does it represent the size of the entire message structure? Does it represent the size of the message without the message type? I find myself having to look up this information in the man pages every time.

The size is indicated in bytes, and it specifies only the size of the `mtext[]` array member in the original structure `msgbuf` that you saw. Another way to state this is that the size does not include the size of the message type, which is a `long` integer type.

The message size of the structure `S_PrintReq`, previously shown, can be computed as follows:

```
sizeof(struct S_PrintReq) - sizeof(long)
```

This size computation is important for successful use of the sending and receiving functions that you are going to examine next.

Sending a Message

You can send a message by using the function `msgsnd()`. Its function synopsis is as follows:

```
#include <sys/types.h>
#include <sys/ipc.h>
#include <sys/msg.h>
```

```
int msgsnd(int msqid,struct msgbuf *msgp,int msgsz,int msgflg)
```

The `msgsnd()` function takes the following four arguments:

- The `msqid` argument specifies the IPC ID of the message queue instance that you want to queue the message to.
- The `msgp` argument is a pointer to a message structured similar to `struct msgbuf`. It points to the message you want to queue.
- The `msgsz` is the size in bytes of the `mtext[]` component of the message. This size does not include the message type component.
- The `msgflg` argument permits the use of special flag option bits.

Argument two in your code usually requires a cast to the type `struct msgbuf`. The cast satisfies the compiler, but you generally need to apply a cast because your structure defines the `mtext[]` component differently. See the example in the next section.

The `msgflg` argument can have the following optional flags:

- `0`, when no option flags are used.
- `IPC_NOWAIT`, which specifies that the function should return with an error if the message queue is currently full. The error returned in this case is `EAGAIN`.

When the option flag `IPC_NOWAIT` is not used, and the kernel message queue buffers are exhausted, the calling process is put to sleep until the call can successfully queue this message. In other words, your process is *blocked*. The `IPC_NOWAIT` option causes an error to be returned instead so that your program can continue with something else.

The return value `0` is returned when `msgsnd()` successfully queues your message. Otherwise, `-1` is returned, and the external integer `errno` contains the posted reason for the error.

Listing 21.1 shows how to use `msgsnd()` to send the print request message illustrated earlier.

Listing 21.1 21LST01.c—Using `msgsnd()` to Send a Priority Message

```
struct S_PrintReq {
    long    mtype;              /* Print priority */
    pid_t   req_PID;            /* Requesting Process ID */
    uid_t   uid;                /* User requesting the print */
    gid_t   gid;                /* The group id of the user */
    char    path[128];          /* File to print */
} req_print;
int msqid;                      /* Message Queue IPC ID */
```

continues

LISTING 21.1 CONTINUED

```
9:   int msgsz;                     /* Message Size */
10:  int z;                         /* Returned status */
11:
12:  msgsz = sizeof req_print - sizeof req_print.mtype;
13:
14:  req_print.mtype = 1;           /* Set top priority */
15:
16:  do  {
17:      z = msgsnd(msqid,(struct msgbuf *)&req_print,msgsz,0);
18:  } while ( z == -1 && errno == EINTR );
19:
20:  if ( z == -1 ) {
21:      perror("msgsnd()");
22:      abort();
23:  }
```

Listing 21.1 assumes that the message is already set up and the value for `msqid` is defined. The steps used are as follows:

1. The size of the message is computed (line 12). Notice that the message type size is subtracted from the total structure size.
2. A message type value is assigned (line 14). Here, you use the message type as a priority value and assign it the highest priority value of `1`.
3. The `msgsnd()` call is invoked in a loop, with the return value assigned to variable `z`. Notice the cast that is necessary in argument two.
4. If `-1` is returned in `z`, and the `errno` value is `EINTR` (line 18), then step 3 is repeated.
5. A test is performed to check for an unrecoverable error (line 20). A returned value of `-1` indicates an error.

This loop is necessary if your program receives any signals, and you should always assume that it does. The `msgsnd()` function call is potentially a blocking call, so the Linux kernel returns error `EINTR` if a signal is received and processed. I will cover this aspect of signals in detail in Hour 22, "Signals." For now, simply understand that you must repeat the system call if it fails on an `EINTR` error.

Receiving a Message

You receive messages with the function `msgrcv()`. Its function prototype is as follows:

```
# include <sys/types.h>
# include <sys/ipc.h>
# include <sys/msg.h>
```

```
int msgrcv(int msqid,struct msgbuf *msgp,int msgsz,
    long msgtyp,int msgflg);
```

The `msgrcv()` function takes the following five arguments:

- The `msqid` argument, which is the IPC ID of the message queue instance that you want to receive a message from.
- The `msgp` pointer to a buffer that will receive the message.
- The maximum size in bytes of the `mtext[]` part of the message that your buffer can accept. Note that this size does not include the size of the `mtype` member of the `msgbuf` structure.
- The message type that you are interested in receiving. See Table 21.1 for more details.
- The optional flag bits for receiving options.

The flag bits can be any of the following:

- Flag `IPC_NOWAIT` indicates that the function `msgrcv()` will return the error code `ENOMSG` if there are no messages to receive. Normally, when this option is not provided, the program is suspended until a message arrives.
- Flag `MSG_EXCEPT`, when used with the `msgtyp` argument greater than zero, causes the first message that differs from `msgtyp` to be received.
- Flag `MSG_NOERROR` indicates that the message should be truncated if necessary to fit the receiving buffer. The error `E2BIG` is returned when this option is used and the message cannot fit into the buffer.

The message type argument `msgtyp` requires special attention. The function `msgrcv()` makes calling variations possible with this argument are what primarily makes the facility so flexible. These variations are listed in Table 21.1.

TABLE 21.1 THE `msgrcv()` MESSAGE TYPE VARIATIONS

`msgtyp`	`msgflg`	*Explanation*
> `0`	`0`	The `msgrcv()` function returns a message only where the `msgtyp` argument matches the message type value of the message.
> `0`	`MSG_EXCEPT`	The `msgrcv()` function returns a message only where the `msgtyp` argument does not match the message type of the message.
`0`	ignored	The `msgrcv()` function returns the first message that has been queued.
< `0`	ignored	The `msgrcv()` function returns the message with the lowest message type that is less than or equal to `abs(msgtyp)`.

From Table 21.1, you can see that `msgrcv()` has a flexible range of ways to select the next message that will be received.

Listing 21.2 shows how you can use `msgrcv()` to receive a priority message.

LISTING 21.2 21LST02.c—USING `msgrcv()` TO RECEIVE PRIORITY MESSAGES

```
1:   union {
2:       struct S_PrintReq {
3:           long    mtype;       /* Print priority */
4:           pid_t   req_PID;     /* Requesting Process ID */
5:           uid_t   uid;         /* User requesting the print */
6:           gid_t   gid;         /* The group id of the user */
7:           char    path[128];   /* File to print */
8:       } req_print;
9:       struct msgbuf msg;
10:  } anymsg;
11:  int msqid;                   /* Message Queue IPC ID */
12:  int maxsz;                   /* Message Size */
13:  int z;                       /* Returned status */
14:
15:  maxsz = sizeof anymsg - sizeof(long);
16:
17:  do  {
18:      z = msgrcv(msqid,&anymsg.msg,maxsz,-16,0);
19:  } while ( z == -1 && errno == EINTR );
20:
21:  if ( z == -1 ) {
22:      perror("msgrcv()");
23:      abort();
24:  }
```

The example shown in Listing 21.2 uses a C union to receive a message (lines 1 to 10). The `union` data type works well when a receiving process can receive several types of messages. Normally, all anticipated message types are defined as part of the `union`.

The sample code uses the following procedure:

1. The maximum size of the `mtext[]` component is computed (line 15).
2. The `msgrcv()` call is made. In this case, the lowest message type less than or equal to 16 is taken off the message queue.
3. A test is performed to check for a `-1` return and error code `EINTR` (line 19). If this result occurs, a signal has been processed. Step 2 is repeated.
4. A test is performed to check for an unrecoverable error (line 21).

This procedure is similar to the message send loop. The only real difference is that `msgrcv()` is called instead of `msgsnd()`. The receiving process, however, has considerable flexibility in which message type it will receive first, depending on how the arguments `msgtyp` and `msgflg` are used.

In this section, you have reviewed the fundamental aspects of message queue operations. In the next section, these concepts will be applied to a paging server.

The Paging Server

To illustrate how message queues can be applied, I've included a simple paging server. The paging server is designed to accept a prioritized message that indicates the pager telephone number to dial and the telephone number that should be called back. The code presented does not actually dial a modem, but it does simulate this action by showing what could be sent to the modem if it had one. This demonstration approach allows anyone to run the demonstration program without worrying about modem setup and access.

One program is used for both the client and the server to keep the program listing small. You can start the server with the following command line:

```
bash$ ./pager -s /dev/tty -k 1234 &
```

The `-s` option indicates that this instance of the program acts as the server. The argument `/dev/tty` is the modem device. For the demonstration, this argument is ignored, but it must be provided.

The `-k` option specifies the IPC key to be used for the message queue. I chose the decimal value 1234 for the example, but any acceptable key can be used. The client program needs this value to queue requests to the server.

The server is put into the background using the ampersand character (&). Moving the server into the background allows the server to wait for and process messages while you run client commands in the same shell session.

The client command is as follows:

```
bash$ ./pager -k 1234 -p5 416-555-1212/905-555-1212x4687
```

The preceding command specifies the following:

- `-k 1234` specifies the server that will service this paging request. The key matches the `-k` option on the server command line.

- `-p5` specifies the paging request priority. The pager program defaults to `-p20`. Lower numbers have greater priority, with `-p1` being the highest priority. Priority 100 is the lowest priority permitted by the program. Lower numbers have priority because the function `msgrcv()` treats lower message type values with greater priority.

Command-line arguments that follow the options are the paging requests themselves:

- `416-555-1212` is the pager telephone number to be called.
- The slash separates the pager telephone number from the callback telephone number.
- `905-555-1212x4687` is the callback telephone number. The `x` will be dialed as an asterisk (*).

The server translates the `x` for the extension number to an asterisk so that it can be dialed by the modem. On many pagers, this character shows up on the display as an asterisk, but on other pagers, it may appear as a hyphen.

Now you're ready to examine the programming behind this paging server.

Implementing the Paging Server

The server reads its messages in priority sequence. For you to see this work, the server first displays the dial string it would send to the modem. It then sleeps two seconds before obtaining the next paging request. A real modem dial-out would take much longer than two seconds, but this example helps to simulate real conditions. Later, you will see how you can queue several requests to exercise its ability to apply priority. Listing 21.3 shows the pager program.

LISTING 21.3 PAGER.C—THE PAGING SERVER LISTING

```
/* Pager.c */

#include <stdio.h>
#include <stdlib.h>
#include <unistd.h>
#include <errno.h>
#include <string.h>
#include <sys/types.h>
#include <sys/ipc.h>
#include <sys/msg.h>

typedef struct {
    long    mtype;          /* Message type */
    char    phone[20];      /* Pager phone number */
    char    callbk[20];     /* Call back number */
} Page;

```

```
typedef union {
    struct msgbuf generic;  /* Generic Message */
    Page    page;           /* Page request */
} Msg;

static char *cmdopt_s = 0;  /* Device to page to */
static key_t cmdopt_k = 0;  /* IPC Key */
static int cmdopt_p = 20;   /* Priority */
static int msqid = -1;      /* Message Queue */

static void
usage(char *cmd) {
    char *cp = strrchr(cmd,'/');

    if ( cp )
        cmd = cp + 1;
    fprintf(stderr,"Server Usage: %s -s tty -k key\n"
        "\tto start server.\n\n",cmd);
    fprintf(stderr,"Client Usage: %s -k key [-p priority] "
        "page#/callbk#...\n"
        "\tto queue a page request\n\n",
        cmd);
    fputs("\t-s tty\t\tDefault /dev/tty\n",stderr);
    fputs("\t-k key\t\tIPC key for server\n",stderr);
    fputs("\t-p priority\tDefault priority=20\n",stderr);
    fputs("\t\t\t(range 1 to 100)\n",stderr);
    fputs("Example:\n",stderr);
    fputs("\t%s -k 23456 -p5 416-555-1212/"
        "416-555-5555x4687\n",stderr);
}

/*
 * Create or access a message queue :
 */
static int
createMsq(key_t key,int perms) {
    int msqid;

    if ( perms )
        perms |= IPC_CREAT|IPC_EXCL;

    if ( (msqid = msgget(key,perms)) == -1 ) {
        fprintf(stderr,"%s: msgget()\n",strerror(errno));
        exit(13);
    }
    return msqid;
}

```

continues

LISTING 21.3 CONTINUED

```
/*
 * Remove a message queue :
 */
static void
rmMsq(int *pmsqid) {

    if ( msgctl(*pmsqid,IPC_RMID,0) == -1 ) {
        fprintf(stderr,"%s: msgctl(%d,IPC_RMID)\n",
            strerror(errno),*pmsqid);
        *pmsqid = -1;
    }
}

/*
 * Queue a Message :
 */
static void
sendMsg(Msg *msg,int msgsz) {
    int msz = msgsz - sizeof(long);
    int z;

    do  {
        z = msgsnd(msqid,&msg->generic,msz,0);
    } while ( z == -1 && errno == EINTR );

    if ( z == -1 ) {
        fprintf(stderr,"%s: msgsnd() mtype=%ld\n",
            strerror(errno),msg->generic.mtype);
        exit(13);
    }
}

/*
 * Receive a Message :
 */
static void
recvMsg(Msg *msg,long mtype) {
    int msz = sizeof *msg - sizeof(long);
    int z;

    do  {
        z = msgrcv(msqid,&msg->generic,msz,mtype,0);
    } while ( z == -1 && errno == EINTR );

    if ( z < 0 ) {
        fprintf(stderr,"%s: msgrcv() mtype=%ld\n",
            strerror(errno),mtype);
        exit(13);
    }
```

```
}

/*
 * Paging server :
 */
static void
server(void) {
    Msg req;

    for (;;) {
        recvMsg(&req,-100L); /* Recv in priority sequence */
        if ( !strcasecmp(req.page.phone,"shutdown") )
            break;
        printf("ATDT%s,,%s\n",
            req.page.phone,
            req.page.callbk);
        sleep(2);            /* Simulate modem delay */
    }
    rmMsq(&msqid);           /* Server removes msgq */
}

/*
 * Client code:
 */
static void
client(int argc,char *argv[]) {
    int x;
    char *cp;
    Msg req;    /* Page request message */

    req.page.mtype = cmdopt_p;  /* Priority */

    for ( x=optind; x<argc; ++x ) { /* Queue each arg */
        while ( (cp = strchr(argv[x],'x')) != 0
          ||    (cp = strchr(argv[x],'X')) != 0 )
            *cp = '*';  /* Dial * instead of 'X' */

        /* Slash separates call from callback number */
        if ( (cp = strchr(argv[x],'/')) != 0 ) {
            *cp = 0;
            strncpy(req.page.phone,argv[x],
                sizeof req.page.phone)
                [sizeof req.page.phone-1] = 0;
            strncpy(req.page.callbk,++cp,
                sizeof req.page.callbk)
                [sizeof req.page.callbk-1] = 0;
            sendMsg(&req,sizeof req.page);
        } else
            fprintf(stderr,
```

continues

LISTING 21.3 CONTINUED

```
                "No call back number given! (%s)\n",
                argv[x]);
    }
}

/*
 * Paging Program:
 */
int
main(int argc,char *argv[]) {
    int rc = 0;
    int optch;
    const char cmdopts[] = "s:k:p:h";

    /*
     * Parse command line arguments :
     */
    while ( (optch = getopt(argc,argv,cmdopts)) != -1 )
        switch ( optch ) {
        case 'h' :  /* -h */
            usage(argv[0]);
            exit(0);
        case 's' :  /* -s /dev/tty */
            cmdopt_s = optarg;
            break;
        case 'k' :  /* -k key */
            cmdopt_k = (key_t) atoi(optarg);
            break;
        case 'p' :  /* -p priority (1 to 100) */
            cmdopt_p = atoi(optarg);
            if ( cmdopt_p < 1 )
                cmdopt_p = 1;
            else if ( cmdopt_p > 100 )
                cmdopt_p = 100;
            break;
        default  :
            rc = 1;
        }

    /*
     * Test for command line argument errors:
     */
    if ( rc )
        exit(1);        /* Bad command options */
    if ( cmdopt_s && optind < argc ) {
        fputs("Server mode does not accept arguments.\n",
            stderr);
        usage(argv[0]);
        exit(1);
```

```
213:     }
214:     if ( !cmdopt_k ) {
215:         fputs("Must supply IPC key in -k option.\n",
216:             stderr);
217:         usage(argv[0]);
218:         exit(1);
219:     }
220:
221:     /*
222:      * Now perform server/client function:
223:      */
224:     if ( cmdopt_s ) {
225:         msqid = createMsq(cmdopt_k,0666);
226:         server();
227:     } else {
228:         msqid = createMsq(cmdopt_k,0);
229:         client(argc,argv);
230:     }
231:
232:     return 0;
233: }
234:
235: /* End pager.c */
```

The main program in Listing 21.3 is divided into the following general steps:

1. The command-line arguments are parsed (lines 181 to 201).
2. The semantics of the options used are checked (lines 206 to 219).
3. A test is performed to check whether the command-line option `-s` is supplied (line 224).
4. The server code is called if the option `-s` is supplied (lines 225 and 226).
5. The client code is called if the option is not supplied (lines 228 and 229).

The server code is shown in lines 120 to 134 of Listing 21.3. The following steps are used by the server loop:

1. The highest priority message is taken off the message queue (line 125). The `-100L` is passed to `msgget()` as a negative value. This fetches the next lowest numbered `mtype` message less than or equal to 100.
2. A check is made for the telephone number `"shutdown"` (line 126). This line instructs the server to shut down. Note that a caseless string comparison is made.

3. The modem dial string is displayed (lines 128 to 130). The two commas that appear between the telephone numbers insert about a four-second pause in the dialing. This way, the modem can dial the pager with the first telephone number and wait for the paging service to answer. Then the callback number is dialed after the four-second pause.
4. The program sleeps for two seconds (line 131). This delay helps simulate modem conditions and demonstrates the priority queuing mechanism at work.
5. Outside the loop, the server removes the message queue in line 133.

The client-side code exists between lines 139 and 167. The steps used in this code are as follows:

1. The priority of all requests is set (line 145). The default value of `cmdopt_p` is **`20`**, unless changed by a command-line option using `-p`.
2. A loop begins (line 147).
3. All capital and lowercase occurrences of the letter `X` are changed to an asterisk (`*`), which can be dialed by the modem (lines 148 to 150).
4. If a slash character is found (line 153), a request is formatted to be queued (lines 154 to 161). Otherwise, a terse error message is provided (lines 163 and 164).

One or more command-line arguments are processed and queued at the same paging priority. Other essential pieces of the program are as follows:

- The `createMsq()` function creates or accesses a message queue, depending on argument `perms` (lines 52 to 64). If `perms` is `0`, a queue is accessed if possible; otherwise, the queue is created.
- The `rmMsq()` function releases the message queue (lines 69 to 77). It is called upon only by the server code.
- The `sendMsg()` function places the given message `msg` on the message queue (lines 82 to 96).
- The `recvMsg()` function receives a message based on the argument `mtype` (lines 101 to 115).

Before you use the server, compile the code:

```
bash$ gcc -Wall -D_GNU_SOURCE pager.c -o pager
```

Now you can start the server, as follows:

```
bash$ ./pager -k 1234 -s /dev/tty &
[1] 1167
bash$
```

Now the paging server is running as process ID 1167. To test it, give it one simple page request:

```
bash$ ./pager -k 1234 -p1 416-555-1212/x4687
ATDT416-555-1212,,*4687
bash$
```

This example shows how 416-555-1212 is paged and leaves extension 4687 as the callback number. Option `-p1` makes it top priority.

To test the priority feature, you need to rapidly queue several paging requests. To accomplish this task, you can write a shell script like the one shown in Listing 21.4.

LISTING 21.4 PAGER.KSH—TEST SCRIPT TO TEST PRIORITY PAGING REQUESTS

```
1:   #!/bin/bash
2:   #
3:   # Queue several paging requests:
4:
5:   ( while read args ; do
6:      ./pager -k 1234 $args &
7:     done
8:   ) <<EOF
9:   -p10 416-555-1212/905-555-1212x10
10:  -p8  416-555-1212/905-555-1212x8
11:  -p6  416-555-1212/905-555-1212x6
12:  -p7  416-555-1212/905-555-1212x7
13:  -p9  416-555-1212/905-555-1212x9
14:  -p30 416-555-1212/905-555-1212x30
15:  -p25 416-555-1212/905-555-1212x25
16:  EOF
```

The loop in lines 5 to 8 of Listing 21.4 reads in the data from lines 9 to 15 of the shell script. By reading the data, it can rapidly invoke the pager client command in line 6 several times. Notice that each paging request has a different priority and that they are not in any particular sequence. So that you can keep track of the priority, each extension number mirrors the priority. When the server receives these requests from the message queue, however, Listing 21.5 shows, by the extension numbers used, that they are received in priority sequence.

Listing 21.5 Testing the Priority Service

```
bash$ ./pager.ksh &
[2] 1195
bash$ ATDT416-555-1212,,905-555-1212*10
ATDT416-555-1212,,905-555-1212*6
ATDT416-555-1212,,905-555-1212*7
ATDT416-555-1212,,905-555-1212*8
ATDT416-555-1212,,905-555-1212*9
ATDT416-555-1212,,905-555-1212*25
ATDT416-555-1212,,905-555-1212*30

[2]+  Done                    ./pager.ksh
bash$
```

Because the shell script is placed in the background, process ID 1195 is displayed, and the bash prompt appears before the server starts displaying modem dialing strings. The first dial string shows extension 10. This result is not unusual because it is the first page request queued. All remaining paging requests that were queued are processed in priority sequence (check Listing 21.4 to see the original sequence).

To shut down the server, you can enter this fake page request:

```
bash$ ./pager -k 1234 shutdown/
[1]+  Done                    ./pager -k 1234 -s /dev/tty
bash$
```

The trailing slash is required to get past the client-side parsing rules for pager and callback telephone numbers. To make sure that it is the last request processed, you could have added `-p100` for lowest priority.

If you do not shut down the server process normally, you need to use the `ipcs` and `ipcrm` commands to destroy the lingering message queue. However, if you shut down the server normally as shown, the message queue is removed automatically.

Summary

In this lesson, you learned how message queues are accessed, created, and used. You used the demonstration program to put a message queue to work as a paging service. Now you are equipped to use the powerful combination of semaphores, shared memory, and message queues under Linux.

In the next lesson, I will cover signals and signal handling. This information will complete the most essential aspects of your Linux programming training.

Q&A

Q Is it possible to queue messages with a `0` or negative value for `mtype`?

A No. The receiving methods available do not permit a way to specifically fetch a `0` or negative value `mtype` message. For this reason, you cannot queue a message with these values.

Q When a message queue is destroyed using `msgctl()` and `IPC_RMID`, is the queue marked for destruction, or is it removed immediately?

A Unlike with shared memory, message queues are removed immediately.

Q What happens if my program is trying to get a message from the message queue, and the queue is destroyed by another process?

A An error indication is returned, and external integer `errno` contains the value `EIDRM`. This error code indicates that the message queue has been removed.

Workshop

To retain what you have learned in this lesson, you are encouraged to work through the quiz and exercises before proceeding to the next lesson.

Quiz

1. What flag do you use to create a message queue when calling `msgget()`?
2. What flag makes sure that the message queue does not already exist when creating a message queue?
3. What flag do you use on the `msgrcv()` call to indicate that the message to be received is not equal to `mtype`?
4. What error code does `msgrcv()` set when option flag `MSG_NOERROR` is used and the message is truncated to fit the receiving buffer?

Exercise

Write a different client program to submit pager requests to the paging server used in this lesson. In your client program, do not permit the priority to be changed to less than `20` if the user is not a root user. Furthermore, screen the pager numbers so that no chargeable calls can be made. This program should get its IPC key value from environment variable `PAGER_KEY`.

Hour 22

Signals

Understanding What Signals Are

A dinner conversation between a husband and his wife could be described as having an order and purpose. That is, until their young child pipes up to interject his needs, which must be taken care of immediately. Sometimes that need can be deferred for a short time, while the parents finish a critical part of the conversation. Eventually, however, their conversation must pause to give their attention to the interrupting child.

In a similar manner, a Linux program executes with order and purpose. At certain points, however, it must be interrupted to carry out something urgent. The *signal*, therefore, is an asynchronous software interrupt.

Upon completion of this lesson, you will know how to ignore some signals so that your program is not terminated, and work with others. You will be able to raise signals of your own, create timers, and learn about some of the problems that signals pose.

Discovering Signal `SIGINT`

When a program is executing and is taking too long, or you change your mind about executing it, you can use the interrupt character to terminate the program. The interrupt character is usually Ctrl+C, but the user can customize it (the default may also vary with different Linux distributions). To find out what your current interrupt character is, execute the following command:

```
bash$ stty -a
speed 19200 baud; rows 0; columns 0; line = 0;
intr = ^C; quit = ^\; erase = ^?; kill = ^U; eof = ^D; eol = <undef>;
eol2 = <undef>; start = ^Q; stop = ^S; susp = ^Z; rprnt = ^R;
➥ werase = ^W;
lnext = ^V; flush = ^O; min = 1; time = 0;
-parenb -parodd cs8 hupcl -cstopb cread -clocal -crtscts
-ignbrk -brkint -ignpar -parmrk -inpck -istrip -inlcr -igncr icrnl
➥ ixon ixoff
-iuclc -ixany -imaxbel
opost -olcuc -ocrnl onlcr -onocr -onlret -ofill -ofdel nl0 cr0 tab0
➥ bs0 vt0 ff0
isig icanon -iexten echo echoe echok -echonl -noflsh -xcase -tostop
➥ -echoprt
-echoctl echoke
bash$
```

Among all this information is this small clause:

```
intr = ^C;
```

This clause appears on the start of the second display line. The caret (^) symbol means "control." So when it displays `^C`, it represents Ctrl+C.

The interrupt character causes an immediate `SIGINT` signal to be raised in the executing program. The default action of the `SIGINT` signal is to terminate the program. You can use `SIGINT` to cancel a program that takes too long to run or stop it if you change your mind about running the program. However, the program can register its own custom action for that signal and issue a message to "go away," for example, and continue executing instead.

To learn the various signal topics, you will use the signal `SIGINT`. Later in the lesson, you will learn about other signals that are defined for Linux.

Understanding Signal Terminology

Because a signal is an asynchronous software interrupt, your program cannot anticipate when or if signals will arrive. For this reason, a function or action is registered in advance for the signal. When the signal arrives, the execution of the present code is suspended while the registered function is called or registered action takes place. This process is known as *catching a signal*. The function that is called as a result of the signal is known as a *signal handler*.

When the interrupt key Ctrl+C is pressed, the signal `SIGINT` is *generated*. Another way of expressing this action is that the signal `SIGINT` is *raised*.

Understanding Reliable and Unreliable Signals

You may have heard or read about *unreliable signals* and *reliable signals*. A brief bit of UNIX history is in order to explain what these terms mean and the difference between them.

The original UNIX signal handling design was not entirely perfect. When a signal was caught by a program, the signal's registered action reverted to its system default. Signal handlers would immediately reregister their required actions but in doing so left a small window of opportunity for the default action to be exercised by bad timing. This is what caused signals to be considered unreliable.

This lesson will focus exclusively on the reliable signal mechanism that is available under Linux. You should avoid the older `signal()` function in new software, except for registering actions `SIG_DFL` and `SIG_IGN`. These actions define the default and ignore actions, respectively, for a signal.

Working with Signal Sets

To register and unregister actions for a specific set of signals, you need to be able to build sets of signals. At other times, you'll need to construct signal masks. All these operations require you to work with signal sets.

The data type that is used for constructing signal sets is the `sigset_t` C data type. This data type is manipulated by a number of functions; the synopsis for these functions is as follows:

```
#include <signal.h>

int sigemptyset(sigset_t *set);
int sigfillset(sigset_t *set);
int sigaddset(sigset_t *set,int signum);
int sigdelset(sigset_t *set,int signum);

int sigismember(const sigset_t *set,int signum);
```

The functions sigemptyset(), sigfillset(), sigaddset(), and sigdelset() all manipulate the sigset_t data type in some way. The last function, sigismember(), allows you to test the sigset_t data type.

The first four functions return a value of 0 if the operation is successful. If the operation fails, -1 is returned, and errno has the posted error code. You will examine the function sigismember() further in the upcoming section "Testing for Signals in a Set."

Emptying a Signal Set

The function sigemptyset() initializes a signal set to the state of "no signal members." This means that no signals are specified in this signal set. Often you use this function when you are about to specify one or more signals to add to the set.

When a signal set is declared, its contents must be considered as garbage data until the set is initialized. The function prototype for sigemptyset() is as follows:

```
#include <signal.h>

int sigemptyset(sigset_t *set);
```

The function sigemptyset() takes one argument and returns a success or failure indication. The following example shows how you can use the function to initialize a new signal set:

```
sigset_t my_sigs;          /* Signal set declaration */

sigemptyset(&my_signals); /* Clear set */
```

This code initializes the variable my_sigs to contain no signals at all.

Filling a Signal Set

The function sigfillset() is similar to sigemptyset(), which you just examined, except that it fills a signal set with all possible signals. Usually, you use this function when creating a signal mask, where only a few signals will be removed from the set. After filling the set with all possible signals, you usually delete one or more signals to be excluded from the mask.

The function prototype for sigfillset() is as follows:

```
#include <signal.h>

int sigfillset(sigset_t *set);
```

This function is used in the same way as the preceding functions. The following sample code shows how to create a set with all possible signals in it:

```
sigset_t all_sigs;

sigfillset(&all_sigs);
```

This function initializes the signal set `all_sigs` to contain every possible signal.

Adding Signals to a Signal Set

The function `sigaddset()` adds a new signal to a signal set. This function is often used after calling `sigemptyset()` to add a signal to the set. The function prototype is as follows:

```
#include <signal.h>

int sigaddset(sigset_t *set,int signum);
```

The following sample code shows how you can declare and initialize a signal set to contain two signals:

```
sigset_t two_sigs;

sigemptyset(&two_sigs);        /* Initialize as empty */
sigaddset(&two_sigs,SIGINT);   /* Add SIGINT to set */
sigaddset(&two_sigs,SIGPIPE);  /* Add SIGPIPE to set */
```

Here, the function `sigemptyset()` is used to initialize the set. Then the signals `SIGINT` and `SIGPIPE` are added to the set by calling the function `sigaddset()`.

Removing Signals from a Signal Set

Signals can also be removed from a signal set with the function `sigdelset()`. This function is often used after using `sigfillset()` to remove one or more signals from the set. The function prototype is as follows:

```
#include <signal.h>

int sigdelset(sigset_t *set,int signum);
```

In the example that follows, the `sig_msk` set is filled with all possible signals by calling `sigfillset()`. Then function `sigdelset()` is used to remove `SIGINT` from this set:

```
sigset_t sig_msk;

sigfillset(&sig_msk);  /* Initialize with all sigs */
sigdelset(&sig_msk,SIGINT);  /* Del SIGINT from set */
```

The resulting signal set `sig_msk` in this example is considered a signal mask because it includes all signals except the few that you have masked out.

Testing for Signals in a Set

The function `sigismember()` tests whether the signal is a member of the given signal set. The function prototype is as follows:

```
#include <signal.h>

int sigismember(const sigset_t *set,int signum);
```

The function `sigismember()` returns the value `1` if the signal given in argument `signum` is a member of the given signal set in argument `set`. Otherwise, `0` is returned to indicate that the signal is not a member of the set. The following code illustrates its use:

```
sigset_t myset;

sigemptyset(&myset);                /* Clear the set */
sigaddset(&myset,SIGINT);           /* Add SIGINT to set */

if ( sigismember(&myset,SIGINT) )   /* Test for SIGINT */
    puts("HAS SIGINT");
if ( sigismember(&myset,SIGPIPE) ) /* Test for SIGPIPE */
    puts("HAS SIGPIPE");
```

In the code shown here, the message `"HAS SIGINT"` is displayed, but because the `SIGPIPE` signal is not a member of the set, the message `"HAS SIGPIPE"` is not shown.

At this point, you have learned how to work with signal sets, whether they are sets of a few signals or mask sets excluding a few signals. Signal sets will be an important concept for the next section, which will teach you how to register actions for signals.

Setting Signal Actions

Function `sigaction()` queries and sets signal actions when using reliable signals. This function replaces the older `signal()` function that you have seen. The function synopsis is as follows:

```
#include <signal.h>

int sigaction(int signum,          /* Signal number */
    const struct sigaction *act,   /* New actions */
    struct sigaction *oldact);     /* Old actions */
```

The function `sigaction()` returns `0` when successful and `-1` if an error occurs. The reason for the error is posted to external integer `errno`.

The argument `oldact` allows you to obtain the original handler state as the new handler is installed. This capability is ideal for use when the new handler is temporary, perhaps within a library function. Before the library function returns, the original signal action can be restored precisely as it was, based on the information captured by the `oldact` argument in the earlier call.

Function argument `signum` is the signal number for which you want to query or modify the action. The second and third arguments both use the structure type `sigaction`. The `sigaction` structure is as follows:

```
struct sigaction {
    void (*sa_handler)(int);    /* Address of signal handler */
    sigset_t    sa_mask;        /* Other signals to block */
    int         sa_flags;       /* Signal handling options */
    void (*sa_restorer)(void); /* Obsolete - don't use */
}
```

A detailed description of each member is given in Table 22.1.

TABLE 22.1 THE MEMBERS OF STRUCTURE `sigaction`

Structure Member	*Data Type*	*Description*
`sa_handler`	`void (*)(int)`	This value represents the address of the signal handler. It may also be the value `SIG_DFL`, which indicates the default action, or `SIG_IGN`, which indicates that the signal will be ignored.
`sa_mask`	`sigset_t`	This value represents the set of other signals that should be blocked while the current signal is being processed. In addition, the signal being processed is blocked unless the `SA_NODEFER` or `SA_NOMASK` flags are used.
`sa_flags`	`int`	This integer value specifies a set of flags that modify the signal handling process.
`sa_restorer`	`void (*)(void)`	This value is obsolete; do not use it.

You also can specify the value of `sa_handler` as the value `SIG_DFL` to specify the system default signal handling instead of a user-supplied function address. Another value that you can use is `SIG_IGN`, which indicates that the signal is to be ignored.

Now you're ready to return to the `sigaction()` function. This function allows you to query the current signal action without modification. Simply specify the second argument, `act`, as shown here:

```
struct sigaction sa_old;
```

```
sigaction(SIGINT,0,&sa_old);
```

Running the following code segment reveals that the program starts with a `SIG_DFL` action registered for `SIGINT`:

```
struct sigaction sa_old;

sigaction(SIGINT,0,&sa_old);

if ( sa_old.sa_handler == SIG_DFL )
    puts("SIG_DFL");
else if ( sa_old.sa_handler == SIG_IGN )
    puts("SIG_IGN");
else
    printf("sa_handler = 0x%08lX;\n",
        (long)sa_old.sa_handler);
```

The code prints the message `"SIG_DFL"`, indicating the current state of the signal `SIGINT`.

Signal Action Flags

Within the structure `sigaction`, the `sa_flags` member allows a number of options to be specified. Table 22.2 outlines the signal-processing flags that Linux supports.

TABLE 22.2 LIST OF `sigaction sa_flags`

Flag	*Description*
`SA_ONESHOT` or `SA_RESETHAND`	These flags cause the signal action to revert to the default when a signal is caught. Note that using these flags is equivalent to using unreliable signals. The AT&T SVID document uses the macro `SA_RESETHAND` for this flag.
`SA_NOMASK` or `SA_NODEFER`	These flags prevent the signal being processed from being blocked automatically when it is processed. Therefore, recursive signals of the same type can occur.
`SA_RESTART`	This flag allows certain BSD signal semantics to occur as it applies to certain system calls.
`SA_NOCLDSTOP`	This flag is applicable only for the signal `SIGCHLD`. When it is used with `SIGCHLD`, no notification occurs when the child process is stopped.

Flags `SA_NOMASK` or `SA_NODEFER` are noteworthy because they allow a signal handler to be called recursively. Normally, when a signal is caught, further signals of the same signal number are blocked until the present signal finishes processing. Using these flags disables this behavior.

Flag `SA_NOCLDSTOP` prevents the parent process from being notified every time a child process is stopped. You can ignore this advanced topic for now.

The flag `SA_RESTART` allows certain function calls not to return the error code `EINTR` and be automatically restarted instead. The `EINTR` error code is discussed later in the section "Processing the `EINTR` Error."

Catching Signals

Using the `sigaction()` function, you can prepare your process to catch a signal. Earlier, you learned that signals are asynchronous. The process cannot anticipate when a signal is going to be raised. For this reason, the process must prepare for the event by registering a function that will be called when the signal is raised. The program in Listing 22.1 shows how this can be done.

LISTING 22.1 CATCHING SIGINT

```
#include <stdio.h>
#include <stdlib.h>
#include <unistd.h>
#include <signal.h>

static int count = 0;

static void
catch_sigint(int signo) {
    ++count;
    write(1,"CAUGHT SIGINT!\n",15);
}

int
main(int argc,char *argv[]) {
    struct sigaction sa_old;
    struct sigaction sa_new;

    sa_new.sa_handler = catch_sigint;
    sigemptyset(&sa_new.sa_mask);
    sa_new.sa_flags = 0;
    sigaction(SIGINT,&sa_new,&sa_old);

    puts("STARTED:");

    do  {
        sleep(1);
    } while ( count < 3 );

    puts("ENDED.");
    return 0;
}
```

The program in Listing 22.1 uses the following basic steps:

1. A signal catching function is declared (lines 8 to 12).
2. Two `sigaction` structures are declared (lines 16 and 17). Structure `sa_old` saves the original values of the signal action, whereas `sa_new` defines the new signal actions that are required.
3. The address of the signal handling function is specified (line 19).
4. The signal set to be blocked is initialized (line 20). In this example, you do not prevent other signals from interrupting while you process `SIGINT`.
5. The flags are set to `0` (line 21). This code has no special requirements.
6. The function `sigaction()` is called to establish a new signal action for signal `SIGINT` (line 22).
7. The function `sleep()` is called in a loop (lines 26 to 28). This loop continues until the count becomes greater than `3`.
8. The program exits (lines 30 and 31).

Compiling and running the program gives you the following display:

```
bash$ gcc -Wall -D_GNU_SOURCE 22LST01.c
bash$ ./a.out
STARTED:
CAUGHT SIGINT!
CAUGHT SIGINT!
CAUGHT SIGINT!
ENDED.
bash$
```

The program enters its loop after the message `"STARTED:"` is displayed. Although it does not show in the session output, the three messages `CAUGHT SIGINT!` are provoked by the user pressing Ctrl+C three times (the interrupt character for this session).

Each time Ctrl+C is pressed by the user, the following events occur:

1. The current program execution is suspended (lines 26 to 28).
2. The signal handler function `catch_sigint()` is called because it is the registered signal handling function for `SIGINT`. The argument `signo` contains the value `SIGINT`.
3. The value of variable `count` is incremented (line 10).
4. A message is written to standard output (line 11). The write call is used because restrictions are placed on what can be called in a signal handler (to be discussed).
5. The function `catch_sigint()` returns, causing the `main` program to be resumed (lines 26 to 28).

6. The `main` program exits the loop (line 28) when the signal handling function `catch_sigint()` has been called at least three times.

Now you have seen how a signal can be caught after registering a signal action with the call to function `sigaction()`. Some restrictions, however, are placed on what can be called when a signal catching function is executing. This is the topic of the next section.

Blocking and Unblocking Signals

When I described the `sigaction()` function, I noted that certain signals are blocked during the call to the signal handler. For example, when `SIGINT` is handled by the signal handler, more `SIGINT` signals are prevented from taking place until the present handler returns (unless flags `SA_NOMASK` or `SA_NODEFER` are used).

In a similar fashion, your application can enter a critical piece of code where signals could cause it problems. An example might be keeping track of child process termination status information in a linked list. However, if the program is in the midst of updating the linked list, you do not want the signal handler to be called until the linked list has been completely updated. Otherwise, the signal handler may stumble on a bad pointer in the list.

For critical sections of code, your program can block certain signals from taking place. After the critical section is finished, then the selected signals can be unblocked. This functionality is supported by the function `sigprocmask()`; its function synopsis is as follows:

```
#include <signal.h>

int sigprocmask(int how,
    const sigset_t *set,
    sigset_t *oldset);
```

This function takes the following three arguments:

- Argument `how` indicates what modification is to be applied to the signal set given in argument two (`set`).
- Argument `set` is the set of signals to apply an action to, based on the value of argument `how`.
- Argument `oldset` is a pointer to the `sigset_t` data type that will receive the original signal set as it was before the current modification is applied.

The valid values for argument `how` are given in Table 22.3.

TABLE 22.3 VALID sigprocmask() ARGUMENT ONE VALUES

Flag	*Description*
SIG_BLOCK	The signals that are members of set are added to the current set of signals that will be blocked. Signals that are generated when they are blocked are "pending" until the signal is unblocked.
SIG_UNBLOCK	The signals that are members of set are removed from the current set of blocked signals (these signals become enabled). You can specify signals that are not currently blocked without ill effect.
SIG_SETMASK	The signals that are members of set are established as the only signals that are currently blocked. The effect is that the signal set given by set replaces the currently blocked signal set.

It is important to note the differences between the value SIG_SETMASK and the other two values SIG_BLOCK and SIG_UNBLOCK in Table 22.3. Values SIG_BLOCK and SIG_UNBLOCK modify the current signal mask; they add to and take away from the current mask, respectively. The value SIG_SETMASK, on the other hand, completely replaces the current signal mask.

The following example shows how you can block signals SIGINT and SIGPIPE from occurring during one statement:

```
sigset_t blk;   /* Signals to block */
sigset_t sigsv; /* Saved signal mask */

sigemptyset(&blk);
sigaddset(&blk,SIGINT);
sigaddset(&blk,SIGPIPE);
sigprocmask(SIG_BLOCK,&blk,&sigsv); /* Block sigs */

/* CRITICAL CODE HERE */

sigprocmask(SIG_SETMASK,&sigsv,0); /* Restore mask */
```

The following steps are applied:

1. Signal set blk is initialized.
2. Signals SIGINT and SIGPIPE are added to signal set blk.
3. The function sigprocmask() is called to block signals in the set blk. They are signals SIGINT and SIGPIPE based on step 2.
4. The critical section of code is executed. At this point, the program is assured that no SIGINT or SIGPIPE is raised.

5. The function `sigprocmask()` is called to restore the signal mask. Note the use of `how=SIG_SETMASK` and that argument two is the pointer to the saved signal mask set. This guarantees that you restore the current signal mask that was in effect before the code was executed.

Obtaining Pending Signals

In the discussion of `sigprocmask()`, I noted that blocked signals become pending signals if they are generated while they are blocked. This point is important because it means that the generated signals do not become lost while they are blocked. Sometimes a program needs to inquire about pending signals. This functionality is provided by the function `sigpending()`; its synopsis is as follows:

```
#include <signal.h>

int sigpending(sigset_t *set);
```

The set of pending signals is written to the set provided in argument one. The following example assumes that signal `SIGPIPE` is blocked and illustrates how to test if the signal is pending:

```
sigset_t pendg;  /* Pending signal set */

sigpending(&pendg);
if ( sigismember(&pendg,SIGPIPE) ) {
    puts("SIGPIPE is pending.");
```

The `sigpending()` function is useful for determining when a program that is in a critical code loop can exit temporarily to safely process the signal.

Using the `sigsuspend()` Function

After noting that a signal is pending with a call to `sigpending()`, you need a reliable way to unblock the signal that you are interested in and allow the signal to be raised. The function for the job is `sigsuspend()`; its function synopsis is as follows:

```
#include <signal.h>

int sigsuspend(const sigset_t *mask);
```

The `sigsuspend()` function temporarily applies the signal mask supplied in argument `mask` and then waits for the signal to be raised. If the mask permits the signal you know to be pending, the signal action takes place immediately.

When the signal action is carried out (assuming a signal has arrived), the original signal mask is reestablished as it was before the call to `sigsuspend()`. This function provides a safe method to control when the signal is raised.

Using the example presented with `sigpending()`, you can extend it to raise and handle the signal when you know it is pending. The following example assumes that signal `SIGPIPE` is currently blocked:

```
sigset_t pendg;              /* Pending signal set */
sigset_t notpipe;            /* All but SIGPIPE */

sigfillset(&notpipe);        /* Set to all signals */
sigdelset(&notpipe,SIGPIPE); /* Remove SIGPIPE */

sigpending(&pendg);
if ( sigismember(&pendg,SIGPIPE) ) {
    sigsuspend(&notpipe);    /* Block all but SIGPIPE */
/* Original signal mask back in effect */
```

In the example shown here, signal set `notpipe` is initialized so that all signals are set except for `SIGPIPE`. You initialize it this way because the mask presented to `sigsuspend()` is the set of signals to *block*. In this manner, when the function `sigsuspend(&notpipe)` is called, the signal `SIGPIPE` is temporarily unblocked and allows the signal to be caught. However, when the signal handler returns, the original signal mask is restored as it was.

The returned value from `sigsuspend()` is always `-1`, and the `errno` value is set to the value `EINTR`. This result reflects the fact that a signal was handled.

When `sigsuspend()` is called, your program is suspended indefinitely until a signal is raised. Sometimes this is the desired behavior when the program has no work to perform, and it is waiting for a signal to arrive.

Using the `alarm()` Function

This point in the lesson is an appropriate place to discuss the `alarm()` function because you can use it with the `sigsuspend()` function just covered. The `alarm()` function can be used as a timeout facility; the function prototype is as follows:

```
#include <unistd.h>

unsigned alarm(unsigned seconds);
```

This function returns the previous alarm setting in seconds, if any, and establishes a new alarm if `seconds` is greater than `0`. After the call to `alarm()` and the specified time elapses, the signal `SIGALRM` is raised. This signal indicates that the timer has expired.

If the function `alarm()` is called before the signal is raised, the current timer is canceled, and a new timer value is established. A value of `0` seconds simply cancels the timer in progress, if any.

The program in Listing 22.2 shows how you can configure a signal handler to process signals `SIGINT` and `SIGALRM`.

LISTING 22.2 22LST02.c—USING `alarm()` AND `sigsuspend()`

```
#include <stdio.h>
#include <stdlib.h>
#include <unistd.h>
#include <signal.h>

static void
catch_sig(int signo) {
    if ( signo == SIGINT ) {
        alarm(0); /* Cancel the timer */
        write(1,"CAUGHT SIGINT.\n",15);
    } else if ( signo == SIGALRM )
        write(1,"CAUGHT SIGALRM.\n",16);
}

int
main(int argc,char *argv[]) {
    sigset_t sigs;                          /* SIGINT + SIGALRM */
    struct sigaction sa_old;
    struct sigaction sa_new;

    sa_new.sa_handler = catch_sig;
    sigemptyset(&sa_new.sa_mask);
    sigaddset(&sa_new.sa_mask,SIGALRM);
    sigaddset(&sa_new.sa_mask,SIGINT);
    sa_new.sa_flags = 0;

    sigaction(SIGINT,&sa_new,&sa_old);   /* Catch SIGINT */
    sigaction(SIGALRM,&sa_new,0);        /* Catch SIGALRM */

    sigfillset(&sigs);
    sigdelset(&sigs,SIGINT);
    sigdelset(&sigs,SIGALRM);

    puts("You have 3 seconds to SIGINT:");

    alarm(3);            /* Timeout in 3 seconds */
    sigsuspend(&sigs);   /* Wait for SIGINT or SIGALRM */

    puts("Done.");
    return 0;
}
```

The basic steps used in the program are as follows:

1. A signal handler is declared (lines 6 to 13). This particular handler accepts either signal `SIGINT` or `SIGALRM`. Note how the alarm is canceled in line 9.
2. The signal handler is configured to call function `catch_sig()` when a signal occurs (lines 21 to 25). Note that signals `SIGINT` and `SIGALRM` are blocked while the signal handler is executing (lines 23 and 24). Blocking them prevents both signals from being processed at the same time.
3. The signal handler is registered for `SIGINT` (line 27).
4. The same signal handler is registered for `SIGALRM` (line 28). Note that signals do not have to share the same handler function, but I wrote them this way to save code in this example.
5. A signal set comprising all signals except `SIGINT` and `SIGALRM` is initialized (lines 30 to 32).
6. A message `"You have 3 seconds to SIGINT:"` is written to standard output (line 34).
7. The alarm is started for three seconds (line 36).
8. The `sigsuspend()` function is called (line 37). The program pauses here either until it is interrupted with `SIGINT` or the alarm `SIGALRM` is raised.
9. The program exits (lines 39 and 40).

Note how care has been taken to make sure that only one signal is processed at a time (lines 23 and 24). When `SIGINT` is being handled, signal `SIGALRM` is blocked. When `SIGALRM` is being handled, `SIGINT` is blocked until the function `catch_sig()` returns.

Because of the way this sample program is written, however, `SIGALRM` still can be raised after `catch_sig()` returns for processing `SIGINT` because the alarm could go off just before the timer is canceled in line 9. The `SIGALRM` signal would be pending until the signal is unblocked, however, by the return from `catch_sig()`. This particular program does not have this problem, but you should pay close attention to race conditions like this in programs that you write.

Compiling and running the sample program and allowing the alarm timer to expire yield the following results:

```
bash$ gcc -Wall -D_GNU_SOURCE 22LST02.c
bash$ ./a.out
You have 3 seconds to SIGINT:
CAUGHT SIGALRM.
Done.
bash$
```

Running the program and interrupting it (Ctrl+C) before the three seconds are up yield the following results:

```
bash$ ./a.out
You have 3 seconds to SIGINT:
CAUGHT SIGINT.
Done.
bash$
```

Note that the library function `sleep()` uses the function `alarm()` also. Be careful that you don't mix the use of `sleep()` and `alarm()` in the same process. Otherwise, the `sleep()` function will cancel the alarm that you may have established.

The next section will cover some advanced signal topics to prepare you for some of the difficulties that signals present to application developers.

Advanced Signal Concepts

The preceding sections have prepared you for using the various signal functions available under Linux. You still need to look at three subjects about signal handling to complete the fundamentals of signal processing. These subjects are working with the reentrant code, working with `errno`, and handling the `EINTR` error code. They are all covered next.

Calling Functions from a Signal Handler

The signal is an asynchronous event, which can arrive at any time. This means that a signal—`SIGALRM`, for example—can arrive while your program is in the middle of executing a call to `malloc()`, `sprintf()`, or code of your own writing. You can never precisely determine when the signal will be raised.

Not knowing when the signal will be raised is a serious issue for many Linux functions that you would normally use in an application. If `malloc()` is being executed, then linked lists of free memory areas may be only partially updated when the signal arrives. Thus, when the signal handler is executed, the memory heap is in an unstable state. If the signal handler were then to call upon `malloc()`, it is likely that corruption of the heap or a program fault would occur. The reason for this problem is that the `malloc()` function is not reentrant code.

A characteristic of reentrant code is that it does not save any state information in itself (static storage) or in global areas. Instead, everything it operates with is provided by the caller. The function `malloc()` relies on a global heap, with global state data, so it cannot be reentrant.

This leads to the rule that you must never call nonreentrant functions from within your signal handler. Otherwise, your application will corrupt itself.

Table 22.4 lists the POSIX.1 standard reentrant functions. Some entries marked with an asterisk are not listed in the POSIX.1 standard; however, they are listed as reentrant by the AT&T SVID standard. Because compiling with `_GNU_SOURCE` includes POSIX and SVID source standards, this table should be a good guide to what functions can be safely called from within a signal handler.

TABLE 22.4 LIST OF REENTRANT FUNCTIONS

_exit	fork	read	tcdrain
abort*	fstat	rename	tcflow
access	getegid	rmdir	tcflush
alarm	geteuid	setgid	tcgetattr
cfgetispeed	getgid	setpgid	tcgetpgrp
cfgetospeed	getgroups	setsid	tcsendbreak
cfsetispeed	getpgrp	setuid	tcsetattr
cfsetospeed	getpid	sigaction	tcsetpgrp
chdir	getppid	segaddset	time
chmod	getuid	segdelset	times
chown	kill	sigemptyset	umask
chroot*	link	sigfillset	uname
close	longjmp	sigismember	unlink
creat	lseek	signal*	ustat*
dup	mkdir	sigpending	utime
dup2	mkfifo	sigprocmask	wait
execle	open	sigsuspend	waitpid
execve	pathconf	sleep	write
exit*	pause	stat	
fcntl	pipe	sysconf	

Avoiding Reentrant Code Issues

The reliable signals interface that has been presented in this lesson does permit you to control when certain signals are raised. You can use this capability to your advantage when a signal handler must call nonreentrant functions. You can apply this method using the following steps:

1. Block the signal of interest using `sigprocmask()`.
2. At certain points within your application, test whether the signal is pending by using `sigpending()`.
3. Call `sigsuspend()` at a safe point to allow the signal to be raised.

By calling `sigsuspend()` at a controlled point in your application, you can eliminate the fact that functions like `malloc()` are executing at the time of the signal. This level of control then permits the signal handler to call nonreentrant functions like `malloc()`.

Working with `errno` in a Signal Handler

Although Table 22.4 lists all the functions that are considered reentrant, technically most of these functions are not purely reentrant. They all can modify the value of the global external integer `errno`. Fortunately, the cure for this problem is simple.

> While you're calling functions that are reentrant within a signal handling function, keep in mind that the external integer variable `errno` still represents an area of vulnerability (a changed `errno` value can make the effect of the call nonreentrant).
>
> A signal catching function should save and then restore `errno` so that when the signal function returns, the `errno` value is undisturbed. Many of the reentrant functions listed in Table 22.4 can alter `errno`. Note also that this type of trouble can be difficult to trace and debug.

The signal catching function code found in Listing 22.1 is repeated here as follows:

```
static void
catch_sigint(int signo) {
    ++count;
    write(1,"CAUGHT SIGINT!\n",15);
}
```

This function breaks the reentrancy rule because the `errno` value could be disturbed by the call to the `write()` function. You can correct this problem by inserting a save and restore statement:

```
static void
catch_sigint(int signo) {
    int e = errno;       /* Saved errno value */

    ++count;
    write(1,"CAUGHT SIGINT!\n",15);
    errno = e;           /* Restore errno value */
}
```

By saving and restoring errno, the application does not see a corrupted errno value when the signal handler returns. Problems like errno corruption can be extremely difficult to track down and debug in an application. For this reason, it is best to code defensively to avoid this problem entirely.

Processing the EINTR Error

You have already seen code in this book that allows for the EINTR error. Now it is time to discover the real purpose of this error code and learn how to apply it.

Except when the sigsuspend() technique is used, a signal can be caught at any time by a signal handler, allowing only reentrant functions to be called. Due to this restriction, one approach that you can use is to have the signal handler post a result to a global flag variable. This flag variable is later polled by the application. In this manner, no reentrancy issues arise because the event is polled instead of asynchronously handled. The following signal handler posts a "true" result to the flag variable gotSIGINT when the signal is handled:

```
static int gotSIGINT = 0;   /* True when SIGINT arrives */

static void
catch_SIGINT(int signo) {
    gotSIGINT = 1;          /* Post the flag */
}
```

This part of the application is simple and works well. The difficulty is that when the program is blocked waiting for another event to occur, it never gets a chance to poll for the SIGINT event. The following example illustrates another part of the program that will wait indefinitely until a message arrives:

```
z = msgrcv(msqid,msgbuf,sizeof msgbuf-sizeof(long),0,0);
```

When the program is waiting for a message, the signal handler can still post its event by assigning gotSIGINT=1, but the application itself cannot break out of the msgrcv() function to see that the event occurred. Instead, the application will wait indefinitely, until a message arrives on the message queue.

To get around this difficulty, the designers of UNIX (and thus Linux) offered the following solution: When a signal handler is executed, upon its return, certain functions immediately have an error returned with the reason EINTR. This solution allows the calling application to regain control from its blocked state and have a chance to poll the value of the gotSIGINT variable, for example. Otherwise, the application can simply ignore the error and try again. The following code illustrates this type of solution for the application waiting for a message:

```
do  {
    z = msgrcv(msqid,msgbuf,sizeof msgbuf-sizeof(long),0,0);
    if ( gotSIGINT )
        doSigINT_Processing(); /* Process the SIGINT event */
} while ( z == -1 && errno == EINTR );
```

This processing loop uses the following steps:

1. The function `msgrcv()`, which is waiting for a message, is called.
2. The signal handler is executed because of a raised signal, and the handler returns.
3. Because no message arrives, the Linux kernel returns `-1` (`z=-1`), and the error is set to `EINTR`.
4. The `if` statement can test `gotSIGINT` and do something about it.
5. The loop continues until a message is received or until an error other than `EINTR` occurs.

Many people have complained about this behavior in various UNIX newsgroups on Usenet news over the years. This behavior, however, is a feature of the operating system, not a defect. Get into the habit of thinking about blocking system calls when you write your applications. If they might block the execution of your program for a long time, check to see whether you should code a loop for the `EINTR` error. The man pages list `EINTR` under the `ERRORS` section if it can occur.

With the knowledge you gained in this section, you are now equipped to apply signals reliably and safely. In the sections that follow, you will learn about other signals Linux has to offer. You will also learn how to raise signals from within your process.

Commonly Used Linux Signals

This lesson has presented you with the "how" part of signal handling. However, it would not be complete without listing some of the other signals that are available to application designers. Some of the common signals are listed for you in Table 22.5. You can find a more complete list in the Linux include file /usr/include/asm/signal.h.

TABLE 22.5 LINUX SIGNALS

Signal	*Description*
SIGHUP	The terminal line has "hung up." Traditionally, this referred to when the modem line experienced a hang up. However, when any terminal device is closed for logout (like with Ctrl+D), then a hang-up signal is delivered to its processes.
SIGINT	The terminal line has received the interrupt character.
SIGQUIT	The terminal line has received the quit character. This action usually produces a core file.
SIGUSR1	User signal one.
SIGUSR2	User signal two.
SIGTERM	The process is being terminated (often from the kill command).
SIGCHLD	A child process has terminated.
SIGPIPE	A write to a half closed pipe has occurred.
SIGALRM	The alarm from `alarm()` has terminated.

Raising Linux Signals

You can raise a Linux signal from your application if you use the `kill()` function. Its function prototype is as follows:

```
#include <signal.h>

int kill(pid_t pid,int sig);
```

This function raises the indicated signal in argument two, in the process given by process ID in argument one. You must have permission to raise the signal in the indicated process to succeed. To raise a user signal like `SIGUSR1` in your own application, you can code the following:

```
kill(getpid(),SIGUSR1); /* Raise SIGUSR1 in current process */
```

The value `0` is returned for success, or `-1` and the posted `errno` value if an error occurs.

Summary

In this lesson, you learned the fundamentals of the advanced topic of signals for Linux. With the knowledge gained in this lesson, you can equip your applications with the capability to deal with signals and process them in a reliable fashion.

Q&A

Q Why must signal handlers save and restore the `errno` values?

A Normally, this action is required to not corrupt the `errno` value for the application that was interrupted by the signal. Event reentrant functions that can be called from a signal handler can modify the `errno` value.

Q What is the reason for returning the `EINTR` error from a function?

A Returning this error gives the application a chance to perform functions after a signal has been received. This error is returned for certain functions that would otherwise block the application program indefinitely, preventing a prompt response to the signal event.

Q What are the signals `SIGUSR1` and `SIGUSR2` used for?

A Any signal application you want. These signals were reserved for use by application developers. However, be aware that the `kill` command is also capable of raising these signals, and the application should not necessarily assume that these signals were raised from within the application.

Q Can a signal handler catch signal `SIGKILL`?

A No. This signal is generated by the command `kill -9` and cannot be caught by an application process. The reason for this is that if the process intercepts all other signals, the `SIGKILL` signal is the only remaining signal that can terminate the process. However, this signal should be used only as a last resort because it prevents the process from performing any cleanup operations.

Workshop

To retain what you have learned, you are encouraged to work through the quiz and the exercises before proceeding to the next lesson.

Quiz

1. What is the C data type used to contain a set of signals?
2. When might you use the function `sigfillset()` instead of `sigemptyset()`?
3. Which function registers a signal handler for a signal?
4. What signal is raised when the timer from `alarm()` runs out?
5. What function do you use to raise a signal?
6. What function waits for a signal to be raised?

Exercises

1. Write a small program that forks into two processes. The child process should then set up a signal handler to handle the signal `SIGALRM`. It should then call on `alarm()` to raise `SIGALRM` in the child process every three seconds with the help of a loop. When the child process signal handler catches `SIGALRM`, it should cause the signal `SIGUSR1` to be raised in the parent process.

   The parent process should catch this signal in its signal handler and report it by writing something to standard output. The parent process must use the function `sigsuspend()` to wait for `SIGUSR1` to arrive and then loop to wait for the next `SIGUSR1` signal.

2. Extend the program from exercise 1 to allow the parent process to handle the signal `SIGINT`. When the parent process receives `SIGINT`, it should send `SIGTERM` to the child process to terminate it and then exit.

HOUR 23

Client/Server Programming

The Advantage of Client/Server

In recent years, much has been said and written about the client/server model. To help you gain some hands-on experience with the client/server model, you will compile and work with a small SQL client and server in this lesson.

The client/server approach can be simply described as splitting an application into a client process and a server process. The client sends its requests to the server, and the server is expected to perform the work. The server, in turn, usually provides some sort of response back to the client, indicating a success or failure. An example might be multiple Windows client applications using a common database that is managed by a Linux host.

Separating the application work between the client and the server process provides a number of advantages:

- The work is divided potentially on different systems or different CPUs of the same system. The client can be a PC, whereas the server can be a Linux server.
- One server can process multiple client processes, providing an economy of scale. The equivalent server code is not required by each client process to perform the same function.
- If the interface does not change between the client and server, the client and server software packages can be updated independently. This approach works because the code for each is separated. An example would be when the database engine is upgraded to a newer database release, while no changes are made to the desktop PCs.
- Separating the client process from the server process provides isolation from critical resources. One example of a critical resource is a database in which access must be strictly controlled and the integrity of the data must be strictly maintained.

Isolation is an important advantage when it comes to protecting critical resources like database data. When a separate server process manages the database, a client program that corrupts itself because of bad programming cannot corrupt the database or the server. Consequently, many relational database management systems (RDBMS) today use this model.

Software economy is another important benefit for RDBMS. The database software performs the complex data management functions that the client program does not need to provide for or manage itself. Instead, the client simply avails itself of the server facilities that it provides.

In the sections that follow, you will look at some of the code behind the demonstration Linux server that has been dubbed the Tiny Query Server (abbreviated TQL). This small SQL server manages a small password database using SQL commands. The purpose of this demonstration software is to illustrate the client/server model as well as to review many of the topics that have been covered in this book.

The TQL Server Design

The TQL demonstration software builds into the following two final executable programs:

- The TQL server daemon (`tqld`)
- The TQL client program (`tqlc`)

To apply these programs, the `tqld` daemon is started first and left running. The SQL server component manages a database of tables.

To access the server, you start the client program `tqlc`. This program attaches itself to the server and waits for you to enter SQL statements to process. After you enter a complete statement, it is sent to the server and executed. The results, if any, are received by `tqlc` from the `tqld` server daemon and displayed on your terminal.

Making the TQL Project

The volume of code for this project prevents me from providing a complete source listing in this lesson. However, you can find all the source code on the CD-ROM. Under Linux, if you have the CD mounted as /cdrom, you can find the source code for the TQL server in the /cdrom/source/chap23 directory. If you are inspecting the CD from DOS or Windows, and D: is your CD-ROM drive, then you should find the TQL source files in the D:\source\chap23 path.

To build the project and use it, you must be running Linux, of course. Simply copy the project files to your work directory and run `make` on the project. Listing 23.1 shows what your `make` session should look like.

LISTING 23.1 RUNNING `make` ON THE TQL SERVER PROJECT

```
bash$ make
gcc  -c -D_GNU_SOURCE -Wall tqld.c
gcc  -c -D_GNU_SOURCE -Wall prepare.c
gcc  -c -D_GNU_SOURCE -Wall server.c
gcc  -c -D_GNU_SOURCE -Wall table.c
gcc  -c -D_GNU_SOURCE -Wall row.c
gcc  -c -D_GNU_SOURCE -Wall select.c
gcc  -c -D_GNU_SOURCE -Wall compare.c
gcc  -c -D_GNU_SOURCE -Wall sort.c
gcc  -c -D_GNU_SOURCE -Wall log.c
gcc  -c -D_GNU_SOURCE -Wall msq.c
gcc  -c -D_GNU_SOURCE -Wall trace.c
gcc  -c -D_GNU_SOURCE -Wall sqerr.c
gcc tqld.o prepare.o server.o table.o row.o select.o compare.o sort.o
➥ log.o msq.o trace.o sqerr.o -o tqld
gcc  -c -D_GNU_SOURCE -Wall tqlc.c
gcc  -c -D_GNU_SOURCE -Wall tqlc2.c
gcc  -c -D_GNU_SOURCE -Wall token.c
gcc tqlc.o tqlc2.o token.o log.o msq.o trace.o sqerr.o -o tqlc
bash$
```

> Older distributions of Linux may not compile with the following statement:
>
> ```
> #include <wait.h>
> ```
>
> If you experience a compile error within the tql.h file at the preceding statement, change it to include sys/wait.h, as shown here:
>
> ```
> #include <sys/wait.h>
> ```
>
> Then invoke the `make` command again, and the program should compile successfully.

After the project is built, you are ready to use it. The next section describes the command-line options supported by the client program.

Using TQL Command-Line Options

Before you start using TQL, take the time to examine some of its features. Listing 23.2 shows the client program's help display.

LISTING 23.2 THE TQL CLIENT HELP DISPLAY

```
bash$ ./tqlc --help
Usage:  tqlc [-x lvl] [-X str] [-h] [-v]
or:     tqlc [--debug lvl] [--trace str] [--help] [--version]

    -h  or  --help              This usage info
    -v  or  --version           Version info
    -x lvl  or  --debug lvl     Debug/trace level 0-9
    -X str  or  --trace str     Subsystem(s) to trace
bash$
```

The command-line options for the `tqlc` client program are shown in Listing 23.2. Note that both the long and short options are supported. Normally, however, you use the `tqlc` client program without command-line options unless you are debugging changes to the project.

Examining Environment Variables for TQL

The `tqlc` client program and the `tqld` server daemon also support a few environment variables that can configure its operation. Table 23.1 lists and describes the environment variables supported.

TABLE 23.1 THE TQL SOFTWARE ENVIRONMENT VARIABLES

Variable	*Default*	*Description*
TQLKEY	0x57305536	Specifies the IPC key value for the TQL server message queue.
TQLLOGFMT	"%Y/%m/%d %H:%M"	Specifies the date and time stamp format to be used in the tql.log file, created by the `tqld` server daemon. This string uses `strftime(3)` format specifiers.
TRACE_LEVEL	0	Specifies the trace level to be given to the `TRACE()` and `TRACEF()` macros. The value `0` disables trace, and the maximum value is `9`.
TRACE_SUBSYS	Not Defined	Specifies the subsystems that are to be traced. When they are not defined, all subsystems are traced at the corresponding debug level.

The client program `tqlc` overrides the environment values `TRACE_LEVEL` and `TRACE_SUBSYS` when client options `--debug` (or `-x`) or `--trace` (or `-X`) are given, respectively. The combination of the environment variables and the trace facilities provided helps you debug any enhancements that you might like to make to the project later. The trace facility itself is fashioned after the code discussed in Hour 9, "Useful Debugging Techniques."

Before you look at the TQL code, you need to understand how to use the SQL language subset that it supports. When you understand SQL, then you can put TQL through its paces.

Understanding SQL

The abbreviation *SQL* stands for *Structured Query Language*, which is often pronounced *SEQUEL*. The SQL language was developed to provide a more natural interface to the data for humans to use. Although the official standard for SQL consists of a large number of statements, the TQL server supports only the following two statements. These statements are enough to demonstrate how client/server processes work.

- The `SHUTDOWN` statement
- The `SELECT` statement

The `SHUTDOWN` statement allows any client program to request that the server daemon be shut down. You will use this statement when you are done with TQL. Here, you can see how to use this statement at the `tqlc` prompt:

```
> SHUTDOWN;
```

The focus of the remainder of this lesson will be on the `SELECT` statement as it applies to TQL. The `SELECT` statement is a very flexible SQL command, and a lot of attention is given to its design in real database systems. The TQL `SELECT` statement supports a subset of what you would find in an Oracle, Sybase, or INFORMIX database management system.

Using SELECT

The `SELECT` statement, as supported by TQL, is composed of four main clauses. The clauses, which must appear in sequence, are as follows:

- The `SELECT` keyword and the columns to be selected
- The `FROM` keyword and the list of tables to select from
- The optional `WHERE` clause, optionally followed by conjunctions and more conditional subclauses
- The optional `ORDER BY` clause, which is used for sorting

Using these clauses, you can specify elaborate queries to obtain the data you are interested in.

Working with Tables and Columns

Modern database technology defines a *table* as a collection of rows of data. Each *row* of data within a table consists of one or more columns of information. Each *column* within a row is like a field within a record. A collection of tables is known as a *database*.

The TQL server considers your whole file system under Linux to be its database. Tables are certain occurrences of the password file, of which /etc/passwd is one such table.

You learned about the format of the password file in Hour 14, "Userid, Password, and Group Management." The TQL server knows about the column names shown in Table 23.2; they map to the corresponding password file fields.

TABLE 23.2 THE COLUMNS OF THE PASSWD TABLE

Column Name	*Data Type*	*Description*
`pw_name`	`string`	The username (also known as the account name)
`pw_passwd`	`string`	The encrypted password data
`pw_uid`	`numeric`	The user number
`pw_gid`	`numeric`	The group number
`pw_gecos`	`string`	The full username and location (GECOS field)
`pw_dir`	`string`	The home directory of the user
`pw_shell`	`string`	The shell to be used for the user

The column names should look familiar. These names were borrowed from the `struct passwd` structure that the password file routines work with (function `getpwent()`, for example).

Starting TQL for the First Time

To start the TQL server, simply invoke it. You don't need to put it in the background with the ampersand (`&`) character because the `tqld` daemon does so by itself:

```
bash$ ./tqld
TQL Server version 1.0
bash$
```

When the daemon is running, you can run the client program to perform SQL queries. The table named passwd is special to TQL. The first time you query it, and the server finds that the file is missing, TQL copies your /etc/passwd file to a local file named passwd so that you can play safely with it. The following code shows how to create your passwd table in the current directory by using a `SELECT` statement:

```
bash$ ./tqlc
> select * from passwd;
```

You start the client program by invoking `tqlc`. Then the greater than prompt is shown to indicate that it is waiting for SQL input. You then enter **`select * from passwd;`** and your whole password file is shown to you. As a side effect, a local password file is created for you to edit for your own experiments. To exit the `tqlc` program, close standard input by pressing your end-of-file character (normally, it is Ctrl+D).

The `tqld` server writes to a log file named tql.log. If you inspect the log file, you should see something like this:

```
bash$ cat tql.log
1999/02/20 19:33 TQL Server version 1.0
1999/02/20 19:33 Written by Warren W. Gay VE3WWG
1999/02/20 19:33 Started as PID 1164
1999/02/20 19:33 Found sort at /usr/bin/sort
1999/02/20 19:37 TQL query for PID 1173.
1999/02/20 19:37 No such file or directory: stat(passwd)
bash$
```

The last log entry shows the message `No such file or directory: stat(passwd)`. Because TQL does not find the file, one is copied from your /etc/passwd file.

Note that TQL is not case sensitive, except for table names. Except where it matters, the text shows SQL statements in uppercase to make them stand out. Table names such as passwd, however, must match the case of the actual filenames residing in your Linux file system.

Now that you have a passwd table to use, it is time to finish the SQL tutorial.

Selecting Specific Columns

TQL lets you select specific columns of the passwd table. You saw the names of the columns in Table 23.2. Listing 23.3 shows how to display only the username, the user number, and the shell program.

LISTING 23.3 SELECTING SPECIFIC COLUMNS

```
> SELECT PW_NAME,PW_UID,PW_SHELL
> FROM passwd;

PW_NAME  PW_UID PW_SHELL

root     0      /bin/bash
bin      1
man      13
www      99     /bin/bash
ftp      404    /bin/bash
guest    405    /dev/null
marlon   502    /bin/bash
bmorsh   501    /bin/crash
durbanky 503    /bin/bash
sid      504    /bin/bash
ken      506    /bin/bash
dan      507    /bin/bash

12 Rows
>
```

Listing 23.3 purposely shows how you can split an SQL query over more than one line. The semicolon character signals the end of the statement and causes it to be submitted to the server. The column selection clause is shown on the first line in this example, and the `FROM` clause chooses the table it is selected from. This technique is often used to give visual distinction to each clause being used. Another reason to split a query over multiple lines is that the query statement can become quite long.

You can use an asterisk (*) in place of the column names to select all columns, as shown here:

```
> SELECT *
> FROM table;
```

One additional SQL construct that is allowed with TQL is the special column name `COUNT(*)`:

```
> SELECT COUNT(*)
> FROM table;
```

This construct allows you to count the rows that would be selected instead of displaying them.

Selecting Specific Rows

Selecting the entire database is not practical if it is large. Usually, part of the query is designed to fetch only those rows that you are interested in. That's why you use a WHERE clause:

```
> SELECT *
> FROM table
> WHERE PW_UID < 100;
```


The query shown here selects only those records where the PW_UID column is less than 100. Listing 23.4 shows how you can put together a more complicated query.

LISTING 23.4 APPLYING A WHERE CLAUSE

```
> SELECT PW_NAME,PW_UID,PW_SHELL
> FROM passwd
> WHERE PW_UID >= 500
> AND PW_NAME <= 'g';

PW_NAME  PW_UID PW_SHELL

bmorsh   501    /bin/crash
durbanky 503    /bin/bash
dan      507    /bin/bash

3 Rows
>
```

Listing 23.4 shows a WHERE clause that also uses the conjunction AND to add another condition to the selection. The result of using the WHERE clause is that only those rows where the PW_UID column has a numeric value greater than or equal to 500 and a PW_NAME that is less than g are selected for display. TQL also supports the conjunction OR to include additional rows in the selection criteria.

Sorting Rows

The last SQL feature supported by TQL is the ORDER BY clause, which causes data to be sorted. The ORDER BY clause is a list of column name references separated by commas. Columns can also be referenced by numbers starting from 1, but TQL restricts its use to table columns only. You cannot reference a column using `COUNT(*)`, for example. Listing 23.5 shows an example of how you can use the `ORDER BY` clause.

LISTING 23.5 USING THE ORDER BY CLAUSE

```
> SELECT PW_NAME,PW_UID,PW_GID,PW_DIR
> FROM passwd
> WHERE PW_UID >= 500
> AND PW_NAME <= 'g'
> OR PW_DIR='/usr/home/ada'
> ORDER BY PW_NAME;

PW_NAME  PW_UID PW_GID PW_DIR

bmorsh   501    100    /home/bmorsh
dan      507    100    /home/dbraun
durbanky 503    100    /home/durbanky
ken      506    102    /usr/home/ada

4 Rows
>
```

With the `ORDER BY` clause set to sort by `PW_NAME`, the results of the query are such that the usernames are sorted. You can sort additional columns by listing the names separated by commas. For example, to sort by the `PW_GID` column and then the `PW_UID` column, you could specify:

```
> ORDER BY PW_GID, PW_UID;
```

The columns can be referenced by number also. If your `SELECT` clause names the columns

```
> SELECT PW_NAME,PW_UID,PW_GID,PW_DIR
```

then you can order by `PW_GID,PW_UID` by specifying

```
> ORDER BY 3,2;
```

This example selects the third column followed by the second, which are `PW_GID` and `PW_UID`, respectively.

If you are new to SQL, you are encouraged to take some time at this point to experiment with queries. Try the `WHERE` and `ORDER BY` clauses to make sure you understand what they accomplish. Just keep in mind that clauses must follow a sequence: `SELECT`, `FROM`, `WHERE`, and `ORDER BY`.

In the following sections, you will learn how the TQL server is implemented. In those sections, you will examine portions of the TQL project code.

Examining the TQL Source Code

The communications link used between the client and the server process for the TQL project is the message queue. For this small demonstration, the message queue is ideal because it can be used to address messages to specific processes.

When the TQL client process makes a request to the server, it sends the request to the message queue. The listening `tqld` server daemon receives the message to be processed. It then prepares the statement, executes the statement, and then sends the results back to the client on the same message queue.

This process is all accomplished on one message queue by using the following steps:

1. The client sends its message to message type one. Inside the message, however, the client places its own process ID (PID 12904, for example).
2. Server `tqld` receives only message type one, so it receives the request from the client as expected.
3. The server services the request for PID 12904. The server knows this PID because it was received in the message.
4. The server sends the response message back to the client by sending it as message type 12904.
5. The client is expecting a response from the server, so it listens for messages of type 12904 (matching its own PID). It therefore receives only the server response(s). It receives this response without picking up any other messages that might occur on this queue from other clients interacting with the server.

The message type is used as an address in this scenario. The server listens only for message type one, and all clients listen only for the message type that matches their own process ID. In this manner, the TQL server can service many clients without the messages being misdirected.

You've now completed the overview of the client and server communication for the TQL project. Next, you will see portions of the TQL server code.

Examining Table Code

Tables in the TQL project refer to password format files. To read and write password rows (records), the TQL server uses the password routines discussed in Hour 14, "Userid, Password, and Group Management." In file table.c, the function `tqlReadTable()` uses the following code:

```
errno = 0;
p = fgetpwent(table->file);
if ( !p && !errno )
    return EOF;      /* EOF */
if ( !p )
    return errno;    /* Error */
```

By using the `fgetpwent()` routine, the code can reference any password format file—not just the /etc/passwd file. Note the familiar tests for end-of-file and the tests for errors.

When the TQL server has to perform selection and sorting, it uses the `putpwent()` function in its function `tqlWriteTable()`:

```
if ( putpwent(&row->pw,table->file) == -1 )
    return errno;
```

When I wrote this lesson, I discovered that the current implementation of `putpwent()` on my system had a bug handling negative values. Newer distributions such as the RedHat 5.2 release may have this problem fixed. In any case, many systems have an entry like this in their password files:

```
nobody:*:-1:100:nobody:/dev/null:
```

When `putpwent()` writes the password entry, the `-1` becomes transformed into a large unsigned value if your system has the bug. Then, when TQL subsequently reads the temporary file back in using `fgetpwent()`, the large `uid_t` value is further mangled by the `fgetpwent()` routine. You might want to experiment with an entry like this added to your test passwd table if your Linux distribution has the bug.

Signal Handling Within `sqld`

The `tqld` server shuts down gracefully when notified by the `tqlc` client program using the `SHUTDOWN` command. When Linux is being shut down, however, the `tqld` process is sent a `SIGTERM` signal as part of the shutdown procedure. For this reason, the `tqld` anticipates signals, makes sure that the message queue resource is removed, and properly closes its log file.

Source file tqld.c contains the following statements in the `main()` program that prepare it for a signal:

```
/*
 * Catch signals SIGTERM, SIGINT and SIGHUP :
 */
sa.sa_handler = catcher;
sigemptyset(&sa.sa_mask);
sa.sa_flags = 0;
sigaction(SIGTERM,&sa,0);
sigaction(SIGINT,&sa,0);
sigaction(SIGHUP,&sa,0);
```

This code anticipates the signals `SIGTERM`, `SIGINT`, and `SIGHUP` and causes the signal handler to be called when signaled. The signal handler looks like this:

```
/*
 * Signal catcher :
 */
void
catcher(int signo) {

    if ( tqld.signo == -1 )
        tqld.signo = signo;
}
```


This function merely stores its signal number in the external integer variable `tqld.signo`. In the message processing loop that might otherwise wait forever, the code checks for the presence of a signal in file server.c:

```
do  {
    z = msgrcv(tqld.msqid,(struct msgbuf *)&msg,
            MAXSQL,1L,0);
    /*
     * 2. Check for signal after EINTR:
     */
    if ( tqld.signo != -1 )
        break;      /* Got signal */
} while ( z == -1 && errno == EINTR );
```

When the signal handler `catcher()` returns, the error `EINTR` is returned from function `msgrcv()`, thus unblocking the program's execution. At this point, the program tests the value of `tqld.signo` and notices that it has been signaled. After exiting the `msgrcv()` loop, the `tqld` daemon takes steps to shut down normally.

Probing the Sort Module

Perhaps the most interesting part of the TQL project is how the sort module works. The normal selection process without an `ORDER BY` clause works as follows:

1. The table identified in the `FROM` clause is opened. It is known as the source table.
2. A temporary table is created by calling on function `tmpfile()`.

3. Rows are read from the source table, and the `WHERE` clause, if any, is evaluated for each row. If the row is accepted by the `WHERE` clause (or its absence), then the row is written to the temporary table.
4. The column widths of the row just written are noted. An array keeps the maximum widths of all columns written. Step 3 is repeated until no source rows remain.

The selected result now sits in a temporary table (which is a nameless temporary file). The temporary table is written using the `putpwent()` function and so it remains in password file format.

The TQL server next calls on its sort module to sort the contents of the temporary table. Listing 23.6 shows the sort module code.

LISTING 23.6 THE TQL SORT MODULE

```
/*
 * Sort the results according to the ORDER BY clause:
 *
 * ARGS:
 *  tbl      I/O     Initially is the table that we are
 *                   sorting from. Later, a switch of
 *                   files is performed.
 *  olist    input   The olist[] array indicates the sort
 *                   order required.
 *  n        input   Indicates how many sort fields there
 *                   are.
 * RETURNS:
 *  True     Succeeded.
 *  False    Sort failed.
 */
Bool
doOrderBy(Table *tbl,OrderBy *olist,int n) {
    short x;
    short ax;                    /* Index into sort_argv[] */
    char *cp;                                 /* Work ptr */
    FILE *tempf;                             /* Temp file */
    pid_t chpid;                             /* Child PID */
    pid_t wtpid;                       /* PID from wait() */
    int termstat;                   /* Termination status */

    /*
     * Begin building the argv[] vector for the sort
     * command. We start by adding argv[2]:
     */
    *(cp = pos_args) = NUL;     /* Buffer for arg data */
    ax = 2;                        /* Start at argv[2] */

```

```
    /*
     * For each ORDER by reference:
     */
    for ( x=0; x<n; ++x ) {
        sprintf(cp,"+%d%s",        /* argv[] = '+POSn' */
            olist[x].fldno, /* Field # in passwd file */
            olist[x].num ? "n" : "");/* Numeric or not*/

        sort_argv[ax++] = cp;      /* Assign to argv[] */
        cp += strlen(cp) + 1;  /* Skip arg & NUL byte */

        sprintf(cp,"-%d",           /* argv[] = '-POS' */
            olist[x].fldno+1);

        sort_argv[ax++] = cp;      /* Assign to argv[] */
        cp += strlen(cp) + 1;  /* Skip arg & NUL byte */
    }

    sort_argv[ax] = NULL; /* Last argv[] must be NULL */

    /*
     * Create another temp file to contain the sorted
     * results:
     */
    if ( !(tempf = tmpfile()) ) {     /* New temp file */
        logf("%s: tmpfile()\n",strerror(errno));
        return False;                      /* Sort failed */
    }

    /*
     * Rewind the table :
     */
    if ( tqlRewindTable(tbl) )  /* Rewind input table */
        goto bail;             /* This shouldn't fail */

    /*
     * Flush pending buffers:
     */
    fflush(stdout);
    fflush(stdin);
    fflush(stderr);
    fflush(tbl->file);
    logFlush();

    /*
     * Fork to create our sort process:
     */
    if ( (chpid = fork()) == -1 ) {
        logf("%s: fork()\n",strerror(errno));
```


continues

LISTING 23.6 CONTINUED

```
            goto bail;   /* System must be short on procs */

    } else if ( !chpid ) {
        extern char **environ;     /* Our environment */

        /*
         * Child process:
         *
         * Close our standard input, so that we can make
         * the input table the standard input instead:
         */
        close(0);   /* stdin */
        if ( dup2(fileno(tbl->file),0) != 0 )
            _exit(10);                          /* Failed */

        /*
         * Close our standard output, so that we can
         * make the standard output the new temp file.
         */
        close(1);   /* stdout */
        if ( dup2(fileno(tempf),1) != 1 )
            _exit(11);                          /* Failed */

        /*
         * At this point in the child process, we have
         * as our standard input the table to be sorted
         * and the new temp table as our standard output.
         * Now we just execute the sort command, with
         * the arguments we set up, and "presto" our
         * new temp file gets the sorted results.
         */
        execve(path_sort,sort_argv,environ);
        _exit(12);                    /* Failed to exec() */
    }

    /*
     * Parent Process :
     *
     * Wait for the sort process to complete.
     */
    do  {
        wtpid = wait(&termstat);
    } while ( wtpid != chpid );

    TRACEF(3,SORT,("Sort PID %ld completed 0x%04lX\n",
        (long)wtpid,termstat))

    /*
```

```
     * See if the sort was successful or not :
     */
    if ( WIFEXITED(termstat) ) {
        x = WEXITSTATUS(termstat);
        if ( x != 0 ) {
            logf("Sort failed with exit code %d\n",x);
            goto bail;
        }
        /* Sort succeeded */

    } else if ( WIFSIGNALED(termstat) ) {
        x = WTERMSIG(termstat);
        logf("Sort failed with signal: %s\n",strsignal(x));
        goto bail;

    } else if ( WIFSTOPPED(termstat) ) {
        x = WSTOPSIG(termstat);
        logf("Sort stopped with signal: %s\n",strsignal(x));
        goto bail;

    } else  {
        logf("Sort failure for X-Files. Status 0x%04lX\n",
            termstat);
        goto bail;
    }

    /*
     * Rewind the new temp file with the sorted results :
     */
    rewind(tempf);
    if ( ferror(tempf) ) {
        logf("%s: Cannot rewind sort tempf\n",
            strerror(errno));
        goto bail;
    }

    /*
     * Pull a switch on the table : The provided table
     * is a temp file, which we can close and consequently
     * allow the system to release. We then put the new
     * sorted temp file in its place.
     */
    fclose(tbl->file);     /* Close unsorted temp file */
    tbl->file = tempf;      /* Put sorted temp file in */
    return True;                /* Sorted successfully */

bail:
    fclose(tempf);          /* Close unused temp. file */
    return False;                    /* Return failure */
```

continues

LISTING 23.6 CONTINUED

```
179: }
180:
181: /* end sort.c */
```

The sort module begins in Listing 23.6 by building up an `argv[]` array to be used to pass to the `sort` command. The declarations not included in Listing 23.6 to support this are as follows:

```
static char pos_args[128];     /* Used for sort_argv[] */
static char *sort_argv[64] = {         /* Sort argv[] */
    "sort",                               /* argv[0] */
    "-t:",                                /* argv[1] */
};           /* The remaining args specify sort fields */
```

Lines 26 to 51 of Listing 23.6 create new `argv[]` values starting with `argv[2]`. For example, the first `olist[]` array member might specify that the third field has to be sorted. Furthermore, because it is a numeric field (`pw_uid`), the `sort` command must be told to sort it numerically. This would effectively cause the following assignment to be made to `sort`'s `argv[2]`:

```
argv[2] = "+2n";
```

This assignment tells the `sort` command to sort field two (zero based) and to sort it numerically. The `sort` command also requires a stop argument, so an additional argument is added in `sort`'s `argv[3]` value:

```
argv[3] = "-3";
```

The pair of options `+2n -3` tells the `sort` command to sort only on the third field (one based). Additional options like these are generated if more `ORDER BY` specifications are given. Each `ORDER BY` specification creates an additional `olist[]` array entry to be set up. Each of these entries results in an additional pair of `sort` command arguments.

Executing the `sort` Command

The following steps outline the remainder of the `sort` procedure:

1. A new temporary file is created (lines 57 to 60). This new temporary file will receive the sorted results.
2. The input temporary file with the selected results is rewound (lines 65 and 66). This temporary file has only those rows that the `WHERE` clause has permitted to be collected. Note that reference `tbl->file` is the `FILE` pointer of the temporary file.

3. Buffers are flushed (lines 71 to 75). This step is necessary to prevent problems after a `fork()` is performed.
4. The `fork()` function is called (line 80). The child process begins executing in line 85.
5. The standard input is closed, and `dup2()` is called to put the temporary file from step 2 on the unit for standard input (lines 93 to 95). This step is taken to make the temporary file appear as standard input to the `sort` command that will be executed.
6. The standard output is closed, and `dup2()` is called to put the new temporary file from step 1 on the unit for standard output (lines 101 to 103).
7. The current child process is replaced using the `sort` command (line 113). The temporary files on standard input and standard output remain open and get processed by `sort` according to the `sort_argv[]` arguments that you set up for it.

The original standard input and output is replaced in the child process with new standard input and output that were existing temporary files.

Understanding the Function of dup2()

This standard input and output swap is accomplished in the TQL sort module with the help of the Linux `dup2()` function. The function prototype is as follows:

```
#include <unistd.h>

int dup2(int oldfd, int newfd);
```

The `dup2()` function takes an existing open Linux file descriptor and makes it available on another file unit. If the input temporary file is currently open on file unit 6, then the following code makes it available as standard input:

```
close(0);    /* Close standard input */
dup2(6,0);   /* Make 6 available as 0 */
```

After this point, unit 6 can be closed if it is not needed because it is still open on unit 0. This is how the sort program takes its nameless temporary file and makes it available as standard input for the `sort` command.

If the output temporary file is open on unit 7, the standard output switch is accomplished in like manner:

```
close(1);    /* Close standard output */
dup2(7,1);   /* Make 7 available as 1 */
```

Notice that the unit has to be available (closed) before `dup2()` can work its magic. Had you not closed unit 1 in the example, the `dup2()` call would have failed.

Waiting for sort

Now you can turn your attention back to the parent process. While the sort executes, the parent process is waiting eagerly to see whether the sort is successful. The parent program paces through the following loop:

```
/*
 * Parent Process :
 *
 * Wait for the sort process to complete.
 */
do  {
    wtpid = wait(&termstat);
} while ( wtpid != chpid );
```

In this loop, the parent process blocks in the wait() function call until the Linux kernel receives notice that its child process has terminated. Using the loop is good programming practice so that other processes do not cause a false notification. The code loops until the process ID matches that of the sort child process. Additionally, this loop protects against exiting because of the error EINTR.

Upon finding that the child process has terminated, the parent process must determine how the sort completed. If the sort failed, then the current query is botched. The following code tests the exit status of the child process:

```
if ( WIFEXITED(termstat) ) {
    x = WEXITSTATUS(termstat);
    if ( x != 0 ) {
        logf("Sort failed with exit code %d\n",x);
        goto bail;
    }
    /* Sort succeeded */
```

When the parent process knows that the child process exited normally, with status code 0, it can then proceed to use the sorted results in the new temporary file. The TQL sort module pulls one more trick out of its hat: The original temporary file is swapped for the new temporary file:

```
/*
 * Pull a switch on the table : The provided table
 * is a temp file, which we can close and consequently
 * allow the system to release. We then put the new
 * sorted temp file in its place.
 */
fclose(tbl->file);     /* Close unsorted temp file */
tbl->file = tempf;      /* Put sorted temp file in */
return True;                /* Sorted successfully */
```

The file swap procedure is outlined as follows:

1. The original temporary file `tbl->file` is closed. This temporary file holds the selected rows. Closing this file discards it because the file is nameless and is no longer open.
2. The new sorted temporary file that was written by the `sort` command now has its `FILE` pointer placed in the `Table` structure that TQL uses. The assignment of `tbl->file=tempf` tricks the calling code into using the new temporary file instead of the old.

Finally, the TQL sort module is able to return `True` to indicate success.

Summary

Unfortunately, there is not enough space remaining in this lesson to explore more of the source code here. However, you have all the source code available on the CD-ROM that is supplied with the book. Table 23.3 outlines some source modules and places of interest that you might visit. Take some time to look at these landmarks and review the lessons that covered them, if necessary.

TABLE 23.3 PLACES TO VISIT IN THE TQL PROJECT

Source File	*Lesson*	*Description*
tqlc.c	6	For an example of `getopt_long()` option processing.
msq.c	21	For message queue functions.
table.c	14	For examples of how the password database routines are used (functions such as `putpwent()`).
table.c	15	For examples of the `stat()` function. It tests to make sure it does not open /etc/passwd for write. Also, the function `access()` is used, which was not covered but is useful to know about.
sort.c	8 & 11	For an example of how to use the `PATH` environment variable. In function `initSort()`, the server discovers where your `sort` command is installed and whether it is executable. The function `strtok()` is also used there.
token.c	11	This module does some difficult string parsing, using many of the usual string favorites: `strchr()`, `strcasecmp()`, `strspn()`, `strcspn()`, `strdup()`, and `strncmp()`.
prepare.c	12	Examples of the functions `strtol()` can be found in the function `value()`.
compare.c	12	More examples of the `strtol()` conversion functions.

In this lesson, you learned about client/server programming and why it is used. You worked through a short tutorial on SQL and built and tested the TQL server. You also examined some of the code highlights, especially the segment on the TQL sort module.

By reading this lesson and experimenting with the TQL demonstration project, you should be well on your way to becoming an accomplished Linux C developer. In the next lesson, I'll provide some guidance about man pages. You will learn how to read between the lines of the man pages themselves and learn what to do when answers don't appear in print.

Q&A

Q What protection does isolating a client process from the server process provide?

A If the services of the server are made available by a shared library instead, then the code that performs the same services share the same memory as the application. This way, the application can overwrite and destroy data if the program has bugs. By performing the same service in a separate process, its memory and data are not vulnerable to client application bugs.

Q What methods do client processes use to communicate with server processes?

A Message queues, shared memory, pipes, and sockets.

Q How do I use SQL to return a count of the rows and not the data?

A `SELECT COUNT(*) FROM table;` where `table` is the table that you are querying.

Workshop

To retain what you have learned, you are encouraged to work through the quiz and the exercises before proceeding to the next lesson.

Quiz

1. What prerequisite is there to using the `dup2()` call to change your standard input?
2. Why is the `wait()` call usually included in a loop?
3. What function call creates a nameless temporary file?

Exercises

1. Discover why the module sort.c calls on the function `_exit()` instead of `exit()`. Force a failure in sort.c by calling `exit(23)` just before calling `execve()`. To provoke the problem, perform a TQL query with an `ORDER BY` clause. Remember that the server log file tql.log might contain clues.

2. Modify the `tqlc` client program to install an alarm with the use of the `alarm()` function and `sigaction()`. Set the timeout to something reasonable like three minutes or more. When the timer expires because of inactivity at the user prompt, catch the signal `SIGALRM`, and terminate the `tqlc` client program gracefully.
3. For the very ambitious: Modify the TQL project to accept the optional ascending or descending keyword after the `ORDER BY` column or numeric references. The new keywords are `ASC` or `DESC` for ascending and descending, respectively. An example of the new `ORDER BY` clause is as follows:

```
ORDER BY PW_NAME DESC
```

4. This clause should cause column `PW_NAME`to be sorted in descending sequence.

HOUR 24

Using the Man Pages

Introducing the `man` Command

This book has covered a lot of ground on the topic of Linux programming. Linux, however, draws on a rich UNIX heritage, and consequently, this is just the beginning of your programming experience. As this book draws to a close, you might be asking yourself, "Where do I go from here?"

When you started reading this book, you may have already been familiar with the `man` command. This important command serves up what are referred to as *man pages*—that is, pages of online documentation.

The man pages provide great assistance to programmers. Although terse and sometimes riddled with errors, the man documentation is a great asset. For this reason, this lesson describes the finer points of the `man` command and the documentation that it serves up.

Using the `man` Command

Throughout this book, I have assumed that you knew how to use the `man` command. To be certain that you are not left in the dark, I'll provide a few examples here. If you are already well acquainted with the command, skip to the next section.

In a man page reference, the man page name is given first, and the section name follows in parentheses. For example, the reference to `ar(1)` refers to the manual page `ar` in section `1`. You therefore type the command as follows:

```
bash$ man 1 ar
```

Many times, you can skip the section number for convenience. Leaving out the section number, you type the following:

```
bash$ man ar
```

By leaving out the section number, however, you may get the incorrect manual page at times. The `man` command retrieves the first page found in a section when no section is specified. For an example, try this:

```
bash$ man chmod
```

Then try this:

```
bash$ man 2 chmod
```

When you omit the section number, you obtain the man page for `chmod(1)`, which describes the `chmod` command. By specifying section number `2`, however, you retrieve the man page for `chmod(2)`, which describes the system call instead.

Discovering the Sections

As you know, the man pages are organized into sections that group functional topics together. In other cases, the groupings are by library. To find out what a section is all about, you can usually look up the man page for `intro(x)`, where `x` is the section number. To look up the page `intro(3)`, you enter the following command:

```
bash$ man 3 intro
```

Table 24.1 summarizes the manual sections that are available under Linux. You may have additional sections because others are being added all the time.

TABLE 24.1 COMMONLY USED MAN SECTIONS

Section	*Library*	*Description*
1	N/A	User commands (`ar`, for example).
2	`libc`	Linux system calls.
3	various	System library functions.
3C	`libc`	Standard C library functions, excluding the section `2` system calls and excluding section `3S`.
3S	`libc`	The standard I/O functions.
3M	`libm`	The arithmetic library. These sections are used by the `f77(1)` FORTRAN compiler by default.
3F	`libF77`	FORTRAN library functions.
3X	various	Special functions. The man page indicates which library these functions are contained within.
4		Special files.
5		File formats.
6		Game documentation.
7		Miscellaneous information.
8		Administration and privileged commands.
9		Kernel reference guide.

Section `9`, shown in Table 24.1, does not have an intro page at the time of this writing.

Linux programmers are usually most interested in the sections for the various libraries. The most referenced sections are sections `2`, `3`, and `3C`. Section `2` describes functions that interface to the Linux kernel, and the sections starting with `3` are library functions provided to save programmers effort.

Finding a Man Page

The most frustrating thing for a programmer is to know what you want but not know what it is called. Say you're a Windows programmer who has become a Linux convert, for example, and you want to call a function that has to do with changing permissions. Which man page do you ask for?

In circumstances like this, you must perform an *apropos search*. An apropos search lists the items that are relevant or related to the topic of interest. Listing 24.1 shows how Linux can help you.

LISTING 24.1 PERFORMING AN APROPOS SEARCH

```
bash$ man -k permissions
access (2)            - check user's permissions for a file
chmod (1)             - change the access permissions of files
chmod, fchmod (2)     - change permissions of a file
ioperm (2)            - set port input/output permissions
access (2)            - check user's permissions for a file
line 1/5 (END)
```

From Listing 24.1, you can see that the `-k` option of the `man` command permits you to perform a search. The text `change permissions of a file` seems to be what you need. Consequently, you can invoke the `man` command a second time to fetch the page `chmod(2)` to answer your need for information.

Debugging Man Pages

Reading man pages is sometimes like debugging a program because the documentation has bugs in it. You need an answer, but you are provided with only a certain number of clues. If you're a resourceful sleuth, you can get the most out of the information presented, however.

Listing 24.2 shows the top portion of a man page that has a few bugs in it.

LISTING 24.2 A PROBLEMATIC MAN PAGE

```
SEMCTL(2)          Linux Programmer's Manual          SEMCTL(2)

NAME
   semctl - semaphore control operations

SYNOPSIS
   # include <sys/types.h>
   # include <sys/ipc.h>
   # include <sys/sem.h>

   int  semctl  ( int semid, int semnun, int cmd, union semun
   arg )

DESCRIPTION
   The function performs the control operation  specified  by
   cmd on the semaphore set (or on the sumun-nth semaphore of
   the set) identified by semid.  The first semaphore of  the
   set is indicated by a value 0 for semun.

   The type of arg is the union
```

```
union semun {
    int val; /* used for SETVAL only */
    struct semid_ds *buf; /* for IPC_STAT and IPC_SET */
    ushort *array;  /* used for GETALL and SETALL */
};
```

The first sentence in the `DESCRIPTION` section starts fine, but then trouble starts within the parentheses. What is meant by the phrase `on the sumun-nth semaphore of the set`? No `sumun` argument is present in the function synopsis. Is it a typing error? If so, does it refer to the argument `semnun`? Alternatively, does it refer to the argument `arg` of type `semun`?

The next sentence reads `The first semaphore of the set is indicated by a value 0 for semun`. The use of `semun` complicates your understanding further. You have no argument named `semun`, but you do have an argument four of type `semun`. Nevertheless, this sentence does offer a clue. It tells you that somehow, under some circumstances, specifying an individual semaphore within a set must be necessary.

Following the Clues

Following the single semaphore hunch causes you to examine the semaphore operations that work on a single semaphore rather than the entire set. Listing 24.3 shows another segment of this man page pertaining to some of the singular semaphore operations.

LISTING 24.3 MORE OF THE `semctl(2)` MAN PAGE

```
GETNCNT     The system call returns the value  of  semncnt
            for  the  semno-th  semaphore of the set (i.e.
            the  number  of  processes  waiting   for   an
            increase  of semval for the semno-th semaphore
            of the set).  The calling  process  must  have
            read access privileges on the semaphore set.

GETPID      The  system  call  returns the value of sempid
            for the semno-th semaphore of  the  set  (i.e.
            the  pid of the process that executed the last
            semop call for the semno-th semaphore  of  the
            set).   The  calling  process  must  have read
            access privileges on the semaphore set.

GETVAL      The system call returns the  value  of  semval
            for  the  semno-th  semaphore of the set.  The
            calling process must have read  access  privi-
            leges on the semaphore set.
```

The three identifiers `GETNCNT`, `GETPID`, and `GETVAL` are different values for argument `cmd`. You can start by examining the `GETNCNT` operation. The opening sentence of its description reads `The system call returns the value of semncnt for the semno-th semaphore of the set....` What is this `semno-th` value? Another different reference?

Turning to the operation for `GETPID`, you find the sentence `The system call returns the value of sempid for the semno-th semaphore of the set....` Again, what is this reference to `semno-th` semaphore?

Finally, looking at the description for `GETVAL`, you get no improvement in the sentence `The system call returns the value of semval for the semno-th semaphore of the set....` Again, you have this reference to the `semno-th` semaphore of the set.

Reviewing the Bugs

Take a moment to review the facts that you've uncovered about this man page:

- The second argument in the synopsis is of type `int` and is named `semnun`.
- The fourth argument in the synopsis is of type `union semun` and is named `arg`.

Within this particular man page, you saw the following:

- The `sumun-nth` semaphore
- Value `0` for `semun`
- Three references to the `semno-th` semaphore of the set

Following a hunch, you also know that a singular semaphore must be specified sometimes. They can be specified in only two possible places; the possibilities are

- Argument two, named `semnun`
- Through argument four, named `arg` via `arg.val`

Now that you have seen the description of the `GETVAL` operation, look at the `SETVAL` operation, which requires a value to be put into the semaphore. Where does that value come from?

Examining Other Semaphore Operations

Previously, I noted that a `SETVAL` operation needs an input value to assign to the semaphore's counter value. Listing 24.4 shows the description of the `SETVAL` operation, extracted from the man page.

Listing 24.4 The SETVAL Portion of the `semctl(2)` Man Page

```
SETVAL      Set  the  value  of  semval to arg.val for the
            semnum-th semaphore of the set, updating  also
            the sem_ctime member of the semid_ds structure
            associated to the set.  Undo entry is  cleared
            for  altered semaphore in all processes.  Pro-
            cesses sleeping on the wait queue are awakened
            if semval becomes 0 or increases.  The calling
            process must have alter access  privileges  on
            the semaphore set.
```

The first sentence, which reads `Set the value of semval to arg.val for the semnum-th semaphore of the set, updating also the sem_ctime member of the semid_ds structure associated to the set`, is interesting for two reasons:

- The value assigned to the semaphore clearly comes from the value `arg.val`. This rules out using this value as a semaphore number.
- The phrase `the semnum-th semaphore` is even more interesting because it is yet another different reference.

At this point, there seems to be little left in the way of clues. In the next section, you will see the evidence so that you can render a judgment.

Rendering a Judgment

Let me restate the different reference types that have been noted so far. The four ambiguous references are as follows:

- The `sumun-nth` semaphore
- The value `0` for `semun`
- The `semno-th` semaphore of the set
- The `semnum-th` semaphore of the set

It seems probable that argument two was intended to be named `semnum` and was mistyped as `semnun`. The reasons for this thinking are as follows:

- If that one small correction is made in argument two to read as `semnum`, then it would agree with the `SETVAL` description.
- The names `semnum` and `semnun` are very similar.
- The letters `n` and `m` are side by side on the keyboard, suggesting that the name was mistyped.

The other references can be judged as follows:

- The use of the phrases `the sumun-nth semaphore` and `the semno-th semaphore of the set` are strikingly similar to the phrase `the semnum-th semaphore of the set`.
- The phrases speak of a specific semaphore, not of a data type. This fact would seem to rule out any reference to argument `arg` of type `semun`.

The last phrase `value 0 for semun` should have been written `value 0 for semnum`. In light of the other evidence presented, it seems likely that this phrase was mistyped as well. Perhaps the author had a problem typing the letters `n`, `u`, and `m`.

The judgment for this case is that argument two is properly named `semnum` in this documentation. The court is adjourned!

I have labored the point somewhat on this one example to show you how manual pages can be ambiguous. You have seen, however, that you can work out the ambiguities if you take the time to study the information in detail.

When you cannot work out the ambiguities, you can draw on other resources. Linux has been built according to industry standards wherever possible. Consequently, you can often scour the Internet to view the man pages for a commercial UNIX platform. Because the commercial man pages have different writers, they often restate the same information in a slightly different manner. Just keep in mind that real differences might exist in the commercial UNIX implementation and the one that Linux uses.

Resolving Conflicts with Documentation

Sometimes your experience might disagree with the documentation. The man pages might tell you one thing, but your program might tell you something different. In Hour 22, "Signals," you learned about the `sigsuspend()` function. The `RETURN VALUES` section of the man page for it reads as follows:

```
RETURN VALUES
   sigaction, sigprocmask, sigpending and sigsuspend return 0
   on success and -1 on error.
```

Although that statement may be true for many of the functions listed, you may discover that it is not, in fact, true for the function `sigsuspend()`.

Assume, however, that you have written a complex project that seems to be encountering a problem near the `sigsuspend()` function call. When you look up the man page for it, you read there that it should return `0`. You suspect otherwise. What do you do?

You have at least three choices:

- Look at commercial UNIX documentation. For example, the UNIX AT&T SVID document reads "Since the function `sigsuspend()` suspends process execution indefinitely, there is no successful completion return value. It returns a value of `-1` and sets `errno` to indicate an error." The error is later listed in the documentation as `EINTR`.
- Put trace statements in your code to find out what is really happening. Some of the techniques shown in Hour 9, "Useful Debugging Techniques," could be applied here.
- Write a small test program.

Using commercial UNIX documentation can often help you see whether you are barking up the wrong tree. After all, Linux is fashioned after existing standards and probably works the same. However, the element of doubt here does not make using this documentation the best choice.

Putting trace statements in a program is often the best course of action. However, using this approach may not always be possible if the project is very large, for example.

Sometimes the best course of action is to write a small test program. I have seen programmers deliberate all day in the workplace about whether this or that happens. Instead, you can write a short program to settle the debate in as little as 5 to 10 minutes. Don't be afraid to write short programs. This trick is often less work than attempting to find out by other means. Listing 24.5 shows a short program that resolves this issue of `sigsuspend()` under Linux.

LISTING 24.5 SIMPLE TEST PROGRAM FOR `sigsuspend()`

```
#include <stdio.h>
#include <stdlib.h>
#include <unistd.h>
#include <signal.h>
#include <string.h>
#include <errno.h>

static void
catch_sigint(int signo) {
    write(1,"CAUGHT SIGNAL!\n",15);
}

int
main(int argc,char *argv[]) {
    int z;
```

continues

LISTING 24.5 CONTINUED

```
16:     sigset_t sigs;
17:     struct sigaction sa_new;
18:
19:     sa_new.sa_handler = catch_sigint;
20:     sigemptyset(&sa_new.sa_mask);
21:     sa_new.sa_flags = 0;
22:     sigaction(SIGALRM,&sa_new,0);
23:
24:     sigfillset(&sigs);
25:     sigdelset(&sigs,SIGINT);
26:     sigdelset(&sigs,SIGALRM);
27:
28:     alarm(3);
29:
30:     errno = 0;
31:     z = sigsuspend(&sigs);
32:
33:     printf("z=%d, errno=%d (%s)\n",
34:         z,errno,strerror(errno));
35:
36:     return 0;
37: }
```

The program in Listing 24.5 is very similar to the ones you saw in Hour 22, "Signals." The important difference about this program is that the returned value from `sigsuspend()` is captured in variable `z` in line 31. The value of `z` indicates what the actual return value is.

Lines 33 and 34 report on the value of `z` and `errno` and provide the interpretation of `errno` by calling `strerror()`. When you compile and run the program, you obtain the following results:

```
bash$ gcc -Wall -D_GNU_SOURCE 24LST05.c
bash$ ./a.out
CAUGHT SIGNAL!
z=-1, errno=4 (Interrupted system call)
bash$
```

It would appear that the AT&T documentation is correct, and that the Linux man page is in error regarding `sigsuspend()`.

The point of this exercise has been to stress the fact that short test programs can often settle the issue. Writing a short program often takes less time than finding the answer by other means.

Examining the ERRORS Section

Many times programmers are focused on the success or failure of an operation rather than on the specific nature of the failure. For this reason, programmers often read only about the returned indication of success or failure in the section `RETURN VALUE`. As a result, they often overlook the `ERRORS` section of the man page, which follows. Reviewing the errors listed there is important, however. Listing 24.6 shows a partial list of errors for the `msgsnd()` function.

LISTING 24.6 THE ERRORS SECTION OF THE MAN PAGE

```
ERRORS
    When  msgsnd  fails,  at  return  errno will be set to one
    among the following values:

    EAGAIN     The message can't be sent due to the msg_qbytes
               limit for the queue and IPC_NOWAIT was asserted
               in mgsflg.

    EACCES     The calling process has no write access permis-
               sions on the message queue.

    EFAULT     The  address  pointed to by msgp isn't accessi-
               ble.

    EIDRM      The message queue was removed.

    EINTR      Sleeping on a full message queue condition, the
               process  received  a  signal  that  had  to  be
               caught.
```

One error that you should always be on the lookout for is the `EINTR` error. If it can occur, then you must program for it in a loop, as you learned in Hour 21, "Message Queues." When signal handlers exit, functions such as `msgsnd()` and `msgrcv()` have the error `EINTR` returned. When you do not see `EINTR` listed as an error, you can safely ignore the issue when the documentation is accurate.

You can probably assume that the errors listed in section `2` man pages make up the complete list. However, as you move out of the system calls and examine the manual pages in the libraries of section `3`, for example, the list may not be exhaustive. The `ERRORS` section for `putpwent()`, for example, lists only one possible error:

```
ERRORS
    EINVAL Invalid (NULL) argument given.
```

However, if you think about the fact that this function writes information, then the `write()` call that it uses possibly can provide other errors indirectly. If you look up the `write(2)` man page, you'll see many possible errors. One that is very likely to occur if you occasionally run out of disk space is the following error:

```
ENOSPC  The  device  containing  the file referred to by fd
        has no room for the data.
```

In summary, my advice for this section is as follows:

- The `ERRORS` section has very important information in it and should not be ignored.
- Think about other error possibilities that may arise from section 2 calls made by the library function.

Note that sometimes the descriptions of the error codes themselves can furnish additional information that helps you understand the document.

Looking at the `SEE ALSO` Section

Sometimes having read the man page, you are left wanting something better. For example, you may have looked at the `wait(2)` man page and wished for a function that provided you with resource utilization information that `wait()` and `waitpid()` cannot supply. Where else do you look?

The `SEE ALSO` section is a veritable gold mine at times because it can refer you to other documentation that you would not have known about otherwise. The `wait(2)` man page shows the following:

```
SEE ALSO
    signal(2), wait4(2), signal(7)
```

From this information, you see three more man page references. The most likely candidate to try is the `wait4(2)` man page, and consequently you can check it out. There you will find just what you are looking for.

This man page section is especially important to someone new to Linux. Even a seasoned programmer who is new to Linux (and UNIX) is not going to be aware of where everything can be found. The `SEE ALSO` section serves as your road map to other places to visit.

Finding Files

Many beginners often don't look past the `SYNOPSIS` and the `DESCRIPTION` sections of the man page. They read the description and understand how the function works. This feeling of understanding seems to make the rest of the documentation seem unimportant to them, so they exit the screen viewer, never seeing the sections at the bottom.

One of the useful bottom sections is the FILES section. There, you can find out about libraries and configuration files. The following is an example taken from the tzset(3) man page:

```
FILES
   /usr/lib/zoneinfo                 system time zone directory
   /usr/lib/zoneinfo/localtime       local time zone file
   /usr/lib/zoneinfo/posixrules      rules for POSIX-style TZ's
```

This information tells you about files that control the defaults for the function tzset(). Like the SEE ALSO section, the FILES section can be another road map to places to be explored.

Documented BUGS

One of the great points about UNIX is its honesty. Linux continues this tradition by documenting its bugs. The following BUGS section was taken from the alloca(3) man page:

```
BUGS
    The alloca function is machine dependent.
```

Knowing the limitations of a function can save you a lot of time and aggravation. This BUGS section tells you that the alloca() function might be a problem for other hardware platforms. The same Intel Linux application using alloca() might not be usable under a different CPU running Linux.

Summary

In this lesson, you reviewed the man command and learned how to use its apropos search option. You learned about the Linux man page sections so that you have a general road map to the documentation that is installed on your system.

You also looked at some documentation with bugs and learned how to apply some detective work to get more out of the information provided. The subdivisions within a specific man page were highlighted so that you will be well acquainted with the documentation format.

Looking Ahead

In this book, you started out by becoming acquainted with the gcc compiler and read about how to make the best use of its warning facilities. Then you learned how to apply source file management using RCS. Modular programming and the make command were discussed after that. All these topics will continue to be important in your Linux programming career.

Further into this book, you learned about command-line option processing. You can refer to this lesson repeatedly until that subject matter becomes instinct.

You also read about Linux error handling and now know all about how to work with `errno` and turn error codes into messages. So much existing library code uses `errno` that this knowledge will serve you well as you write new programs.

The `main` program and its environment were covered in detail as it applies to Linux. You saw how `argv[]` was formed and where your exported environment variables came from. This information tied in well with the lesson that covered the `fork()` and `exec()` function calls. You got the complete picture of how a new process begins.

You also learned about debug and trace techniques to help you with those difficult projects. Static and shared libraries were covered to provide you with the advantages that they offer in large projects. Again, you will use these techniques for the rest of your Linux programming life.

To round out your knowledge, you read about many of the more advanced string functions. You later tested the numeric conversion functions that Linux has to offer. Date and time conversions were also covered, leaving out nothing essential.

Linux programs must also manage users and groups. You learned about the facilities that Linux provides for working with the password and group files. This knowledge will help you when you frequently need to covert a `uid_t` number into a username or a `gid_t` number into a group name.

You became a master of linking, moving, and unlinking files from a C program. The programs you write can now also create directories and remove directories. Using the `stat()` function, your programs can test files and links.

Temporary file facilities were discussed and used. You saw how useful they were in the TQL project for sorting the results for the `ORDER BY` clause. Applications you write will also frequently need temporary files.

Toward the end of this book, you learned about pipes, semaphores, shared memory, and message queues. These facilities were demonstrated in various ways. These subjects tend to be more difficult. Yet the rewards can be great when you understand and apply them correctly. When your applications demand a client/server approach, you will now have the necessary skills to incorporate that approach.

So where do you go from here? The direction you take is primarily up to you and your interest in Linux. However, I can suggest a few ideas for you:

- Practice what you have learned. This book has covered a lot of material. Now is a good time to have some fun with projects of your own choosing.
- Explore, explore, and explore! Many related topics fell by the wayside in this book to make way for the most important topics. Keep a sharp eye on those `SEE ALSO` sections of the man pages for other places to visit.
- Look at other people's code. The Internet is a wonderful resource, providing you with access to volumes of publicly available source code.
- Join other Internet Linux development efforts. Many projects are still outstanding on the wish list for Linux. Everyone has something to contribute.
- Teach others. Teaching others can be both rewarding and help you to refine your own knowledge in the process.

Be sure to thank those people who have selflessly given themselves to the GNU and Linux programming efforts. Many people have expended countless hours to make the current Linux distributions possible. We also need to be grateful to the many people who contributed to the development and growth of the Internet. The Internet has played a large part in the development of Linux. I thank you for reading this book. It is my hope that this book will greatly increase your enjoyment of your programming experience under Linux.

Q&A

Q Why is the `man` command not called something like `help`?

A The `man` command is short for *manual*. Its role is to serve documentation rather than help.

Q What does it mean to perform an apropos search?

A It means to search for all relevant topics.

Q How can I find out more about the `man` command?

A You can execute the command `man man`. This way, you can see how the `man` command describes the `man` command.

Workshop

You are encouraged to work through the quiz and the exercises to practice what you have learned.

Quiz

1. How do you invoke an apropos search using the `man` command?
2. Which manual section describes the system calls?
3. Which manual section describes user commands?
4. Which section are the standard I/O library routines described in?
5. What part of the man page is the library file indicated in, if any?
6. Where do you look in a man page when you want to know if the function requires `EINTR` handling?

Exercises

1. Read the man page for the `wait(2)` function. Determine whether the error `EINTR` is returned by this function.
2. Write a small program to prove the truth of what you found in exercise 1. This program needs to call on `fork(2)` to create a child process. Otherwise, the parent process gets an error indicating that you have no child process to wait for when it calls `wait(2)`. The child process must sleep for at least four seconds and then exit.
3. The parent process must be set up to catch the signal `SIGALRM`. The signal handler will simply return. Then you must call `alarm(2)` to create a two-second timer. This way, `SIGALRM` can be raised before the child process exits. Now enter a loop that calls on `wait(2)`. Test for error returns, and report the error. Is the error `EINTR` returned? Is it documented?

APPENDIX A

Answers to Quiz Questions

Hour 1

1. The gcc command is the compiler. It also acts as a front end to the linker command.
2. A *.c file is a C source program file. A *.h file is a C include file, which is also known as a header file.
3. A *.o is a compiled object file. It is the C compiler's translated output file.
4. The a.out file is an executable image file.
5. A compiler error is a message that indicates why a compile cannot succeed. A warning message, on the other hand, indicates something that you should investigate, even though the compile suceeds.

6. The dot slash method tells the shell explicitly that your command to be executed is in the current directory. Normally, the shell looks for the command in every directory listed in the PATH environment variable. For root users, this capability is especially important because running a different program found by the PATH variable could invoke a harmful program that has root access.
7. The `void` cast simply means that no result is returned. It is useful to the compiler because it tells the compiler that you don't expect to use the result, if any. This cast suppresses warnings that might otherwise be generated by the compiler.

Hour 2

1. The `ci` command checks in a new source module.
2. The `co` command with no `-l` option checks out a read-only working copy of a source module.
3. The `co -l` command checks out and locks a source module for editing.
4. The `rcs -u filename` command cancels the lock for the named file.
5. The `ci` command checks in a changed source module.
6. A locked checkout prevents other users from accidentally checking out the same file for editing. The owner of the locked file is presumably in the process of making changes to the file. An unlocked checkout can grant any number of read-only copies of the same source file.

Hour 3

1. The value of `argc` is `3` because the value of `argv[0]` counts as one. The additional values `argv[1]` and `argv[2]` count as two more, resulting in a value of `argc=3`.
2. There is no difference between command-line arguments and options. In this case, the `argv[0]` value counts as one, the option counts as the second, and the two additional arguments result in a total of `argc=4`.
3. Use the command `ls -i file1 file2`. If the i-node numbers differ, then they do not point to the same file.
4. The file may not exist, or you may lack permissions to open it.
5. If the output is being directed to a file, the file system may run out of disk space.
6. The bash shell is a program that runs on top of the Linux kernel, as all programs do.
7. In bash, you set vi command-line editing mode by entering the command `set -o vi`.
8. You can use the command `fc -l` to list your command-line history.

Hour 4

1. A program becomes modular when it is composed of more than one source file. This is in contrast to a nonmodular program, which is contained entirely in one source file.
2. Modularity causes one large component to be broken down into smaller components. The reduced size makes the modules easier to edit. Additionally, when changes are made to a module, only the modules affected require a recompile.
3. External definitions form the linkages to other components that are defined in other modules. For example, a global `int` value defined in the `main` program is not defined in a subroutine module of a different source module. The external reference, however, indicates that the global `int` value is defined somewhere else. This satisfies the compiler's needs and indirectly directs the linker when the program is linked later.
4. Static definitions keep the global names out of the link phase. If a global reference is not static, it is external. External names are used by the linker to link different object modules together. Unnecessary use of external names can introduce linking conflicts.

Hour 5

1. A reference to an undefined macro in a make file is not an error. The `make` command supplies the value `""` (null string) when the macro reference is not defined.
2. The target is the object that is to be created from its dependents. Therefore, if it is newer than its dependents, it is considered up-to-date, and the actions for creating it are not carried out.
3. Yes. Make file macro assignments overrule values supplied from the environment. The `make -e` option, however, does allow the environment values to overrule the `make` macro assignments.
4. No. The target can be a directory, a link, or a symlink, for example. Additionally, some targets may never exist, such as the quasi-standard targets `clean` and `clobber`.
5. A tab character must precede an action line in the make file. Space characters are not acceptable.
6. The at (`@`) character causes `make` to suppress printing the command line to standard output.
7. One or more blanks separate multiple dependents on a target specification line.

Hour 6

1. Options that follow a single hyphen consist of a single character for each option given.
2. A long option is indicated by two leading hyphen characters.
3. Precede the problem argument with another argument that consists solely of two hyphens (`--`).
4. The pointer to the option's argument is supplied by the external character pointer `optarg`.
5. The pointer to the option's argument is still supplied by the external character pointer `optarg`.
6. The application can set external integer `opterr` to `0` to disable error messages from `getopt()` or `getopt_long()`.
7. The character `?` is returned when an option is not supported by the `getopt()` argument three.

Hour 7

1. Use the function `strerror()` to translate the `errno` value into a message, and then copy that message to a holding buffer. Another method uses `errno` as a subscript into the external array `sys_errlist[]`, which does not need to be concerned about long-term use.
2. The external integer `sys_nerr` contains the highest `errno + 1` value. Therefore, the highest `errno` value is `sys_nerr - 1`.
3. An error is indicated when `fopen()` returns a `null` pointer. At this point, `errno` contains a posted error code.
4. The standard I/O package often uses buffers to improve the performance of input/output operations. The `fflush()` call is necessary to force out a buffer of unwritten data. After forcing a write with `fflush()`, the `ferror()` call can detect whether a write error occurred.
5. The `ferror()` function can indicate that an error has occurred long after its cause. However, the precise cause of the error found in `errno` will be lost if the test is not made close enough to the point of failure. Only the value of `errno` can tell you the nature of the error.
6. The `perror()` function always prints to `stderr`, and its output format is simple and noncustomizable. Sometimes you need to format a string or provide a more detailed message. These are the primary reasons that discourage its use.

7. The `strerror()` should not be used more than once in any argument list, including the `printf()` function because the pointer returned from `strerror()` could point to a static buffer. This buffer could be overwritten with subsequent calls to `strerror()` and is therefore considered unsafe.

Hour 8

1. The program's return code or exit status is posted to the Linux kernel's process table.
2. The size of the `argv[]` array is `argc`. Array element `argv[argc]` contains a `null` pointer.
3. No. The new environment variables and values are stored in another location, determined by the library routines `putenv()` and `setenv()`. These functions probably call on `malloc()` to allocate storage for the new values. When `unsetenv()` is called, a flag value within the library's data area flags the indicated variable as undefined.
4. The function `setenv()` permits the caller to conditionally define a value for an environment variable if it does not exist.
5. The `unsetenv()` function marks the environment variable as destroyed. Subsequent calls to `getenv()` will return a `null` pointer to indicate that the variable does not exist.
6. This value indicates that your program is returning a garbage return code. You usually get this result when the main program does a simple return without specifying a value. Compiling with maximum warning levels turned on helps you spot these problems ahead of time.

Hour 9

1. The C preprocessor has made no provision for a macro to accept a variable number of arguments. All macro definitions have a fixed number of arguments.
2. The variable number of arguments problem is solved by passing a bracketed list of arguments in the place of one macro argument.
3. The debugging or trace level is used to eliminate trace output when it is not required. By specifying various levels of trace output, you can control how much detail you want to trace.
4. The trace level range is entirely arbitrary. It is simply general practice for the levels to be given in a range of `0` to `9`.

5. The debug or trace command-line option does not have to be the option `-x`. Some commands use the option `-d` to indicate a debug option. Others may choose to use a long option such as `--debug`. The `make` command uses the `-d` option to display debugging output. The `gcc` command also supports various forms of the `-d` option for debugging.

Hour 10

1. Only the modules necessary to resolve undefined external references are extracted from an archive file. In this manner, only the modules required are loaded from a static library.
2. Because functions `funa()`, `funb()`, and `func()` are compiled as one unit, the three of them exist in the object module produced by the compiler. A library containing this object module loads all three functions if any of the function names are referenced. This situation occurs because the archive program can only extract object module files and cannot split up object module files into smaller components.
3. The `-shared` option indicates that the output of the link operation will be a shared library instead of the default executable library.
4. Any external global variables, structures, unions, or functions are visible to the calling program.
5. The `LD_LIBRARY_PATH` environment variable can be used to control the search order of shared libraries.
6. The `-fPIC gcc` option permits the compiler to produce position independent code.

Hour 11

1. The `strdup()` function duplicates a string.
2. The leftmost matching character in a string is returned by `strchr()`.
3. The function `strcspn()` function returns a `size_t` numeric offset value.
4. The second argument to the `strtok_r()` call specifies the set of delimiter characters.
5. The first call to `strtok_r()` has a non-null argument one to begin parsing a string into tokens. When the first argument is null on successive calls to `strtok_r()`, the parse is resumed based on information it picks up from argument three.

Hour 12

1. The sscanf() function cannot tell you where a conversion failed. The %n format specifier can only indicate how many successfully processed characters were converted.
2. The value to be converted is too small. Another way to state this is that the exponent has underflowed.
3. This result tells you that the function strtoul() successfully converted an unsigned long value that just happens to be the value represented by macro ULONG_MAX.
4. When the returned string pointer points to the start of the string being converted.

Hour 13

1. The time() function returns the current system date and time.
2. You can use the localtime() and gmtime() functions to convert the time_t value into its date and time components.
3. The mktime() function takes date and time components as input and computes a time_t value from them.
4. The ctime() and asctime() functions return string format dates.
5. The strftime() function permits you to format a custom date and time string.
6. First, you must be certain that the function tzset() has been called directly or indirectly. When the external integer variable daylight is true (nonzero), then daylight saving time is in effect. When variable daylight is false (0), then daylight saving time is not in effect.
7. Environment variable TZ overrides your session's time zone.

Hour 14

1. The subfields of the GECOS field are the full name, the office location, office extension or phone number, and home phone number.
2. The first four fields of the password database are pw_name (or username), pw_passwd (or password), pw_uid (or uid number) and pw_gid (or gid number).
3. The pathname of the group database is /etc/group.
4. The group name is the first field, and the group number is the third field in the group database.

5. The user list is composed of usernames separated by a comma in the group database.
6. The `setpwent()` function rewinds the password database so that `getpwent()` returns the first entry.
7. You use the `getpwnam()` function to look up the password entry by username directly.
8. You use the function `getgrgid()` to look up a gid number directly.

Hour 15

1. The `unlink()` function indicates success by returning a value of `0`.
2. You link the first pathname to the second pathname. Then you unlink the first pathname.
3. The practice of passing a `null` pointer in argument one of `getcwd()` is not portable to other platforms. It is not portable because this practice is a GNU extension to the standard for `getcwd()`.
4. The second argument must include the terminating `NUL` byte in its buffer size count.
5. Permission bits and file type information are saved in the `mode_t` data type.
6. You should include the include file sys/stat.h to define macros such as `S_IRUSR`.
7. The C macro `S_IXGRP` represents execute permission for the group.
8. You use the `or` operator to combine multiple permission bits. For example, `S_IRUSR|S_IRGRP` combines the two bits.
9. The current `umask` setting determines the final resulting permissions for the `mkdir()` function.
10. The `stat` structure member `st_mtime` contains the date and time that a file or directory was last modified.
11. The `stat` structure member `st_size` contains the size in bytes of a file.

Hour 16

1. The function `atexit()` registers a cleanup function that is called before all file streams are closed.
2. Cleanup functions are called in the reverse order that they were registered in.
3. Calling `tmpnam()` with a `null` argument returns a pointer to a static buffer internal to the function.

4. The returned non-null pointer from tempnam() is allocated by malloc(). This pointer should be freed when the pathname string is no longer required.
5. The environment variable TMPDIR overrides the directory chosen for temporary files by the function tempnam().
6. The value P_tmpdir is defined in the include file stdio.h.
7. You open the file, and then while it remains open, you unlink all pathname references to it. While the file remains open, it exists as a nameless file.

Hour 17

1. Because you are reading the output of the sort command, the sort process is attached to the other end of your pipe.
2. Your written output is being read by the mailx command, and therefore the mailx command is reading the other end of the pipe.
3. You should clear the errno value to 0 before calling function system().
4. This value means that the command was executed and that it returned the exit status of 3.
5. No. You must use the pclose() function to close FILE streams created by popen() because the process created by popen() must be waited on in order to pick up the process termination status. The call to pclose() also synchronizes the flow of the calling program, so it does not proceed until the child process has terminated.

A

Hour 18

1. The child process is returned the value 0 from the function fork().
2. If the function execve() is successful, there is no return from this function. Only an error indication of -1 is ever returned to indicate that the execve() function failed.
3. The wait() function blocks the calling process until the Linux kernel has a termination status to report. The wait() function also does not report any resource utilization of the process that terminated.
4. No. When the Linux kernel has reached the maximum process ID value possible, it starts over with the number 4 and works upward until it finds a process ID that is not currently in use. Therefore, although child processes usually have higher process IDs than their parents, this relationship is not always true.
5. If the parent of a child process is terminated, the process ID of the parent for the child becomes process ID 1. This is normally the process ID of the init process.

6. You use the macro `WIFEXITED()` to see whether the process terminated normally.
7. You must use the macro `WIFSIGNALED()` first to determine that the process was signaled. If this macro evaluates `true`, then you can use macro `WCOREDUMP()` to determine whether a core file was produced.

Hour 19

1. The wait operation is the opposite of the notify operation.
2. The `semctl()` function is used to initialize semaphore values.
3. An atomic semaphore operation means that an operation on a set of semaphores is performed in an indivisible fashion. It is therefore impossible to partially succeed at a semaphore operation.
4. The write permission indicates that the user of the semaphore is able to alter the value of the semaphore counter. This implies that the user may both wait on and notify the semaphore.

Hour 20

1. The function `shmget()` accesses or creates shared memory.
2. You use the function `shmat()` to attach shared memory.
3. Pointer values should be avoided in tables because their use requires that all users of the shared memory table attach the table at the same starting address.
4. You use the `shmctl()` function to destroy shared memory.
5. The `shmat()` function returns the value `(char *)(-1)`—that is, an address with all 1-bits.

Hour 21

1. You use the `IPC_CREAT` flag to create a message queue when calling `msgget()`.
2. You use the `IPC_EXCL` flag to make sure that the message queue does not already exist when creating a message queue.
3. You use the `MSG_EXCEPT` flag to return a message where the message `mtype` value does not match the `msgtyp` argument of the `msgrcv()` call.
4. The `E2BIG` error code is returned when the `MSG_NOERROR` flag is used in the `msgrcv()` call and the message is truncated to fit the receiving buffer.

Hour 22

1. The `sigset_t` data type is used to contain a set of signals.
2. You use `sigfillset()` to create a set of all signals. In this manner, you need to remove only the few signals necessary to create a signal mask set.
3. The `sigaction()` function registers a signal handler for a specific signal.
4. The `SIGALRM` signal is raised when the `alarm()` timer runs out.
5. You can use the `kill()` function to raise a signal.
6. The `sigsuspend()` function waits for a signal to be raised.

Hour 23

1. The standard input (file unit 0) must be closed. You cannot specify a new file descriptor that is already open.
2. The `wait()` call is coded in a loop because other child processes may return exit status information. For this reason, you should loop until the matching process ID is returned. Additionally, the error `EINTR` can be returned.
3. The function `tmpfile()` creates a nameless temporary file.

Hour 24

1. You perform an apropos search by using the `man` command with the option `-k string`, where `string` is the search string to use.
2. System calls are described in section `2`.
3. User commands are described in section `1`.
4. The standard I/O library routines are described in the section `3S`.
5. The library file is described in the `FILES` section of the man page.
6. To look for the error code `EINTR`, you examine the `ERRORS` section of the man page.

INDEX

Symbols

A

D

G

H

I

K

L

N

Q

R

S

T

What's on the Disc

The companion CD-ROM contains all of the author's source code and Red Hat Linux 5.2.

Install from Boot Floppies

1. Using DOS or Windows, format two 1.44MB floppies.
2. Copy three files to a temporary location on your hard drive, such as TEMP: \IMAGES\BOOT.IMG, \IMAGES\SUPP.IMG, and \DOSUTILS\RAWRITE.EXE.
3. Type `RAWRITE` and press <ENTER>.
4. When prompted to do so, type in the name `BOOT.IMG` and press <ENTER>.
5. When prompted to do so, type in the drive letter of the disk(s) you are going to prepare and press <ENTER>. Since you are going to be booting from this disk, it's typically `A:`.
6. Most CD-ROM drives are supported by the information found on the boot disk. However, you may want to create the supplementary disk just in case. Repeat step 3. When prompted to do so, type in the name `SUPP.IMG` and press <ENTER>.
7. Repeat step 5.
8. If you don't already have the boot floppy in your disk drive, insert it now.
9. Restart your computer.
10. You may need to change your BIOS settings to boot from the floppy drive. Typically, you enter your BIOS setup program with the F2 or DEL keys.
11. Make your changes (if any) and exit the BIOS setup utility.
12. If your computer is set up properly, you will boot into the Red Hat Linux setup program.
13. Follow the onscreen prompts to complete the installation.